New Religions

New Religions

Emerging Faiths and Religious Cultures in the Modern World

VOLUME I: A–L

Eugene V. Gallagher and Lydia Willsky-Ciollo

An Imprint of ABC-CLIO, LLC
Santa Barbara, California • Denver, Colorado

Copyright © 2021 by ABC-CLIO, LLC

All rights reserved. No part of this publication may be reproduced, stored in a retrieval system, or transmitted, in any form or by any means, electronic, mechanical, photocopying, recording, or otherwise, except for the inclusion of brief quotations in a review, without prior permission in writing from the publisher.

Every reasonable effort has been made to trace the owners of copyright materials in this book, but in some instances this has proven impossible. The editors and publishers will be glad to receive information leading to more complete acknowledgments in subsequent printings of the book and in the meantime extend their apologies for any omissions.

Library of Congress Cataloging-in-Publication Data

Names: Gallagher, Eugene V., author. | Willsky-Ciollo, Lydia, author.
Title: New religions : emerging faiths and religious cultures in the modern world / Eugene V. Gallagher and Lydia Willsky-Ciollo.
Description: Santa Barbara, California : ABC-CLIO, 2021. | Includes bibliographical references and index. | Contents: v. 1. A-L — v. 2. M-Z.
Identifiers: LCCN 2020015897 (print) | LCCN 2020015898 (ebook) | ISBN 9781440862373 (v. 1 ; hardcover) | ISBN 9781440862380 (v. 2 ; hardcover) | ISBN 9781440862359 (hardcover) | ISBN 9781440862366 (ebook)
Subjects: LCSH: Cults.
Classification: LCC BP603 .G356 2020 (print) | LCC BP603 (ebook) | DDC 209—dc23
LC record available at https://lccn.loc.gov/2020015897
LC ebook record available at https://lccn.loc.gov/2020015898

ISBN: 978-1-4408-6235-9 (set)
 978-1-4408-6237-3 (vol. 1)
 978-1-4408-6238-0 (vol. 2)
 978-1-4408-6236-6 (ebook)

25 24 23 22 21   1 2 3 4 5

This book is also available as an eBook.

ABC-CLIO
An Imprint of ABC-CLIO, LLC

ABC-CLIO, LLC
147 Castilian Drive
Santa Barbara, California 93117
www.abc-clio.com

This book is printed on acid-free paper ∞

Manufactured in the United States of America

Contents

Alphabetical List of Entries   vii

Guide to Related Topics   xiii

Preface   xix

Introduction   xxiii

Chronology   xxix

A–Z Entries   1

Index   691

Alphabetical List of Entries

VOLUME ONE
Adi Da Samraj
Aetherius Society, The
African New Religious Movements
Ahmadiyya Movement, The
Alamo, Tony
Ali, Noble Drew
Al-Qaeda
Amana Society
Amish, The
Anamadim
Anthroposophy
Anticult Movement, The
Apostates
Applewhite, Marshall, and Bonnie Lu Nettles
Art and New Religious Movements
Asahara, Shoko
Ásatrú
Aum Shinrikyō
Aurobindo, Sri
Ayahuasca
Baba, Meher
Babism
Bahá'í
Ballard, Guy W.
Bey, Hakim

Black Judaism
Blavatsky, Helena Petrovna
Book of Mormon, The
Brahma Kumaris
Brainwashing
Branch Davidians
Breatharianism
Caddy, Eileen
Candomblé
Cao Dai
Cayce, Edgar
CESNUR (The Center for the Study of New Religions)
Channeling
Chaos Magick
Charisma and Leadership in New Religious Movements
Chen Tao
Children and New Religious Movements
Children of God (The Family International)
Chinese New Religious Movements
Christadelphians
Christian Identity
Christian Science
Church of All Worlds, The

Church of Jesus Christ of Latter-day Saints, The
Church of Satan, The
Church of the Lord (Aladura)
Church Universal and Triumphant, The
Conspiracy Theories
Conversion
Cosmotheism
Course in Miracles, A
Courts and New Religious Movements
Crowley, Aleister
Crystals
Cult
Cult Awareness Network
Cultic Milieu
Damanhur
Deprogramming
Diamond Mountain Center
Diamond Way, The
Dianetics
Disaffiliation and Ex-membership in New Religious Movements
Divine Principle
Druidry
Dudeism
Eckankar
Eco-Paganism
Eddy, Mary Baker
Elan Vital (Divine Light Mission)
Environmentalism and New Religious Movements
Essene Groups
Exclusive (Plymouth) Brethren
Exit Counseling
Falun Gong
Farm, The
Farrakhan, Louis
Father Divine
Findhorn Foundation, The
Food and New Religious Movements
Fortune, Dion
Fourth Way, The
Fox, Kate, and Margaret
Fraud and Deception in New Religions
FREECOG (Free the Children of God)
Freemasonry
Freezone Scientology
Fundamentalist Mormons
Gardner, Gerald
Gender and New Religious Movements
Ghost Dance Movement (Wovoka)
Ghosts, the Paranormal, and New Religious Movements
Globalization and New Religious Movements
Gnostic Groups
Goddess Worship
Grant, Kenneth
Guénon, René
Gurdjieff, G. I.
Hassan, Steven
Healing, Health, and New Religious Movements
Heaven's Gate
Hermetic Order of the Golden Dawn, The
Hermeticism
Hindu New Religious Movements
Holy Order of MANS, The
Holy Piby, The
Hoodoo
Hubbard, L. Ron

Alphabetical List of Entries

I AM Activity, The
Indigo Children
Info-Cult/Info-Secte
INFORM (The Information Network on Religious Movements)
Insider/Outsider Problem, The
Integral Yoga
International Cultic Studies Association, The (The American Family Foundation)
International Peace Mission Movement
International Society for Krishna Consciousness (ISKCON)
ISIS
Japanese New Religious Movements
Jediism
Jews for Jesus
Jones, Rev. Jim
Judge, William Quan
Kabbalah
Kardecism (Spiritism)
Kimbangu, Simon
Knight, JZ (Ramtha)
Kopimism
Korean New Religious Movements
Koresh, David
Landmark Forum, The (est)
LaVey, Anton Szandor
Law Enforcement and New Religious Movements
Lee, (Mother) Ann
Lévi, Éliphas
Love Israel Family, The

VOLUME TWO

Magic and New Religious Movements
Malcolm X
Marian Apparitions
Marriage and Relationships in New Religious Movements
Mathers, Samuel Liddell
Media and New Religious Movements
Mediums
Membership and New Religious Movements
Mesmerism
Messianic Judaism
Messianism and New Religious Movements
Millennialism
Miller, William
Millerites, The
Moon, Rev. Sun Myung
Moorish Science Temple of America, The
Movement for the Restoration of the Ten Commandments of God, The
Movement of Spiritual Inner Awareness
Muhammad, Elijah
Mungiki
Music and New Religious Movements
Mysticism
Nation of Gods and Earths, The (The Five Percent Nation)
Nation of Islam, The
Nation of Yahweh, The
Native American Church, The
Neopaganism
New Age, The
New Cathar Church, The
New Church, The
New Religions on/and the Internet
New Scriptures and New Religious Movements

New Thought
Noyes, John Humphrey
NXIVM
Oahspe
Occultism and Esotericism
Odinism
Olcott, Henry Steel
Oneida Community, The
Order of the Solar Temple, The
Ordo Templi Orientis
Otherkin
Ouspensky, P. D.
Parsons, John Whiteside
Pastafarianism (The Church of the Flying Spaghetti Monster)
Patrick, Ted
Pentecostalism
Peoples Temple
Prabhupada, A. C. Bhaktivedanta
Prophecy in New Religious Movements
Prophet, Elizabeth Clare
Pursel, Jach (Lazaris)
Quimby, Phineas
Race and New Religious Movements
Raëlians, The
Rajneesh, Shree Bhagwan/Osho
Rajneesh/Osho Movement, The
Ramakrishna Mission
Rastafari
Rosicrucianism
Ross, Rick Alan
Russell, Charles Taze
Salafism
Santería
Satanic Panic
Satanism
Sathya Sai Baba Movement, The
Science and Health with Key to the Scriptures
Science Fiction and New Religious Movements
Science, Technology, and New Religious Movements
Scientology
Sect
Seekers
Self-Realization Fellowship (Yogananda)
Seventh-day Adventism
Sex, Sexuality, and New Religious Movements
Seymour, William
Shakers, The
Shamanism
Shembe, Isaiah
Singer, Margaret Thaler
Smith, Joseph
Soka Gakkai
Spiritual but Not Religious
Spiritualism
Starhawk
Steiner, Rudolf
Subud
Sufi New Religious Movements
Swedenborg, Emanuel
Tantrik Order, The
Temple of Set, The
Thelema
Theosophical Society, The
Theosophy
Thoreau, Henry David
3HO
Transcendental Meditation

Transcendentalism
Twelve Tribes, The
UFO Religions
Umbanda
Unarius Academy of Science, The
Unification Church, The
Unitarian Universalism
United Nuwaubian Nation of Moors, The
Unity School of Christianity
Urantia Book, The
Utopianism in New Religious Movements
Valley of the Dawn, The
Vampirism
Vedanta Society, The
Violence and New Religious Movements
Vivekananda, Swami
Vodou
Vorilhon, Claude (Raël)
Waite, Arthur Edward
Watch Tower Bible and Tract Society, The (Jehovah's Witnesses)
White, Ellen G.
Wicca
Women in New Religious Movements
World Church of the Creator, The
World's Parliament of Religion, The
Yoga
Yogi, Maharishi Mahesh
Zionist Churches (Africa)

Guide to Related Topics

GROUPS AND MOVEMENTS

Aetherius Society, The
African New Religious Movements
Ahmadiyya Movement, The
Al-Qaeda
Amana Society
Amish, The
Anamadim
Anthroposophy
Anticult Movement, The
Ásatrú
Aum Shinrikyō
Ayahuasca
Babism
Baháʼí
Black Judaism
Brahma Kumaris
Branch Davidians
Breatharianism
Candomblé
Cao Dai
CESNUR (The Center for the Study of New Religions)
Channeling
Chaos Magick
Chen Tao
Children of God (The Family International)
Chinese New Religious Movements
Christadelphians
Christian Identity
Christian Science
Church of All Worlds, The
Church of Jesus Christ of Latter-day Saints, The
Church of Satan, The
Church of the Lord (Aladura)
Church Universal and Triumphant, The
Cosmotheism
Crystals
Cult Awareness Network
Damanhur
Diamond Mountain Center
Diamond Way, The
Druidry
Dudeism
Eckankar
Eco-Paganism
Elan Vital (Divine Light Mission)
Essene Groups
Exclusive (Plymouth) Brethren
Falun Gong

Farm, The
Findhorn Foundation, The
Fourth Way, The
FREECOG (Free the Children of God)
Freemasonry
Freezone Scientology
Fundamentalist Mormons
Ghost Dance Movement (Wovoka)
Gnostic Groups
Goddess Worship
Heaven's Gate
Hermetic Order of the Golden Dawn, The
Hermeticism
Hindu New Religious Movements
Holy Order of MANS, The
Hoodoo
I AM Activity, The
Indigo Children
Info-Cult/Info-Secte
INFORM (The Information Network on Religious Movements)
Integral Yoga
International Cultic Studies Association, The (The American Family Foundation)
International Peace Mission Movement
International Society for Krishna Consciousness (ISKCON)
ISIS
Japanese New Religious Movements
Jediism
Jews for Jesus
Kabbalah
Kardecism (Spiritism)
Kopimism
Korean New Religious Movements
Landmark Forum, The (est)
Love Israel Family, The
Marian Apparitions
Mesmerism
Messianic Judaism
Millerites, The
Moorish Science Temple of America, The
Movement for the Restoration of the Ten Commandments, The
Movement of Spiritual Inner Awareness
Mungiki
Mysticism
Nation of Gods and Earths, The (The Five Percent Nation)
Nation of Islam, The
Nation of Yahweh, The
Native American Church, The
Neopaganism
New Cathar Church, The
New Church, The
New Thought
NXIVM
Odinism
Oneida Community, The
Order of the Solar Temple, The
Ordo Templi Orientis
Otherkin
Pastafarianism (The Church of the Flying Spaghetti Monster)
Pentecostalism
Peoples Temple
Raëlians, The
Rajneesh/Osho Movement, The
Ramakrishna Mission

Rastafari
Rosicrucianism
Salafism
Santería
Satanic Panic
Satanism
Sathya Sai Baba Movement, The
Scientology
Self-Realization Fellowship (Yogananda)
Seventh-day Adventism
Shakers, The
Soka Gakkai
Spiritual but Not Religious
Spiritualism
Subud
Sufi New Religious Movements
Tantrik Order, The
Temple of Set, The
Thelema
Theosophical Society, The
Theosophy
3HO
Transcendental Meditation
Transcendentalism
Twelve Tribes, The
UFO Religions
Umbanda
Unarius Academy of Science, The
Unification Church, The
Unitarian Universalism
United Nuwaubian Nation of Moors, The
Unity School of Christianity
Valley of the Dawn, The
Vampirism
Vedanta Society, The

Vodou
Watch Tower Bible and Tract Society, The (Jehovah's Witnesses)
Wicca
World Church of the Creator, The
Zionist Churches (Africa)

PEOPLE

Adi Da Samraj
Alamo, Tony
Ali, Noble Drew
Applewhite, Marshall, and Bonnie Lu Nettles
Asahara, Shoko
Aurobindo, Sri
Baba, Meher
Ballard, Guy W.
Bey, Hakim
Blavatsky, Helena Petrovna
Caddy, Eileen
Cayce, Edgar
Crowley, Aleister
Eddy, Mary Baker
Farrakhan, Louis
Father Divine
Fortune, Dion
Fox, Kate, and Margaret
Gardner, Gerald
Grant, Kenneth
Guénon, René
Gurdjieff, G. I.
Hassan, Steven
Hubbard, L. Ron
Jones, Rev. Jim
Judge, William Quan
Kimbangu, Simon

Knight, JZ (Ramtha)
Koresh, David
LaVey, Anton Szandor
Lee, (Mother) Ann
Lévi, Éliphas
Malcolm X
Mathers, Samuel Liddell
Miller, William
Moon, Rev. Sun Myung
Muhammad, Elijah
Noyes, John Humphrey
Olcott, Henry Steel
Ouspensky, P. D.
Parsons, John Whiteside
Patrick, Ted
Prabhupada, A. C. Bhaktivedanta
Prophet, Elizabeth Clare
Pursel, Jach (Lazaris)
Quimby, Phineas
Rajneesh, Shree Bhagwan/Osho
Ross, Rick Alan
Russell, Charles Taze
Seymour, William
Shembe, Isaiah
Singer, Margaret
Smith, Joseph
Starhawk
Steiner, Rudolf
Swedenborg, Emanuel
Thoreau, Henry David
Vivekananda, Swami
Vorilhon, Claude (Raël)
Waite, Arthur Edward
White, Ellen G.
Yogi, Maharishi Mahesh

TERMS

Apostates
Brainwashing
Conspiracy Theories
Conversion
Cult
Cultic Milieu
Deprogramming
Dianetics
Exit Counseling
Insider/Outsider Problem, The
Mediums
Millennialism
New Age, The
Occultism and Esotericism
Sect
Seekers
Shamanism
World's Parliament of Religion, The
Yoga

TEXTS

Book of Mormon, The
Course in Miracles, A
Divine Principle
Holy Piby, The
Oahspe
Science and Health with Key to the Scriptures
Urantia Book, The

THEMES

Art and New Religious Movements

Charisma and Leadership in New Religious Movements

Children and New Religious Movements

Courts and New Religious Movements

Disaffiliation and Ex-membership in New Religious Movements

Environmentalism and New Religious Movements

Food and New Religious Movements

Fraud and Deception in New Religions

Gender and New Religious Movements

Ghosts, the Paranormal, and New Religious Movements

Globalization and New Religious Movements

Healing, Health, and New Religious Movements

Law Enforcement and New Religious Movements

Magic and New Religious Movements

Marriage and Relationships in New Religious Movements

Media and New Religious Movements

Membership and New Religious Movements

Messianism and New Religious Movements

Music and New Religious Movements

New Religions on/and the Internet

New Scriptures and New Religious Movements

Prophecy in New Religious Movements

Race and New Religious Movements

Science Fiction and New Religious Movements

Science, Technology, and New Religious Movements

Sex, Sexuality, and New Religious Movements

Utopianism in New Religious Movements

Violence and New Religious Movements

Women in New Religious Movements

Preface

These volumes are intended as an overview of new and emerging religious movements, often pejoratively called "cults." No single volume could provide a comprehensive account of new religions, of course. The entries included aim to provide basic information about a wide variety of movements, religious leaders, texts, and topics while also nodding at different and extended lines of inquiry that the reader might take. In this way these books are intended to be employed by those with interest ranging from casual to avid and can be used in undergraduate and high school classrooms as a primer for knowledge or a source for student research.

The authors of this volume, as historians of religion, take an historical approach to the topic. More than keeping an eye to dates, this means that the entries encompass the most prominent "new religions," so called either because they are relatively recent traditions or because they exhibit certain characteristics, like existing in a high state of tension with society, that qualify (or qualified) them as minority or alternative traditions, which can include traditions that are centuries, even millennia old in certain instances. For example, Freemasonry, Sufism, and Gnostic Christianity are by all accounts established as ancient traditions. However, each of these traditions is included because at the time of its emergence the group exhibited new or innovative ways of being religious, generated a great deal of interest or hostility, claimed to be the "truest" version of an established tradition, or all of the above. Additionally, each of these traditions has also spawned new religious movements in recent centuries or even recent decades. Our focus is also comparative. In many entries we make comparisons not only between one new religion and similar ones but also between new, alternative, and emergent religions and more established ones.

It may be helpful to consider new religions as experiments in being religious and in being human. They experiment with new ways of thinking about individuals, new ways of forming social groups, and new doctrinal, ritual, and ethical emphases. Many times new religions reach back to the past for their accounts of the origins of a certain group, but they give traditional materials a new twist. The past is very important to new religions, but they also remake the past to provide themselves with an anchor in a legitimate lineage. For example, many new religions propose new interpretations of familiar texts, such as the Bible, Qur'an, or the Bhagavad Gita, even while they claim they are not innovating but merely bringing out of the text what has already been there. Many new religions also produce their own theological literature, with some of it, such as *The Book of Mormon* or *Science and Health with Key to the Scriptures*, attaining the status of scripture within their respective groups. Overall, new religions develop, expand, and respond to their social environments and other social groups in the same ways that more established religions have. Although their newness is distinctive, their characteristics assure that they have much more in common with older and more established religions than they do not. Accordingly, they are susceptible to the same kinds of description, analysis, and interpretation as any other religions, new or old.

These volumes also take a global approach to the study of new religions. Though many of the traditions examined herein found root or prominence in the so-called West, particularly the United States, significant attention is paid to those traditions that emerged in other areas of the globe. More significantly, the authors seek to show how many, if not all, new religions emerged at the nexus of global influences. For example, Helena Petrovna Blavatsky (1831–1891), Henry Steel Olcott (1832–1907), and William Q. Judge (1851–1896) founded the Theosophical Society in New York in 1875. However, both Blavatsky and Olcott had traveled to South Asia and dabbled in Hindu and Buddhist religious ideas and sources in the years before and after the founding of their movement. (In fact, Blavatsky's writings earned accusations of plagiarism, when similarities emerged between them and certain Sanskritic texts.) And after the major institutional center of the Theosophical Society in the United States, its other hub is in Adyar, India. Thus, rarely is a new religious movement a geographical or ideological island. More recently, although the Church of Scientology developed in the United States in the early 1950s, it quickly set up an outpost in Great Britain and soon had centers throughout the world. Many new religions are "world" religions in the sense that they both have been shaped by forces of globalization, such as the Atlantic slave trade that displaced thousands of Africans to the New World and led to the formation of multiple hybrid new religions that drew on traditional African religions and major traditions such as Christianity, and have used processes of globalization to spread their messages far and wide.

The entries are listed alphabetically; however, they are also grouped by category, namely, groups/movements, people, terms, texts, or themes. The aim is to move beyond a simple encyclopedic catalog of new religions, showing instead how various new religions compare and connect to one another. For example, entries on marriage, children, and health or healing bring together numerous new religions highlighting how historical, geographical, and societal trends helped to produce these movements and, in various cases, sustain or sink them.

Entries are also cross-listed; each ends with a "See also" section listing entries directly or indirectly mentioned in the text or which the authors believe bear thematic or historical relevance to the topic. Were students to read the entry on Mary Baker Eddy (1821–1910), they would be directed to entries on, among others, Christian Science; Healing, Health, and New Religious Movements; and New

Thought. The purpose of such connections is to provide greater context for each individual movement or figure as well as to aid students in researching subjects of their choice. This is also aided by the suggestions for "Further Reading" included at the end of each entry, which provides a list of two to six sources should students wish to deepen their knowledge of a particular topic.

Introduction

All religions were once new religious movements. The history of religion is, from one perspective, the history of new religions. Religions are born from need, opportunity, innovation, disagreement, context—both internal and external—revelation, crisis, and change, among other forces. New religions are shaped both by efforts of their founders or original groups and by the social, cultural, political, economic, and religious contexts in which they develop. From a modern and scholarly vantage point, however, new religions are those that arose relatively recently (for many scholars of new religions this means religions that have arisen in the last 150 years), exist in a high state of tension with the surrounding society, cannot be categorically subsumed by a larger world religion, or all of the above.

While it is certainly possible to study early Christianity or Christianity in schism and transition or early Buddhism and Buddhism in schism and transition over the years as new religious movements, to say that Christianity or Buddhism is a "new religion" is too broad of an assertion. Still, it is important to examine new religious movements as both a discrete set of religious groups and as an historical phenomena that sheds light on how and why religions form; what they do to attract, maintain, and increase members; and why certain religions survive and others fizzle.

The study of new religions as an academic discipline (in Western nations, specifically) emerged in the latter half of the twentieth century, spurred by the extraordinary boom of religious innovation occurring at that time, the result of globalization and immigration trends that prompted religious diversity, movement away from mainstream religious institutions, new technologies and discoveries, and, on occasion, global events or crises. Many could cite the U.S. Immigration and Nationality Act of 1965, which lifted draconian immigration bans on certain, predominantly Asian, countries to the United States as a major factor in the increase of new religions as well as the interest in studying them. Interest in Asian, esoteric religious sources and ideas had long been a feature of "Western" new religious movements, such as the Theosophical Society, the Tantrik Order, and the Fourth Way, which were born in the nineteenth and early twentieth centuries. However, with an influx of immigration to the United States, not only ideas but people crossed oceans to found and foster new religions.

Additionally, a series of tragedies beginning with the mass, revolutionary suicide of more than nine hundred members of Peoples Temple in Guyana in 1978, and including the fiery demise of the Branch Davidian sect of Waco, Texas, in 1993, the deadly attack on the Tokyo subway by members of the Japanese new religion Aum Shinrikyō in 1995, the suicides of members of the UFO group Heaven's Gate in 1997, and the deaths of members of the Order of the Solar Temple in 1994, 1995, and 1997, led to public outcry and the branding of all new or alternative religions as dangerous "cults." That increased the desire and need for scholars to understand such groups on their own terms as viable religious groups to provide a counterweight to public stereotyping of new religions as uniformly threatening.

The desire to debunk pejorative stereotypes regarding new religions—such as the tropes that all leaders are megalomaniacal, manipulative, and power driven, rather than genuinely devoted religionists, and that all members are brainwashed sheep incapable of agency or authentic belief—led naturally to a look backward at other new religious movements whose experiences were similar to those of the present cultic milieu. Entire academic subfields, such as Mormon studies, were spawned from such endeavors. Not only that, but the field of new religious movement studies was a cross-disciplinary endeavor; historians, sociologists, psychologists, and anthropologists examined from different perspectives groups such as the Latter-day Saints, the Nation of Islam, and the Branch Davidians, among many others.

Historians, for example, could discern connections not only between historical context and a particular group but between new religious movements at a specific historical moment or across time. For example, the mid-to-late nineteenth century in the United States witnessed the birth of a number of new religious movements whose focus was on the mastery of body by mind or spirit. "New Thought" emerged at a moment when science and medicine were advancing, providing a spiritual complement or, on many occasions, an alternative to traditional medical practices. Among social scientists, sociologists explore the evolution and maintenance of new religious movements, as well as public hostility to new religious movements, as functions of group or societal behavior. The notion that some religions are labeled as "cults," whereas others are denoted "churches" or viable "religions," has more to do with the perception of such groups by society than by any intrinsic "deviance."

As various entries in these volumes will show, there is nothing intrinsically dangerous about new religions; however, when a tragedy does occur, there is a higher likelihood that such an incident will be used to universalize behavior if the perpetrators hail from a fringe or minority religious group (which often includes religions that are a minority in certain contexts, such as Islam in the United States, but a numerical majority elsewhere). In other words, context matters as much as belief—religious groups might be pushed to extreme actions that they would not have entertained in a different time or place.

Variation due to geographical context can also occur within new religions, a phenomenon that Roland Robertson called "glocalization" (1992). There are numerous Hindu sects in south Asia, for example, but some become viable new religions in Europe or the United States. Such was the case for the Vedanta Society—Vedanta societies existed in India long before they were established in the late nineteenth century in the United States—which adapted to its Western context, combining Hindu practice with Christian ecumenical language then in vogue. Vedantists in the United States were practicing something that differed from the Vedantists in India, while still sharing the same lineage.

Neither are new religions static over time. In most cases, adaptation is necessary for survival or for the carrying out of central crucial beliefs. Change often occurs as new religions grow and expand, requiring institutionalization to keep a diffused religious system together. Ole Nydahl (1941–), a Danish lama, spread the Diamond Way of Tibetan Buddhism in the West, creating numerous centers for the practice and streamlining the practice of the movement in the process. Of course, institutionalization does not mean that consistency is guaranteed; the Diamond Way, for example, employed teachers who lacked the deep training Nydahl had experienced, leading to variation in practice from center to center. In some cases, standalone religious traditions emerge as a religion expands and institutionalizes, with those establishing a particular "branch" believing that they are the true heirs to a particular religious lineage. Pentecostalism, which exploded in membership during the nineteenth century, witnessed the creation of numerous denominations, each providing a particular pathway to Pentecostal practice.

Often the death of a religion's founder can be devastating to a new religion, leading to its dissolution, as was the case for the Oneida Community, which dissolved as the health of its founder, John Humphrey Noyes (1811–1886), began to fail. In some cases, such as that of Babism and its offshoot, Bahá'í, the death of a leader may mark the end of the original tradition as well as the beginning of a new movement. However, those religions that are able to channel a leader's magnetism into a sustainable religious system, a process also known as the "routinization of charisma," are often more likely to survive (Weber 1947). Christian Science (or Church of Christ, Scientist), for example, though never numerically dominant has sustained itself for more than a century due in great part to the efforts of its founder Mary Baker Eddy (1821–1910). Eddy eventually declared Christian Science's primary sacred text, *Science and Health with Key to the Scriptures* (1875), the "pastor" of the church, thus ensuring uniformity between congregations and authority outside of herself.

Change may also occur out of necessity, due to hostility from the outside. Such was the case for the Church of Jesus Christ of Latter-day Saints, which abandoned the practice of plural marriage to avoid further penalization by the U.S. government. In many instances, such change may spur innovation by those left disgruntled by such adaptation, which was the tack of many so-called Mormon "fundamentalists" who founded new religions, which they believed held onto original Mormon doctrine where plural marriage was still allowed. Occasionally, the lack of hostility or public notice may also spur change. Combined with a shift in theology and the appearance of the Hale-Bopp Comet, their inability to spread the message that the earth was about to experience a "recycling" further than a few dozen members (by its end) led the members of Heaven's Gate to initiate their own "graduation" to The Evolutionary Level Above Human through ritual suicide.

The growth of new religions or innovation within new religious groups is also spurred by external or environmental factors. Much has been made of the fact that new religions are often born during times of crisis or upheaval. Many millennialist new religions—those that look forward to the return of Jesus Christ or, more generally, to some major, world-shifting event—appear during moments of societal uncertainty or are pushed to act when they view such changes as supernatural signs. However, the opposite is also true according to Peter Clark (2006): that new religions are "born of insufficient change." Numerous "new new religions" in Japan emerged without prompting from societal factors, which, among other reasons, has often led to them being overlooked by scholars (Melton). The contexts in which new religions arise, therefore, are as diverse as the religions themselves.

It is difficult to measure the "success" or significance of new religions from any specific metric. How others may define success—numerical significance, acceptance by society, stable institutions—may not be important for new religions. Certainly, new religions that are able to grow numerically could be called successful, but one should not discount smaller new religious movements for whom mission may not be expansion but consolidation or purity. No one would doubt that Falun Gong, which claims over one hundred million followers in China by some counts, has succeeded in spreading its message. However, it is also the target of historic persecution by the Chinese government, compelling many to practice in secret and rendering its organization inherently vulnerable (its leader lives in the United States to avoid extradition and trial by China, for example). Then there are traditions like the Church of Satan, which are inherently iconoclastic and satiric in nature, enabling them to feed off (and often enjoy) negative attention and suppression. The Farm in Tennessee and the Findhorn Foundation in Scotland, both community beacons of New Age spirituality, count full-time members in the hundreds only. However, their cultural, ecological, and spiritual impact extends far beyond their numerical strength and has enabled these groups to maintain themselves relatively unimpeded by outside forces for decades. Additionally, the survival of a group may not be a marker of success for its members. The death of its members (often by martyrdom) or the group's dissolution might mean that the religion has succeeded in its ultimate goal. Suicide is considered by most to be a tragedy if not a grievous sin; however, the effective end of a group by suicide might mark, for its members, a new beginning for them or for the world. Thus, it is exceedingly important to pay attention to the theological and practical aims of a group rather than simply turning to traditional measures of sustainability and impact to determine a group's significance.

The study of new religions is a rich and fascinating field. These volumes provide a starting point for that study.

Further Reading

Clark, Peter. 2006. *Encyclopedia of New Religious Movements.* London: Routledge.

Melton, J. Gordon. 2007. "Perspective New New Religions: Revisiting a Concept." *Nova Religio* 10, no. 4: 103–112.

Robertson, Robert. 1992. "Globalization or Glocalization." *Journal of International Communication* 1: 33–52.

Weber, Max. 1947 [1922]. *Theory of Social and Economic Organization.* Translated by A. R. Anderson and Talcott Parsons. New York: Oxford University Press.

Chronology

1614
First Rosicrucian texts are published

1693
The Amish emerge from a schism in the Anabaptist group, the Swiss Brethren, and are led by Jakob Amman

1744
Emanuel Swedenborg begins to experience visions, including one where he ascended to the heavens

1774
Franz Anton Mesmer cures a patient through use of magnets and coins, "animal magnetism"

1774
May
Mother Ann Lee and the Shakers sail for the New World

1787
May
The New Church is founded in England

1791
August
Haitian Revolution begins with the performance of a Vodou "Petro" ritual

1820
Joseph Smith Jr. is visited by God and Jesus (known as the "First Vision")

1830
April
The Church of Jesus Christ of Latter-day Saints is founded

c. 1830
Candomblé emerges in Brazil

1836
"Hedge's Club" (or the Transcendental Club) is founded

1844
May
Siyyid 'Alí Muhammad claims to be "the Báb" or the "Gate" to God

1844
June
Joseph Smith Jr. and brother Hyrum are murdered in an Illinois jail cell

1844
October
"The Great Disappointment"; William Miller's third failed prediction of Christ's Second Advent

1848
Kate and Margaret Fox hear a series of "rappings" by a spirit and initiate the Spiritualist movement

1848
John Humphrey Noyes founds the Oneida Community in Oneida, New York

1850
The Báb is executed, bringing an end to the Bábist movement

1852
Bahá'ú'llah's mission begins

1855
The Amana Colonies are founded in Iowa

1858
February
Bernadette Soubirous is visited by the Virgin Mary in Lourdes, France

1861
Ellen G. White founds the Seventh-day Adventists

1862
Mary Baker Eddy apprentices under Phineas Quimby who practiced "Mind Cure"

1863
The Bahá'i religion is established

1866
February
Mary Baker Eddy suffers a fall, discovers "Divine Science," and makes a miraculous recovery

1875
November
Helena Petrovna Blavatsky, Henry Steel Olcott, and William Q. Judge found the Theosophical Society

1875
Mary Baker Eddy publishes *Science and Health with Key to the Scriptures*

1879
Eddy founds the Church of Christ, Scientist (Christian Science)

1881
The Oneida Community dissolves

1881
Charles Taze Russell establishes the Watch Tower Bible and Tract Society (Jehovah's Witnesses)

1881
Charles and Myrtle Fillmore found the Unity School of Christianity

1882
Oahspe: A New Bible is published

1888
The Order of the Golden Dawn is founded

1889
Wovoka (né Jack Wilson) has a vision during a solar eclipse, prompting the Ghost Dance movement

1890
The Church of Jesus Christ of Latter-day Saints ceases the practice of plural marriage

1890
December
The massacre at Wounded Knee brings the Ghost Dance movement to a close

1893
September
The first World's Parliament of Religion is held; Swami Vivekananda speaks at the Parliament, leading to a lecture tour and the establishment of the Vedanta Society in the United States

1904
April
Aleister Crowley is visited by a messenger and transcribes the message into *The Book of Law*, the major text of Thelema

c. 1905
Pierre Bernard founds the Tantrik Order of America

1906
April
Asuza Street Revival marks the beginning of Pentecostalism

1907
The Rosicrucian Fellowship is founded

1910
Hazrat Inayat Khan "introduces" Sufism to the United States

1910
Isaiah Shembe founds the Nazareth Baptist Church

1912
Rudolf Steiner breaks with the Theosophical Society and founds the Anthroposophical Society

1913
Noble Drew Ali establishes the Moorish Science Temple of America

1914
Father Divine claims to be God incarnate and takes the name Rev. Major Jealous Divine

1914
Sri Aurobindo founds his first ashram in India

1915
P. D. Ouspensky begins to study under G. I. Gurdjieff, creator of the esoteric religious practice, "The Fourth Way"

1918
Independent ministry of Simon Kimbangu begins

1924
The Holy Piby is published

1924
Beth B'Nai Abraham congregation of black Jews founded in New York City

1924/5
The Zionist Christian Church, South Africa's largest Zionist Church, founded

1925
July
Meher Baba begins a lifelong vow of silence

1928
The Moorish Science Temple formally incorporated

1930
Guy Ballard visited by Saint Germain on Mount Shasta

1930
Soka Gakkai is founded in Japan

1930
The Church of the Lord (Aladura) is formally established

1930

November

Ras Tafari Makonnen is crowned emperor Haile Selassie I of Ethiopia, inspiring and galvanizing Rastafari, a Jamaican revitalization religion

1931

"Sleeping Prophet" Edgar Cayce founds the Association for Research and Enlightenment

1931

Meher Baba visits the United States for the first time

1931

August

Elijah Poole meets W. D. Fard; Poole determines Fard is Allah made flesh and Fard makes Poole his prophet, naming him Elijah Muhammad

1934

Guy Ballard establishes I AM Activity

1935

Sun Myung Moon experiences his first vision

1938

Dada Lekhraj founds Brahma Kumaris

1940

Sathya Sai Baba first performs miraculous feats and declares himself to be the reincarnation of Sai Baba of Shirdi

1948

Malcolm X converts to the Nation of Islam while in prison

1950

L. Ron Hubbard publishes *Dianetics*

1952

Jim Jones founds Community Unity (later Peoples Temple Christian Church Full Gospel)

1954

L. Ron Hubbard founds the Church of Scientology

1954

Sun Myung Moon establishes the Holy Spirit Association for the Unification of World Christianity (the Unification Church)

1954

May

George King, founder of the Aetherius Society, is contacted by the "Cosmic Masters," who told him he was to become the voice of an "interplanetary parliament"

1955
The Urantia Book is published

1955
The Branch Davidians, led by Ben and Lois Roden, break from the Davidian Seventh-day Adventists founded by Victor Houteff

1956
Ernest Norman, cofounder with his wife Ruth Norman of Unarius Academy of Science, publishes the messages he received from extraterrestrials in *The Truth About Mars* and *The Voice of Venus*

1958
George King receives *The Twelve Blessings*, dictated by Jesus Christ

1958
Maharishi Mahesh Yogi begins a global tour to spread Transcendental Meditation

1961
Rev. Sun Myung Moon of the Unification Church conducts the first "Blessing" (mass marriage) ceremony

1962
New Age group the Findhorn community first gathers

1965
Philip Berg and Yehuda Tzvi Brandwein found the Kabbalah Centre in New York

1965
The U.S. Immigration and Nationality Act is passed, leading to increased religious diversity from Asian immigrants

1965
Malcolm X is assassinated

1965
ECKANKAR is established

1966
A. C. Bhaktivedanta Prabhupada founds the International Society for Krishna Consciousness (ISKCON) in New York

1966
Rev. Sun Myung Moon publishes *Divine Principle*, the central sacred text of the Unification Church

1966
Anton LaVey founds the Church of Satan

1967
The Children of God (the Family International) begins its ministry in California

1968
The Mother (Mirra Alfassa) establishes Auroville as the spiritual retreat of Sri Aurobindo

1968
The Church of All Worlds is incorporated

1968
The Love Israel Family begins

1969
Anton LaVey publishes *The Satanic Bible*

1969
Yogi Bhajan founds 3HO in the United States

1971
John-Roger Hinkins formally incorporates the Movement of Spiritual Inner Awareness (MSIA)

1971
Stephen and Ina May Gaskin found the Farm in Tennessee

1971
Ted Patrick founds FREECOG to cope with conversions of young people to "cults"

1971
One of the first Dianic Wiccan covens is founded

1972
The Findhorn Foundation is formally founded in Scotland.

1973
Ruth Norman is recognized as the healing archangel, Queen Uriel

1973
December
Claude Vorilhon (Raël) receives first visit from the Elohim

1974
The Cult Awareness Network (originally the Citizens' Freedom Foundation) is created

1974
Elizabeth Clare Prophet takes leadership of the Summit Lighthouse, renaming it the Church Universal and Triumphant

1974
Shree Bhagwan Rajneesh (Osho) establishes his first ashram in India

1974
October
Jack Pursel makes contact with Lazaris, begins channeling him shortly thereafter

1975
Michael Aquino splits with the Church of Satan to found the Temple of Set

1976
Helen Schucman publishes *A Course in Miracles*

1977
Jim Jones and nearly one thousand members of Peoples Temple move to Guyana from California

1977
JZ Knight first encounters Ramtha

1978
Louis Farrakhan leads a group of followers to reestablish the Nation of Islam apart from the group led by Warith Dean Muhammad, who aligned the movement with Sunni Islam following Elijah Muhammad's death

1978
November
More than nine hundred members of Peoples Temple commit revolutionary suicide at the Peoples Temple Agricultural Project ("Jonestown") in Guyana

1980
Michelle Remembers is published, setting off the Satanic Panic

1980
Deprogrammer Ted Patrick is convicted of false imprisonment, kidnapping, and conspiracy for his actions taken to remove an individual from a new religious movement

1981
The Osho Movement creates the incorporated city of Rajneeshpuram in Oregon

1983
At the height of the Satanic Panic, several teachers at the McMartin Preschool in California are charged with Satanic abuse of children; the case is ultimately thrown out in court

1984
Ron's Orgs, for practice of Scientology independent of the Church of Scientology, founded

1985
Rajneeshpuram dissolves

1985
June
Bonnie Lou Nettles dies, prompting Marshall Applewhite, cofounder of Human Individual Metamorphosis (later Heaven's Gate) to rethink the movement's theology

1987
Shoko Asahara founds Aum Shinrikyō in Japan

1987
The American Psychological Association denies the validity of the "brainwashing" hypothesis of membership in new religious movements

1988
CESNUR (the Center for Study of New Religions) is founded as the first European institution for scholars of new religious movements

1989
The Temple of the Vampire is granted tax-exempt status in the United States

1990
March
The predicted time of the end-times according to Elizabeth Clare Prophet, prompting members to move to a compound in Montana prior to the event

1992
The Federation of Damanhur reveals their excavation and construction of the Temple of Humankind

1992
Falun Gong is created by Li Hongzhi

1993
February
Bureau of Alcohol, Tobacco, and Firearms serves a warrant to the Branch Davidians; siege of Mount Carmel Center begins

1993
April
Siege of Mount Carmel Center ends in fire; more than eighty Branch Davidians perish

1994
October
The Order of the Solar Temple is involved in a ritual murder-suicide, believing the end-times were near

1995
The Cult Awareness Network declares bankruptcy following their loss in a civil suit

1995
March
Aum Shinrikyō carries out sarin gas attack on Tokyo subway

1997
March
Members of Heaven's Gate commit ritual suicide with appearance of the Hale-Bopp Comet

1998
March
Predicted time of Christ's return according to Hon-Ming Chen, founder of Chen Tao

1999
ISIS emerges separately from al-Qaeda in Iraq

1999
April
Falun Gong holds a silent protest outside Communist headquarters in China

2000
March
Predicted beginning of the apocalypse by the Movement for the Restoration of the Ten Commandments turned into a date of mass murder of Movement members by group leaders

2001
About 450,000 people in the United Kingdom and New Zealand identify as "Jedi" on a census survey, initiating Jediism as a religion

2001
September
Al-Qaeda carries out terrorist attacks on the World Trade Center

2002
The Raëlians claim to have successfully cloned the first human baby

2004
The American Family Foundation is renamed the International Cultic Studies Association

2005
The Church of the Flying Spaghetti Monster (Pastafarianism) emerges as an internet phenomenon

2008
April
Texas Child Protective Services raids the Yearning for Zion Ranch (Fundamentalist Church of Latter-day Saints [FLDS]) following allegations of statutory rape and child abuse

2011
August
Warren Jeffs (prophet of FLDS Church) is convicted of sexual assault on a child and begins serving two life sentences

2012
January
The Missionary Church of Kopimism is formally recognized as a religious institution in Sweden

2017
The death of a member leaves only two Shakers left in the world

2019
May
Founder of NXIVM, Keith Raniere, is convicted of sex trafficking and racketeering

A

Adi Da Samraj (1939–2008)

The repeal of the Asian Exclusion Act in 1965 brought with it an influx of gurus and religious teachers into the United States. But the religious traffic between Asia and the United States had never been one way. In the nineteenth century, New England Transcendentalists like Henry David Thoreau (1817–1862) were fascinated by what they perceived to be the wisdom of the East. In the mid-twentieth century, the Beats developed a fascination with Zen. Thus, the career of the religious teacher known most recently as Adi Da Samraj should be read against the background of American fascination with Eastern religions.

As his consciousness of his identity developed, Adi Da contributed to the mythologization of his own life. Born Franklin Albert Jones on Long Island in 1939, he adopted a sequence of honorific names that were designed to signal his religious significance; they included Bubba Free John, Da Free John, Da Love-Ananda, and Da Avabhasa. As the names suggest, he progressively came to identify with the broad Hindu tradition, seeing himself as an avatar of the divine. His particular mission, as he understood it, was to awaken individuals from the dreams in which they were living so that they could realize their true identity. As his teaching career progressed, he attracted followers and established centers where they could take up residence to concentrate on mastering his teachings. His status as a guru, however, also provoked controversy, with Adi Da being accused of mismanagement and sexual improprieties.

In his own telling, Adi Da was aware of his special status virtually from his birth. He reported that even as a small child he was conscious of being a manifestation of the "Bright," or the ultimate Divine Reality. As he grew up, however, that heightened awareness of his true identity faded and only flickered into light occasionally. Although he studied diligently with his own guru, Rudrananda in New York City and with Rudrananda's own Indian masters, Swami Muktananda and Swami Nityananda, Adi Da would only return to his full consciousness of the Bright in 1970.

During meditation in a Hindu temple in southern California, Adi Da reports that he came to a full realization that he himself was a complete and fully realized being. That, however, was not the end of his extraordinary experiences. In 1986, for example, he claimed to have experienced a "yogic death" that completed his understanding of himself as a divine avatar. Later, in 2000, he experienced another "yogic event" during which he entered directly into the Bright. Adi Da's various religious experiences supported his claim to be a contemporary guru.

Despite his involvement with Hindu gurus, Adi Da insisted that his teachings constituted a distinctive new religious message. One of his final written works, *The Gnosticon*, draws together those elements of Indian traditions that he believed informed his own teaching while simultaneously making the case for its novelty.

Followers' encounters with Adi Da through meditation and study are crucial because he has asserted that being in his company is the only true spiritual practice through which individuals can themselves come into contact with the Bright. He has called his teachings an unparalleled revelation of the truth. Accordingly, residence at one of the sanctuaries in Fiji, Hawaii, and northern California, among which Adi Da himself circulated, has been highly desirable for his followers. Those who could not interact with the guru directly have been instructed to perform their acts of worship (puja) before a photograph of him. The devotee's discipline of devotion to Adi Da through meditation and study is also complemented by a recommended vegetarian diet and yogic regulation of sexuality.

By stating that Adi Da can still be encountered through his writings, recordings of his teachings, and the artwork that he produced, the guru and his followers have tried to ensure that his personal charisma would continue to be communicated, even after his passing. Consequently, the Adidam movement maintains an extensive website (https://www.adidam.org), including audio and video recordings, and some selected texts. In addition, the Dawn Horse Press keeps his many books, as well as video and audio recordings, available for purchase.

See also: Charisma and Leadership in New Religious Movements; Hindu New Religious Movements.

Further Reading

Adi Da Samraj. 2009. *The Aletheon*, 8 vols. Lower Lake, CA: The Dawn Horse Press.

Adi Da Samraj. 2010. *The Gnosticon*. Lower Lake, CA: The Dawn Horse Press.

Sheinfeld, Gerald. 2017. *At the Feet of the Spiritual Master: Stories from My Life with Avatar Adi Da Samraj*. NP: Gerald Publications.

Aetherius Society, The

Founded in 1956 by George King (1919–1997), the Aetherius Society is designed to promote human evolution to a higher spiritual level, guided by revelations that King received from extraterrestrial sources. On May 8, 1954, in London King experienced a call from the "Cosmic Masters" that told him to prepare to become the voice on earth of the "Interplanetary Parliament." Over the course of his life, King would receive more than six hundred "transmissions" from extraplanetary figures. King's teachings, and commentaries on them, are available from the society's website (www.aetherius.org) in print, audio, and video formats in multiple languages.

TEACHINGS AND PRACTICES

The Aetherius Society affirms the existence of advanced extraterrestrial intelligences, such as the Cosmic Master Aetherius who first contacted King and others who subsequently communicated with him. Accordingly, the society contends that there are other planes or realms in which life exists. All life has within it the divine spark of God, who is known by different names in different religions but remains the same being. Humans should strive toward becoming increasingly aware of their divine nature, which will increase the spiritual powers that they can use in the service of others. Prayer, for example, can summon spiritual energy and direct it to positive purposes, such as healing and directing positive energy toward social improvement.

The society draws on eclectic sources in addition to King's experience. King himself is presented as extraordinarily adept at yoga, which prepared him to act as the earthly recipient of cosmic wisdom. The society recommends the practice of yoga as a route to enlightenment. It also endorses the concepts of karma and reincarnation, along with ideas about chakras and auras. Jesus is also accepted as a Cosmic Master, who delivered the group's most important text to King.

The society understands itself as undertaking five "Cosmic Missions." The first is Operation Prayer Power, which aims to concentrate healing spiritual energy on earth through chanting and visualization. The society also sponsors pilgrimages to sites identified as holy mountains, where the power of individuals' prayers can combine with the inherent power of the mountains to promote personal and social well-being. The society provides lectures and workshops on a variety of topics and holds hour-long services, which include visualization, prayer, and chanting as well as an address by King or an official of the group. One specific form of group meeting is devoted to the teachings of *The Twelve Blessings*.

The Twelve Blessings is considered the major religious work of the Aetherius Society. The slim volume is intentionally portrayed as "an extension of the Sermon on the Mount" and is said to have been delivered directly from Jesus himself to King between July 27 and October 12, 1958. As with other scriptures from new religious movements, *The Twelve Blessings* claims both direct ties to an authoritative past and an innovative message tailored exactly for the present. For example, King ends the foreword of the book with a statement from Jesus himself: "Oh, adorable little children, take these. My texts—and read them well. Accept them as your Bible—and ACT upon these—and you will be of great service to your brothers" (p. 10).

The connection of *The Twelve Blessings* to the canonical Christian scriptures is strengthened by its contents. The blessings themselves appear in a form that directly recalls the beatitudes of the Sermon on the Mount. Among those who are counted as blessed are those who work for peace, those who love and those who heal, the givers of thanks, and those who have wisdom. The Earth, Sun, Galaxy, Lords of Karma and Lords of Creation, and the Absolute itself are also blessed. Like the biblical text on which it is built, *The Twelve Blessings* sketches out a desired set of virtues at the same time that it affirms the cosmology of the Aetherius Society.

In a similar attempt to depict itself as the clearest contemporary expression of the message first given by Jesus in the Bible, the Aetherius Society also offers a New Lord's Prayer, which was received by King directly from the Cosmic Master Jesus in 1961. While it loosely follows the form of the biblical prayer, opening with praise of God and continuing with a series of petitions, the new version distinctly reflects the society's worldview and goals. For example, the petitioner requests to be made a channel for God's light and energy so that those on earth may be helped, healed, and uplifted so that they can realize their Higher Selves.

Participation in the activities of the Aetherius Society is largely based on personal interest and initiative. To full members, who must pay annual dues of sixty dollars in the United States and Canada, the society offers an array of information and opportunities, but only requires of them participation in several holidays on the group's ecclesiastical calendar. At least in part because it is largely an "audience cult" in which members can determine their own degree of participation rather than a fully mobilized "cult movement" which monopolizes the time of its members, the Aetherius Society has largely been able to steer clear of the controversies that have dogged many new religions.

See also: Cult; Millennialism; New Scriptures and New Religious Movements.

Further Reading
Aetherius Society, The. 1958. *The Twelve Blessings: The Cosmic Concept for the New Aquarian Age as Given by the Master Jesus in His Overshadowing of George King*, rev. ed. Los Angeles: The Aetherius Press.
King, George. 2000. *The Nine Freedoms*, rev. ed. Los Angeles: The Aetherius Press.
King, George, with Richard Lawrence. 1996. *Contacts with the Gods from Space: Pathway to the New Millennium*. Los Angeles: The Aetherius Press.
Rothstein, Mikael. 2007. "Hagiography and Text in the Aetherius Society." In Diane G. Tumminia, ed., *Alien Worlds: Social and Religious Dimensions of Extraterrestrial Contact*, pp. 3–24. Syracuse, NY: Syracuse University Press.

African New Religious Movements

The African continent, with its more than two thousand ethnic groups and more than fifty nation-states, has long been involved in the global exchange of people, goods, and ideas. Africa's ethnic diversity has produced a wide variety of traditional religious practices, some of which are being revived today. The continent's interactions with people beyond its shores through trade, forced relocation by slavers, military clashes, colonialism, and other contacts exposed its inhabitants to religions that had never been practiced in Africa.

Despite the efforts of many missionaries and other bearers of new religious ideas and practices, transplanted religions almost always went through some alterations in their new, African contexts as local African populations sought to make sense of newly encountered religions on their own terms. Such encounters produced not only adaptations of foreign religions but also spurred the development of indigenous forms of those religions by African religious leaders.

Imported religions, such as various forms of Christianity and Islam, and those developed locally have been used both to support political powers and to challenge them. Colonial political regimes, for example, frequently supported missionary efforts to "civilize" native populations and in turn were supported by the efforts of missionaries. On the other hand, indigenous religious groups, in part because of their ability to mobilize large groups of people, have often been seen as threats to established regimes. New religions in Africa, as elsewhere, have never been confined solely to the "spiritual" realm but have always been involved with a full range of social and political issues.

The African religious economy, with the focus here on sub-Saharan Africa, has been in a continual state of dynamic transformation. It is not surprising, then, that some estimates suggest that there are as many as twelve thousand new religious movements in Africa today.

ISLAMIC MOVEMENTS

Islam came to Africa from the Arabian peninsula soon after the prophet Muhammad received his call in the early seventh century. At that time Islam was still a new religious movement in its original context, just as it was in its new African contexts. Sufi forms of Islam, especially the Qadiriyyah and Tijaniyyah orders, flourished in West Africa and still have a strong presence there. More recently, forms of militant Islam have appeared in several African countries. Some observers see Sufi groups as providing a potential counterweight to jihadist groups, but both forms of Islam have been practiced peacefully and have inspired violent actions.

Nigeria is the most populous country in Africa, with more than two hundred million inhabitants. Although the Nigerian constitution guarantees freedom of religion and the government operates on secular principles, the country is roughly divided between Muslims and Christians, with Muslims concentrated in the north. Clashes between the two groups and between religious groups and the state have been frequent, with some Islamic groups successfully arguing for the implementation of Sharia law in some northern provinces. The history of Islam in Nigeria from the eighteenth century to the present captures at least some of the forms that Islam has taken in Africa and its interactions with other religious groups and with the state.

Islam was first practiced in Nigeria in the tenth century. It attracted the rulers of Hausa city-states in the fourteenth century, though they also tended to retain elements of their traditional religions. Fulani people from the Senegambia region introduced a stricter form of Islam in the sixteenth century, setting the stage for a sequence of Islamic reform movements that continues to the present. Central to that story is Usman dan Fodio (1754–1817). He was a Sufi reformist with an Islamic education who wanted to establish a theocratic state in which there would be no oppression or vice. Usman located himself in the strain of Islam that looked forward to the appearance of the Mahdi, the "rightly guided one" who, according to the traditions in the hadith, would appear just before the Day of Judgment to establish a just society.

Usman was particularly critical of the local Hausa kingdoms that, he claimed, were not practicing pure forms of Islam. He declared a jihad in 1804. His war against the local kingdoms led to him establishing the Sokoto caliphate, which lasted until 1903 when it was conquered by the British.

Usman has been a lasting inspiration for individuals and groups who want to create what they see as a more pure form of Islam in Nigeria. For example, the Izala Society, formally known as the Society for the Removal of Innovation and Re-establishment of the Sunna, formed in the northern Nigerian city of Jos in 1978 and spread to neighboring states in the 1980s. It explicitly follows Usman's example and has been critical both of what it sees as the unfounded religious innovation practiced by Sufi orders and the secular state. Izala sees Usman as the true Sunni and shares his goal of conforming politics and society to Islam, arguing that being nominally Islamic is not enough.

The internationally notorious jihadist group, Boko Haram, likely developed out of the Izala Society in the early 2000s. Although the group was originally known as "People Committed to the Prophet's Teachings and Jihad," the common name of the group combines a Hausa term that broadly encompasses modern, Western, secular education ("Boko") and the Arabic term for things that are forbidden ("Haram"). Accordingly, the group is strongly anti-Western and endorses reliance on the Qur'an for guidance in all matters. Boko Haram is one of many groups that have protested the poverty, radical income inequality, corruption, and abuses of power by state officials that have characterized contemporary Nigerian society. Founded by Muhammad Yusuf (1970–2009), Boko Haram seems not to have been involved in violent incidents until 2009. Although it clashed with Nigerian security forces before then, until that time it had focused on preaching, proselytization, and recruitment of new members.

An incident between police and Boko Haram members in June 2009 during a funeral procession, however, touched off a new, violent phase for the group. The preaching of Salafist Islam, a fundamentalist orientation focused on the purported practices of Muhammad's closest companions, had previously set other groups in conflict with the Nigerian government. For example, the Maitatsine movement, a Mahdist Islamic group that rejected the secular state, desired to purify the practice of Islam, and was also inspired by Usman dan Fodio, had sparked popular uprisings in 1980, 1982, 1984, and 1985. But the government's violent attempts to control Boko Haram provoked its call for jihad and escalating acts of violence, including the murder of male and the kidnapping of female school children. Boko Haram even targeted the Izala Society, which had criticized its turn to violence.

The complex religious situation in Nigeria is also signaled by the formation of groups in the southwest, near Lagos, that espouse distinctive blends of both Christianity and Islam called Chrislam. Such groups argue, for example, that since the same God is worshipped by both Christians and Muslims, it therefore makes sense that the two religions are compatible.

Although Islam in many forms has been practiced throughout Africa in a peaceful manner, it is the occasional outbreaks of violence undertaken in the name of Islam that have attracted widespread public attention. Like other spasms of violence, they need to be carefully investigated in their particular contexts and the temptation to use them to support blanket condemnations of entire categories such as new religious movements or Islam needs to be strenuously resisted.

CHRISTIAN MOVEMENTS

Modern Western missions to Africa began in earnest in the early nineteenth century. While they had some success, there greatest impact has been in inspiring the development of independent Christian churches founded and led by Africans.

Christian religious movements in Africa have also frequently come into conflict with the state. For example, the incarceration of the prophet Simon Kimbangu (1887–1951) in the former Belgian Congo in 1921 was a failed attempt to diminish the perceived threat that his African-Initiated Church posed to the colonial authorities.

Such attempts to make Christianity speak to African people go back to the late seventeenth century, but the African "reformation" of Christianity gained momentum in the late nineteenth century with the formation of a variety of Ethiopianist churches in South Africa. Those churches broke away from mission churches in search of an authentically African form of Christianity. Psalm 68:31, "Let Ethiopia hasten to stretch out it hands to God," served as an organizing concept for the formation of independent churches led by and designed for Africans and the African diaspora.

The late nineteenth and early twentieth century saw the formation of a variety of independent Zionist churches, particularly in southern Africa. Those churches promote a conservative morality, focus on healing and protection from evil, and practice baptism in rivers and the ocean. The specific theological ideas differ from one group to another. The South African Nazareth Baptist Church founded by Isaiah Shembe (c. 1865–1935), for example, observes the Sabbath on Saturday; practices ritual dancing based on its understanding of Psalm 150; has members take the Nazirite vows described in Numbers 6; identifies the holy city of Ekuphakameni, outside of Durban, as the New Jerusalem; and promotes an annual pilgrimage to a second sacred site, the mountain Nhlangakazi, where Shembe received his call to form a new religion.

Zionist churches continue to attract millions of members throughout southern Africa and abroad. In terms of total membership, however, they have been surpassed by the dramatic growth of Pentecostalism throughout sub-Saharan Africa. Pentecostalism reached several African countries soon after the Asuza Street Revival in 1906. Various foreign Pentecostal groups continue to send missionaries to save souls. But Africa also has had its own Pentecostal preachers. William Wadé Harris (c. 1860–1929), for example, began his missionary career in 1913 after he received a vision of the angel Gabriel. He traveled from Liberia to Ghana, preaching that people should get rid of their traditional religious objects and adopt an orthodox form of Christianity. Harris ultimately founded hundreds of church communities. Among the prominent Pentecostal groups in Africa today is Brazil's Universal Church of the Kingdom of God, which has a robust missionary presence throughout the world, preaches a prosperity gospel, and practices healing.

OTHER MOVEMENTS

Although Christianity and Islam dominate the religious economy of sub-Saharan Africa, many other sectarian groups and new religions claim members.

Some groups, such as the Jehovah's Witnesses and the Mormons, have been subjected to state regulation, for example, when Ghana banned them from 1989 to 1994. But the generally tolerant official policies toward religion in Africa have enabled many groups to gain at least a foothold. In Nigeria alone there are members of the Aetherius Society, the International Society for Krishna Consciousness, the Raëlians, the Brahma Kumaris, Eckankar, Rosicrucian groups, and Scientology, among many others. The African-influenced Brazilian religion of Candomblé has been brought back to Africa by Africans who visited Brazil. As befits a continent with the size and population of Africa, religious diversity is thriving and new religions continue to be formed.

See also: Al-Qaeda; Church of the Lord (Aladura); Globalization and New Religious Movements; Kimbangu, Simon (1887–1951); Movement for the Restoration of the Ten Commandments of God, The; Mungiki; Pentecostalism; Shembe, Isaiah (c. 1865–1935); Sufi New Religious Movements; Violence and New Religious Movements; Zionist Churches (Africa).

Further Reading

Clarke, Peter B. 2012. "New Religious Movements in Sub-Saharan Africa." In Olav Hammer & Mikael Rothstein, eds., *The Cambridge Companion to New Religious Movements*, pp. 303–319. Cambridge: Cambridge University Press.

Hackett, Rosalind I. J. 2004. "Prophets, 'False Prophets' and the African State: Emergent Issues of Religious Freedom and Conflict." In Phillip Charles Lucas & Thomas Robbins, eds., *New Religious Movements in the Twenty-First Century: Legal, Political, and Social Challenges in Global Perspective*, pp. 151–178. New York: Routledge.

Hansen, William. 2017. "Boko Haram: Religious Radicalism and Insurrection in Northern Nigeria." *Journal of Asian and African Studies* 52: 551–569.

Jules-Rosette, Bennetta, ed. 1979. *The New Religions of Africa*. Norwood, NJ: Ablex Publishing Corporation.

Tishken, Joel E. 2008. "A Brief History and Typology of the African Reformation." *Nova Religio* 13: 4–10.

Ahmadiyya Movement, The

Described as a "revival movement within Islam" on its website, the Ahmadiyya movement has attracted numerous converts (reported as "tens of millions" in over two hundred countries) and censure from the global Muslim community (https://www.alislam.org/library/ahmadiyya-muslim-community/). As a movement that claims to fulfill Muslim prophecy of the end-times, its members employ ideas common to many millennialist groups and world religions, even as it claims to be the culmination of all of them.

Named for its founder, Mirza Ghulam Ahmad (1835–1908), the Ahmadiyya movement began in India in 1899. Ahmad claimed that he was the Messiah predicted to appear before the end-times, as foretold in the Qur'an and by the prophet Muhammad, as well as the figure who would bring an end to bloodshed and reform Islam and the (metaphorical) second coming of Christ. Since childhood, Ahmad had been receiving revelations regarding his own role and sacred knowledge of all the world's religious traditions. He attracted a number of followers who pledged allegiance to him as the Messiah and who became the first among a wide number of Ahmadiyya members who vowed to spread Ahmad's message and the news of his arrival.

Following Ahmad's death, an electoral council was convened to elect a caliph, who would lead the Ahamiddya community as its spiritual head. Unlike historical Muslim caliphates that often did not separate religious from secular authority, the Ahmadiyya caliph did not (nor was he expected to) preside over state issues. Mirza Masroor Ahmad (1950–), the fifth caliph, currently leads the movement. Though the movement began in India and has its highest concentrations in South Asia and Africa, its headquarters are in London, where it has maintained a presence since the fourth caliph was exiled from India in 1984.

Muslim believers sit in the evening waiting for a lecture in the courtyard of the Ahmadiyya Shaykh. (Dmitriy Feldman/Dreamstime.com)

BELIEFS AND PRACTICES

Like most millennialist groups, the Ahmadiyya movement maintains that the end of the world is imminent. It holds that these last days are predicted in scripture and will result in the definitive triumph of Islam in the world. Similar to many Christian millennialist groups, Ahmadiyya Muslims believe that mass conversion to Islam will serve as both proof of and a catalyst for the impending end-times. Thus, the movement is fundamentally missionary in nature, focusing on proselytization efforts among Muslims (to convince them of the truth of Ahmadiyya) and non-Muslims alike. They maintain that all proselytization must occur through peaceful means, thus rejecting any militarization of Islam—a fact that divides them from millennialist groups like ISIS. Further, as a messianic and revitalization movement, Ahmadiyya Muslims believe that it was Ahmad who ushered in these last days and prompted a reform movement within Islam.

Beyond its millennialist focus, the Ahmadiyya movement maintains a relatively traditional system of Islamic belief and practice. Its members adhere to the six axioms of faith, which are the belief in the existence and unity of God (Allah); the belief in angels; the belief that the Qur'an (and other sacred texts, such as the Bible) is the word of God; the belief that there have been many prophets, with Muhammad serving as the last; the belief in a final Day of Judgment; and the belief in predestination. Diverging from traditional Islamic theology, however, Ahmadiyya Muslims believe that Jesus was crucified but survived until an old age. They also believe that the prophecy of his second advent was metaphorical in nature and is fulfilled in the person of Ahmad. They also believe that the Qur'an is divinely inspired but maintain that God continues to speak to chosen individuals, such as Ahmad.

Ahmadiyya Muslims also practice the five pillars of Islam: the statement of faith in Allah and the prophet Muhammad (Shahada), prayer (*salat*), charity (*zakat*), fasting during Ramadan (*sawm*), and pilgrimage to Mecca (*hajj*). They also follow the practices (sunnah) and teachings (hadith) of Muhammad, though they reject strict adherence to the rulings of any Muslim clerics since Muhammad and until Ahmad. They also practice traditional Muslim holidays, such as the end of Ramadan (*Eid al-Fitr*), while incorporating their own annual ceremonies. Jalsa Salana, for example, is an annual (though not required) gathering of the Ahmadiyya community, or "Promised Messiah Day," which marked the date (March 23) when the first individuals took an oath of allegiance to Ahmad. Additionally, as a missionary movement, it is unsurprising that the Ahmadiyya movement has foregone the traditional sanction against translation of the Qur'an into vernacular languages. Through the movement, the Qur'an has been published in over seventy languages. Ahmadiyya Muslims maintain a respect for other world religions, believing that they are simply incomplete versions of Islam whose members should be approached peacefully.

CONTROVERSY AND CULTURE

Given its controversial beliefs regarding the person of Ahmad as the Messiah and the second coming of Christ among others, the Ahmadiyya movement has experienced criticism and outright persecution in certain instances since its inception in the nineteenth century. Non-Ahmadiyya Muslims have protested the movement and even, in some countries such as Algeria and Pakistan, refused to recognize it as a religion or its members as Muslims. Ahmadiyya Muslims have been subjected to violence, most recently in the United Kingdom in 2016. Christians, though not as virulently, have denounced the belief that Ahmad was the second Coming of Christ or that Christ somehow survived the cross.

Over against the persistent pressure to fold, Ahmadiyya Muslims maintain a global presence and retain a commitment to peaceful proselytization and to sustaining a vital caliphate for the spiritual guidance of the world's Muslims.

See also: ISIS; Messianism and New Religious Movements; Millennialism.

Further Reading
Hanson, John H. 2017. *The Ahmadiyya in the Gold Coast: Muslim Cosmopolitans in the British Empire.* Bloomington: Indiana University Press.

Irawan, Andi Muhammad. 2017. "'They Are Not Muslims': A Critical Discourse Analysis of the Ahmadiyya Sect Issue in Indonesia." *Discourse & Society* 28, no. 2: 162–181.

Khan, Adil Hussain. 2015. *From Sufism to Ahmadiyya: A Muslim Minority Movement in South Asia.* Bloomington: Indiana University Press.

Valentine, Simon Ross. 2008. *Islam and the Ahmadiyya Jama'at: History, Belief, Practice.* New York: Columbia University Press.

Alamo, Tony (1934–2017)

The entertainment industry centered in Hollywood plays an important role in American mythology. It frequently attracts individuals who aspire to "make it" in films, television, or the recording industry. So it was with Bernie LaZar Hoffman who moved there from Missouri in 1964. Seeking his fortune in entertainment, Hoffman would call himself Marcus Abad, perhaps to minimize his Jewish ancestry, then Tony Fortunato and finally Tony Alamo in imitation of the then-popular Italian crooners. Hoffman's aspirations were frustrated, but he did prosper as an owner of a string of health clubs. He did not have a religious upbringing and had no religious inclinations. Thus, it came as a shock when during a business meeting in 1964 he experienced a vision that told him that Jesus was soon coming back. He also had a vision of heaven and hell.

As Alamo wrestled with the implications of his experience, he turned to a friend, Edith Opal Horn (1925–1982), to help him figure out what it meant. Horn herself had failed to realize her dream of becoming an actress and was working as an itinerant preacher. In the current view of Tony Alamo Christian Ministries (see www.alamoministries.com), Horn had been marked for a special role from birth. She had been miraculously healed of tuberculosis as a child, had received visions of events in the Book of Revelation, and was informed by God that she would be preaching the Gospel in the last days before Jesus's return. Horn helped confirm Alamo's Christian conversion and the two married in 1966.

In Alamo's mythology, Horn, who took the name Susan Alamo, was the driving force behind the Jesus Movement of the 1960s and 1970s. Susan and Tony did minister to the members of the youth subculture in the Hollywood area. Much of their message fit well with the evangelical Christianity with which Susan was familiar from her birthplace in Arkansas and her time in southern California.

The Alamos' message was simple. They asserted that Jesus was the way, the truth, and the life and that no one could be saved by any other means (see John 14:6). They also asserted that Jesus had come to earth to restore his lost holiness in humans. Beyond that, they asserted based on their understanding of texts like Matthew 5:17 ("Do not think that I have come to abolish the law or the prophets; I have come not to abolish but to fulfill") that the fulfillment of the entire law outlined in both the Hebrew Bible and the Christian Scriptures was incumbent on true Christians. None of that really set the Alamo's preaching outside the evangelical mainstream. A third conclusion, however, definitely did.

Despite their references to commissioning visions, neither Tony nor Susan particularly emphasized their prophetic status. Tony took a literalist approach to the scriptures in the King James translation, emphasizing that "God's word means what it says." He eventually drew from that some startling conclusions. Based on the examples of the patriarchs Abraham and Isaac, Tony concluded that the ancient Hebrews practiced polygamy. Moreover, since he could find no direct condemnation of such a practice in the New Testament, save for the injunction that bishops and deacons should have only one wife (see I Timothy 3), he decided that early Christians followed the examples of the patriarchs and took multiple wives. Unlike the early Mormon Church or the Fundamentalist Latter-day Saints, Alamo did not appeal to direct revelation to support his exegesis. He simply claimed to be relaying the clear statements of scripture.

Another bit of interpretation took his argument further. Commenting on the injunction in Genesis 1:28 to be fruitful and multiply, Alamo argued that girls at or even under the age of puberty could be taken as wives because it would increase their opportunities to be fruitful by bearing children.

Alamo moved his center of operations to Dyer, Arkansas, in 1976, where he kept his followers isolated except for missionary efforts. External opposition and internal dissent led to a raid on the community in nearby Fouke, Arkansas, in 2008 on charges of child pornography. In 2009, Alamo was found guilty of transporting underage girls across state lines for sex and was sentenced to 175 years in prison. He died in prison in 2017, but a website keeps his teachings alive.

See also: Fundamentalist Mormons; Sex, Sexuality, and New Religious Movements.

Further Reading
Allen, Spencer L. 2014. "The Anomaly of Tony Alamo Christian Ministries: A New Testament-based Call for Christian Polygamy." *Nova Religio* 17: 61–82.

Ali, Noble Drew (1886–1929)

The prophetic persona that Noble Drew Ali and his followers crafted for him makes it difficult to extract accurate biographical details from the pious legends about his life. The founder of the Moorish Science Temple of America was born in 1886 in North Carolina, purportedly to a Cherokee mother and a "Moorish" father who named him Timothy Drew. At sixteen, he traveled to Egypt with merchant marines and, while there, was initiated into an ancient magical cult. He then received the name Noble Drew Ali.

Drew Ali next surfaced in New Jersey around 1913 when he founded the Canaanite Temple, a precursor to the Moorish Science Temple, which would only be formally incorporated in Chicago in 1928. Drew Ali's teaching was consistent throughout his life. He asserted that Americans of African descent were not "Negroes" or any other common designation but rather descendants of an Asiatic race that had come to Africa from ancient Canaan. As "Moors," they had a history that was not restricted to their suffering under slavery and colonial domination; they also had a true religion, Islam.

Drew Ali recorded his teachings primarily in what he called a new edition of the Koran that he had "divinely prepared." That Koran, however, looked nothing like the Arabic Qur'an and instead heavily relied on passages taken from Levi

Dowling's *The Aquarian Gospel of Jesus Christ* and the Rosicrucian *Unto Thee I Grant*. Drew Ali's eclectic teaching blended esoteric sources with elements of Freemasonry and Islamic ideas and practices that he likely derived from black Shriners, particularly The Ancient Egyptian Arabic Order and Nobles of the Mystic Shrine. His distinctive synthesis is captured in the statement that the Moorish Science Temple honored all the prophets, particularly Jesus, Muhammad, Buddha, and Confucius.

Some texts from the movement suggest that Drew Ali went so far as to indicate that he himself was an incarnation of both Jesus and Muhammad. The underlying theory was apparently that there was only one God and all prophets, despite superficial differences, were unified in the message about Him. Similarly, all scriptures were also unified in what they conveyed. From that perspective, Drew Ali became the particular prophet for a specific people, the Moors, who had lost their true identity.

While Drew Ali was successful in attracting as many as thirty thousand members in the 1920s, his time as the head of the Temple was cut short by his death in 1929 under uncertain circumstances. No single figure succeeded in replacing him and the Temple broke into factions. Drew Ali, however, is still revered as the founding prophet by Moorish Science practitioners throughout the world.

See also: Moorish Science Temple of America, The; Nation of Islam, The; New Scriptures and New Religious Movements; Race and New Religious Movements.

Further Reading

Dorman, Jacob S. 2020. *The Princess and the Prophet: The Secret History of Magic, Race, and Moorish Muslims in America*. Boston: Beacon Press.

Drew Ali, Noble. 1927. *The Holy Koran of the Moorish Science Temple of America*. Available at: hermetic.com/moorish/7koran.

Gomez, Michael A. 2005. *Black Crescent: The Experience and Legacy of African Muslims in the Americas*. Cambridge: Cambridge University Press.

Al-Qaeda

ORIGINS

In the twenty-first century, al-Qaeda, translated as "the Foundation" or "the Base," has become synonymous with one word: "terror." Following major terror attacks in the United States and Indonesia, al-Qaeda served as the prime example of militant Islamism and a central target of the modern "war on terror." However, the movement's founders and members have consistently maintained that their use of violence represents a defensive response to global apostasy from Islam, in general, and Western imperialism and atrocity, specifically. Most Muslims deny al-Qaeda's connection to Islam, which they say promotes peace over violence, but members of al-Qaeda believe that it is they who are preserving Islam.

Before al-Qaeda was formalized, Osama bin Laden provided a support network for Muslims fighting against the Soviet Union during the 1979 war in Afghanistan. Seeing the need for a more organized structure—particularly given the network's multinational membership by the late 1980s—Osama bin Laden officially founded al-Qaeda in 1988. Its formal purpose was to oppose intervention in Muslim countries. Bin Laden led al-Qaeda until his assassination in 2011.

At various points in its history, al-Qaeda has been affiliated and even merged with other Islamist groups whose aims aligned with its own, particularly with groups that target the United States. During the 1990s, U.S. involvement in the Gulf War and its continued engagement in the Israeli-Palestinian conflict heightened tensions between the United States and global Islamist movements, particularly al-Qaeda, prompting bombings of several U.S. embassies in Nairobi, Kenya, and Dar es Salaam, Tanzania in 1998.

BELIEFS AND PRACTICES

Like many Islamist groups, al-Qaeda derives much of its ideology from the work of Sayyid Qutb, a former leader of the Muslim Brotherhood in Egypt. Qutb opposed what he saw as the westernization of Muslim countries, which represented a weakening of Islamic law and a reversion to "jahiliyyah," or the time before the founding of Islam. He admonished Muslims to reestablish godly, Sunni order in formerly Muslim nations and advocated for lesser jihad, or "defensive jihad," which emphasized the need to protect Islam, with violence if necessary, when the religion was threatened. This ideology is often referred to as Salafism, which represents the belief that Islam needed to experience a revival of the fierce commitment of the earliest Muslims. Salafists generally argue that all Muslims not seeking such ends are in a state of apostasy or "kafir," making them equally liable to be targeted by groups like al-Qaeda.

Members of al-Qaeda believe that they are acting in accordance with the principles of Islam based on their interpretation of the Qur'an, the Muslim holy text. Their willingness to employ violence, which they view as righteous, has led most Muslims to condemn their actions as heretical and antithetical to the principles of Islam. Al-Qaeda uses violence or terror to provoke Western nations, particularly the United States, into conflict, thus thinning the resources of these countries and ultimately fueling the economic and political collapse of the West. Such a collapse will leave room for Islam to ascend as the only viable religion and governing system in the world.

Though al-Qaeda maintains a central chain of command, with Ayman al-Zawahiri as its current leader, the organization of al-Qaeda is purposefully diffuse and organized into "affiliates," which are generally organized by country or territory (such as al-Qaeda in Syria or al-Qaeda in Gaza). Though connected in ideology and tactics, members are often kept separate and unaware of each other, to ensure practices and plans are kept secret. Given this lack of transparency, it is difficult to estimate the number of al-Qaeda members who are currently active.

9/11 AND TERROR IN THE TWENTY-FIRST CENTURY

On September 11, 2001, nineteen al-Qaeda operatives hijacked four planes, three of which hit their intended targets, killing nearly three thousand people and becoming the deadliest day in American history since the Japanese attacked Pearl Harbor in 1941. The event instantly raised the global profile of al-Qaeda. However, al-Qaeda has had its greatest impact by inciting sectarian violence among Muslims, a fact that is often missed in portrayals of al-Qaeda by the media.

See also: ISIS; Salafism; Violence and New Religious Movements.

Further Reading
Holbrook, Donald, ed. 2018. *Al-Qaeda 2.0.* Oxford; New York: Oxford University Press.
Lawrence, Bruce, ed. 2005. *Messages to the World: The Statements of Osama bin Laden.* London; New York: Verso Books.
Wright, Lawrence. 2007. *The Looming Tower: Al-Qaeda and the Road to 9/11.* New York: Vintage Books Edition, Random House.

Amana Society

Like the Oneida Society, the Amana Society or Amana Colonies began as a communal religious movement that transformed into a for-profit business, the result of both religious innovation and financial necessity. Today, both are better known for their commercial products (respectively, Oneida silver and Amana crafts, crops, and energy, among other items) than their religious roots. Like the Mansion House of Oneida, New York, the Amana Colonies are now national heritage sites and represent Iowa's largest tourist attraction.

The movement arose out of a subset of eighteenth-century German Pietists known as the Community of True Inspiration, who believed, among other things, that their members received direct inspiration from God and served as "instruments" for the will of God. After years of persecution, instrument Christian Metz and other prominent members of the group determined that their survival depended upon immigration to the United States. The movement arrived in New York in the 1840s, first settling outside of Buffalo, New York. However, the success of the group prompted further immigration and led its founders to purchase territory near the Iowa River, where the Amana Colonies were established in 1855, incorporated as a business, as was required under Iowa law. "Amana" translates to "faithful" and "constant" in Hebrew.

The colonies were divided into villages run by a set of elders who answered to the Great Council of Brethren who oversaw the entire enterprise. Gender generally dictated the positions one held, with women having less variety than men and rarely doing hard agricultural labor or serving skilled positions, such as medical personnel. All colony members were expected to work and received an annual salary to be spent in the various village stores; members also invested money in a "common fund" intended for the running of the society. They were not totally self-sufficient, however; they relied on the outside community for certain goods and sold their wares as well. Meals were taken together and jobs were usually assigned according to age and gender. Members spoke English, German, and Kolonie-Deutsch, a dialect specific to Amana. Despite the individualistic bent of German Pietism, which emphasized the personal connection of each believer to

God, the society quite intentionally dissolved rank (save for the governing elders) and sought to live communally—to create a godly society focused on good work for God and for each other.

Besides being the economic arm of Amana, the church was the central governing institution of the colonies. Services were held every day, sometimes twice a day. During worship services, men and women sat separately and then according to age (young mothers with children sat toward the back and elders sat toward the front). Seating denoted status, as did the service one attended. Different services were held for different age groups or for people with positions of prominence in the community. Like other communal religious groups, including Oneida, the Amana Colonies reconfigured relationships between their members. Marriage, and its ensuing sexual relationship, was viewed with disdain and seen as a sign of spiritual "weakness." For those who did fall victim to human foibles such as sexual desire, marriages were allowed, but weddings were rarely joyous occasions and procreation was discouraged.

In 1932 and as a result of the Great Depression, the movement split into the Amana Church Society and the for-profit Amana Society. Today there are seven Amana Colonies, or villages, still existent, though communal living stopped when the group split. According to the most recent U.S. Census in 2010, the largest village comprises nearly six hundred members and the smallest nearly sixty; altogether there are around fifteen hundred people remaining in the Amana Colonies, which is considerable given that, in their heyday in the 1910s, there were around two thousand colonists. Those who remain are engaged in the maintenance of the colonies as tourist sites and participate in the various industries, including the creation of handcrafts, energy production, food services, and farming. However, the religious thread is not lost, as the Amana Church Society proclaims on its website that it continues "to be the religious foundation of the community" (www.amanachurch.com).

See also: Marriage and Relationships in New Religious Movements; Oneida Community, The; Utopianism in New Religious Movements.

Further Reading
Hoehnle, Peter. 2003. *The Amana People: History of a Religious Community.* Iowa City, IA: University of Iowa Press.
Shambaugh, Bertha M. H., & Deb Schense. 2010 [1908]. *Amana: The Community of True Inspiration.* Iowa City, IA: Penfield Books.
Webber, Phillip E. 2009. *Kolonie-Deutsch: Life and Language in Amana.* Iowa City, IA: University of Iowa Press.

Amish, The

The public's engagement with the Amish is often reduced to either curiosity, because of their perceived antimodernism, or consumerism, because of the vast array of Amish "goods" one can purchase online or at farmer's markets. Living a simple life, close to God and without the trappings of modern convenience, the Amish are a self-consciously "old" new religion.

An Amish farmer. The Amish generally avoid using mechanical tools and frequently employ organic practices. (Corel)

ORIGINS AND HISTORY

The Amish descend from the Anabaptist tradition, a strain of Protestantism from the sixteenth century that produced multiple sects. Specifically, the Amish derive their name and trace a lineage from Jakob Amman (1644–c. 1712), a member of the Anabaptist sect known as the Swiss Brethren, who split from the group over questions of membership and relationships to those in the outside world. Amman desired a more exclusivist tradition, with strictures placed on communication with those who sin or leave the community and the society at large.

Due to a rise in religious persecution in Switzerland during the eighteenth century, the Amish began to immigrate to North America, specifically Pennsylvania, which was a colony founded on principles of religious toleration. During the nineteenth century, the Amish community fractured into two primary groups: the Amish Mennonites and the Old Order Amish. The Amish Mennonites were those who favored assimilation into American society and ultimately merged with the Mennonite Church (another Anabaptist denomination), often dropping the name "Amish" altogether. The Old Order Amish were those who wished to retain their traditional way of life and practice apart from external society. Fractures would continue to occur throughout the twentieth century over issues of language (to retain their specific dialect), the adoption of a select few modern amenities, and service during wartime.

Today, there are many Amish sects, not all of which would fit the picture painted of Amish life. Each Amish community functions with its own degree of autonomy or "Ordnung," as there is no central governing body. Most members of Amish communities have contact with the outside world (whom they call "English"), out of necessity and proximity, though the strictest sects regulate the degree and type of contact with those who are non-Amish. In total, there are around two hundred thousand Amish living in the United States.

BELIEFS AND PRACTICES

The Amish maintain that simplicity is key to a good and godly life. They believe that people must remain humble (Demut) and submit to the will of God with composure (Gelassenheit). The crime of arrogance (Hochmut) is seen as a major sin against God and the community. In everything, the individual is subordinated to the group. Though they do not live communally, this view is reflected in their desire for equality among neighbors and the rejection of accumulated wealth and status symbols, such as clothes. They are pacifists as well, believing that taking up arms is both a violation of God's law and the result of hubris.

Central to all Anabaptist traditions is the practice of believer's baptism. In contrast to infant baptism, members of the Amish church are baptized sometime in their late teens through early twenties, because members should enter the community of their own free will and usually after an experience of the saving grace of God. Prior to baptism, Amish teenagers can live outside the community to determine whether they wish to be formally baptized and renounce life outside (also known as Rumspringa).

Maintaining a cohesive community is central to Amish practice. The Amish maintain their own separate language, known as Pennsylvania Dutch, a German dialect, though they often use High German for worship services and are fluent in English to interact with outsiders. Those who violate rules are called to confess and repent of their behavior before the entire congregation, since Amish hold the belief that the sin of one member taints the entire community. Those who refuse to confess or do not change their ways may be excommunicated and "shunned," meaning those who remain in the community are forbidden from contact with them. The same would occur for those who have been baptized, but then choose to renounce their faith and leave—a violation viewed as a broken vow against God and community.

Community unity is also furthered through self-sufficiency, which some would characterize as isolation from society. The Amish are encouraged to work from home and to focus on working the land around them, a reflection of their belief that God blesses those who live in harmony with nature. Their eschewing of modern technology is also reflective of the desire to unite the community, not out of any inherent belief that modern devices are evil. If distracted by modern conveniences or the ability to travel long distances in cars, the community may suffer. It is the Old Order Amish who are the strictest in their adherence to these principles and practices, whereas others, such as the Beachy Amish, allow cars and certain modern amenities.

IN CONTEMPORARY CULTURE

During the late twentieth and early twenty-first century, the Amish became unwitting fodder for pop culture. *Witness*, a film starring Harrison Ford and Kelly McGillis, portrayed a fictional Amish community whose world is disrupted when one of their group witnesses a violent crime. Though the film was a critical and box office hit, many Amish expressed concern at their portrayal and fear over what this publicity would do to their communities. More recently, the television show *Breaking Amish* purported to trace the experience of young Amish people on Rumspringa; however, it was discovered later that the series was staged and that most of the cast had been living outside of the community for some time.

With their buggies and their simple way of life, the Amish will continue to evoke a degree of cultural fascination, however undesired.

See also: Membership and New Religious Movements; Sect.

Further Reading
Hostetler, John. 1993. *Amish Society*. Baltimore, MD: Johns Hopkins University Press.
Kraybill, Donald B., Karen M. Johnson-Weiner, & Steven M. Nolt. 2013. *The Amish*. Baltimore, MD: Johns Hopkins University Press.
Nolt, Steven M., & Thomas J. Myers. 2007. *Plain Diversity: Amish Cultures and Identities*. Baltimore, MD: Johns Hopkins University Press.

Anamadim

Religions have always addressed the full range of human experiences, including the lifecycle from birth through death (and possible rebirths and redeaths). Few if any aspects of life escape behavioral prescriptions enforced by religions to promote human progress toward specified goals, whether they are defined as salvation, enlightenment, or something else. Among other things, religions have been particularly interested in regulating what and how individuals eat, or not.

That perspective at least partially lessens the shock of discovering a new religion that exists primarily online and addresses individuals who are experiencing the eating disorder of anorexia. There is no central organization for the religion but rather a variety of expressions of it in personal blogs and other formats on the internet. "Project Shapeshift," probably the earliest website, is now devoted to being a "Pro-Ana/Pro-Reality/Ana Acceptance Community" (see https://project-shapeshift.net/index.html), which offers both publically available content and a private Community Forum. It is now run by an individual who has taken the name "AnaEmpathGirl." What takes Project Shapeshift and related internet sites out of the realm of health and wellness and into the realm of religion is the presence of texts and practices that take distinctly religious forms.

The creator of the Project Shapeshift website, writing under the name of "Narcissa," is generally credited with being the first to write of "Ana" as a distinct entity named "Anamadim," though there are discrepancies concerning whether Narcissa created Anamadim or actually contacted her through occult rituals. Narcissa described Ana as an "Entity within" who had an existence separate from the individual self. The personification of Ana led easily to the perception of her as a deity, the goddess of anorexia. Other goddesses, such as "ana" and "mia" (the second is related to bulimia and both typically written in lower case) have also been identified.

Pro-Ana websites feature such religious practices as an invocation of the goddess, which is to be undertaken at 1:47 a.m. on the night of the new moon. The invocation, in one form, includes a plea to help the practitioner's body shed density and become a light vessel. Expressions of faith can also be found. One version of "Ana's Creed," clearly modeled on the Christian Nicene creed, begins "I believe in control, the only force mighty enough to bring order in the chaos that is my world" (see https://anastart.weebly.com/ana-creed-and-thin-commandments.html). The same website presents a set of "thin commandments," doubtlessly patterned on those of the Hebrew Bible. The first asserts that "If you aren't thin, you aren't attractive" and the second strikingly emphasizes that "Being thin is more important than being healthy." For individuals attuned to the religious rhetoric of the Jewish and Christian traditions, the religious character of Pro-Ana websites is unavoidable. Echoes of the Lord's Prayer, for example, appear in this comment: "I shall not be tempted by the enemy (food), and I shall not give into temptation should it arise. Should I be in such a weakened state and I should cave, I will feel guilty and punish myself accordingly, for I have failed her" (see https://theproanalifestyle00.wordpress.com/about/).

Since eating disorders are classified as mental illnesses in the *Diagnostic and Statistical Manual of Mental Disorders* published by the American Psychiatric Association, it is imperative to figure out what the adoption of religious practices and textual forms does for the Pro-Ana community. It is clear that texts like the Thin Commandments and Ana's Creed offer those who accept them a sense of power and agency. Instead of being at the mercy of a disease, they have chosen a way of life. Moreover, they can enlist the power of entities greater than themselves to support their choices and practices. Like other religions, then, the religion of the Pro-Ana community is about using available power to set oneself on the path toward a religiously desirable goal.

See also: Food and New Religious Movements; New Religions on/and the Internet; Women in New Religious Movements.

Further Reading

Alderton, Zoe. 2018. *The Aesthetics of Self-Harm: The Visual Rhetoric of Online Self-Harm Communities.* New York: Routledge.

Singler, Beth. 2011. *"Skeletons into Goddesses": Creating Religion, The Case of the Pro-Ana Movement and Anamadim.* MA Thesis, The University of Cambridge.

Singler, Beth. 2017. "No Leader, No Followers: The Internet and the End of Charisma?" In Eugene V. Gallagher, ed., *Visioning New and Minority Religions: Projecting the Future*, pp. 61–73. New York: Routledge.

Zeller, Benjamin E., Marie W. Dallam, Reid L. Neilson, & Nora L. Rubel. 2014. *Religion, Food, and Eating in North America.* New York: Columbia University Press.

Anthroposophy

An offshoot of Theosophy, Anthroposophy shares a great deal with its parent tradition. Both are religions that place a premium on the innate human ability to discover occult knowledge, particularly that gleaned from higher, spiritual dimensions. Both believe that Great Masters have been visiting the earth throughout history to help humanity in their spiritual development and from whom much of this occult knowledge derives. Both have been critiqued for an evolutionary theory of race that seems to place the "Aryan" race above others. Where the two religious movements diverge can be traced to the founder of Anthroposophy, Rudolf Steiner (1861–1925).

Steiner joined the Theosophical Society at the turn of the twentieth century, even serving as secretary of its German chapter from 1902 to 1912. However, Steiner grew increasingly critical of Theosophy's privileging of Asian religious sources. In particular, he was perturbed by the Theosophical position that Jesus was simply the chosen Avatar of Great Masters and not the turning point of all spiritual history. In part, Steiner founded Anthroposophy in 1912 to highlight the importance of Jesus and to emphasize the Christian esoteric tradition. The name "Anthroposophy," meaning "human wisdom," versus "Theosophy," meaning divine wisdom, reflected the belief that human beings had once possessed divine abilities, but had lost them over time. Reclamation of these divine powers began through belief in Jesus Christ and his miraculous abilities.

Steiner was also greatly influenced by the natural sciences, wishing to apply spiritual knowledge to the practice of medicine, agriculture, and education, not only to the advancement of the individual soul. Combining science and religion from the start, Steiner proposed Anthroposophy as a "research method" into the nature of reality and the human psyche. Steiner argued that the spiritual world was comprehensible and observable by all people once they had developed their mental faculties properly. By methodically developing mental faculties, one could perceive the spiritual realm, ultimate truths, and track gains in physical and intellectual ability, which were quantifiable measures of spiritual development. Those who achieved the highest levels of divine ability could experience clairvoyance and heightened senses as well as the ability to receive inspiration directly from the spiritual realm. Like Theosophy (and in contrast to the Christian worldview it privileged), Anthroposophy maintains a belief in reincarnation and the effects of karma, arguing that each human being not only evolves in a particular lifetime on earth but over successive lifetimes spent on earth and in the spiritual realm.

However, defying the individualistic nature of this practice, Steiner advocated for a more socially conscious worldview and believed spiritual development implied community development. This led to a number of institutions based on anthroposophical beliefs. The most renowned of these programs is the Waldorf school program. At Waldorf schools, students are encouraged to develop their own interests at their own pace, with a premium placed on developing their imagination and creative faculties. Though the schools have experienced scrutiny for their position on standardized testing and, more recently, vaccines, the Waldorf schools are still considered the most successful independent school program in the world.

Steiner and Anthroposophy came under scrutiny for providing language and inspiration to Nazi theories of Aryan racial superiority. In Helena Petrovna Blavatsky's (1831–1891) original description, there were seven "root races" that represented different stages in spiritual and human evolution. At their particular historical moment, argued Blavatsky and Steiner, those representing the highest stage of evolution were Aryan, or the fifth root race. Steiner, however, reportedly associated Aryanism with Christianity and whiteness, thus marking all other religious and racial groups as inferior.

Conversely, Anthroposophy has been touted for its role in the modern environmentalism movement, particularly in sustainable organic farming. Steiner also advocated for the creation of cooperative and socially conscious financial institutions aimed at eliminating disparities in wealth and promoting community. There is also a society for doctors of Anthroposophical medicine (though the latter has faced critique from the medical community as peddling pseudoscience). The Anthroposophical Society, which was established in 1912 in Germany, but whose largest chapter is now in the United States, spans fifty countries and counts over fifty thousand active members.

See also: Blavatsky, Helena Petrovna (1831–1891); Occultism and Esotericism; Race and New Religious Movements; Science, Technology, and New Religious Movements; Theosophical Society, The; Theosophy.

Further Reading

Chyrssides, George D. 2011. "Anthroposophy." In *Historical Dictionary of New Religious Movements*. Lanham, MD: Scarecrow Press.

McKanan, Dan. 2018. *Eco-Alchemy: Anthroposophy and the History and Future of Environmentalism*. Berkeley: University of California Press.

Steiner, Rudolf. 1908. *How to Know Higher Worlds: A Modern Path of Initiation*. London: Theosophical Publishing Society.

Anticult Movement, The

Whenever and wherever new religions have appeared, they have experienced skepticism and resistance from the surrounding society. The opposition to new religions is not a recent phenomenon.

In 186 BCE, for example, the Roman Senate issued a decree that prohibited the worship of Dionysus or Bacchus. The rites were identified as *superstitio* (roughly "superstition" or ritual practice outside the official Roman religion), which threatened the Roman political and religious order. Early forms of Christianity would also be identified as *superstitio* in the Roman Empire and were subject to occasional, regional persecution. Of the many broad critiques written against Christianity before it achieved legal favor in the fourth century, one of the fullest was written by the philosopher Celsus in the second century. He both questioned the status imputed to Jesus, whom he saw as a common magician, and mocked the gullibility of those who accepted him as their savior.

Early American history reveals a similar suspicion about new religions. In the late eighteenth century, Valentine Rathbun produced a pamphlet against the Shakers, who had begun proselytizing in New York and New England. *An Account of the Matter, Form, and Manner of a New and Strange Religion, Taught and Propagated by a Number of Europeans, Living in a Place Called Nisqueunia, in the*

State of New-York described the group as being held in thrall by their leader, Mother Ann Lee, whom they identified as a figure in the Book of Revelation (see Rev. 12:2) and the second coming of the Christ. Like Celsus before him, the author excoriated the blindness of the Shaker converts who could not see the falsity of Lee's claims. He further accused the Shakers of everything from practicing magic to committing murder.

Crucial to Rathbun's attack on the Shakers was his claim to have spent time among them as a potential convert. The appeal to personal experience, even from a disgruntled former member, was designed to be unimpeachable. Further, Rathbun claimed only to be interested in serving the public good, with no ulterior motives of his own. Both of those positions, the privileged knowledge of former members and the claim of having no agenda other than helping others, remain important elements of anticult arguments today.

Broadsides against "new and strange" religions continued to be published in the nineteenth century, with the Church of Jesus Christ of Latter-day Saints receiving sustained criticism of things like Joseph Smith's claim to have experienced visions and a divine commission as a prophet to the historical inaccuracies of *The Book of Mormon*.

From an historical perspective, then, the contemporary anticult movement that began in the early 1970s in the United States and is now present throughout the world is a continuation of a long-established antipathy to the appearance of religious innovations. The vocabulary of invective has changed somewhat from the Roman use of *superstitio*, but the general approach of casting doubt on the motives of the leaders of new groups, emphasizing the gullibility of converts, and warning about the negative impact that new religions can exert on the religious, social, and political status quo has remained constant for more than two thousand years.

COUNTERCULT MOVEMENTS

One of the distinctive elements of the contemporary anticult movement has been its ability to invest the term "cult" itself with powerful, negative signifying power. The negative use of the term itself can be found in the late nineteenth-century Christian writings that identify new and alternative religions as dangerous heresies. In fact, the contemporary anticult movement was preceded by and exists alongside a vigorous Christian ministry that strives to identify and combat what it perceives as doctrinal errors that threaten the true (conservative, evangelical) expressions of Christian faith. In many instances, Christian countercult activists employ a more elastic conception of what counts as a cult than even their secular counterparts. It is not uncommon, for example, to find the Roman Catholic Church lumped in with the International Society for Krishna Consciousness (ISKCON), Neopaganism, and the Unification Church as "cults."

Since the 1970s there has also been an active Jewish countercult movement. In 1972, for example, Rabbi Maurice Davis founded Citizens Engaged in Reuniting Families, which focused on retrieving individuals who had joined the Unification Church. Davis also participated in the American Family Foundation, which later became the International Cultic Studies Association. Since 1985, Jews for

Judaism has been the most prominent organization resisting efforts to convert Jews to various new religions, including Jews for Jesus.

Although countercult organizations have a particular focus on maintaining and defending what they perceive as religious orthodoxy and preventing the loss of members through conversion, they have frequently focused their attention on the same groups as the secular anticult movement, though for different reasons.

THE CONTEMPORARY ANTI-CULT MOVEMENT

In its current form, the contemporary anticult movement dates to the early 1970s in California. Several parents were alarmed when their young adult children left college or jobs to join the group of evangelizing "Jesus people," then known as the Children of God, and began to seek ways to "recover" their "lost" family members. Their efforts remained disjointed and ad hoc, but they soon found a champion in Ted Patrick (1930–), a California state official who himself had become concerned about the recruiting practices of the Children of God. Patrick, along with one of the parents, William Rambur, helped to form the first contemporary anticult group, eventually known as FREECOG, or Free the Children of God.

Over time, the developing anticult movement broadened its scope to include other groups that were actively proselytizing at the time, including ISKCON and the Unification Church, among others. Even as FREECOG changed its name to the Citizens Freedom Foundation and then in 1986 to the Cult Awareness Network (CAN), anticult organizations remained largely regional, dependent on the actions of volunteers, and consequently prone to short lifespans. Only CAN, which lasted in its original form until 1996, and the American Family Foundation, founded in 1979 and now known as the International Cultic Studies Association, succeeded in establishing a national presence.

At the core of the contemporary anticult movement is a distinctive set of propositions. First, many new religious movements are, in fact, dangerous cults, and there are few, if any, significant differences among them. Second, they pose a danger to individuals by subjecting them to processes of brainwashing or coercive persuasion, which they are virtually powerless to resist. Third, that deception is practiced by manipulative and deceptive leaders who are interested primarily in their own gratification. Fourth, consequently, dangerous cults deprive individuals of their free will and exploit them for labor, money, and even sex. Fifth, the negative influence of dangerous cults extends to families, which are ripped apart when individuals convert, and to society as a whole, which loses productive members. Sixth, because individuals are kept in dangerous cults by processes of irresistible brainwashing or thought reform, they need outside intervention to be "rescued" and returned to their families, to their free will, and to being productive members of society. Seventh, that intervention originally took the form of involuntary "deprogramming," which attempted to wrench individuals away from their cult membership and return them to their "right minds." Over time, more sophisticated, and purportedly therapeutic approaches, such as voluntary deprogramming and, more recently, exit counseling have developed to accomplish the same ends.

The concept of deprogramming, which has been central to the anticult movement in various forms, depends on the related concept that individuals had somehow been programmed or brainwashed by devious cult leaders. By the mid-1980s, however, the power of the brainwashing explanation of conversion, and with it the argument in favor of deprogramming, began to suffer serious challenges. In 1987, the American Psychological Association declined to accept a report from a task force led by Margaret Singer (1921–2003) that endorsed the brainwashing hypothesis. In 1995, a civil judgment in a deprogramming case led to the bankruptcy of CAN and further undermined the credibility of the brainwashing theory.

Despite the events that seriously undermined the credibility of some of its central assumptions, the anticult movement remains vigorous in the United States and has experienced noteworthy successes in Europe. While cruder forms of the brainwashing theory have largely been abandoned, the movement in general still sticks to the contentions that some groups exercise undue influence over their members and therefore pose individual and social dangers.

See also: Apostates; Brainwashing; Cult; Cult Awareness Network; Deprogramming; Exit Counseling; FREECOG (Free the Children of God); Patrick, Ted (1930–); Shakers, The.

Further Reading

Cowan, Douglas E. 2003. *Bearing False Witness? An Introduction to the Christian Countercult.* Westport, CT: Praeger.

Gallagher, Eugene V., ed. 2017. *"Cult Wars" in Historical Perspective.* London: Routledge.

Shupe, Anson D., Jr., & David G. Bromley. 1980. *The New Vigilantes: Deprogrammers, Anti-Cultists, and the New Religions.* Beverly Hills, CA: Sage.

Shupe, Anson, & Susan E. Darnell. 2006. *Agents of Discord: Deprogramming, Pseudo-Science, and the American Anticult Movement.* New Brunswick, NJ: Transaction Publishers.

Zablocki, Benjamin, & Thomas Robbins, eds. 2001. *Misunderstanding Cults: Searching for Objectivity in a Controversial Field.* Toronto: University of Toronto Press.

Apostates

Disaffiliating from a religion or religious institution does not necessarily mean that a person has abandoned its particular belief system. A former member may disagree with the current hierarchy's administration of the religion or may, for time or other reasons, feel that practicing the religion on one's own or in a smaller group is better suited to his or her needs. Apostasy, on the other hand, represents a true and often formal renunciation of this former belief system by an individual. The term derives from the Greek work "apostasia," which means revolt or defection.

Apostasy is a two-way street, of course. Those who leave a particular group or institution may charge their former religion with apostasy; in other words, it is not they who have left who are in error, but it is the entire system that has strayed. Groups like ISIS take this idea even further, arguing that the entire non-Sunni

Islamic world exists in a state of *al-Jahiliyya*, or apostasy, thus justifying its subjugation by any means. On the other hand, those people who have left the institution are often labeled as apostate by those who remained. This is complicated when individuals leave and continue to practice what they perceive as the "true" version of a particular faith, as have Freezone Scientologists who split from the Church of Scientology. While they may consider themselves the true believers, they are likely to be labeled as apostates by those who remained. In a broad sense, many new religious movements would be considered apostate by the religions from which they broke or against which they build their religion. Some resent their portrayal as apostate, whereas others, such as the Church of Satan (which emerged autonomously, not out of a particular religion), court the moniker, reveling in their role as provocateur of major religious institutions, such as the Catholic Church.

There are numerous reasons why a person might become an apostate of a mainstream as well as of a new religious movement. When it comes to the latter, apostates may be those who joined the religion in its earliest stages of development and who felt as though the direction of the movement is leading away from its original intentions. Such was arguably the case when some of the earliest members of the Church of Jesus Christ of Latter-day Saints (LDS Church) left when its founder, Joseph Smith (1805–1844), introduced the practice of plural marriage. Years later in the late nineteenth century, when the doctrine of plural marriage became standardized in the Church, only to be abandoned due to governmental pressure, many Latter-day Saints split from the Church, eventually forming their own groups, generally referred to as Fundamentalist Mormon sects. The LDS Church does not recognize these groups and considers them to be apostate. Within these sects, however, the view of the mainstream LDS Church varies: some see it as existing in a state of apostasy, whereas others still see the mainstream Church as the "true" Church, even hoping that they could be again absorbed into the larger body (provided the Church allows the practice of plural marriage).

Often new religions may offer immediate results, such as those traditions that promise healing or the development of special abilities. When those abilities do not materialize, former members may leave and even become vocal detractors of their former religious home. Several famous exposés emerged during the early twentieth century written by former Theosophists who argued that the phenomena claimed by the Theosophical Society to be the result of spirits or supernatural entities were hoaxes. Apostates may also emerge when new information or revelation contradicts their sense of reality. This occurred for several well-known Scientologists who became disillusioned about the Church when they learned of certain theological propositions or allegedly questionable practices by its administration.

It is important to note that the vast majority of apostates do not openly denounce their former religions. For most who have apostasized, they leave quietly and without event.

See also: Church of Jesus Christ of Latter-day Saints, The; Church of Satan, The; Conversion; Disaffiliation and Ex-membership in New Religious Movements; Freezone Scientology; Fundamentalist Mormons; ISIS; Membership and New Religious Movements; Scientology; Smith, Joseph (1805–1844); Theosophical Society, The; Theosophy.

Further Reading

Introvigne, Massimo. 1999. "Defectors, Ordinary Leave-takers, and Apostates: A Quantitative Study of Former Members of New Acropolis in France." *Nova Religio* 3, no. 1: 83–99.

Wright, Stuart A. 2014. "Disengagement and Apostasy in New Religious Movements." In Lewis R. Rambo & Charles E. Farhadian, eds., *The Oxford Handbook of Religious Conversion*. New York: Oxford University.

Applewhite, Marshall (1932–1997), and Bonnie Lu Nettles (1927–1985)

When Marshall Herff Applewhite and Bonnie Lu Nettles met in 1972, each of them had already embarked on a spiritual search. Applewhite was the son of a Presbyterian preacher. He attended Union Theological Seminary in Virginia for two years but left to study music, eventually earning a Master's degree. In the 1960s, he worked in Houston directing the chorus at St. Mark's Episcopal Church and directing the fine arts program at the University of St. Thomas. Toward the time he met Nettles, Applewhite was broadening his religious interests to include UFOs, astrology, and ancient mysticism.

Nettles had a more eclectic religious background. Although raised a Baptist, she was not a dedicated churchgoer. But the occult fascinated Nettles. For a time, she was a member of the Houston branch of the Theosophical Society of America. Her wide-ranging religious interests also included astrology, UFOs, and the channeling of spirits. Both Nettles and Applewhite had been married and had children, but each was single by the time they met. Applewhite was also coming to grips with his bisexuality. Freed from their former lives and commitments, they were ready to follow a new path. Eventually, they would found the group known as Heaven's Gate.

THE TWO

Applewhite and Nettles quickly forged a strong bond and provided each other emotional, psychological, and religious support. Over time, they came to believe that their meeting was part of a larger plan and even that they had known each other in previous lives. In 1972, they founded the short-lived Christian Arts Center, which sold books and offered classes on a variety of religious topics related to their mutual interests. A distinctive mix of Christian and "New Age" elements would continue to characterize their religious lives.

When their first venture failed, Applewhite and Nettles opened a retreat center called "Know Place," where they taught classes, met with individuals, and worked on their own spiritual development. It did not last very long either, and closed at the beginning of 1973. But Applewhite and Nettles continued their spiritual search. They gradually began to attract a cluster of students.

In the early to mid-1970s, both Applewhite and Nettles were involved in trying to figure out precisely what their sense of calling meant for them. In July 1973, they concluded that they were the "two witnesses" mentioned in Revelation 11. That text states that the two witnesses will prophesy for 1,260 days before they are killed by a "beast from the bottomless pit." But after three and a half days, they will be resurrected and go "up to heaven in a cloud." The idea of entering the heavenly kingdom held a particular attraction for them.

Applewhite's and Nettles's identification with the two witnesses had far-reaching implications. The Book of Revelation is a key text of Christian millennialism. By seeing themselves in that text, Applewhite and Nettles were aligning themselves with the view of the millennium that sees the destruction of this world as a necessary precursor to the establishment of a new heaven and new earth (Rev. 21:1). That form of millennialism differs notably from the more progressive form that anticipates the gradual amelioration of the world through human effort and is often found in the "New Age" milieu. Their catastrophic millennialist conviction would continue to deepen, even as Applewhite and Nettles adjusted their sense of who they actually were.

Applewhite and Nettles understood their joint leadership as a single effort and identified themselves as "the Two." They gave their understanding of Revelation a distinctive inflection that merged their disparate religious influences into a coherent message. They believed that the particular means of ascent to the heavens of the two witnesses and anyone who believed their message would be a spaceship, a UFO.

Applewhite and Nettles would continue to try out often whimsical self-designations, such as Bo and Peep, Guinea and Pig, and Ti and Do (for musical notes), until they settled on the latter. But the merging of Christian millennialism and belief in UFOs, first expressed in their self-understanding as the two witnesses of Revelation 11, continued to characterize their message.

FROM SEEKERS TO LEADERS

Initially Ti and Do did not invest much effort in either vigorous proselytizing or the formation and maintenance of a group. In May 1974, they gained their first follower, a woman whom they had known at the Christian Arts Center and Know Place. But their subsequent efforts to spread the word met with no success. Their first convert subsequently returned to her family, and her husband accused Applewhite of fraudulently using her credit card. The police declined to charge him, but Applewhite was eventually convicted of another count, which led to him spending time in jail. During that time, he claimed to have achieved another insight into his true identity. He and Ti, Do reported, were not really human at all. Instead, they were extraterrestrial beings who were incarnated in human bodies to spread the message about humans' true home in The Evolutionary Level Above Human.

The Two preached that individuals needed to abandon their attachments to the physical body to prepare themselves to enter their true heavenly home. Continuing to read the Bible through the lenses supplied by their conviction that the Kingdom of God could be found in the literal heavens, Ti and Do also developed a new understanding of the mission of Jesus. The Christ, in their interpretation, was actually a representative of the next level who merged with Jesus of Nazareth in Mary's womb. Jesus himself experienced a gradual awakening to his true nature, which culminated in his transfiguration. Jesus's task on earth, before he returned to the Kingdom of Heaven, was to alert individuals to the possibility of their own self-transformation. Ti and Do had the same task in their time that Jesus had in his.

Ti and Do's message found a receptive audience when they spoke to a Los Angeles area group in April 1975. They came away with some two dozen converts. In October, a large crowd turned out to hear the Two in Waldport, Oregon. That meeting produced more than twenty additional converts. Although the number of people who accepted the idea that they would have to train their bodies to be ready to enter the physical Kingdom of God was growing, Ti and Do were still not focused on making them into a cohesive group. Only in April 1976 did Ti turn to making the disparate followers a single community. Declaring that the "harvest" was over and that no more informational meetings would be held, the Two invited their followers to join them at the Medicine Box National Forest in Wyoming.

Only at that point did the loose collection of seekers then known as Human Individual Metamorphosis coalesce into a religious movement. Ti and Do concentrated authority in themselves and laid down a strict set of behavioral rules. The new emphasis on conformity and maintenance of group boundaries set the group apart from the general New Age milieu that had nurtured it. In a frequently used metaphor, they saw their followers as a "class" that would need to pass a "final exam" to "graduate" to the next level of the Kingdom of God.

Nettles's death in 1985 was unexpected. She did not resurrect, as Revelation predicts the two witnesses would. Consequently, Applewhite had to adjust the group's theology, in particular the idea of a bodily entrance into the kingdom of Heaven. Between 1985 and 1994, the possibility was considered that Do's followers might have to shed their human bodies to enter The Evolutionary Level Above Human, just as Ti had, to merge with God the Father. With that acknowledgment suicide became a possibility.

THE END OF HEAVEN'S GATE

Virtually from the beginning, Applewhite and Nettles had focused on a literal heavenly kingdom. As late as 1996, Applewhite articulated a position against suicide as a way of abandoning the human body and entering that kingdom. But other options were not attractive or did not seem possible. Death from natural causes or random accidents would not enable the whole class to "graduate" at the same time. An expected attack from government forces, prompted by the treatment of other minority religious groups such as Peoples Temple and the Branch Davidians, did not materialize. Suicide as a way of reaching the next level became a real possibility. When the Hale-Bopp Comet became visible in 1996, Do took it as a sign that it was time for the entire class to move on from this world. On March 26, 1997, police called to a home in the San Diego suburb of Rancho Santa Fe found the bodies of thirty-nine people, including Do, who had decided to leave behind their earthly bodies.

See also: Heaven's Gate; Millennialism; UFO Religions.

Further Reading

Chryssides, George D, ed. 2011. *Heaven's Gate: Postmodernity and Pop Culture in a Suicide Group.* Burlington, VT: Ashgate.

Zeller, Benjamin. 2014. *Heaven's Gate: America's UFO Religion.* New York: New York University Press.

PRIMARY SOURCE DOCUMENT

"Last Chance to Evacuate Earth before It's Recycled," Edited Transcript of a Videotape by "Do" (Marshall Applewhite Jr.), Founder of Heaven's Gate (1996)

On September 29, 1996, Heaven's Gate founder Marshall Applewhite Jr. (known as "Do") created a videotape meant to introduce watchers to the Heaven's Gate website and teachings. The transcript below reflects the founder's urgency in recruiting and informing his followers.

This is the 29th of September, 1996. I'm "Do." "Do" probably doesn't mean anything to many of you. To those who have heard of "Do," I might relate "Do" to "Ti and Do," of the "UFO Two," or of what the media dubbed the "UFO cult" that made some splash in the news in 1975 and disappeared from the scene shortly after that. And some of you might have heard of some efforts that we have made to try to share a little bit of what we have learned with the public, periodically, between 1975 and now. We put out a statement called '88 Update, and we did a videotape series a little while after that, I think it was 1992, 1991–1992, called "Beyond Human." Now, today we have quite a different urgency. It's urgent to me, and it's urgent to the students that sit before me. Our reason for speaking to you is because we feel to warn you of what is just around the corner.

I'll try to just put it as briefly as I can and as clearly as I can. This planet is about to be recycled, refurbished, started over. That doesn't mean it's going to be destroyed, it doesn't mean it's the end of the world. But it does mean that it is going to be spaded under. Now, you can say, "Well, who are you to say that?" And I'll tell you who I am. As to whether or not you believe who I am is up to you. And whether or not you believe that this civilization is going to be recycled or refurbished is up to you. Now, the purpose of this tape is to warn you that this is about to happen, and that it's going to happen very soon.

If I would title this tape, it would be "Last Chance to Evacuate Planet Earth Before It Is Recycled"—last chance to evacuate Earth before it is recycled. If you've read any of our teachings—the information that we have—you know that our discipline is strict, that we teach "overcoming human ways," overcoming human addictions. The purpose of that is not for religious reasons, or for morality, or in order to become "righteous." The purpose of that is to go to the heavens. Humans have some idea, because of what the negative forces have let them believe, or have led them to believe—humans have the idea that through religion, if I live a good life, then I get to go to Heaven when I die. And they don't know what Heaven is, but they think that Heaven is where God is, and Heaven is where whoever the leader of their religion is, and they'll get to go be with them if they've lived a good life by whatever standard their religion teaches.

The fact is, that there is only one Kingdom Level—a Kingdom Level, just like there's a human kingdom—there's only one Kingdom Level above the human kingdom, and that Kingdom Level made the human kingdom, and designed the planet, designed all of its resources, designed all of its life forms, designed humans, and even designed humans with the potential of leaving the human kingdom in order to go to the Kingdom Level Above Human.

Now, the startling thing to many is that the Kingdom Level Above Human is physical. There's some idea that the Kingdom Above Human is spiritual, as if it is limited to being spiritual. It is spiritual in the sense that, if you think of "mind" as synonymous with "spirit," and you become something that identifies with your mind instead of the "suit of clothes" you wear, then it is spiritual, because that mind/spirit becomes your identity. Even in the human world—if humans identify with the mind that they have, or the spirit that they have (remember, those two are synonymous)—if they identify with that mind, then they don't think that they die when the body they are wearing drops. They think that they move into another world. When they move out of the body, whether they do, in fact, move into another world depends upon whether they're connected or not, or what their information is, or what they are capable of knowing or doing, what they've been willing to learn.

You know, the Next Level, or the Evolutionary Level Above Human—oops, I said that bad word: Evolutionary Level. Because religious people think, "Oh, "evolution," does this mean that you don't believe in creation?" That's the most ridiculous thing that someone could think—that evolution is not a part of creation. That Kingdom Level created everything that is, or made everything that is, and among those things it made, it made a number of things that advance in an evolutionary progression. So to speak of that Level Above Human, we shouldn't be afraid to use the word "Evolutionary" Level Above. It's not really an Evolutionary Level Above Human, in that creatures here can, on their own, advance into that Kingdom Level, because they can't. That sounds strange. Well, they can advance, but they can't do it—on their own. . . .

Now, the only time we have an opportunity to leave the human kingdom and go to the Kingdom Level Above Human, is when there is a Member from that Kingdom Level, incarnate in human form, saying to you, "I'll tell you about a Kingdom Level beyond here, and if you want to go there then you have to follow me, because I am the guy who's got the key at the moment." Whatever Representative is sent from that Kingdom Level and comes into the human kingdom, then that's the Representative who has that key to that Kingdom, for that period of time. And it requires, if you move into that Evolutionary Kingdom, that you leave behind everything of human ways—human behavior, human ignorance, human misinformation.

Source: "Do." "Last Chance to Evacuate Earth Before It's Recycled." Available at: http://www.heavensgate.com/misc/vt092996.htm.

Art and New Religious Movements

Religion and the visual arts have a close relationship. One need look no further than the stained glass and high gothic arches of European cathedrals, to the intricate depictions of Hindu deities, to the vibrant costumes worn by religious practitioners in certain rituals. Some religious groups, such as the Puritans, eschew the visual, arguing that it distracted congregants from hearing the word of God. However, even the aversion to visual stimuli in the context of religious practice highlights the fact that religion, for many, is sensory. Art, some would argue, has the ability to move people spiritually, to enlighten, and even to reveal sacred truths.

Not only does visual art appear often in religious spaces, but religion often inflects and influences art and artists. Religious themes and ideas have appeared in the works of major artists for centuries and, like Michelangelo's "David" or Hieronymus Bosch's "The Garden of Earthly Delights," are often counted as masterpieces. It is no surprise that, given the inspirational and revelatory nature of many religions, such inspiration could touch those with artistic ability as well as those with specifically clerical vocations.

From a Western standpoint, specifically, the notion of art and religion most likely conjures specifically Judeo-Christian or Abrahamic religious themes. However, there are a number of new religious movements whose practitioners or whose ideas have found a place in the realm of visual art.

ART AS SPIRITUAL PRACTICE

Not all art needs to be explicitly religious in theme to be made with religious intent. Many abstract artists were devoutly religious, such as Catholics Georges Mathieu (1921–2012) and Kim En Joong (1940–) and Marc Chagall (1887–1985) who was a Jew. If one accepts the notion that human beings represent part of a larger sacred history or grand spiritual scheme, then it would make sense that those with artistic ability would conceive of their art as an extension of their spiritual lives, if not the primary means for engaging or advancing their spiritual selves. In this vein, there are new religious movements, many of which were born in the nineteenth and twentieth centuries, that take seriously the notion that art is a viable spiritual practice.

Russian painter Kazimir Malevich (1879–1935) created his own religious practice, Suprematism, which doubled as a style of art. A form of abstract art created from geometric shapes in a limited set of colors, its purpose was to experience God not through typically sacred sites or rites but through art itself. That the art was abstract enabled one to see each piece as encompassing the entire universe, whereas pictorial art was naturally narrative and delimiting. Malevich believed that both God and Suprematism as God's primary form of expression were compatible with Communism—facts he laid out in his book, *God Is Not Cast Down* (1920). However, his government disagreed and he was imprisoned for six months. He continued to spread the idea that Suprematism was a new kind of religion that could operate even in the most secular societies (or, conversely, as a result of them).

The Federation of Damanhur, located near Turin, Italy, is an esoteric religious community, where members live communally and focus spiritual practice on detachment from material reality in the hope of realizing their original, spiritual selves. There are numerous pathways for achieving this former state, each suited to a particular person's talents and abilities. One such path is art, which is unsurprising given that Damanhur's founder, Oberto Airaudi (1950–2013), was a painter. Damanhur self-admittedly takes a cue from the Renaissance notion that art signifies humanity's rebirth. While in the community, members may engage in "art of the popolo," or art engaged by the community, thus revealing one's shared history. Members may also participate in artistic endeavors on an individual basis.

Damanhur maintains its own art school (http://www.damanhur.org/en/art-and-creativity/art-school). However, it was Damanhur's most ambitious artistic undertaking that earned it fame, namely, the construction of the Temples of Humankind. An underground temple often touted as the "Eighth Wonder of the World," the Temple comprises eight halls, each decorated to accord with a particular theme or spiritual principle, such as the Hall of Earth, which celebrates the masculine element of humanity and the cycle of reincarnation. Both the creation of the halls and the experience of them represent art as a very human pathway to spiritual catharsis.

NEW RELIGIOUS MOVEMENTS' INFLUENCE ON ARTISTS

Art historians and critics have been somewhat averse to attribute artistic inspiration to alternative or occult religious sources; in fact, art historians such as Sixten Ringbom (1935–1992) who brought attention to this fact were often panned by the art historical and curatorial communities. In fact, some new religious movements seem to attract or produce a significant number of artists. Theosophy, and its institutional vehicle, the Theosophical Society, for example, have influenced numerous artists and, in turn, various artists have counted themselves Theosophists. Theosophy emerged in the nineteenth century, the child of Spiritualism, which posited that human beings could communicate with spirits or the spiritual realm, and esoteric religious beliefs, particularly those emerging from South Asia. Believing that a series of Masters (Mahatmas) who were spiritually advanced had been guiding human beings in their spiritual evolution for millennia, Theosophists sought contact with these Masters to gain special, sacred knowledge and to further their own enlightenment.

Abstract artists Hilma af Klint (1862–1944), a Swede, and Georgiana Houghton (1814–1884), an Englishwoman, claimed to paint under the influence of spirit guides when they painted. In other words, what they painted was sacred knowledge; as esoteric knowledge, it was sensible to those of similar spiritual inclinations. Much like automatic or trance writing, which occurred when a spirit inhabited a medium's body and communicated a message in writing, painting while under spiritual influence was intended to be revelatory. Houghton believed that she was being guided by deceased artists, such as Titian (1488–1576), who influenced her less in style than in the underlying spiritual message of her works.

Wassily Kandinsky (1866–1944), one of the pioneers of modern art, was deeply influenced by Spiritualism, Theosophy, and its offshoot Anthroposophy (which emphasized the Christian esoteric tradition over against Asian occult ideas and sources). Kandinsky read deeply in Theosophical and Anthroposophical texts, coming to the belief that art, more than words or other forms of expression, could convey the essence or "inner sound" of existence, which underlined all matter. Abstract art was the ideal form of expression for this underlying reality, since it did not adhere to conventional methods for communicating a particular theme or message. Drawing upon Theosophical beliefs that sacred truth lay within all reality, Kandinsky helped to birth the idea that need not be realistic to be religious or spiritually relevant. Increasingly, Kandinsky was convinced that a new age, called the "Epoch of the Great Spiritual," would soon arrive, which would usher in an era of unprecedented spiritual knowledge and access.

Christian Science, a nineteenth-century religious movement that posited that God was Mind and, thus, all matter an illusion, was hugely influential on a variety of artists who ultimately joined the Church. Assemblage artist, Joseph Cornell (1903–1972), converted to Christian Science after reading *Science and Health with Key to the Scriptures*, the central sacred text alongside the Bible for Christian Scientists. His own history was riddled with family illness, which initially drew him to the new religion, which posited that disease was illusory, the result of wrong thinking or "sin." After his conversion, his art became a means of acting upon his faith. Assemblage art comprises two-dimensional images with three-dimensional objects extruding from or featured prominently in the foreground of the piece. Cornell believed that by organizing matter in a way that was conceptual, rather than practical, he could remake matter into thought, both for himself and for the observer. Muralist Violet Oakley (1874–1961), while providing two portraits of Christian Science founder, Mary Baker Eddy (1821–1910) and illustrations to accompany a poem by Eddy, also cited Christian Science influence in her secular works of art. For example, her mural *Unity*, which appears in the chamber of the Pennsylvania Senate and depicts the end of slavery, is intended to convey a sense of harmony for the beholder.

Numerous new religious movements have encouraged and influenced artists in various ways and continue to act as both source and artistic subject.

See also: Anthroposophy; Christian Science; Damanhur; Eddy, Mary Baker (1821–1910); Occultism and Esotericism; *Science and Health with Key to the Scriptures*; Spiritualism; Theosophical Society, The; Theosophy.

Further Reading

Coleman, Earle Jerome. 1998. *Creativity and Spirituality: Bonds Between Art and Religion.* Albany: SUNY Press.

Introvigne, Massimo. 2016. "New Religious Movements and the Visual Arts." *Nova Religio* 19, no. 4: 3–13.

Introvigne, Massimo. 2018. "The Sounding Cosmos Revisited: Sixten Ringbom and the 'Discovery' of Theosophical Influence on Modern Art." *Nova Religio* 21, no. 3: 29–46.

Versluis, Arthur. 2011. *Esotericism, Art, and Imagination.* East Lansing: Michigan State University Press.

Zoccatelli, PierLuigi. 2016. "'All the Heavens in Your Hands': Oberto Airaudi and the Art of Damanhur." *Nova Religio* 19, no. 4: 145–146.

Asahara, Shoko (1955–2018)

At first glance, the history of Shoko Asahara (né Chizuo Matsumoto) seems unlikely to have prepared him for religious leadership. Born into a family that was supported by his father's fabrication of *tatami* mats, Asahara was blind in one eye and had only partial sight in the other. Consequently, he spent fourteen years, from age six, in a state boarding school, where his partial sight gave him an advantage among his completely blind peers.

Asahara's desires for further education were frustrated when he was unable to secure sufficiently high grades on the entrance examinations at prestigious universities. Instead, he worked as a masseuse, acupuncturist, and dispenser of herbal remedies. Asahara joined one of Japan's postwar new religions, Agonshū, in 1981 but left in 1984 with a handful of followers to start a group dedicated to meditation and yoga. In the next year he attracted some attention by claiming in an occult journal that he was able to levitate.

Asahara awakened to his true, religious calling in 1985, during a session of meditation. He believed that he had been appointed by a deity to lead the armies that would establish the Buddhist millennial kingdom of Shambala on earth. From that point on, Asahara, who officially changed his name in 1987, continued to develop his prophetic persona by appealing to a number of other supernatural experiences. He emphasized that it was only through him, as guru, that salvation could be earned.

As his experience in 1985 suggests, Asahara developed a millennialist message that situated his followers as the vanguard that would transform the earth into a paradise. By 1988, however, his prophecies were taking a darker turn and he began to preach about the catastrophic end of the world through a battle between Japan, the United States, and other forces.

Although Asahara predicted that the end could at least be postponed if enough people joined Aum and became renunciants, he was never able to gain anywhere near the thirty thousand committed members that he claimed to need. As Asahara's recruitment efforts continued to fall short and as opposition to his movement mounted, he began to rely on violence to silence dissent and eliminate enemies.

Asahara continued to move the date of Armageddon closer to his present and eventually sponsored the spasm of violence that took thirteen lives and injured thousands when five Aum members released sarin gas in the Tokyo subway on March 20, 1995—a crime for which he was executed in 2018.

Despite the eclectic and evolving theology that he espoused, Asahara was able to recruit a group of largely young and well-educated members and engage them in both extreme ascetic practices that often damaged their health and acts of violence against their perceived enemies.

See also: Aum Shinrikyō; Charisma and Leadership in New Religious Movements; Millennialism.

Further Reading

Reader, Ian. 2000. *Religious Violence in Contemporary Japan: The Case of Aum Shinrikyo.* Richmond, Surrey, UK: Curzon Press.

Wessinger, Catherine. 2000. *How the Millennium Comes Violently: From Jonestown to Heaven's Gate.* New York: Seven Bridges Press.

Ásatrú

Contemporary Paganism has taken diverse forms as individuals have recovered, reconstructed, and invented religious beliefs and practices that hark back to pre-Christian times. As a whole, Paganism lacks a single, generally acknowledged organizational structure. Consequently, significant variations in practice and belief exist among groups and individuals who claim to be following a Pagan way.

One particular strand of contemporary Paganism, found specifically in northern Europe and in North America, focuses on the Old Norse and Germanic gods and goddesses, such as Odin, Thor, Freyr, and Freya. The revived form of Old Norse religion is generally known as Ásatrú or Heathenry and sometimes as Odinism. Ásatrú roughly connotes "belief in the Gods (*Aesir*)." The *Aesir*, the deities who reside in the highest of the nine worlds at the top of the world-tree Yggdrasil, can be distinguished from the *Vanir*, who are associated with fertility, though the two groups are often merged under the term "Aesir." The ethos of Ásatrú is summarized in a list of nine noble virtues: courage, truth, honor, fidelity, discipline, hospitality, industriousness, self-reliance, and perseverance. Practitioners participate in rituals such as the blot, an offering of mead or other alcoholic beverages to the gods, and seasonal celebrations.

Central to Ásatrú is the conviction that there is an essential connection between an ethnic group and the worship of a certain pantheon of gods. The website of the Ásatrú Folk Assembly (asatrufolkassembly.org), for example, asserts that the worship of the Norse gods is the "native religion" of "ethnic European folk," no matter how distant they now may be from their homelands. Similarly, the website of the Ásatrú Alliance (www.asatru.org) identifies Ásatrú as the "original or native religious belief" of people of northern European ancestry. Other forms of contemporary Paganism make similar connections to Celtic or central European forms of pre-Christian religion. They all share the desire to reject what they see as universalizing and oppressive forms of Christianity and to reestablish a pre-Christian religion that has an intrinsic connection to people of a particular ethnicity.

Yggdrasil is the tree of life that links the nine worlds and preserves the structure of the cosmos in Old Norse mythology. Various forms of contemporary Germanic Paganism, including Ásatrú, include Yggdrasil in their adaptations of ancient mythology. (Jozef Klopacka/Dreamstime.com)

The ethnic emphasis of such forms of Paganism, however, has been understood in multiple ways. In some formulations it has overlapped with ideologies of white supremacy, as in the thought of Wotansfolk, cofounded by David Lane (1938–2007), a former member of the domestic terrorist group, The Order, and one-time proponent of Christian Identity. The connection of Ásatrú with white supremacist identity has also proven attractive to incarcerated people who identify as white and poses a challenge to law enforcement.

A milder form of ethnic exclusion simply emphasizes that each ethnic group has its own deities and representations of the divine. In general, ethnic forms of Paganism reject the eclecticism that characterizes some other Pagans and the broader cultic milieu in favor of worship of ancestral gods. Other strands of Ásatrú, however, welcome individuals of all ethnicities to worship the Norse gods.

As elsewhere in Paganism, there are solitary practitioners of Ásatrú. But several important organizations have developed. The Odinist Fellowship was founded by Else Christensen (1913–2005) in 1969. Founded in 1969 by Stephen McNallen (1948–), the Ásatrú Free Assembly lasted until 1987 and was then reestablished in 1996 as the Ásatrú Folk Assembly. The group's website maintains an extensive library of its journal, *The Runestone*, and related texts and offers a selection of books and paraphernalia for purchase.

Other notable Ásatrú groups include the Ásatrú Alliance (www.asatru.org), which was launched by Valgard Murray (1950–), who had been a member of Christensen's Odinist Fellowship, and Robert N. Taylor (1945–) in 1987 after the Ásatrú Free Assembly dissolved. Taylor went on to found the Wolfling Kindred. Ásatrú remains a vital element of Neopaganism.

Ásatrú has also experienced a resurgence in contemporary Iceland, where Christianity had been the only officially recognized religion since 1000 CE. The Icelandic Ásatrú Fellowship was founded in 1972 and achieved legal recognition in the following year. In 2019, there were more than four thousand members; the growing popularity of the revival of ancient Icelandic Paganism has also led to the construction of a temple or hall (*hof*) outside of Reykjavík (see http://magnus.jensson.is/?page_id=141 for drawings and photos).

See also: Christian Identity; Neopaganism; Odinism; Race and New Religious Movements.

Further Reading

Anonymous. 2000. "Who Are the Asatruar?" *Beliefnet*. Available at: https://www.beliefnet.com/faiths/pagan-and-earth-based/2001/04/who-are-the-asatruar.aspx.

Bellamy, Seamus. 2018. "Interview: Dr. Karl E. H. Seigfried Talks Ásatrú, Heathenry and Beards." May 25, 2018. Available at: www.boingboing.net.

Gardell, Mattias. 2003. *Gods of the Blood: The Pagan Revival and White Separatism*. Durham, NC: Duke University Press.

Aum Shinrikyō

On March 20, 1995, five members of a Japanese new religion released deadly sarin gas on three separate lines of the Tokyo subway system during rush hour. Thirteen people eventually died and more than five thousand were injured by the attack. Previously little known, Aum Shinrikyō immediately became an internationally notorious example of a dangerous, millennialist cult.

ORIGINS

Aum was one of the "new, new religions (*shinshinshūkyō*)" that formed in Japan after World War II. Its founder was born Chizuo Matsumoto (1955–2018) but changed his name to Shoko Asahara in 1987 to reflect his religious calling. Asahara was born blind in one eye and with only partial sight in the other, and from the age of six, he spent fourteen years in a state boarding school. Frustrated in his attempts to gain admission into prestigious university programs he turned to massage, acupuncture, and herbal remedies to support himself. Asahara joined the new religion of Agonshū in 1981 but left in 1984, and with fifteen followers, he started his own group dedicated to yoga and meditation.

Over time, Asahara claimed various extraordinary experiences that legitimized his religious leadership. While meditating in 1985, for example, he claimed to have been told by a deity that he would be the god of light and lead the armies of the gods in the effort to establish the Buddhist millennial kingdom of Shambala.

In 1986, Asahara visited India and came back proclaiming that he had accomplished final liberation. In 1987, he met the Dalai Lama and later used a photo of the two together to reinforce his legitimacy. From 1987 on, Asahara also depicted himself as a Buddha. Asahara's various claims to charismatic authority made him the focal point of the groups he led, including Aum Shinsen no Kai (Aum Wizards/Daoist Sages Society), which became Aum Shinrikyō in 1987.

BELIEFS AND PRACTICES

From the outset, Asahara professed an eclectic set of beliefs. He drew on Japanese folk religion from his early days as an herbalist, Hindu yoga practices and associated ideas, and Mahayana and later Vajrayana Buddhist beliefs particularly focused on the benefits of asceticism. Asahara held a specific reverence for the deity Shiva and even saw himself as an avatar of that God.

Asahara's beliefs had a consistently millennialist character. He initially hoped that the kingdom of Shambala could be established in Japan and then throughout the world. In pursuit of the goal he hoped to establish a network of "Lotus Villages" throughout Japan, whose residents would soon enter the glorious new world.

By 1988, however, Asahara's millennialism began to take a more catastrophic form, prompted in part by his reading of the biblical Book of Revelation. He added Christian ideas to his eclectic mix and even wrote a book called *Declaring Myself the Christ* (1992). Several years before David Koresh, he saw himself as the Lamb mentioned in Revelation 5.

Although he first set the time of the end sometime around the end of the twentieth century, Asahara gradually moved the date closer to his present in an attempt both to attract more followers and to retain and enhance the commitment of members.

Asahara's grand desires for mass conversion never materialized. Neither did his attempts to gain political power by sponsoring a party (*Shinrito*, the "Truth Party") and a slate of candidates in the 1990 elections for the Japanese Diet. Aum had around four thousand members when it was incorporated in 1989 and by 1995 counted some ten thousand members in Japan and another thirty thousand in Russia. Those numbers, though substantial, paled in comparison to other Japanese new religions, such as Soka Gakkai. The perceived failures of Aum's missionary efforts increased Asahara's suspicion of those outside the group and eventually led him to entertain broad conspiracy theories about worldwide opposition to Aum led by the United States and prominently featuring, like so many conspiracies, the Jews. Asahara's growing paranoia about external enemies contributed to the group's violent actions.

Those attracted to Aum were generally young and highly educated. Many had scientific backgrounds, which Aum would put to work in its manufacture of biological weapons. For individuals often alienated from their lives in a materialist consumer culture, Aum offered the possibility of mystical experience, enlightenment, and personal salvation. But the demands were also stringent. Aum had a two-tier membership, in which the most dedicated members became renunciants (*shukkesha*) who cut off contact with their families, donated their wealth and possessions to the group, lived communally, and adopted very rigorous ascetic practices. Asahara predicted that Armageddon would occur in 1999 unless thirty thousand people became renunciants. Indications that Aum would clearly fall far short of that number contributed to Asahara's negative evaluation of the world outside Aum.

The austerities imposed on Aum members, such as fasting, being immersed in extremely hot or cold water, and even being hung upside down, were so severe that some members actually died. Apparently, Terayuki Majima, in 1988, was the first to die, but scholars suspect that perhaps dozens of others suffered a similar fate. Such events, should they have become widely known, would have been extraordinarily damaging to both Asahara and Aum. Accordingly, Asahara directed trusted Aum members to take extraordinary, even criminal, actions to keep them from widespread public knowledge.

The crackdown addressed both internal and external critics. For example, a member with knowledge of Majima's death, Shuji Taguchi, was perceived as a potential leak for what had happened. Taguchi was brutally murdered at Aum headquarters in February 1989. Later that year, a lawyer for a society of Aum victims was killed in his apartment, along with his wife and young son. In 1994, Aum used sarin gas in Matsumoto in an attack aimed at judges who were hostile to the group and the general populace, many of whom had opposed Aum's attempt to set up a factory in the town. Aum had thus consistently engaged in violence against its members and enemies in the years before the subway attack.

Borrowing from Tibetan Buddhism, Asahara developed a theological justification for violence focused on the concept of *poa* (or *phowa*). In Aum's usage, *poa* reflects the focus on the guru (Asahara) as the key to salvation. Aum held that although the fate of the individual soul after death was based on its karma, the guru could transfer spiritual merit and thus help the soul enter a higher spiritual realm. Asahara extended the concept to cover killings that he ordered; his rationalization was that by killing certain individuals he kept them from accumulating even more bad karma and saved them from an even worse fate in the afterlife. Aum's increasing reliance on violence directed at both real and perceived enemies thus acquired a religious gloss.

THE SUBWAY ATTACK AND ITS AFTERMATH

The 1995 attack in the Tokyo subway was part of a longer history of Aum's reliance on violence. Fortunately, Aum was unable to manufacture sarin of high purity or the casualties would have been far greater. The perpetrators, and Asahara, were quickly rounded up by law enforcement. In the end between 1995 and 2011, nearly two hundred people were tried for Aum's crimes. Asahara was eventually executed, along with twelve others, in 2018.

After the subway attack some members of Aum tried to reestablish the movement as Aleph in 2000 (see http://english.aleph.to/); they rejected the controversial uses of some Vajrayana concepts and also the New Testament. They also apologized to the victims of the subway attack and established a compensation fund for victims. In 2007, Aleph split into factions, with Joyu Fumihiro (1962–) leading a new group, Hikari no Wa ("The Circle of Light").

Aleph, however, remained controversial and in 2017 Japanese police raided Aleph's offices as part of an investigation into its recruiting practices. On January 1, 2019, in Tokyo, an Aum sympathizer trying to exact revenge for the 2018 executions ran his car into a crowd injuring nine people.

Although Aleph tried to purify Aum of the violent teachings developed by Asahara, the successor organization has failed to gain either the public prominence or the number of members that Aum had in the 1980s and 1990s. Asahara's distinctive views have largely been repudiated and the eclectic millennialist movement that he created has virtually been extinguished. Nonetheless, Aum, despite its evident distinctiveness, is frequently used by anticult activists as a cautionary example of the dangers posed by new religious movements to both individual members and society as a whole.

See also: Asahara, Shoko (1955–2018); Millennialism; Soka Gakkai; Violence and New Religious Movements.

Further Reading

Baffelli, Erica, & Ian Reader, eds. 2012. "Aftermath: The Impact and Ramifications of the Aum Affair." Special Issue of the *Japanese Journal of Religious Studies* 39, no. 1: 1–199.

Lifton, Robert Jay. 1999. *Destroying the World to Save It: Aum Shinrikyo, Apocalyptic Violence, and the New Global Terrorism*. New York: Henry Holt.

Murakami, Haruki. 2000. *Underground: The Tokyo Gas Attack and the Japanese Psyche*. New York: Vintage Books.

Reader, Ian. 2000. *Religious Violence in Contemporary Japan: The Case of Aum Shinrikyo*. Richmond, Surrey, UK: Curzon Press.

Aurobindo, Sri (1872–1950)

Aurobindo Ghose was born in Calcutta, India, in 1872 at the height of British colonial rule. At the age of seven, his parents sent him to be educated in England, where he excelled in his studies. Though surrounded by English culture and with little direct connection to his homeland, Aurobindo began to develop a pronounced interest in India, as well as the Indian Independence Movement, which sought freedom from British rule. His interest grew until he returned to India, where he continued his studies while working as a teacher and secretary to an Indian prince. Soon thereafter, he became the first Indian intellectual to make a public statement regarding the need for India's independence from Britain, prompting his firing from his current position, and, in 1908, his arrest and imprisonment for activism.

It was during his incarceration that he experienced a religious transformation, which would ultimately change his professional path and ideological focus. Since his return to India, he had become increasingly interested in Hindu sacred texts and practices, but his year-long imprisonment compelled him to turn inward and practice pranayama or yogic meditation and breathing. Eventually, he was released

A collective meditation on February 28, 1998, at the Auroville ashram founded by Sri Aurobindo in the Tamil Nadu state of India. The ashram continues to attract devotees more than seventy years after Aurobindo's death. (Catherinelprod Catherine/Dreamstime.com)

from prison, but fearing reimprisonment (his political activities did not simply cease despite his spiritual turn), he traveled to Pondicherry, which was then the French part of India, where his religious practice intensified and where he would remain for the duration of his life.

Between 1914 and 1922, Aurobindo composed the majority of his major works, which were originally published in the journal *Arya*, then later as books, including *The Life Divine* (1944) and *The Synthesis of Yoga* (1948). In these works, he laid out his religious philosophy, which posited that all beings proceed through an evolution of "consciousness," beginning as matter, then as animals, then humans, and ultimately, through sustained spiritual practice over lifetimes, as the "supermind" (terminology that some argue reveals the influence of Friedrich Nietzsche [1844–1900]). To rise to the level of supermind, practitioners must liberate their human minds from their unstable state; this evolution was achieved through yoga and with the help of a guru.

As a result of his discovery regarding the supermind, Aurobindo became more reclusive and desirous of focusing on his own spiritual path. However, since arriving in Pondicherry, Aurobindo had begun to attract disciples, though he was reticent to call them that. Chief among them was Mira Richard (née Alfassa; 1878–1972), who traveled to India in 1914 with her husband Paul, prompted by their esoteric religious interests. Aurobindo and Richard became increasingly close through spiritual practice, so much so that he began to refer to her as "The Mother," maintaining that the two were actually one soul, simply appearing in different aspects. Following a brief return to England, Mira ultimately arrived back (and permanently) in Pondicherry without her husband. She and Aurobindo founded and opened the Sri Aurobindo Ashram (a site that would eventually be called "Auroville") in 1926. Shortly thereafter, Aurobindo retreated from most public engagements to focus exclusively on liberating his mind; he also began to compose commentaries on major Hindu sacred texts, such as the Upanishads and Bhagavad Gita, which would be published posthumously. Mira became the public face of the movement and took over as guru and administrator of the ashram up to and following Aurobindo's death in 1950.

Though he had long since retreated from politics and activism—and somewhat ironically given his opposition to British rule—Aurobindo showed public support for England and the allied powers during World War II. Aurobindo believed that there existed a cosmic battle between the progressive, "supranational" forces for change and the antidivine forces for stasis, of which the Allied-Axis conflict was simply the current iteration. He would also live to see India achieve independence in 1947 (on his seventy-fifth birthday).

Aurobindo's teachings had wide circulation, particularly during the 1960s and 1970s, though by that point there were similar Hindu or South Asian new religious movements and multiple versions of yoga with which to contend for disciples. Nonetheless, many still traveled to Auroville, with some choosing to remain to feel closer to the guru's presence.

See also: Hindu New Religious Movements; Integral Yoga; Occultism and Esotericism; Yoga.

Further Reading

Aurobindo, Sri. 1973 [1944]. *The Life Divine.* Pondicherry, India: Sri Aurobindo Ashram.

Aurobindo, Sri, & Rishabhchand. 1959. *The Integral Yoga of Sri Aurobindo.* Pondicherry, India: Sri Aurobindo Ashram.

Heehs, Peter. 2008. *The Lives of Sri Aurobindo.* New York: Columbia University Press.

Ayahuasca

Both established and alternative religions have used multiple methods to foster individuals' achievement of altered states of consciousness. Dancing, drumming, and singing have frequently been used. So has the ingestion of psychoactive substances. The ancient Indian *Rigveda*, for example, mentions a drink called soma, which some believe has hallucinogenic properties. The same goes for the ritual drink consumed in the ancient Greek Eleusinian mysteries. Similarly, the sacramental smoking of marijuana helps the Rastafari attain insights during their reasoning sessions. Ayahuasca is another psychoactive substance originally used during shamanic rituals by indigenous peoples in the Amazon area of Brazil.

Several religious groups focus on the ritual use of ayahuasca. They have helped move the use of the tea concocted from the *Banisteriopsis caapi* vine and leaves of the *Psychotria viridis* shrub out of the Amazon into Brazil's urban areas and from

Practitioners of Santo Daime use the psychoactive plant ayahuasca in ritual settings to promote visionary experiences. It is usually brewed into a tea. (Eskymaks/Dreamstime.com)

there to South America, Europe, and North America. The most influential among these groups has been Santo Daime (from the Portuguese for "Holy" and "Give me [Light, Love]").

Santo Daime originated in the experiences that Raimundo Irineu Serra (1890–1971), known among his followers as Mestre Irineu, had with ayahuasca. In his first vision, he saw the moon as a female figure. He later identified her as the Queen of the Forest and Our Lady of Conception, which signaled the mix of Christian and indigenous religious ideas that would characterize the new religion. The formal foundation of Santo Daime occurred in 1930 when Mestre Irineu and two others conducted the first formal ritual or "work."

Both Mestre Irineu and ayahuasca quickly gained a reputation for healing and the ritual work became more elaborate. Mestre Irineu and other elders composed hymns that could be sung at ayahuasca ceremonies. The hymns are perceived to have come directly from the astral or spiritual realm. They help to manify the presence of Christ within the community. The ritual centers on drinking the tea, accompanied by hymns, prayers, and moments of meditation.

When Mestre Irineu died in 1971, Santo Daime split into factions. The group with the largest international presence was led by Sebastião Mota de Meio (1920–1990), who had met Mestre Irineu in 1965 and quickly established his own Santo Daime Center. He then founded The Eclectic Center of Flowing Universal Light

Raimundo Irineu Serra (known as CEFLURIS from the Portuguese), which performed its first formal ritual in 1975.

The movement of ayahuasca outside of Brazil, aided by immigration from Brazil and abetted by spiritual tourists who come to Brazil seeking authentic religious experiences, has set up a complex flow of people, ideas, and practices between Brazil and the rest of the world.

See also: Rastafari; Shamanism.

Further Reading

Dawson, Andrew. 2013. *Santo Daime: A New World Religion.* London: Bloomsbury.

Labate, Beatriz, & Clancy Cavnar, eds. 2014. *Ayahuasca Shamanism in the Amazon and Beyond.* New York: Oxford University Press.

Lowell, Jonathan Thomas, & Paul C. Adams. 2017. "The Routes of a Plant: Ayahuasca and the Global Networks of Santo Daime." *Social and Cultural Geography* 18: 137–157.

B

Baba, Meher (1894–1969)

Meher Baba was born Merwan Sheriar Irani to Zoroastrian parents of Persian descent in Poona (now Pune), India. While attending college in Poona, he met a Muslim woman named Hazrat Babajan (?–1931), who became the first of five "Perfect Masters" (those who exist in a state of spiritual enlightenment, or God-consciousness) and who over the next seven years would help Baba awaken to his true spiritual identity. He discovered that he was the divine avatar of his age—serving the role that Zoroaster, Buddha, Jesus Christ, and Muhammad had before him, which was to spur human beings to spiritual evolution. Reportedly, Baba said, of his role as a divine avatar, that he came "not to teach, but to awaken."

In 1921, after taking the name "Meher Baba" (which means "loving father" in Persian), he began to gather disciples, with the aim of universalizing religion. He taught religion without a creed, instead arguing that all religions bore elements of truth but now, with greater knowledge facilitated by him, those divisions could dissolve. He established an ashram in Bombay (now Mumbai), which also focused on social outreach for the poor, based upon the idea that all people were ultimately one (a critique of the Hindu caste system that surrounded him in India). By 1930, he began traveling to the West, ultimately establishing ashrams in the United States and Europe and gathering followers as he went.

From 1925 until his death, Baba did not speak, communicating via an alphabet board, then through a series of hand gestures, and through his writings. He fell silent, in part, to show that humanity has been deaf to God, who has been speaking constantly throughout history. Ironically, he titled his most important treatise, *God Speaks* (1955), which still serves as the major religious text for Baba acolytes. The book, written as a collection of discourses, details the history of the universe, from creation until the present. Evolution of all created forms proceeds through seven stages beginning with stone or metal, to plant, to insect, to fish, to bird, to mammal, and, finally, to human. For humans who are more progressed in their spiritual journeys, either across incarnations or in their current state, they are moving toward becoming one with the "Over-soul," or God-consciousness.

The fact that God is one with everything, including the self, or "Real Existence" is the foundational reality of Baba's spiritual platform; "Real Love" refers to the actual union with God, which is the aim of Baba's message and the focus of spiritual practice. These are two of seven "realities" taught by Baba. The others are: Real Sacrifice and Real Renunciation (referring to the steps people must

Though he was born in India and established an ashram there, Meher Baba attracted a worldwide audience for his message that all religions held elements of the truth and that their differences could be overcome. (Library of Congress)

take to rid themselves of attachments and selfish wants), Real Knowledge (understanding the nature of "Real Existence"), Real Control (mastering one's emotions and mind through practice), and Real Surrender (total submission to God). Those who became followers of Baba aim to exist in all seven realities at once, which would mean attainment of God-consciousness. There is no creed or specified path for achieving this, however, though Baba advocated the power of service to others as a means of expressing total love for God through love of creation.

Later in his life, Baba became well known for his stance against drug use. At the height of the counterculture in the 1960s, drugs and religion often intersected. On several occasions, recreational drug users, primarily from the United States, sought out Baba for aid in their spiritual quest. Baba admonished them for their use of these substances, arguing against the idea forwarded by some during that time that psychedelic substances aided spiritual awakening; in fact, he argued, drugs distracted from the correct spiritual path.

Besides his teachings, which are still widely circulated among his followers, Baba enjoyed a certain pop cultural relevance at the close of the twentieth century. For example, Baba's life and teachings were commemorated by Pete Townshend of The Who, who became a disciple of Baba in the 1960s, invoking the spiritual master's message in song and naming the song, "Baba O'Riley," for him.

See also: Mysticism; Seekers.

Further Reading

Baba, Meher. 1955. *God Speaks, The Theme of Creation and Its Purpose.* New York: Dodd, Mead, and Company.

Muhkerjee, Sumita. 2017. "Indian Messiah: The Attraction of Meher Baba to British Audiences in the 1930s." *Journal of Religious History* 41, no. 2: 215–234.

Purdon, C. B. 1964. *The God-Man: The Life, Journeys and Work of Meher Baba with an Interpretation of His Silence and Spiritual Teaching.* Myrtle Beach, SC: Sheriar Foundation.

Babism

Babism, or the Babi movement, was a nineteenth-century Iranian religious movement born from Shia Islam and led by Siyyid Ali Muhammad Shirazi (1819–1850) who claimed to be the Bab or the "Gate" to God. Though the movement itself was relatively short-lived—ending following the Bab's execution in 1850—the religious system lives on through the Bahá'í tradition, whose founder Mirza Husayn Ali Nuri (1817–1892) or Bahá'u'lláh ("Glory of God") was an early follower of the Bab.

ORIGINS AND HISTORY

During the 1840s, the Bab began experiencing religious visions, which provided him with special divine knowledge of the Qur'an. Around that time he was visited by a member of the Shaykhi movement, a messianic Shia movement that believed that the arrival of the "Mahdi" or the Hidden Twelfth Imam, the redeemer of Islam, would soon appear. This visitor, named Mullá Husayn (1813–1849) became convinced that the Bab was the awaited Mahdi, becoming his first disciple. Though the Bab would originally claim to be the "Gate" to the Mahdi, he eventually declared himself to be this individual and therefore a divine manifestation and messenger. He gathered a small group of devoted followers to him known as the Letters to the Living, for their role in disseminating the Bab's message. The Bab also wrote extensively, and his teachings are still used among the Bahá'í.

Soon, the Bab's claims to secret knowledge of the Qur'an and to divine, messianic status spread, bringing both further followers and increased pressure from the Iranian government. This led to violent clashes between the government and the Babis, during which the latter were massacred by the tens of thousands. Those who died were viewed as martyrs by those in the movement, since Babism had a pronounced sense of defensive or lesser jihad. Ultimately, he was imprisoned and tried for his teachings. During the trial, he was asked to recant his teachings, but refused, only to recant later following prolonged torture. Shi'ite clergy called for his execution for heresy, a fact that placed the government in a difficult position as the Bab had grown in popularity among the laity. Despite some reticence by the government (and sparked by a political regime change), the Bab was executed on July 9, 1850. A number of people claimed to be his successor, spawning sectarian offshoots, with the most successful being led by Bahá'u'lláh, but Babism as an autonomous entity effectively died with its founder.

BELIEFS AND PRACTICES

Central to Babism is its messianic and millennialist nature. Most Shi'ite Muslims believe that there are twelve imams who represent the successors to the prophet Muhammad. The last imam, the Mahdi, will be hidden and will reappear concurrently with the Second Coming of Christ, who will fight alongside the Mahdi to defeat the *Masih ad-Dajjal* (the false Messiah). The Mahdi is believed to be hidden (or in a state of "occultation") and communicates only through chosen messengers or gates. Numerous people have claimed to be the Mahdi, including the Bab. In this way, Babism aligns with Shia Islam.

However, Babism diverges from its parent religion in several key respects. As the Mahdi, the Bab claimed to bear special knowledge of the Qur'an, thus enabling him to clarify its murkier points. His method of interpretation impacted some of the alterations made to belief and practice as he tended to deny the more literal interpretations of the text, focusing instead on the letters of each word as symbolic entry points to divine knowledge. One of his major theological claims based on this kind of Qur'anic interpretation was that rather than redeem Islam, the Mahdi would introduce a new prophetic dispensation, and that, in fact, the apocalypse would mark an end not to the world, but to Islam and the beginning of something new. Rather than a literal realization of all of the events in the Qur'an, they would occur symbolically: the Last Judgment represented the appearance of a new prophet and manifestation of God, and the resurrection of believers referred to a mass spiritual awakening of those on earth. Further, the Bab predicted that further messianic figures would emerge, a fact that directly undercut the notion of the Mahdi's and the apocalypse's finality.

This new period, which would also realize the Kingdom of God on earth, would mean the end to traditional Islamic practice as well, much of which would still exist, but in revised form. In some respects, he demanded more of practitioners, requiring additional prayers, for example. This increased burden reflected the fact that Babism emphasized a turn inward, toward the self and soul, as a means of serving God and progressing spiritually. Yet, many of the changes would seem to move Babism outside of Islam entirely, at least as his critics would contend. He changed the traditional calendar, which instead of following a lunar cycle, followed a nineteen month solar cycle with the last month, which lasted for nineteen days, to serve as the traditional month of fasting (Ramadan). He also seemed to elevate the status of women, discontinuing laws requiring them to be veiled, ending concubinage, and providing women more private and public autonomy.

Though precise numbers of the Babi movement are unknown, during its short span the movement managed to gather a significant following. Though more syncretic than specifically Islamic in nature—a fact that reflects Babism's own divergence from Shia—Bahá'í extends the Babi tradition of looking for divine messengers and seeking progressive religious knowledge. The Bab's writings are considered to be scripture by those who practice Bahá'í, and certain of its practices (like the nineteen-month religious calendar) have been adopted.

See also: Bahá'í; Messianism and New Religious Movements; Millennialism.

Further Reading
MacEoin, Denis. 1992. *The Sources for Early Babi Doctrine and History.* Leiden: Brill.
MacEoin, Denis. 2009. *The Messiah of Shiraz: Studies in Early and Middle Babism.* Leiden: Brill.

Sharon, Moshe. 2004. *Studies in Modern Religions and Religious Movements and the Babi-Bahai'i faiths.* Leiden: Brill.

Smith, Peter. 1987. *The Babi and Baha'i Religions: From Messianic Shi'ism to a World.* Cambridge: Cambridge University Press.

Bahá'í

ORIGINS AND BACKGROUND

Similar to other new religious movements born in the nineteenth century that emphasized the unity of all religions, such as Theosophy, the Bahá'í faith is a religion that emphasizes the essential truth and worth of all religions, particularly the major world religions such as Islam, Christianity, Buddhism, and more. Bahá'í developed in the mid-nineteenth century out of the Bábi religion. In 1844, the Iranian Siyyid Ali Muhammad Shirazi claimed to be the Báb, or the "Gate" to God, and began recording a series of divine revelations. His teachings began as an alternative interpretation of Shia Islam, a fact reflected in the many echoes of Muslim beliefs and practices in Bahá'í. His most important message was that God would soon send a new messenger. For his claims, the Báb was executed in 1850. However, his beliefs lived on through one of his earliest followers, Mirza Husayn Ali Nuri (1817–1892), who took the name Bahá'u'lláh (meaning "Glory of God") and formally founded the Bahá'í faith in 1863. In 1866, Bahá'u'lláh claimed to be the messenger whose coming the Báb had promised and whose role was to aid in humanity's spiritual advancement.

Under Bahá'u'lláh, the religion spread throughout the Persian and Ottoman empires. Leadership spread through the paternal line; thus, it was Bahá'u'lláh's successor, his son Abdu'l-Baha (1844–1921), who furthered the spread of the movement into Asia and Africa. However it was through the work of arguably the most significant leader of the new religious movement, Abdu'l-Baha's grandson, Shoghi Effendi (1897–1957), whose translation of Bahá'u'lláh's writings into English enabled the spread of the movement into Europe and North America.

Though their expansion into other countries has been steady, Bahá'ís have faced persistent persecution, particularly in those Muslim countries in which the movement grew and where the greatest number of Bahá'ís were concentrated. As late as 1998, Bahá'ís were being publicly executed in Iran and still face imprisonment in countries like Iran and Egypt, where the religion is illegal. In Egypt in 2009, Bahá'ís were reportedly required to hold religious identification cards, though the consistency of distributing such cards is unclear. Nonetheless, carrying a card means that a Bahá'í may be stripped of certain civil rights, such as the right to vote.

BELIEFS AND PRACTICES

Similar to major monotheistic traditions, such as Christianity and Judaism, the Bahá'í faith believes in a single, omniscient, omnipotent, and eternal deity who created the universe. In fact, Bahá'ís maintain that the God of Christians, Jews, and so forth is this one, divine Creator, who sent a succession of "Divine Messengers" (human manifestations of God), since He is inaccessible. These Messengers, including Abraham, Jesus, Buddha, Muhammad, and, most recently, Bahá'u'lláh, created the various world religious traditions to guide humanity toward knowledge of the one God.

Bahá'ís also believe that revelations of religious knowledge are progressive, meaning that the later Divine Messengers introduce a more complete knowledge than those who had come before, mirroring humanity's readiness to know and understand divine truth. This also means that revelation has not ended and that there will be a new Divine Messenger at some point in the future. From this perspective, Bahá'ís argue that while religions may differ in belief, history, and practice, all are simply manifestations of the one true faith revealed by the Bab and Bahá'u'lláh. Bahá'ís differentiate the one, true faith from its denominational iterations by parsing the "Greater" and "Lesser Covenants." The Greater Covenant is an eternal and universal promise by God to all of humanity, wherein He will come to humans' aid during times of crisis and to generally take a care for their wellbeing. The Lesser Covenant (or, more accurately, Covenants) refers to individual covenants between the various Divine Messengers and their followers, which relate to the specifics of practice and belief in respective religious traditions.

Bahá'ís believe that humans possess not simply eternal, but rational souls. This fact has produced two essential and related conclusions. First, since human beings are inherently rational, they are capable of accepting and understanding divine truth, shaped though by the particular religious manifestation (Islam, Buddhism, etc.) to which they subscribe. This lays the groundwork for the second conclusion that all human beings are equal and the pursuit of truth should be free and unfettered. Translator of much of Bahá'u'lláh's writings and leader of the religion from 1921 to 1957, Shoghi Effendi made it a personal mission to argue for peace among religions and disseminated the Bahá'í message as a means of eradicating religious prejudice. Even today, the Bahá'í website (www.bahai.org) lists "Universal Peace" as a primary belief of the religion.

Though Bahá'ís consider scriptures such as the Bible or the Qur'an to be divine and true, for Bahá'ís, themselves, they consider the writings of the Báb, Bahá'u'lláh, and their various successors, such as Shoghi Effendi, as canonical and authoritative. The most important texts are the *Kitab-i-Aqas*, or *The Most Holy Book*, which lays out guidelines for daily living and standards for religious practice, and the *Kitab-i-Iqan*, or *The Book of Certitude*, which is considered the primary source of Bahá'í belief.

Much of Bahá'i practice is individual in nature, focusing on daily obligatory prayers and study of Bahá'i scripture. Though Bahá'i gatherings often occur in private homes, there are Bahá'i houses of worship, known as Mashriqu'l-Adhkars, where devotional gatherings occur, particularly for important holy days (such as the birthdays of the Báb and Bahá'u'lláh). As of 2018, there are only about two dozen of these structures around the world, reflecting that more local and private element of most Bahá'i practice.

Bahá'ís observe a nineteen-month holy calendar, with each month measuring nineteen days (and a few interim days, known as "intercalary" dates to round out the solar year). During March each year (which corresponds to the first month of the Bahá'i calendar), Bahá'is fast from sunrise to sunset to come closer to God. Similar to the nineteen-day fast, which corresponds with the Muslim practice of fasting during Ramadan, Bahá'is are prohibited from drinking alcohol and from extramarital (or homosexual) sex. Abstention from politics is also recommended. However, Bahá'is' adherence to these proscriptions often depends on the culture in which they live, acting differently in more socially progressive versus socially conservative contexts. In other areas, Bahá'is have long held reformatory positions, particularly when it comes to gender equality, health and educational reform, and global poverty. As of 2017, Bahá'is are involved in numerous development projects focused on socioeconomic advancement.

INSTITUTIONS AND CULTURE

The Bahá'i religion is organized into two related branches, one filled with elected officials and the other with appointed officials. The aim of this dual system, according to Shoghi Effendi, was to mix elements of both democracy and autocracy, which have their benefits and pitfalls; the aim of the Bahá'is is to keep the good of each system and avoid the bad. The highest body of the religion is the Universal House of Justice, whose members are elected and which has the power to supplement (though not to alter) and administer the religious laws laid out by Bahá'u'lláh. Alongside this group are those hereditarily appointed to the Institution of Guardianship and who have the sole authority to interpret the religion's holy texts.

Outside of the top-down structure of religious governance, the religion is rather democratic in its devotional and day-to-day practices. There is no ordained clergy. Instead, local community leaders are elected to councils who help with the day-to-day issues of religious governance. These local spiritual authorities also serve in regional and, occasionally, in national capacities, where they may serve as a member of a Bahá'í National Spiritual Assembly (usually representing the Bahá'is of a particular country. As of 2010, there were a little more than 7.3 million Bahá'is living in 221 countries.

Culturally and popularly, often little is known or understood about Bahá'is. However, Bahá'is have appeared as fictional characters, primarily in literature, but more recently in film. Khalil Gibran was reputedly influenced by Bahá'i ideas, which factored into some of his greatest works, such as *The Prophet*. The film *The Matrix* bore parallels to the Bahá'i faith, though the filmmakers did not cite Bahá'i sources directly, and the iconic show *The Simpsons* featured the Bahá'i religion in an episode titled "She of Little Faith," where Lisa Simpson debates which religion to join. Though these pop cultural iterations rarely delve into the nuances of Bahá'i faith (and often arguably subscribe to Orientalist tropes), they show how far the religion has extended in its short lifespan thus far.

See also: Babism; Theosophy.

Further Reading

Baha'u'llah. 1873. *The Kitab-i-Aqdas: The Most Holy Book*. Available at: http://www.bahai.org/library/authoritative-texts/bahaullah/kitab-i-aqdas/.

Baha'u'llah, & Shoghi Effendi, trans. 1931. *The Kitab-I-Iqan: The Book of Certitude*. Available at: http://www.bahai.org/library/authoritative-texts/bahaullah/kitab-i-iqan/.

Esslemont, J. E. 2006. *Baha'u'llah and the New Era: An Introduction*, 4th ed. Wilmette, IL: Baha'i Publishing.

Smith, Peter. 2013. *An Introduction to the Baha'i Faith*. Cambridge: Cambridge University Press.

Warburg, Margit. 2003. *Baha'i: Studies in Contemporary Religions*. Salt Lake City, UT: Signature Books.

Ballard, Guy W. (1878–1939)

Like many others, Guy Ballard entered the ranks of American prophets as the result of an extraordinary experience. Although he had previously been interested in Spiritualism, Theosophy, and other currents of alternative religious thought, Ballard's life changed in August 1930. While hiking on Mount Shasta in northern California, whose esoteric associations he was well aware of, Ballard stopped to drink from a stream. He was interrupted, however, by what he thought was a young man who offered a different drink. That drink infused Ballard with an amazing feeling. The young man, whom Ballard later recognized as the Ascended Master, Saint Germain, told him that it came from the Universal Supply of Life itself.

Ballard understood Saint Germain as one of the Ascended Masters of the Great White Brotherhood, one of the many perfected beings who had fully identified with their God Selves and who desire to spread their special esoteric knowledge, or Light, to humankind. Saint Germain was also one of the Mahatmas or Masters associated with Theosophy, but Ballard's understanding of them differed from the foundational sources of Theosophy. Saint Germain remained the most important of many masters for the Ballards, but the master Jesus, distinguished from the Christ for theological reasons, was also important.

Ballard's initial encounter with Saint Germain led to a continuing relationship and an intense tutorial over the next three months. Ballard learned from the Ascended Master about the divine presence that lies within every human being. Saint Germain told Ballard that if humans could realize the God Self within them they could achieve extraordinary things. In fact, Ballard learned that whatever humans could think and feel, they could bring into being. Those ideas were influenced by the New Thought movement, associated particularly with Emma Curtis Hopkins (1849–1925), which affirmed the inherent divinity of each individual.

During his meetings with Saint Germain and his continuing reception of messages from him and other masters, Ballard learned many other things, including the doctrine of reincarnation, details of his own past lives, the history of ancient civilizations, and the central role of America in an imminent Golden Age. But the focal point of Saint Germain's teaching was on the potential of each individual to realize her or his God Self. God became known as the mighty "I AM" presence, which also associated Ballard with the prophet Moses, who received God's self-disclosure in Exodus 3:14.

When Ballard returned to his Chicago home and told his wife, Edna (1886–1971), about his experiences, she quickly joined him in promoting the message of Saint Germain. Edna had herself long been interested in the occult and had also associated with the white supremacist and anti-semitic Silver Legion of America or "Silver Shirts" founded by William Pelley. Pelley's goal of a Christian Commonwealth in the United States influenced the pronounced American patriotism in the developing movement led by the Ballards.

Quickly, Edna, too, became an "accredited messenger" of the Ascended Masters. By 1932, they had established the Saint Germain Foundation to promote the teachings Ballard had received. In 1934, writing under the pen name Godfré Ray King, Ballard published his own detailed account of his interactions with Saint Germain in *Unveiled Mysteries*. Many more publications would follow.

The I AM religious movement that the Ballards led spread the message of the Ascended Masters through publications, public appearances, special classes held by the Ballards, and by local groups devoted to the study of the Ascended Masters' teachings. By the end of the 1930s perhaps as many as a million people were engaged with the I AM Activity.

Guy's death in 1939 left Edna as the leader of the movement. Very quickly, she proclaimed that he had himself joined the Ascended Masters and would even come back again. Though that return has not yet happened, Guy's teachings continue to be promulgated by the Saint Germain Foundation (www.sanitgermainfoundation.org). In addition, the I AM Activity has influenced a number of groups in the Theosophical and New Age milieus, including The Summit Lighthouse and the Church Universal and Triumphant.

See also: Church Universal and Triumphant, The; I AM Activity, The; New Age, The; New Thought; Theosophy.

Further Reading

Braden, Charles Samuel. 1949. *These Also Believe: A Study of Modern American Cults and Minority Religious Movements.* New York: Macmillan.

King, Godfré Ray (Guy Ballard). 1934. *Unveiled Mysteries.* Schaumburg, IL: Saint Germain Press.

Rudbøg, Tim, 2013. "The I AM Activity." In Olav Hammer & Mikael Rothstein, eds., *Handbook of the Theosophical Current*, pp. 151–172. Leiden: Brill.

PRIMARY SOURCE DOCUMENT

"Guy Ballard's Initial Encounter with Saint Germain" from *Unveiled Mysteries* (1934)

Guy Ballard was a student of Theosophy who founded the "I AM" Activity. In 1934, he penned an account of his interactions with Saint Germain, writing under the pen name Godfré Ray King. An excerpt from his text, Unveiled Mysteries, *follows.*

MOUNT SHASTA stood out boldly against the western sky, surrounded at its base by a growth of pine and fir trees that made it look like a jewel of diamond shining whiteness held in a filigree setting of green. Its snow covered peaks glistened and changed color from moment to moment, as the shadows lengthened in the sun's descent toward the horizon.

Rumor said there was a group of men, Divine men in Fact, called the Brotherhood of Mount Shasta, who formed a branch of the Great White Lodge, and that this Focus from very ancient times had continued unbroken down to the present day.

I had been sent on government business to a little town situated at the foot of the mountain, and while thus engaged occupied my leisure time trying to unravel this rumor concerning The Brotherhood. I knew, through travels in the Far East, that most rumors, myths, and legends have, somewhere as their origin, a deep underlying Truth that usually remains unrecognized by all but those who are Real students of life.

I fell in love with Shasta and each morning, almost involuntarily, saluted the Spirit of the Mountain and the Members of the Order. I sensed something very unusual about the entire locality and, in the light of the experiences that followed, I do not wonder that some of them cast their shadows before. . . .

As the day advanced, it grew very warm and I stopped frequently to rest and enjoy to the full the remarkable stretch of country around the McCloud River, Valley, and town. It came time for lunch, and I sought a mountain spring for clear, cold water. Cup in hand, I bent down to fill it as an electrical current passed through my body from head to foot.

I looked around, and directly behind me stood a young man who, at first glance, seemed to be someone on a hike like myself. I looked more closely, and realized immediately that he was no ordinary person. As this thought passed through my mind, he smiled and addressed me saying:

"My Brother, if you will hand me your cup, I will give you a much more refreshing drink than spring water." I obeyed, and instantly the cup was filled with a creamy liquid. Handing it back to me, he said:

"Drink it."

I did so and must have looked my astonishment for, while the taste was delicious, the electrical vivifying effect in my mind and body made me gasp with surprise. I did not see him put anything into the cup, and I wondered what was happening.

"That which you drank," he explained, "comes directly from the Universal Supply, pure and vivifying as Life Itself, in fact it is Life—Omnipresent Life—for it exists everywhere about us. It is subject to our conscious control and direction, willingly obedient, when we Love enough, because all the Universe obeys the behest of Love. Whatsoever I desire manifests itself, when I command in Love. I held out the cup, and that which I desired for you appeared.

"See! I have but to hold out my hand and, if I wish to use gold—gold is here." Instantly, there lay in his palm a disc about the size of a ten dollar gold piece. Again he continued:

"I see within you a certain Inner understanding of the Great Law but you are not outwardly aware of It enough to produce that which you desire direct from the Omnipresent Universal Supply. You have desired to see something of this kind so intensely, so honestly, and so determinedly, it could no longer be withheld from you.

"However, precipitation is one of the least important activities of the Great Truth of Being. If your desire had not been free from selfishness and the fascination of phenomena, such an experience could not have come to you. When leaving home this morning, you thought you were coming on a hike, that is, so far as the outer activity of your mind was concerned. In the deeper—larger sense—you were really following the urge of your Inner God Self that led to the person, place, and condition wherein your most intense desire could be fulfilled.

"The Truth of Life is you cannot desire that which is not possible of manifestation somewhere in the universe. The more intense the feeling within the desire, the more quickly it will be attained. However, if one is foolish enough to desire something that will injure another of God's children or any other part of His Creation, then that person will pay the penalty in discord and failure somewhere in his own Life's experience.

"It is very important to realize fully that God's intent for every one of His children is abundance of every good and perfect thing. He created Perfection and endowed His children with exactly the same power. They can create and maintain Perfection also and express God—dominion over the earth and all that is therein. Mankind was originally created in the Image: and Likeness of God. The only reason all do not manifest This dominion is because they do not use their Divine Authority—that with which each individual is endowed and by which he is intended to govern his world. Thus, they are not obeying the Law of Love by pouring out peace and blessing to all creation.

"This comes about through their failure to accept and acknowledge themselves—Temples of the Most High Living God—and to hold this acknowledgment with eternal recognition. Humanity—in its present seeming limitation of time, space, and activity—is in the same condition a person in need would be to whom some one held out a handful of money. If the needing one did not step forward and accept the money held out to him—how in the world could he ever have the benefit—which it could bring.

"The mass of mankind is in exactly this state of consciousness today—and will continue in it—until they accept the God within their hearts as—the Owner—Giver—and Doer—of all the Good—that has ever come into their lives and world. . . .

"Then close the meditation by the command:—*I am a Child of the 'Light'—I Love the 'Light'—I Serve the 'Light'—I Live in the 'Light'—I am Protected,*

> *Illumined, Supplied, Sustained by the 'Light,' and I Bless the 'Light.'* Remember always—'One becomes—*that*—upon which he meditates'—and since all things have come forth from the 'Light'—'Light'—is the Supreme Perfection—and Control—of all things."
>
> **Source:** King, Godfre Ray (Guy Ballard). *Unveiled Mysteries*. Chicago: Saint Germain Press, 1934. Available at: https://www.sacred-texts.com/eso/um/index.htm.

Bey, Hakim (1945–)

Better known by his pen name, Hakim Bey, Peter Lamborn Wilson was propelled into spiritual and philosophical experimentation in the 1960s, as were many Baby Boomers, in reaction to the dominant conservatism of American culture. As a college student in New York, Bey was introduced to Islam through the Moorish Science Temple, though he would ultimately split along with several other members to found the Moorish Orthodox Church.

Not content to limit his religious evolution to the United States and perturbed by American culture and politics, Bey left for Lebanon in 1968 and spent the better part of a decade traveling to India, Pakistan, and Iran. In his travels, he studied Sufism, Kriya yoga (central to Tantric practice), and Islam. While in Iran, he began translating Persian texts as well as Sufi poetry.

The vast majority of Bey's written work, however, is original. He writes under both his given name and his pen name. He derived the latter from the sixth Muslim caliph and renowned alchemist, il-Hakim, and the traditional attachment of the surname "Bey" by Moorish Science Temple members. He has published over fifty books and many more articles, ranging from translations of Sufi poems to political manifestos to postanarchist philosophy.

Most influential of his theoretical writings are those dealing with "temporary autonomous zones" (TAZ) or "ontological anarchy," also known as "immediatism." Bey apparently got the inspiration for his theory of TAZ from Timothy Leary's (1920–1996) commune (the Moorish Orthodox Church had ties to Leary). Noting the tendency of such utopias to dwindle after the death of their founding members, Bey posited a number of theories on the nature of time and space in these short-lived utopias. Immediatism represents the idea that only chaos exists (and that all claims for nonchaotic states are false), thus any governance is an illusion. To this end, Bey recommends that people "awaken" and create each day out of total, existential freedom. Though indebted in part to European philosophy, most of Bey's works are influenced by occult and mystical religious ideas that he learned in his travels.

Bey has come under fire for his open endorsement of pederasty—the relationship of an older man with a younger, even adolescent, boy. His seeming alignment of pedophilia with the freedom invoked by his postanarchist theory has led critics to view his political views as serving his sexual proclivities. Bey, for his part, is open and unapologetic about these views.

Bey resides in upstate New York and continues to write prolifically on eclectic subject matter.

See also: Moorish Science Temple of America, The; Occultism and Esotericism; Utopianism in New Religious Movements.

Further Reading

Bey, Hakim. 2003. *TAZ: The Temporary Autonomous Zone, Ontological Anarchy, Poetic Terrorism*, 2nd ed. Brooklyn, NY: Autonomedia.

Bey, Hakim (as Peter Lamborn Wilson). 2014. *Spiritual Journeys of an Anarchist*. Brooklyn, NY: Autonomedia.

Greer, Joseph Christian. 2013. "Occult Origins: Hakim Bey's Ontological Post-Anarchism." *Anarchist Developments in Cultural Studies* 2: 166–187.

Williams, Leonard. 2010. "Hakim Bey and Ontological Anarchism." *Journal for the Study of Anarchism* 4: 109–137.

Black Judaism

In the late nineteenth and twentieth centuries many different religious movements arose among African Americans that aimed to give them a meaningful sense of identity and history beyond what had been imposed on them first by slaveholders and then by other colonialists in the aftermath of slavery. Some found that they could effectively reframe the Christianity that they were forced to practice by their masters. Others adopted some elements of Christianity but mixed them with the traditional religions of their homelands, forming new hybrid religions like Santería, Vodou, and Candomblé. Still others, like the Moorish Science Temple and the Nation of Islam, sought religious roots beyond Christianity and declared that some form of Islam was the appropriate religion for people of African descent. And some other African Americans looked for their roots in Judaism, identifying themselves variously as Jews, Hebrews, or Israelites. Different forms of Black Judaism have expressed and shaped African American identity and will likely continue to do so.

Since Christianity at its beginnings presented itself as the true Israel, the claim to be Israelites was engrained in the Christian scriptures. Many Christian groups throughout the world have emphasized their connections with ancient Israel, such as the Seventh-day Adventists or the Zionist churches of southern Africa. In the United States various forms of Anglo-Israelism influenced the Holiness movement and later Pentecostal Christianity. Some African American Christians amplified the connection to Israel and mixed it with an eclectic set of other influences, including Freemasonry, Spiritualism, Ethiopianism, New Thought, African American folk traditions, and, eventually, black nationalism.

William Saunders Crowdy (1847–1908), for example, founded the Church of God and Saints of Christ in 1893 after receiving various divine visions and communications that directed him to establish God's true church. Crowdy asserted that the ancient Israelites, the patriarchs, and Jesus himself were black and that African Americans were descended from the ten lost tribes of Israel. Over time Crowdy's group incorporated various Jewish practices, including observation of the Sabbath on Saturday, adoption of the Jewish ritual calendar including the week-long observance of Passover, and following Jewish dietary laws. Crowdy traveled throughout the Midwestern and Eastern United States preaching his message, which eventually included the belief that Jesus was a prophet rather than a divine figure. After his death, the Church split into two factions and congregations are still in operation (see, e.g., www.cogasoc.org and www.saintsofchrist.org).

Crowdy preached in New York City in 1899 where, similar to Chicago, the rich and diverse black intellectual life in the city after World War I would give rise to several prominent Black Jewish congregations. For example, Arnold Josiah Ford (1877–1935), originally from Barbados, immigrated to New York in 1912. Ford was active in Marcus Garvey's (1887–1940) Universal Negro Improvement Association and was also a Mason. In 1924, he established the Beth B'Nai Abraham congregation. Ford's story of origins placed the ancient Israelites first in Nigeria from which they moved east through Carthage and Egypt to Palestine—a journey that gave African Americans a connection to ancient blacks. Ford's group adopted many Jewish ritual practices, including the use of Torah scrolls, prayer shawls, and Jewish prayer books, but also added Islamic elements, such as observing Ramadan. Ford attempted to set up a separate colony in Ethiopia with some of his followers, but it never came to fruition.

Also active in New York around the same time and influenced by Ford was Wentworth Arthur Matthew (1892–1972), who founded The Commandment Keepers Church of the Living God, the Pillar and Ground of Truth. Like Ford's congregation, Matthew's followers observed the Jewish ritual calendar but they also had a variety of ritual practices that included foot washing, use of incense and special oils, and other elements of what Matthew called his "cabbalistic science." Although Matthew aspired to lead all of the black Jews in the United States, his influence did not extend that far. His students formed their own congregations that did not always recognize his authority, and some of them pursued rapprochements with white Jewish groups. In 1973, one of his students formed the International Israelite Board of Rabbis (see www.blackjews.org), which continues Matthew's tradition of Black Judaism.

Congregations of black Jews have continued to form. Reprising the theme of exodus that prompted Ford's move to Ethiopia and also animates Rastafarian discourse, in May 1967 three leaders of the Abeta Hebrew Israel Cultural Center in Chicago flew to Liberia and eventually secured three hundred acres of land on which they could establish a settlement in the land of their ancestors. Like Ford's experiment, that move did not work out, but a member who took the Hebrew name Ben Ammi (né Ben Carter, 1939–2014) led the group to Israel in late 1969. Their petition to take up residence under Israel's "right of return" policy was initially rejected by the Israeli government, initiating a long period of tension that was partially resolved by granting the group permanent residency status in 2003. The group of some two thousand members, the African Hebrew Israelites of Jerusalem, remains in the southern Israel towns of Dimona, Arad, and Mitzpe Ramon (see http://africanhebrewisraelitesofjerusalem.com/), and there are communities in major American cities. Seeking a meaningful history for his followers, Ben Ammi connected African Americans with the ancient Israelites by claiming that many of the Israelites dispersed to Africa, becoming the ancestors of tribes like the Ashanti. Also, like other groups of Black Israelites, the Hebrew Israelites observe what they understand to be the legal requirements stipulated in the Hebrew Bible, adopting a style of dress designed to express their Jewish identity.

See also: African New Religious Movements; Candomblé; Freemasonry; Moorish Science Temple of America, The; Nation of Islam, The; Race and New Religious Movements; Rastafari; Santería; Vodou.

Further Reading

Chireau, Yvonne, & Nathaniel Deutsch, eds. 1999. *Black Zion: African American Encounters with Judaism.* New York: Oxford University Press.

Dorman, Jacob S. 2013. *Chosen People: The Rise of American Black Israelite Religions.* New York: Oxford University Press.

Landing, James E. 2001. *Black Judaism: Story of an American Movement.* Durham, NC: Carolina Academic Press.

Blavatsky, Helena Petrovna (1831–1891)

EARLY LIFE

Though it is established that Helena Petrovna Blavatsky was born in Ukraine (then part of the Russian empire) on August 12, 1831, much of her life story has been consigned to the realm of speculation and myth. Some of this arises from Blavatsky herself, who provided conflicting accounts of her past, painting a picture that makes her later spiritual and professional life the natural progression of her early precocity and psychic abilities. For example, Blavatsky said that she felt protected and guided by something outside of herself at a very early age. By her teens she was traveling regularly and extensively, encountering those who she had known appeared in visions throughout her childhood, such as the Mahatma ("Great Master") Morya, with whom she met in London in 1851 and who told her that she had great work in store for her.

However, it was her travels in southeast Asia with Morya (or "M," as she called him), particularly India and Tibet, during the 1850s and 1860s that would bear lasting effects on both her personal spiritual growth and the religious movement that she would soon lead, Theosophy. While in Tibet, Blavatsky reportedly spent time with Master Koot Hoomi who, along with Morya, began her education in the world of occult or "hidden" knowledge. Under their guidance, Blavatsky claimed to learn a language called Senzar used in the various texts curated by the monks of a Tibetan monastery, all the while focusing her psychic powers, particularly those that allowed her to project her consciousness into other, metaphysical planes of existence.

FROM SPIRITUALISM TO THEOSOPHY

Blavatsky's travels eventually took her to the United States in 1873, where by the next year, she entered into Spiritualist circles. Emerging in the mid-nineteenth

One of the founders of the Theosophical Society and its primary religious thinker, Helena Petrovna Blavatsky was both a formidable and mysterious figure. Her claimed encounters with a variety of Masters formed the basis of her religious authority. (Blavatsky, Helena Petrovna, *Isis Unveiled: A Master-Key to the Mysteries of Ancient and Modern Science and Theology*, 1891)

century, Spiritualism was a religious movement premised on the belief that the deceased now residing in the spirit world were capable and desirous of communicating with the living. Already primed to believe that human beings were capable of psychic connections to other planes, Blavatsky felt at home in the movement, which also forged her introduction to Theosophy's future cofounder, Colonel Henry Steel Olcott. However, Blavatsky would take Spiritualist practices a step further, arguing that those who were mentally and spiritually prepared could communicate with "The Great Masters," those with vast stores of esoteric knowledge about both the natural and supernatural world. From this notion, Theosophy, and its institutional base, the Theosophical Society, were born.

After amassing a following in the United States, first among Spiritualists and increasingly among a sizable population of religious "seekers," Blavatsky and Olcott traveled to India, where they resided from 1879 to 1885 and enjoyed a continued measure of success in gaining Indian converts to Theosophy. Eventually, Blavatsky returned to Europe due to her weakening physical condition, where she oversaw the growing network of Theosophical "lodges." Aware that her health was fragile, Blavatsky began to concern herself with finding a successor to the movement. She found such a figure in Annie Besant, who would publish several of her predecessor's works after Blavatsky's death.

LATER YEARS AND LEGACY

The years between the founding of the Theosophical Society and Blavatsky's death were filled with triumphs and controversies. Among the former were Blavatsky's numerous publications, particularly those considered versions of "automatic writing," or texts written under the agency of a spirit (or Great Master). While writing her first book, *Isis Unveiled* (1886), Blavatsky claimed to be aided, but not overcome, by a spiritual presence. The contents of the book's two volumes formed the basis of Theosophical thought. It argued that there was a higher, sacred knowledge available through communion with the Great Masters, which would synthesize and expand upon the truth of the world's major religious traditions. *The Secret Doctrine* (volumes I and II, 1888; volume III edited by Annie Besant, 1897) soon followed, which laid out an evolutionary theory of human development, as people progressed along the path to greater spiritual enlightenment. With Olcott, Blavatsky edited *The Theosophist*, a periodical that enjoyed a rather large readership, beyond those who claimed membership in the Theosophical Society. These accomplishments were marred by accusations of plagiarism in Blavatsky's major writings. Specifically, *Isis Unveiled* was apparently rife with passages from various ancient texts she may have encountered in her travels. Additionally, these years brought with them several explosive reports claiming the fraudulent nature of Theosophy, generally, and, Blavatsky herself, including a highly critical report by the Society of Psychical Research that accused Blavatsky of falsifying supernatural phenomena. Though Blavatsky and Olcott denied the reports outright, this led to a number of defections from the organization.

Described as eccentric in manners, Blavatsky purportedly had a fearsome charisma and seemingly endless energy for her work. Her appearance and sexuality were often the subject of speculation, however. Blavatsky reputedly refused to allow tabloid fodder to distract from the dissemination of Theosophical beliefs and practices. Deteriorating health did not slow down the rate of publication nor the zeal with which she combated Theosophy's detractors (she sued a paper for libel during the last months of her life). Despite her vigor, Blavatsky contracted and succumbed to the flu, dying on March 8, 1891.

See also: Olcott, Henry Steel (1832–1907); Theosophical Society, The; Theosophy.

Further Reading

Blavatsky, H. P., & Michael Gomes. 1997. *Isis Unveiled: Secrets of the Ancient Wisdom Tradition, Madame Blavatsky's First Work; A New Abridgement by Michael Gomes.* Wheaton, IL: The Theosophical Publishing House.

Blavatsky, H. P., & Michael Gomes. 2009. *The Secret Doctrine: The Class Work, Abridged and Annotated.* Los Angeles: TarcherPerigee.

Lachman, Gary. 2012. *Madame Blavatsky: The Mother of Modern Spirituality.* Los Angeles: TarcherPerigee.

Lubelsky, Isaac. 2012. *Celestial India: Madame Blavatsky and the Birth of Indian Nationalism.* Translated by Yael Lotan. Sheffield, UK: Equinox Publishing.

Book of Mormon, The

REVELATION AND TRANSLATION

The Christian canon was officially closed by the fifth century. At this point, the age of revelation was declared over and the books of the Bible were set; nothing would be added, nothing subtracted. Since that time, the boundaries of this canon would be tested, but perhaps none would do so as brazenly as Joseph Smith who defied the closed canon by first adding to it a new testament of Jesus Christ, *The Book of Mormon*.

In 1820, a confused fourteen-year-old Joseph Smith went to the woods near Palymyra, New York, and asked God which Christian denomination he should join. God and Jesus appeared to him and told him that none of the existing churches were the true church and that Smith would have to found it. Then in 1823, Smith received a second vision, this time of the angel Moroni who told him that buried in a nearby hill was a set of golden plates, which he must excavate and then translate. Smith proceeded to the hill, found the plates, but was unable to take them for, as Moroni told him, he desired the plates for their monetary value (they were pure gold, after all). Only in 1827 would Moroni declare Smith worthy of retrieving the plates, along with two seer stones, the Urim and Thummim, to enable him to read the unfamiliar, ancient text; he did and immediately set about the task of translation.

New religions are prolific producers of new scriptural texts. The supernatural means by which Joseph Smith received, and then translated, *The Book of Mormon*, underscored its religious authority. (Library of Congress)

Though he originally intended to undertake the task of translation by himself—Moroni having warned him that no one must see or handle the plates but himself—Smith quickly realized that he lacked funding to ensure its swift translation and publication. Thus, he enlisted the help of a wealthy local farmer, Martin Harris, who, besides serving as both benefactor and first scribe, would become one of the earliest converts to Smith's burgeoning religious movement. From April to June of 1828, the two set about the work of translation. However, disaster occurred when Smith entrusted Harris with the first 116 pages of the manuscript, which the latter promptly lost (they were never recovered). Next, he would turn to his wife Emma to help him translate. She, sitting behind a cloth barrier, described hearing the sound of the plates as Joseph turned them, while never seeing them herself. Finally, it was Oliver Cowdery, another early convert, who would serve as scribe and help Smith complete the project of translation in a mere three months—April to June 1829.

Due to increasing pressure from his expanding inner circle, Smith prayed for and received revelation enabling him to allow three of the fold (known as "The Three Witnesses") to handle and touch the text while covered and, later, for eight individuals ("The Eight Witnesses") to see the golden plates. The lucky individuals recorded and affixed their names to statements affirming what they had felt or seen; these statements of the witnesses are included in every edition of *The Book of Mormon*, bolstering its authenticity. The first edition was published in April of 1830; Joseph Smith founded the Church of Jesus Christ of Latter-day Saints (LDS Church) a month later.

A NEW SACRED HISTORY: CONTENT AND RECEPTION

The Book of Mormon tells the story of an ancient civilization that lived and perished in America. The narrative follows the story of the righteous Nephites and wicked Lamanites, who originated from the Middle East (perhaps descending from the ten lost tribes of Israel). Repeated squabbles over a period of twenty-six hundred years ultimately led to their mutual destruction—which is why it is their record and not their descendants who have survived to tell the story. The original "golden bible" was reportedly written in "Reformed Egyptian," set down by the prophet Mormon (for whom the text is named) and his son, the last prophet, Moroni. The primary purpose of the text, as stated in the book's title page, is to convince both "Jew and Gentile that Jesus is the Christ, the Eternal God, manifesting himself unto all nations." So this new sacred text represented the Gospel "restored," and the central purpose of Smith's LDS Church was to preach it far and wide as, to this point, the Church had been unsuccessful in convincing everyone of this essential truth.

The text reads similarly to the Old Testament—both in terms of organization and style and the overlap in historical periods during which both narratives take place—while maintaining a distinctive focus on the life and work of Jesus Christ. It effectively merges both Jewish and Christian sacred histories into the same text. Besides providing a new sacred history that centered the action in the American continent, *The Book of Mormon* opened the canon and made continuing revelation a major feature of the LDS Church. In the years that followed, Smith would add *The Book of Moses* (the beginning of his translation of the Bible), *The Book of Abraham* (translated from recovered Egyptian scrolls), and the *Doctrine and Covenants*, which is a living compendium of revelations made by the prophet. So, the canon still grows. Though the LDS Church still considers the Bible as sacred scripture, they have dispensed with the idea that it, alone, bears canonical status.

Proponents of the book point to Joseph Smith's lack of education as proof that its pages must be true, for how could an uneducated man have woven together an intricate, six-hundred-page history in the span of two months? Conversely, critics of the text have argued, variously, that Joseph Smith plagiarized the text, that he conceived it from his own imagination, that its pages tell of ancient civilizations for which there is no archaeological evidence, and that, the story of a primitive people coming to America in rickety boats is, simply, fantastical. For LDS, the text is simply scripture and one that points to a lost history, now restored, which they must spread to the world.

See also: Church of Jesus Christ of Latter-day Saints, The; Smith, Joseph (1805–1844).

Further Reading

The Book of Mormon. Available at: https://www.lds.org/scriptures/bofm?lang=eng.

Gutjahr, Paul C. 2012. *The Book of Mormon: A Biography.* Lives of Great Religious Books Series. Princeton, NJ; Oxford: Princeton University Press.

Holland, David. 2011. *Sacred Borders: Continuing Revelation and Canonical Restraint in Early America.* Religion in America. Oxford: Oxford University Press.

Brahma Kumaris

Brahma Kumaris, also known as the "Daughters" of Brahma, is a syncretic Hindu new religious movement with a millennialist bent. Founded in the 1930s, it is known for the crucial (and overwhelming) role women play in the movement and, more recently, for its advocacy of sustainable farming practices and ecological initiatives. Those involved often eschew the idea that Brahma Kumaris is a religion, preferring to think of it as a lifestyle or pathway to spiritual perfection.

Between 1934 and 1937, Dada Lekhraj (1876–1969), a wealthy jeweler, had a series of spiritual visions, prompting him to found a religious community in Hyderabad, India (now part of Pakistan). Living as a member of the merchant class, Dada was surrounded primarily by women and children, since men were often called away to work. His inner circle, often called "Om Mandali," for their repeated chanting of "Om," comprised primarily of women, with whom he began to unpack the meaning of his revelations. Many of his disciples also experienced visions, often entering trances and serving as mediums for supernatural beings or deities. Eventually, through these gatherings (called *satsangs*) and repeated metaphysical experiences, Dada determined that a deity (sometimes determined to be Krishna, at others, Shiva) was working through him to create a new world; the world itself was at a point of transition where either good or evil could prevail across humanity. Different from traditional Hindu belief, which posits that a so-called golden age will rise and fall in perpetuity, Dada argued that the world currently stood on the brink of destruction. He also determined that perfection, rather than enlightenment, and rebirth in this golden age could only be achieved by those who adopted a pure, pseudoascetic lifestyle, which included abstention from alcohol, vegetarianism, and celibacy.

Women (*kumaris*), in particular, were urged to live celibately—a recommendation that flew in the face of societal norms and led to "anticult" activity spearheaded by men. Due to this persecution, the group retreated from society for a time until the partition of India and Pakistan in 1947, after which, the movement focused on disseminating its message of imminent world change, focused meditation, and a pure lifestyle. However, the movement did not begin its global spread until 1971, when missionaries created inroads among Indian immigrants in other countries.

Founded in 1937, the Brahma Kumaris World Spiritual University is the formal institutional structure of the movement. Unsurprisingly, women comprise the majority of administrative and spiritual positions (known as "sisters"), a system that continues to the present. As of 2019, the movement has spread and founded retreat centers in 110 countries, spanning every continent, with an administrative center in Mount Abu, India and an international center in London. At these centers, practitioners usually take a seven-day course that instructs them in the basic beliefs and practices of the movement. Raja-yoga meditation is the primary spiritual exercise practiced by Brahma Kumaris. According to their website (www.brahmakumaris.org), raja-yoga requires no ritual or mantra and is "accessible to people of all backgrounds"; its primary intention is to attain "open eyes" to one's mental and emotional state, enabling better control of oneself and to merge with God. The vast majority of people who practice Brahma Kumaris are what could be described as dabblers, participating in a workshop or seminar at the university and then incorporating these methods into their daily lives. Only a select few, mainly women, live and teach at the centers. Full-time members often wear white to symbolize purity.

In recent years, Brahma Kumaris has earned accolades for its environmentalism. They have spearheaded efforts to employ solely solar or other sustainable sources of energy, developing a solar power plant in Mount Abu. Combining the practice of raja-yoga with sustainable farming practices, the Sustainable Yogic Agriculture program was initiated in 2009. Farmers are trained in organic and sustainable farming as well as meditation techniques; a belief abounds that proper meditation increases the likelihood of a healthy crop.

See also: Environmentalism and New Religious Movements; Hindu New Religious Movements; Mediums; Millennialism; Women in New Religious Movements; Yoga.

Further Reading

Ramsay, Tamasin, Wendy Smith, & Lenore Manderson. 2012. "Brahma Kumaris: Purity and the Globalization of Faith." In Lenore Manderson, Wendy Smith, & Matt Tomlinson, eds., *Flows of Faith: Religious Reach and Community in Asia and the Pacific.* Dordrecht: Springer Netherlands.

Walliss, John. 2002. *The Brahma Kumaris as a "Reflexive Tradition": Responding to Late Modernity.* Burlington, VT: Ashgate.

Whaling, Frank. 2012. *Understanding the Brahma Kumaris.* Edinburgh: Dunedin Academic.

Brainwashing

Prior to and during World War II, intelligence services in both Nazi Germany and the United States were intrigued by the possibility of inducing dramatic psychological changes in individuals. In the United States, the Central Intelligence Agency (CIA) continued that interest after the war. At the same time, the Chinese Communists were developing strategies of their own, which were employed in North Korean prisoner of war camps during the Korean conflict.

In the decade from the mid-1950s through the mid-1960s a series of scholarly and popular examinations of brainwashing or thought reform were published. They included journalist and CIA propagandist Edward Hunter's *Brainwashing in Red China* (1951), psychiatrist Robert Jay Lifton's *Thought Reform and the Psychology of Totalism* (1961), and psychologist Edgar Schein's *Coercive Persuasion*. Those works, and others, used different theoretical models and made different analytical points, and for the anticult movement that began in the early 1970s, they provided a powerful explanation for why young people joined alternative religions.

BRAINWASHING AS AN EXPLANATION FOR CONVERSION

The debate about whether conversion to new religions results from brainwashing or personal choice focuses on the issue of individual agency, including when it is exercised and whether it can be overcome.

The contention that converts to new religions have been brainwashed or suffered coercive persuasion has several implications. It absolves individuals and, importantly, their families from any responsibility for the unorthodox religious choices they make. Consequently, it paves the way for the reintegration of former cult members, who could not have been in their "right mind" while in the cult, into mainstream society. It also lays the groundwork for a specific intervention in response to cult membership. Since converts have been brainwashed or "programmed" by unscrupulous cult leaders, they need to be "deprogrammed" and returned to their preconversion state. That chain of reasoning led to the invention of a new role, the freelance deprogrammer, and eventually a new profession in which entrepreneurs, like the early deprogrammer Ted Patrick (1930–), could make a living.

The notion of brainwashing, or its rough equivalents, was embraced by the anticult movement, which publicizes the pervasive danger that cults pose to individuals, families, and American society. Such a succinct, dramatic, and terrifying explanation for why individuals would join strange, new religions and forsake their previous lives and the futures their parents had imagined for them succeeded in attracting support for anticult work from the general public and some professionals, including psychiatrists, psychologists, and lawyers. The news and entertainment media also accepted and promulgated dramatic stories of individuals who had been "saved" from cults by the heroic efforts of deprogrammers. Brainwashing remains the template for most stories about cult membership in the news media.

The brainwashing theory also made its way into the courts as parents sought legal means of compelling their adult children to abandon cult membership. Anticult activists, like the clinical psychologist Margaret Singer (1921–2003), provided expert testimony that reinforced the conception that cult members had been coerced into membership and deceived about the true nature of their groups. But the prominence of the brainwashing theory also invited critical scrutiny from scholars in multiple disciplines. By the late 1970s and early 1980s, their findings began to undermine the simplistic use of the concept of brainwashing by members of the anticult movement to explain cult membership. A decisive turn occurred in 1987 when the American Psychological Association declined to accept the report of a task force headed by Singer that endorsed the general outlines of the brainwashing theory. That damaged the credibility of expert witnesses who tried to introduce the brainwashing theory in court and their testimony began to be excluded.

At the same time, several researchers subjected the brainwashing explanation of conversion to empirical examination. The most thorough test was conducted by sociologist Eileen Barker, who focused on the Unification Church in England. Her conclusions were devastating to the brainwashing theory. Barker found that even starting with those who actually visited a Unification center, no more than one in two hundred of them would be involved with the Church in any fashion two years later. From that perspective, the purported brainwashing practiced by the Unificationists appeared eminently resistible.

THE FALL AND RISE OF BRAINWASHING

Despite the rejection of the anticult movement's version of brainwashing theory by the courts and the undermining of the theory by empirical studies, it continues to exert attraction. In popular news and entertainment media it still provides a simple, compelling, and dramatic explanation for participation in groups as diverse as the Fundamentalist Latter-day Saints and NXIVM. It is used to elicit sympathy for members, former members, and their families and to stoke outrage about predatory and deceptive groups.

Some scholars have also tried to rehabilitate the brainwashing theory of cult membership. In a series of publications in the 1990s and 2000s, sociologist Benjamin Zablocki (1941–2020) has shifted the focus from unsophisticated claims of "on-the-spot hypnosis" advanced by some early deprogrammers to what he terms the "exit costs" of cult membership. Zablocki uses the theory of brainwashing to explain how cultic groups induce obedience in and retain the loyalty of members who have already joined. Steven A. Kent is another sociologist who has used the brainwashing theory to explain rehabilitation programs in the Children of God and the Church of Scientology. Neither has persuaded many other scholars, though Kent has received a positive welcome in the anticult movement.

See also: Anticult Movement, The; Deprogramming; Exit Counseling; Fundamentalist Mormons; Media and New Religious Movements; NXIVM; Singer, Margaret Thaler (1921–2003); Unification Church, The.

Further Reading
Barker, Eileen. 1984. *The Making of a Moonie: Choice or Brainwashing.* Oxford: Basil Blackwell.
Richardson, James T., & David G. Bromley, eds. 1983. *The Brainwashing/Deprogramming Controversy.* Lewiston, NY: Edwin T. Mellen Press.

Shupe, Anson, & Susan E. Darnell. 2006. *Agents of Discord: Deprogramming, Pseudo-Science, and the American Anticult Movement*. New Brunswick, NJ: Transaction Publishers.

Zablocki, Benjamin, & Thomas Robbins, eds. 2001. *Misunderstanding Cults: Searching for Objectivity in a Controversial Field*. Toronto: University of Toronto Press.

Branch Davidians

Until nearly eighty heavily armed agents of the U.S. Bureau of Alcohol, Tobacco, and Firearms (BATF) conducted a botched raid on the Mount Carmel Center outside Waco, Texas, on February 28, 1993, the Branch Davidians were a little-known sectarian group within the Christian Adventist tradition. During the ensuing fifty-one day siege, members of the Federal Bureau of Investigation (FBI) attempted to negotiate the departure of those whom they had barricaded inside the Center and saw as hostages. Fourteen adults and twenty-one children left the Center during that time, but on April 19, 1993, seventy-six people died in a fire that consumed the Mount Carmel Center. Nine people survived. The cause of the fire remains disputed.

The Branch Davidians quickly became assimilated to the image of a "dangerous cult" that had been cemented into the public consciousness by the tragedy at Jonestown in Guyana in November 1978. David Koresh (1959–1993) was

During the siege of the Mount Carmel Center in 1993, the Branch Davidians flew a distinctive flag over the building. The Star of David signals their connection to the land of Israel, and the stylized serpent refers to the Book of Revelation and its message of the Seven Seals. (Liskonogaleksey/Dreamstime.com)

understood as another deranged cult leader; "Waco" became "another Jonestown." The popular understanding of the Branch Davidians, however, ignores their religious context and exaggerates their distinctiveness.

ROOTS

The roots of the Branch Davidians go back to the mid-nineteenth century when the Baptist layman William Miller (1782–1849) became convinced that he had deciphered the meaning of the Book of Revelation and could predict the second coming of Christ. He believed that the momentous event would occur between March 21, 1843, and March 21, 1844. When the latter date passed without observable consequences, Miller adjusted the date to October 22, 1844. When Christ again failed to return, the Adventists experienced the "Great Disappointment."

That disillusionment, however, did not eliminate the anticipation of the imminent end of the world. Out of the Great Disappointment arose another millennialist religious movement. Near the end of 1845, a small group of former Millerites in New Hampshire coalesced around Ellen G. White (1827–1915), who was seen as a prophet who could deliver "present truth." They also observed Saturday as the Sabbath. The group would become the Seventh-day Adventist Church (SDA). The Branch Davidians continued the Seventh-day Adventists' openness to prophetic claims to deliver "present truth" or "new light." They also continued the SDA interpretive strategy of seeing the Bible as a mosaic of passages that when put into proper relations with each other would reveal God's hidden plan for the end-times and their commitment to spreading the word about Christ's imminent return.

DAVIDIANS

The immediate precursor of the Branch Davidians was the sectarian Davidian movement begun by Victor Houteff (1889–1955) in the 1930s. Houteff recorded his own present truth in *The Shepherd's Rod* and other self-published titles. He argued that the Seventh-day Adventists had become hopelessly complacent and could not represent the 144,000 who would be saved (Rev. 7:4; 14:1, 3) when Christ returned. By 1934, Houteff's teachings had been rejected and he was excommunicated from the SDA.

Nonetheless, he collected a small but dedicated group of disciples and, in 1935, moved with them to a large tract of land outside of Waco, Texas, where they established the Mount Carmel Center. Houteff remained committed to reforming the SDA and to assembling the 144,000 who would soon occupy God's kingdom. The term "Davidian" was very important to Houteff and his followers, since it signaled their expectation that they would set up a new messianic Davidic kingdom in Israel prior to Christ's return.

When Houteff died in 1955, he was succeeded by his wife Florence (1919–2008). Failing to heed the cautionary example of the Millerite movement, Florence announced that the end would come on April 22, 1959, and summoned all

Davidians to Mount Carmel for Passover. But her prophecy was not fulfilled, an event that nearly destroyed the Davidians. Florence retreated from leadership; some Davidians argued for extending their proselytization efforts beyond the SDA, and a group splintered off to form a separate body of Davidian Adventists that continues to this day.

FROM DAVIDIANS TO BRANCH DAVIDIANS

The ensuing leadership vacuum in the Houteff's group was filled by Ben Roden (1902–1978). He, too, understood himself as a prophet. Casting himself as "the Branch" mentioned in Isaiah 11:1 and elsewhere, Roden imagined himself as the one who would rebuild the temple and rule over a restored kingdom. Roden's inclination to see himself in scripture remained an important theme in the Davidian group that, under his leadership, came to be known as the Branch Davidians.

When Ben Roden died in 1978, he was succeeded by his wife. Relying on visionary experiences and styling herself "the Branch she," Lois Roden (1916–1986) claimed that the Holy Spirit was female, an innovation that threatened to divide the community. Like her predecessors, Lois was also a dedicated missionary. She saw her work as the last stage of the reformation of the SDA and as necessary preparation for Christ's imminent return. Lois also welcomed into the group another former Seventh-day Adventist, then known as Vernon Howell.

DAVID KORESH AND THE BRANCH DAVIDIANS

Like Victor Houteff, Howell had been "disfellowshipped" from the SDA in part because of his claim to have received revelations from God. Despite his limited formal education and apparent learning disability, Howell knew the Bible very well. Impressed with his knowledge and dedication, by 1983, Lois Roden was treating him as her potential successor, despite the continued opposition of her son George. Howell both learned from Lois through her Bible studies and began to develop his own distinctive theology.

A turning point for Howell came during a visit to Israel in 1985. Though he never fully described what happened, Howell apparently had a profound visionary experience, probably in the form of an ascent into the heavens. It led him to identify himself as the Lamb mentioned in Revelation 5 as the only one able to unseal the scroll sealed with seven seals. In 1990, Howell even formally changed his name to David Koresh to link his mission to both King David and the "messiah" Cyrus (see Isa. 45:1).

LIFE AT MOUNT CARMEL WITH DAVID KORESH

The cult stereotype conveyed an image of Koresh as a mentally unstable and manipulative leader who browbeat his followers into joylessly listening to his incomprehensible ranting about the seven seals of Revelation when he wasn't exploiting them sexually or training them for Armageddon. Testimony from surviving Branch Davidians, however, tells a rather different story.

Most of the Branch Davidians had been Seventh-day Adventists, and they were eager to discover what the Bible said about the imminent end. They saw themselves as students of the Bible and wanted to hear what Koresh could teach them. Koresh's Bible studies, sometimes going on for hours, were the focal point of life at Mount Carmel. For Koresh, like previous leaders, his function as a religious teacher was paramount.

But Koresh also saw himself as playing another role in the coming kingdom. In the summer of 1989, he communicated to the group a troubling revelation of "New Light." He informed the community that those who were married would have to separate from their spouses and adopt a celibate way of life. In addition, he proclaimed that his own children, both present and future, would become the elders mentioned in Revelation 4:4 and 5:10 as the priests and kings who would rule over the coming kingdom. Koresh created a situation in which he had a sexual monopoly over all the women in the group, even those under the age of consent. His consolidation of sexual power created tension within the group and, for the general public, became a sign of his true motives and one of the most prominent marks of the illegitimacy of his leadership.

Although the Texas Department of Human Services had investigated charges of child abuse at Mount Carmel, nothing came of their visit. The actual pretext for the BATF raid was that some of the Branch Davidians were illegally converting semiautomatic weapons to full automatic as part of their business of selling guns and other paraphernalia at gun shows. Such an infraction, however, involved filling out paperwork and paying a fine. The BATF's extraordinary show of force on February 28, however, provoked the Branch Davidians' armed response and triggered the fifty-one day siege and the fire that virtually destroyed the community.

THE BRANCH DAVIDIANS AFTER APRIL 19, 1993

The few surviving Branch Davidians and a smattering of new converts keep alive their millennialist hope. Livingstone Fagan continues faithfully to represent Koresh's teaching. Others, like the self-proclaimed "Chosen Vessel," offer a new present truth. Though dramatically reduced in numbers, the Branch Davidian tradition continues to generate new visions of the coming millennium.

See also: Koresh, David (1959–1993); Millennialism; Miller, William (1782–1849); Seventh-day Adventism.

Further Reading

Doyle, Clive, with Catherine Wessinger, & Matthew D. Wittmer. 2012. *A Journey to Waco: Autobiography of a Branch Davidian.* Lanham, MD: Rowman & Littlefield.

Newport, Kenneth G. C. 2006. *The Branch Davidians of Waco: The History and Beliefs of an Apocalyptic Sect.* Oxford: Oxford University Press.

Tabor, James D., & Eugene V. Gallagher. 1995. *Why Waco? Cults and the Battle for Religious Freedom in America*. Berkeley: University of California Press.

Thibodeau, David, & Leon Whiteson. 1999. *A Place Called Waco: A Survivor's Story*. New York: PublicAffairs.

Breatharianism

Fasting is a practice common to many world religions. Specifically, the act of abstaining from food and drink for prescribed periods of time shows humility or penitence toward a higher power, operates as a rite of purification, or prepares the body for communion with the divine. For most, the fast ends. This is not the case for Breatharians.

Breatharianism, or inedia, posits that human beings do not need food, and in some cases, water, to survive. Rather, the only substance one needs to live is prana, a Sanskrit term that means "life force" or "life air" and appears in Hindu sacred texts. Breatharians are fed spiritually and, quite literally, breath in their sustenance. As a standalone religious movement, Breatharianism is a relatively recent phenomenon. However, inedia, as a practice of religious ascetics, has appeared in ancient religious texts, from those of Rosicrucianism, to Christianity, to Hinduism. Breatharianism emerged alongside many New Age religions, which often combined spiritual advancement with health and wellness. The aim of Breatharian practice is to subsume bodily functions into religious practice—to discipline the body in such a way that it enables, rather than distracts from, spiritual enlightenment.

Breatharianism does not have a singular, organizational hierarchy. Rather, there are a variety of Breatharian groups and leaders, such as The Breatharian Institute led by Wiley Brooks or Breatharian life coaches, Akahi Ricardo and Camila Castillo. Ricardo and Castillo, for example, invite potential converts to "Pranic Living Retreats," which promote an 8-Day process for achieving "ultimate health and spiritual realization" (https://breatharianschool.com/). After a day of orientation, those who attend the retreats, which are offered all over the world, participate in an "initiation fast," whereby they abstain from all food and water for three days and then subsist on juice for the next four, a process overseen only by a device called a "Bio-Well," which monitors chakra alignment. Fasting is accompanied by meditation and other exercises intended to focus spiritual energy.

The religious movement has been historically criticized, most often by scientists who cast Breatharianism as a dangerous pseudoscience and who debunk the idea that humans can subsist on air alone. There are cases where Breatharians have died due to starvation or dehydration, and www.snopes.com, a site that seeks to disprove pseudoscientific claims among other things, has reportedly debunked Breatharianism on several occasions. However, most Breatharians claim that they do eat; they simply reject the idea that reliance on food is necessary for survival. By making food "optional," people can transcend bodily wants and focus on spiritual needs. Thus, in a sea of diets that purport to change the body, Breatharians are those who see the ability to change both body and soul by a new relationship to food.

See also: Food and New Religious Movements; Hindu New Religious Movements; New Age, The; Rosicrucianism.

Further Reading

Inedia Musings. 2015. *The Complete Science of Breatharianism: Metabolic Energy from the Sun in the Form of ATP*. Benson, VT: The Book Shed.

Nash, Jo. 2006. "Mutant Spiritualities in a Secular Age: The 'Fasting Body' and the Hunger for Pure Immanence." *Journal of Religion and Health* 45, no. 3 (Fall): 310–327.

Caddy, Eileen (1917–2006)

One of the founders of the Findhorn community in Northeast Scotland near the Moray Firth, Eileen Caddy discovered her religious vocation only in her mid-thirties. While visiting one of the sanctuaries in Glastonbury, England in 1953, Eileen heard an inner voice that she identified as God. She was informed by the voice that she had a religious mission to undertake. Although Eileen was initially hesitant to act on what she heard, that generative experience of divine revelation quickly led her to divorce her husband, Andrew Combe, with whom she had five children. She then joined with Peter Caddy (1917–1994), who would become her second husband and partner in exploring spiritual realms.

From 1953 until 1971 Eileen received and reported to Peter a growing corpus of daily communications from the same voice. Their topics ranged from practical advice about how to tend a garden to abstract considerations of the nature of love. Eileen quickly developed the habit of quietly waiting to be contacted by God each morning and then transcribing what she heard from the voice immediately after.

Although Eileen at first functioned as an apprentice to Sheena Govan (1912–1967), who had been with her and Peter at Glastonbury, she soon eclipsed Govan, and she and Peter established themselves as independent teachers.

A NEW AGE COMMUNITY

By 1957 Eileen had completely accepted that she was being guided by the voice of God. In March of that year, she and Peter had taken over the management of the Cluny Hill Hotel near Forres, Scotland. In late 1962, their employment at the hotel ended, but they continued living nearby in a caravan or camper park near the village of Findhorn. They were joined there in 1963 by Dorothy Maclean (1920–2020), a former student of Govan who had been working at the hotel as a secretary. The small encampment of the Caddys and MacLean would form the nucleus of the Findhorn community.

Although MacLean claimed a remarkable ability to communicate with the "devas" or overseers of the natural world, particularly in connection with the extraordinary yield of the Findhorn garden, Eileen provided the central religious guidance for the growing intentional community that was taking shape around the three founders. What she learned from the voice would be read aloud to the community every day.

Although her understanding of her prophetic role continued to evolve throughout her lifetime, Eileen was insistent that the voice that communicated to her was the voice of the biblical God who revealed himself to Moses and was the Word of the Gospel of John. More dramatically, Eileen reported that God had informed her that she was, in some way, the reincarnation of Mary, the mother of Jesus. Although that claim was understood in different ways by different people, including David Spangler (1945–) who quickly rose to prominence in Findhorn and became an important New Age teacher himself, it is clear that Eileen understood her vocation against the backdrop of the Bible, no matter how unorthodox her claims. The appropriation of biblical models extended to Peter as well, with one of Eileen's messages identifying him with the Peter of Matthew 16:18. Peter Caddy, too, would become the rock on which a new religious community would be established.

Eileen's teaching mission was transformed in October 1971, when she was informed by the voice that it was no longer necessary for her to receive daily messages for the community and for those beyond Findhorn. It was time for her audience to put Eileen's teachings into action. That shift of responsibility for guidance from Eileen to individuals had a particularly dramatic impact on Peter, who floundered without Eileen's direct guidance. He sought other teachers and eventually left both Eileen and the Findhorn community.

Although Eileen had always recorded the communications she received from the voice, a turning point occurred in 1965 when Eileen concluded that the voice had encouraged her to spread her teachings beyond the small community at Findhorn. Over time, Eileen would reach a much larger audience through her published writings. The Findhorn Foundation (www.findhorn.org) continues to print short excerpts from Eileen's *Opening Doors Within* as daily guidance.

See also: Channeling; Findhorn Foundation, The; New Age, The.

Further Reading
Caddy, Eileen. 1992. *God Spoke to Me*, 3rd ed. Forres, Scotland: Findhorn Press.
Caddy, Eileen. 2007a. *Flight into Freedom and Beyond: The Autobiography of the Co-Founder of the Findhorn Community*, rev. ed. Forres, Scotland: Findhorn Press.
Caddy, Eileen. 2007b. *Opening Doors Within: 365 Daily Meditations from Findhorn*, 20th anniversary ed. Forres, Scotland: Findhorn Press.

Candomblé

During the nineteenth and twentieth centuries in Brazil, a complex array of overlapping religious systems developed. They drew upon the practices and beliefs that enslaved Africans brought with them to the New World and also forms of Catholicism practiced by the Portuguese colonists. The rich, diverse, and thriving tradition of Candomblé is one of them. The term Candomblé has multiple meanings. Originally referring to a specific drum rhythm, it can be used to refer to the religious tradition but also to ritual practices, the community of worshippers, a specific *terreiro* (consecrated space, temple, or house of worship), and complex interchange in which individuals offer sacrifice to the *orixás* (or *orishas*, deities) who in turn offer their power or *axé* to the worshippers.

The rich symbolism of Candomblé is indicated by the items in the basket, including the Roman Catholic statue and the cowrie shells, associated with Africa, worn by the person holding the basket. (Alf Ribeiro/Dreamstime.com)

ORIGINS

Around 1830 Candomblé emerged in the northeastern Brazilian state of Bahia, which continues to be its stronghold. More than one-third of the three and a half million African slaves forcibly brought to Brazil entered through Bahia. As they did in Cuba, both slaves and free people of color participated in social clubs, *irmandades*, which served particular ethnic groups. Those clubs facilitated the remembering and continued practice of African religions subverting the intent of the colonial administration, which aimed to suppress African religious practices in part because of the fear that they could lead to uprisings like the Haitian revolution that began in 1791. Extensive trade connections between Bahia and Africa have also helped Afro-Brazilians maintain their ties to the homeland, a distinctive feature of Candomblé. In many instances, the strength and purity of an individual group's ties to Africa provides a measure of its prestige within Candomblé.

In Brazil "Africans," both slaves and free, were originally grouped into "nations" according to their perceived ethnic background and connections to a particular region in Africa. Over time the term came to denote a group of fellow worshippers who constituted a kinship network based on religious practice rather than an ethnicity. In the irmandades religious practices, known as *calundus*, were the direct predecessors of practices in the various Candomblé communities that developed in local groups throughout Bahia. Candomblé features eight primary nations and multiple subgroupings. The nation with Yoruba origins, the Nagô or Quêto, has been particularly influential in Bahia.

Although Candomblé originated in northeastern Brazil, it has spread through the country and beyond. Candomblé now has a substantial presence in southern cities, such as Rio de Janiero and São Paulo. Its primary clientele comes from the urban, lower classes. There is no overarching hierarchy for all of Candomblé and consequently there is substantial diversity among individual houses or terreiros. Ongoing connections to specific African groups and the knowledge, skills, and style of individual leaders contribute to that diversity. Each terreiro is presided over by a *maes de santo* (mother of the saints) or *pai de santo* (father of the saints). Female leadership predominates. Priests and priestesses, who have undergone long initiations, maintain the religious and cultural life of the community and cultivate the axé of the orixás within it.

PRACTICES AND BELIEFS

Ritual activity in the terreiros revolves around the reciprocal relations between the community and the orixás. Worshippers offer sacrifices to nourish the deities or spirits and the orixás, in turn, give the worshippers access to their nurturing divine power, which provides protection from misfortune, prosperity, and physical and mental health. Worshippers can interact directly with the orixás when the latter manifest themselves in individuals through the process of spirit possession. A person, frequently a woman in Candomblé, who serves as a medium must first experience a calling by a particular orixá and then go through an extensive initiation, which can last a few years. Each medium is connected to a particular deity and must learn the special music, songs, and dances associated with that figure. During possession, the medium speaks as the orixá and can offer advice and diagnose physical, moral, and social problems. The manifestation of the orixá thus knits the community together and at the same time binds it to the orixás. The services that any Candomblé provides through consultation, divination, and dispensing of healing herbs are not limited to initiates but are available to anyone who is interested and can pay for them.

Of the many orixás who were prominent in African religions, only a handful play important roles in Candomblé. They are frequently endowed with royal characteristics, which appear in their demeanor, actions, and dress during ceremonies. The most prominent male figure is Xango (Shango). He is a warrior deity associated with fire, thunder, lightning, iron, and steel. He has a temper and is a strong leader. He therefore supports his followers' resistance to slavery and colonialism. The female deity Oxum (Oxun) is the goddess of freshwater and protector of rivers and streams. In Brazil, she has multiple forms and is associated with many different Catholic saints.

Healing is important to the practitioners of Candomblé. Priestesses need to master an extensive body of knowledge about the properties of various plants, each of which is associated with a particular orixá to put patients back into a harmonious relationship with the orixas, no matter what the presenting complaint.

The ingestion of herbal remedies may be complimented by prescriptions to undertake sacrifices.

Although Candomblé has frequently been the object of repression, since the 1970s it has experienced a growth in prestige in Brazilian society. It now numbers more than two million followers in Brazil and several other South American countries.

See also: Race and New Religious Movements; Santería; Umbanda; Vodou.

Further Reading

Capone, Stefania. 2010. *Searching for Africa in Brazil: Power and Tradition in Candomblé*, Lucy Lyall Grant, trans. Durham, NC: Duke University Press.

Matory, J. Lorand. 2005. *Black Atlantic Religion: Tradition, Transnationalism, and Matriarchy in the Afro-Brazilian Candomblé*. Princeton, NJ: Princeton University Press.

Parés, Luis Nicolau. 2013. *The Formation of Candomblé: Vodun History and Ritual in Brazil*, Richard Vernon, trans. Chapel Hill, NC: University of North Carolina Press.

Schmidt, Bettina E., & Steven Engler, eds. 2016. *Handbook of Contemporary Religions in Brazil*. Leiden: E. J. Brill.

Cao Dai

Cao Dai, or Caodaism, is a syncretic Vietnamese religious movement that was founded in 1925 by Ngo Van Chieu (1878–1932). It combines the traditional religions practiced in Vietnam (Buddhism, Confucianism, and Taoism) with Spiritualist practice and Theosophical ideas. In 1921, Chieu experienced a vision of the Supreme Being, also known as the Jade Emperor or Cao Dai ("highest power"), in which he was asked to spread the truth of the unity of all religions. Soon joined by several others who claimed to have been contacted by Cao Dai, Chieu determined to found a new religion, which was called "the Great Way of the Third Era of Redemption." According to Cao Dai, Chieu was to be named the first "Pope"—a position he declined to focus on his own spiritual practice, effectively leaving the running of the movement to others. From that point, the history of Cao Dai was tumultuous, due in great part to the efforts of various powers—first France, then the Communist regime—to retain control of Vietnam, which stymied the spread and practice of the religion and even led to periods of outright persecution. Finally, in the late 1990s, various Cao Dai groups were finally recognized by the Vietnamese government and permitted to practice in peace.

Similar to Theosophy, Caodaism posits that Cao Dai, who created the universe, has been sending spiritual teachers (or "Masters") to humanity throughout history. Problems arose when separate religious traditions arose around a particular teacher (such as Christianity or Buddhism); Caodaism argues that all of these discrete religious traditions have been corrupted, making it necessary to restore unity between them. Thus, Caodaism combines elements of numerous religions. For example, from Buddhism, its members take "refuge" in the Buddha, the sangha (community), and dharma (teachings); from Confucianism, practitioners aspire to

Many individual denominations of the Vietnamese new religion Cao Dai are associated with particular temples. The temple depicted is outside of Tay Ninh, about sixty miles northwest of Ho Chi Minh City. The architecture of the temple resembles a Christian cathedral, though its decorations use elements from the various traditions upon which Cao Dai draws. (Corel)

five virtues—love, justice, respect, wisdom, and loyalty; and from Spiritualism, they go by the belief that people can communicate with the spirit realm through mediums and séances. Much like the automatic writing and revelation of divine knowledge that occurred for Theosophists, new scriptures were a common feature of these spirit contacts and were the most common means of merging the distinctive belief systems of religions, such as Christianity and Buddhism. Caodaism's belief that humanity has entered the "third age of redemption" echoes Christian millennialism, a system that posits the imminent return of Christ and the beginning of the Kingdom of God. Christ, as a spiritual teacher and son of Cao Dai, is also included in Cao Dai doctrine.

Séances have been illegal in Vietnam since the 1970s, though this has not stopped the practice entirely; most now occur in private. Much more publicly, Caodaism holds thrice daily worship services at its various temples, of which there were approximately fourteen hundred in Vietnam as of 2015. Similar to Buddhist services, worshippers chant the names of deities and supernatural entities in unison, while burning incense and making various offerings. Its members celebrate a variety of holidays, merging the liturgical calendars of various religious traditions with several holy days of its own, including the commemoration of the religion's founding and the birthday of Victor Hugo (1802–1885), who was a follower of Kardecism or Spiritism and participated in séances.

In Vietnam, Caodaism is divided into denominations, often affiliated with a particular temple. Because of the restrictions on practice that existed for many years, no "Pope" of the religion was ever elected. The organization is overseen by the highest ranking Cardinal, thus mimicking the Roman Catholic Church's hierarchy. Additionally, only séances could officially confirm new mediums and spiritual leaders; since séances were banned for many years, the religious hierarchy could not grow for many years. However, as of 2014, Cao Dai is recognized as Vietnam's third largest religion, counting around 4.5 million members (a number that has undoubtedly grown since then). There are Cao Dai organizations that exist outside of Vietnam, many of which have sought to distance themselves from their Vietnamese counterparts who they feel have been compromised by restrictive government regulations; in return, Vietnamese Cao Dai groups have refused to recognize these groups as well as any revelations that have occurred in "unauthorized" séances.

See also: Kardecism (Spiritism); Mediums; Millennialism; Occultism and Esotericism; Spiritualism; Theosophy.

Further Reading

Hoskins, Janet Alison. 2015. *The Divine Eye and the Diaspora: Vietnamese Syncretism Becomes Transpacific Caodaism*. Honolulu: The University of Hawaii Press.

Hoskins, Janet Alison. 2017. "Caodaism," World Religion and Spirituality Project. Available at: https://wrldrels.org/2017/08/10/caodaism/.

Tran, Anh-Tuyet. 2015. *Cao Dai: The Grand Cycle of Esoteric Teaching*. Garden Grove, CA: Cao Dai Temple Overseas.

Cayce, Edgar (1877–1945)

Many attribute the advent of New Age religion to Edgar Cayce. Known as the "Sleeping Prophet," the result of his psychic flights while in a trance-like sleep, Cayce is often hailed as the founder of holistic medicine, early advocate of the spiritual power of food, and one of the most prolific clairvoyants of the twentieth century. Cayce was able to build on Spiritualism and Theosophy, both of which promoted the ability of human beings to connect to spiritual realms as well as the ability of mediums to access sacred, esoteric knowledge.

Cayce was born in Kentucky in 1877. From an early age, he reported seeing spirits and supernatural beings, who appeared to call him for some special work. Though he was raised Christian and was an avid Bible reader, soon these supernatural beings began communicating to him knowledge of special and religious significance. He first experienced this when he fell asleep while studying for school and miraculously awoke knowing all the answers, which were supposedly given to him by a "woman with wings." His abilities soon extended to the diagnostic: he was able to locate and diagnose illnesses while asleep.

In his adult life, Cayce served as a Bible teacher and an occasional businessman, and at the same time he cultivated his psychic abilities. He became an expert at putting himself in a somnanbulistic state, which activated his clairvoyant abilities. He also performed "self-cure" on numerous occasions, once curing himself of laryngitis. Soon people sought Cayce for his diagnostic and healing abilities, asking for remedies or "readings" when Western medicine had failed; this prompted him to form his own practice of psychic healing. He refused to take money for his readings. He also was accused by the medical community of quackery and was forced to close his burgeoning practice. Nonetheless, his fame grew as did the demand for his work.

It was not long after that Cayce began to cross into the realm of theology and metaphysics. While asleep, he reportedly received information regarding the truth of reincarnation, for example. At times, Cayce, still an avowed Christian, surprised himself at the heretical and even non-Christian nature of these proclamations. In fact, he was so troubled over the doctrines he received while in a trance, so much so that he almost considered stopping his trances altogether for fear that he could not reconcile his Christian beliefs with non-Christian ideas.

Nonetheless, he continued his work. During the 1920s, much of his later work focused around issues of healing and health. He began experimenting with different modes of healing as revealed to him while asleep. Crystals, massage, and exposure to certain spectrums of light became staples of his practice. Diet would also play a significant factor in his healing practice. Cayce specified an eating plan that would enable the digestive system, the source of bodily energy, to operate at peak performance, thus ensuring spiritual alignment and enlightenment. His cures were at a premium, but the Depression dampened demand and brought Cayce back to spiritual questions and pursuits. He began holding "Study Groups," during which he dispensed received knowledge on a number of religious and metaphysical subjects and on which numerous publications emerged. While under a trance, he reportedly viewed the "Akashic records," a sacred compendium of all human events throughout time and into the future; several of his books are devoted to describing Akashic knowledge.

Cayce founded several institutions in Virginia, where he lived for the remaining two decades of his life, including a hospital devoted solely to the techniques he had developed while asleep. Most significant was the establishment of the Association for Research and Enlightenment (ARE), which merged his spiritual and physical practices. ARE owns the rights to most of Cayce's works and operates the various healing, publishing, and religious institutes he created.

Cayce had his critics. Some critiqued his supposed racial theories, which he claimed derived from Helena Petrovna Blavatsky's work on "Master Races," and others simply did not believe he was psychic. Still, none can dispute his lasting mark on New Age religion.

See also: Blavatsky, Helena Petrovna (1831–1891); Food and New Religious Movements; Healing, Health, and New Religious Movements; New Age, The; Occultism and Esotericism; Spiritualism; Theosophy.

Further Reading

Cayce, Edgar. 1996 [1946]. *A Search for God: 50th Anniversary Edition*. Books 1 & 2. Virginia Beach, VA: A.R.E. Press.

Duncan, Ann W. 2015. "Edgar Cayce's Association for Research and Enlightenment: 'Nones' and Religious Experience in the Twenty-first Century." *Nova Religio* 19, no. 1: 45–64.

Sugrue, Thomas. 2015 [2003]. *There is a River: The Story of Edgar Cayce*. Virginia Beach, VA: A.R.E. Press.

CESNUR (The Center for the Study of New Religions)

As the public debate about whether new religious movements posed a danger to individuals and society as a whole continued from the 1970s into the 1980s, various individuals claiming expertise attempted to sway public opinion. The ensuing clash of opinions exacerbated the need for accurate, fully researched, and up-to-date information about groups called "cults."

With support from a sympathetic Roman Catholic bishop and from one of its founders, Massimo Introvigne, CESNUR (the Center for Study of New Religions) was established in Torino, Italy, in 1988 to promote scholarly research. Introvigne maintains his position as managing director. CESNUR held its first conferences in 1988 and continues to sponsor annual conferences throughout the world. CESNUR often cooperates with other research-oriented groups, such as INFORM in the United Kingdom.

Since the later 1990s, CESNUR has increasingly addressed public issues, both through publications and hosting conferences. Introvigne himself is a prolific writer on new religious movements, secret societies and esoteric groups, and religious diversity in Italy and Europe. CESNUR established a website (www.cesnur.org) in 1997, which archives an extensive collection of conference proceedings, primary texts, and scholarly writings in both Italian and English.

CESNUR has also sponsored a book series focused on new and alternative religions.

Although Introvigne originally participated in an Italian Catholic counter-cult group, he split from it when he learned that the organization did not take seriously how religious groups represented themselves. Introvigne took a similar stance in criticizing a 1996 French report on cults. With that, he and CESNUR earned the continuing ire of the European and international anticult movement.

Although CESNUR still focuses on new religious movements, since the 1990s, it has also undertaken several large-scale projects that mapped the religious diversity of Italy, and extensive investigations of secret societies and esoteric groups, inspired in part by their prominence in novelist Dan Brown's *The DaVinci Code*.

In 2011, CESNUR's work earned Introvigne, who also holds a law degree, a position as a representative for the Organization for Security, and Co-operation in Europe, which combats racism, xenophobia, and discrimination against Christians and members of other religions. Following that, in 2012, he was appointed by the Italian Ministry of Foreign Affairs as chair of the newly established Observatory of Religious Liberty.

Through the work of its Managing Director and affiliated scholars, its sponsorship of publications, including *The Journal of CESNUR*, initiated in 2017, and the maintenance of its website, CESNUR remains a trustworthy source of information about new religions.

See also: Anticult Movement, The; Cult; Deprogramming; INFORM; Media and New Religious Movements; Sect.

Further Reading

Barker, Eileen. 2002. "Watching for Violence: A Comparative analysis of Five Types of Cult-Watching Groups." In David G. Bromley & J. Gordon Melton, eds., *Cults, Religion, and Violence*, pp. 123–148. Cambridge: Cambridge University Press.

Gallagher, Eugene V., ed. 2017. *"Cult Wars" in Historical Perspective*. London: Routledge.

Introvigne, Massimo, with David G. Bromley. 2016. "CESNUR: The Center for Studies on New Religions." Interview. Available at: https://wrldrels.org/wp-content/uploads/2017/03/Interview-with-Massimo-Introvigne-on-CESNUR.pdf.

Channeling

Many major religions have been founded on individuals' claims to have experienced contact with a world beyond the mundane. New religious movements are no different. The Church of Jesus Christ of Latter-day Saints, for example, stems from Joseph Smith's (1805–1844) experiences during his first and second visions when he was commissioned to dig up and translate *The Book of Mormon*. Similarly, African prophets like Simon Kimbangu (1887–1951) have been spurred to their missions by visionary experiences. Since the nineteenth century, the Spiritualist movement has promised its eager audiences contact with their deceased loved ones. The phenomenon of channeling, closely associated with the milieu of New Age religious and spiritual practices, has to be understood in the context of many other claims to be in contact with unseen worlds and entities.

Although it has antecedents in the work of various Spiritualists and Edgar Cayce (1877–1945), in the narrow sense, channeling is associated with the activities of a variety of figures from the 1970s to the present in New Age circles.

EMERGENCE AND SIGNIFICANT FIGURES

One of the first prominent channels was Jane Roberts (1929–1984). In 1963, Roberts began to receive communications from a disembodied entity or "energy personality essence" named Seth while she and her husband, Robert Butts (1919–2018), experimented with a Ouija board. Seth, along with other figures who contacted Roberts less frequently, continued to speak through Roberts until her death. When contacted, Roberts would enter a trance state and her husband would transcribe or tape the messages received. The publication of *Seth Speaks: The Eternal Validity of the Soul* in 1970 brought Roberts's message to a broad audience. The many volumes that followed expanded that audience.

The most influential assertion in the Seth material is the contention that "you create your own reality," which gained a wide currency in the New Age

JZ Knight remains one of the most popular channels since she began receiving messages from a thirty-five-thousand-year-old resident of Atlantis, Ramtha, in the late 1970s. (Special Collections, Davidson Library, University of California, Santa Barbara)

movement. In the Seth material, this world is presented as a classroom in which individuals can learn that they are actually manifestations of the Universal Spirit and that they, too, can become gods (see www.sethlearningcenter.org).

Robert Butts continued to publish messages from Seth after his wife's death, and after his own death, others continue to publicize Seth's teachings through conferences and online courses (see www.sethcenter.com). Although some have claimed that they have also been contacted by Seth, Roberts was adamant during her lifetime that she was Seth's only channel.

In 1978, JZ Knight (née Judith Hampton; 1946–) introduced another channeled teacher. Although Knight had several experiences that led her to the mystical conviction that God was everywhere in the world, including within her and all other individuals, her career as a channel was inaugurated by a vision in February 1977. At that time, she first encountered Ramtha, who thirty-five thousand years ago had lived in Lemuria on the northern part of the continent of Atlantis. Ramtha's origin story is complex, but through a prolonged process, the former warrior eventually conquered himself and transformed into a god. His goal is to teach humans all that he had learned and enable them to make the same kind of transformation.

In its general outlines, Ramtha's message resembles Seth's. Ramtha emphasizes that humans have forgotten who they really are. Through his teachings and associated practices, individuals can realize that their physical incarnation is a trap and recapture their divine identities. Ramtha's teaching bears a pronounced resemblance to ancient Gnostic systems of thought, which also devalued the material world and asserted that individuals contained within themselves a spark of the divine, though over time they had forgotten who they really were.

Knight has established Ramtha's School of Enlightenment at her headquarters in Yelm, Washington. Those who want something beyond the print and electronic presentations of Ramtha's teachings can attend retreats and workshops at the school. Ramtha continues to teach and publish books, audio, and video resources (see www.ramtha.com).

Another prominent channeled teacher, Lazaris, made his debut in October 1974 by contacting Jach Pursel (1947–). In contrast to Ramtha, Lazaris identifies himself as a "spark of consciousness" and claims never to have been a physical being. Like other channeled teachers, Lazaris wants to help his audience understand the reality they have already created and to help them build a reality that better promotes their well-being. Lazaris denies that he is any sort of guru or savior and identifies himself as a loving friend who wants to promote hope, healing, and human development. In 1977, Jach, his wife, and a friend established the Synergy Foundation to promote and distribute Lazaris's teachings. It became Concept:Synergy in 1980 and continues to serve as the clearing house for Lazaris's channeled messages and related activities (see https://lazaris01.worldsecuresystems.com/).

The three channels mentioned practice a form of trance channeling in which their conscious mind appears to be displaced so that the channeled entity can speak directly to an audience. Observers report multiple ways in which the behavior of the channeled entity differs from the behavior of the channel, including the use of distinctive vocabulary, accent, gestures, and the overall message. Trance channeling is therefore very different from conscious channeling, in which channels simply speak in their own voices. Some channels, like Roberts, Knight, and Pursel, claim to be the only individuals who can communicate the teachings of entities that speak through them. Lazaris, for example, makes it very clear that he will only communicate through Pursel. Other teachers, like Kevin Ryerson (see www.kevinryerson.com/), channel several different entities. Still other teachers encourage their students to strive to channel any entities with whom they can make contact and are less concerned with limiting channeling to a few individuals.

In addition to the compiled authoritative utterances of channeled entities, some contemporary scriptures also have been produced through a process of channeling. Helen Schucman (1909–1981), for example, served as the "scribe" for *A Course in Miracles*, which was delivered by a voice identified with Jesus Christ. *The Urantia Book* was communicated through an anonymous channel known only as "the sleeping subject." Schucman, however, was much more ambivalent than many channels about publicizing the course and the channel for *The Urantia Book* and played no role in the dissemination of its message.

RECEPTION AND CONTROVERSIES

Although the heyday of the New Age may be in the past, New Age beliefs and practices have become part of popular culture, and many channeled entities continue to attract audiences. Like other religious innovations, channels have also provoked their share of criticism. As with others who claimed to have communicated with other worlds, channels have been widely accused of fabricating their messages. There have been lampoons of channels, as in the comic strip *Doonesbury* where Barbara Ann Boopstein ("Boopsie") channeled Hunk-Ra. But channeling also received a substantial boost from celebrities, especially Shirley MacLaine (1934–) in her various autobiographical publications that recount her interactions with multiple channels.

One of the most controversial aspects of channeling has been the decision of many prominent channels to charge for their services, whether they are individual sessions, workshops, lectures, or the many materials that are offered for sale on their websites. JZ Knight, for example, argues that she was informed directly by Ramtha that she should charge anyone seeking to consult her, at least in part to give her some control over the demands on her time and energy. But the decision to charge money has exposed many channels, as it has other leaders of innovative religious groups, to accusations that they are in it only for profit. Knight's former husband, for example, has accused her of running a money-making scam. In response, channels appeal to the testimonies of those who have benefited from their teachings. The debate about the reality and benefits of channeling thus echoes many of the same themes that have come to dominate the public discussion of new religious movements in general. It is fueled by similar passions and has been similarly inconclusive, with partisans remaining unwavering in their dedication, former participants often ruing their involvement, some outsiders seeking to expose what they perceive to be deceptive activities, and the general public leaning toward a widespread skepticism.

See also: Cayce, Edgar (1877–1945); Church of Jesus Christ of Latter-day Saints; *Course in Miracles, A*; Kimbangu, Simon (1887–1951); Knight, JZ (Ramtha) (1946–); Mediums; New Age, The; Pursel, Jach (Lazaris) (1946–); Smith, Joseph (1805–1844); Spiritualism; *Urantia Book, The.*

Further Reading

Albanese, Catherine L. 2007. *A Republic of Mind and Spirit: A Cultural History of American Metaphysical Religion.* New Haven, CT: Yale University Press.

Brown, Michael F. 1999. *The Channeling Zone: American Spirituality in an Anxious Age.* Cambridge, MA: Harvard University Press.

Klimo, Jon. 1998. *Channeling: Investigations on Receiving Information from Paranormal Sources,* 2nd ed. Berkeley, CA: North Atlantic Books.

Knight, J. Z. 2004. *A State of Mind: My Story / Ramtha: The Adventure Begins.* Yelm, WA: JZK Publishing.

Lazaris. 2017. "Awakening the Love." Available at: https://www.youtube.com/watch?v=_yGaRFXbiSc.

Seth. 1994 [1972]. *Seth Speaks: The Eternal Validity of the Soul.* San Rafael, CA: Amber-Allen Publishing.

Urban, Hugh B. 2015. *New Age, Neopagan, and New Religious Movements: Alternative Spirituality in Contemporary America*. Berkeley: University of California Press.

Chaos Magick

Chaos Magick, often called "results-based magic," arose during the height of New Age religious innovation. Founded in England in the 1970s, itself the center of twentieth-century occult religion, Chaos Magick took as its credo the idea that objective truth is either unknowable or a fallacy. Rather than emphasize some authoritative occult tradition from which all sacred knowledge emerged, practitioners are encouraged to experiment with a variety of magical and occult practices and beliefs and to craft their own, unique magico-religious system. Defying a "one-size-fits-all" model of religion, Chaos magicians believe that the validity of a particular system is measured by the results it produces for the individual practitioner.

The founders of Chaos Magick, Peter J. Carroll (1953–) and Ray Sherwin (1952–), drew upon the work of Austin Osman Spare (1886–1956). Spare was a member of fellow British occultist Aleister Crowley's (1875–1947) group Argenteum Astrum for a time; Crowley's eclecticism when it came to the uses and sources of magical knowledge also influenced Chaos Magick at its outset. An artist by trade, Spare developed a system of sigils (symbols used in magical ritual), which he believed became empowered in different ways depending upon the individual employing them. Each individual learned to communicate a particular desire through these symbols, which imbued the sigils with meaning and empowered them (hence the name for these symbols as the "alphabet of desire"). Carroll and Sherwin adapted these techniques to challenge the hegemony of Wicca in England or what they perceived as any exclusive occult or religious tradition. And though their system advocates for variety in practice and belief, Carroll and Sherwin adopted the term "chaos" to denote that the universe is chaotic and each practitioner must seek to order it in his or her own way.

Defying most magical traditions (and often irking other magicians), Chaos Magick does not argue that magical power derives from some supernatural source; neither does it deny this possibility. However, many Chaos magicians, influenced by a variety of religious, scientific, and philosophical sources, also see human agency as a factor in producing magical results. This is reflected in their central belief that all beliefs are simply tools for creating an effect, without holding any objective truth of their own. In other words, it is what practitioners do with or because of these beliefs that matters. The individual consciousness, or "Kia," draws upon the forces of the universe (Chaos) and channels them to varying effect.

Any practice or magical system can be employed to achieve results, from meditation, to crystals, to Wiccan ritual, to gnostic or mystical religious practices from major world traditions. Nonetheless, most Chaos Magick involves achieving a "gnostic state," where the mind is singularly focused on a particular desire, end, or idea (similar to many techniques of meditation). Sigils are often employed to focus attention and are also believed to be "charged" with power through this process.

Though there is no single institution of Chaos Magick, the most established is the Illuminates of Thenateros (IOT), which was the organization created by Carroll and Sherwin in 1978. In general, however, Chaos magicians may practice on their own or in small groups, never affiliating with a formal group. Though there is no central sacred text—reflecting the subjective nature of Chaos Magick—Carroll's book, *Liber Null* (1978), and Sherwin's book, *The Book of Results* (1981), among other publications, are viewed as valuable sources for Chaos technique. Others from the IOT circle followed suit, publishing their own set of magical techniques or advertising their own brand of Chaos Magick.

Many magicians argue, however, that the age of Chaos Magick has passed. Whereas Chaos Magick felt like the ideal new religious tradition for the era of postmodernism—where all truth and knowledge is believed to be personally and historically located—some Chaos magicians, including occult author Phil Hine (1960–), have begun to challenge that idea that magic should exist only as a set of diffuse techniques. Some are calling for a return to historical, magical lineages, rooted in a particular tradition or style of magic—in essence, reversing the initial premise of Chaos Magick.

See also: Crowley, Aleister (1875–1947); Magic and New Religious Movements; New Age, The; Occultism and Esotericism; Wicca.

Further Reading

Chyrssides, George D. 2011. "Chaos Magic." In *Historical Dictionary of New Religious Movements.* Lanham, MD: Scarecrow Press.

Hine, Phil. 1998. *Prime Chaos: Adventures in Chaos Magic.* Scottsdale, AZ: New Falcon Publications.

Urban, Hugh. 2006. *Magia Sexualis: Sex, Magic, and Liberation in Modern Western Esotericism.* Berkeley: University of California Press.

Charisma and Leadership in New Religious Movements

The origin of a new religion can often be identified. In many, but not all, instances it involves an appeal to extraordinary events or experiences that set the founder apart from other human beings. The experience of visions, auditions, or other uncanny phenomena often triggers the proclamation of a new message and the formation of a new religious group. In 610, the prophet Muhammad (c. 570–632), for example, was visited by the angel Gabriel while he was in solitary prayer in a cave outside of Mecca. There Muhammad received the first of many revelations, which would give rise to Islam and was recorded in the Qur'an.

Although there have been psychological theories about leadership, even within new religions, the scholarly understanding of such claims and their recognition has been decisively shaped by the German sociologist of religion, Max Weber (1864–1920). Weber was interested in the ways that claims to authority were supported or legitimated. He identified three "ideal types" of legitimate authority, though he acknowledged that in practice they could be blended. The first was rational-legal authority, which vests power in widely acknowledged rules and offices, such as the presidency in the United States. The second was traditional authority, which vests power in time-honored customs or lineages, as with the royal succession in the United Kingdom and elsewhere.

Weber's third type of legitimate authority was charismatic authority. Although it is used imprecisely in public discourse, the word "charisma" derives from the Greek term for "gift," frequently from a divine source. Charismatic authority, then, is supported by an individual's claims to somehow be in touch with a world beyond the mundane. Joseph Smith, for example, in the accounts of his first visions claimed to have conversed with God, Jesus, and the angel Moroni. Similarly, the author of *The Holy Piby*, Robert Athyli Rogers, claimed to have been given his mission by the angel Douglas.

Such arresting claims, however, do not constitute authority on their own. They need to be recognized, and acted on, to have any social efficacy. Otherwise claimants to charismatic authority would remain legends in their own minds. *The Book of Mormon*, for example, includes at the beginning short texts called "The Testimony of the Three Witnesses" and "The Testimony of the Eight Witnesses," in which various individuals testify to the reality of the "gold Bible" that Joseph Smith recovered and translated and their own commitment to his new religious group. Their support was essential to the success of Smith's new church.

Followers may increase their perception of a leader's charisma, as their sentiments become supported and amplified by other, more experienced members in a group. The speeches of the Rev. Sun Myung Moon (1920–2012), in Korean and accompanied by apparently dramatic gesticulations, could be off-putting on first encounter to those who could not understand the language. But through a process of "charismatization" potential or fledgling Unificationists learned from others within the movement how to understand them as part of Moon's charisma. Those who could not understand Moon as manifesting charisma were less likely to be attracted to or stay within the movement.

Charismatic authority, then, rests on a dynamic relationship between leaders and the claims that are made by and for them, and followers who hear the claims made, deliberate about them, and accept or reject them. From that perspective, followers do much to constitute the charismatic authority of any individual. Consequently, they can also erode, diminish, or even destroy the credibility of charismatic claims. Charismatic authority, therefore, is produced, maintained, and transformed in an ongoing process of interaction between individuals to whom it is attributed and others who weigh those claims.

CLAIMING CHARISMA

The supernatural encounters that authorize claims to charismatic authority come in a variety of forms. For example, Shoko Asahara (1955–2018), the founder of the Japanese new religion Aum Shinrikyō, claimed in 1985 to have received a divine appointment to lead the armies that would establish the Buddhist millennialist kingdom of Shambala on earth. Ellen G. White (1827–1915), the founding prophet of the Seventh-day Adventists experienced multiple visions. In her first, she felt herself rising into heaven and seeing the 144,000 mentioned in Rev. 7:4 as being worthy of entering the New Jerusalem. In another, she beheld a card on which were written in gold fifty passages from Scripture, many of which had to do with individuals being given the power to proclaim the word of God.

Charismatic authority is not limited to individuals who claim a prophetic vocation. It can be attributed to objects and places, among other things. *The Urantia Book*, for example, stands alone as an authority for all who read it. Although it was delivered through an individual known as the "sleeping subject," that person is understood to have been merely a conduit for the intergalactic wisdom that the book offers and to have no prophetic status at all. Similarly, Mary Baker Eddy (1821–1910), the founder of Christian Science, declared that her central text, *Science and Health with Key to the Scriptures* would serve as the "pastor" of all Christian Science churches. The Sikh tradition, begun by Guru Nanak (1469–1539), presents an interesting mixed case. Guru Nanak was succeeded by a sequence of nine gurus, but the tenth, Gobind Singh (1666–1708), declared that after him authority would be vested in a scriptural text, the Adi Granth or Guru Granth Sahib. A similar transfer of charisma from prophet to book occurred on the passing of Adi Da Samraj (né Franklin Jones, 1939–2008) whose followers now claim that he can still be encountered in the pages of his books.

When they are recognized, such claims to charismatic experience can forge a charismatic relationship between an aspiring leader and potential followers. Acceptance gives social legitimacy and power, while rejection can make them wither and vanish.

MAINTAINING CHARISMA

Holding onto and extending charismatic authority, especially within a new religious group, is virtually a daily challenge. New religions change frequently, in response to both internal developments, such as the reception of further revelations, and external pressures, such as opposition from various factions of the anticult movement. An initial demonstration of charisma is thus insufficient to maintain a leader's tenuous hold over a group of followers.

David Koresh's (1959–1993) tenure as the leader of the Branch Davidians provides a good example. Although Koresh could claim some traditional legitimacy from his close association with the prior leader of the small Adventist group, Lois Roden (1916–1986), his identity as the Lamb of God who could open the scroll sealed with seven seals (see Rev. 5) derived from his extraordinary experience of ascent into the heavens, which happened in Jerusalem in 1985.

Koresh's charisma enabled him to make sense of the Bible in ways that no one before him ever had. He demonstrated his command of the text virtually daily in often marathon "Bible Studies," showing how every bit of the Bible confirmed his interpretation that the Book of Revelation predicted the imminent end of the world. Every time someone attended one of those sessions and responded positively to Koresh's prompts, it reaffirmed that Koresh was who he claimed to be.

The charismatic capital that Koresh built up in the Bible Studies supported his other theological innovations. But it proved insufficient to convince some members that he should have a sexual monopoly over all the women in the group so that he could sire the twenty-four elders who would rule over the Kingdom of God. Such rejection of charismatic claims can lead to voluntary withdrawal or excommunication from a group.

Other leaders of new religions strive to maintain and extend their charismatic authority through the performance of miracles. Sathya Sai Baba (1926–2011), for example, was well known for his ability to "materialize" various small objects, which his followers took as evidence of his divinity, even while others dismissed them as sleights of hand.

ROUTINIZING CHARISMA

Weber emphasized that charisma is always in the process of transformation and that it tends toward routinization or domestication into other forms of authority. At no point is that more evident than when an individual charismatic leader nears or reaches death. The transition to a second generation of leadership is especially fraught for new religions that rest uneasily on charismatic foundations. They must face questions such as whether charismatic authority will continue to be manifested in the leadership, consigned to the time of the founder, or perhaps manifested in a different way, such as a scriptural text. Frequently enough, leaders have made no or inadequately concrete plans for succession. In such cases, a welter of contenders for leadership can emerge, each with a distinctive claim for authority. Groups that effectively weather the succession crisis may well last for generations to come; those that bungle it risk their dissolution.

When L. Ron Hubbard (1911–1986) died, the Church of Scientology needed to establish succession. It took several steps to ensure both that Hubbard's status as "the source" of Scientology would remain unchallenged and that a smooth organizational transition would occur. Among other things, Scientology declared that every word of Hubbard's teachings about Dianetics and Scientology constituted the scripture of the church. It cannot be altered in any way and must be taught and implemented exactly as he initially laid it out. The Religious Technology Center was tasked with the preservation of Hubbard's teaching and David Miscavige (1960–), a longtime church member, serves as its Chairman of the Board. Having successfully consolidated his power, Miscavige is seen as the ecclesiastical leader of the religion of Scientology. While he is not credited with the insights into human nature that Hubbard achieved, Miscavige controls the preservation, dissemination, and even the release of new elements of Hubbard's teachings. While he has effected a successful organizational transition, Miscavige's sometimes high-handed behavior has provoked some defections of high profile Scientologists.

Not all transitions go that smoothly. Joseph Smith's (1805–1844) murder in June 1844 left the community of Latter-day Saints without a leader or a clear way forward. Multiple potential successors came to the fore. Smith's brother Hyrum (1800–1844) had died with him and other brothers and Joseph's sons were unsuitable for various reasons. Some of Smith's first converts had already left the church.

Eventually, Brigham Young, the senior member and president of the Quorum of the Twelve Apostles, led the majority of Smith's followers on to the Utah territory. But some members followed either Sidney Rigdon (1793–1876) or James J. Strang (1813–1856) into smaller groups that claimed to preserve Smith's true legacy. Finally, in some cases, the death of a leader makes it difficult or impossible for a group to continue. After David Koresh died in the fire that consumed the Mount Carmel Center in April 1993, several contenders tried to fill the leadership void, but none has mustered a substantial following. Heaven's Gate did not survive the death of Marshall Herff Applewhite (1931–1997).

See also: Applewhite, Marshall (1932–1997), and Bonnie Lu Nettles (1927–1985); Aum Shinrikyō; *Book of Mormon, The*; Christian Science; *Holy Piby, The*; Heaven's Gate; Hubbard, L. Ron (1911–1985); Koresh, David (1959–1993); Millennialism; Moon, Rev. Sun Myung (1920–2012); Samraj, Adi Da (1939–2008); Sathya Sai Baba; Seventh-day Adventism, The; Smith, Joseph (1805–1844); *Urantia Book, The*.

Further Reading

Barker, Eileen. 1993. "Charismatization: The Social Production of an Ethos Propitious to the Mobilisation of Sentiments." In Eileen Barker, James A. Beckford, & Karel Dobbelaere, eds., *Secularisation, Rationalism, and Sectarianism*, pp. 181–201. New York: Oxford University Press.

Dawson, Lorne L. 2002. "Crises of Charismatic Legitimacy and Violent Behavior in New Religious Movements." In David G. Bromley & J. Gordon Melton, eds., *Cults, Religion, and Violence*, pp. 80–101. Cambridge: Cambridge University Press.

Lindholm, Charles. 1990. *Charisma*. Oxford: Basil Blackwell.

Prophet, Erin. 2016. "Charisma and Authority in New Religious Movements." In James R. Lewis & Inga B. Tøllefsen, eds., *The Oxford Handbook of New Religious Movements*, vol. II, pp. 36–49. New York: Oxford University Press.

Wessinger, Catherine. 2012. "Charismatic Leaders in New Religions." In Olav Hammer & Mikael Rothstein, eds., *The Cambridge Companion to New Religious Movements*, pp. 80–96. Cambridge: Cambridge University Press.

Chen Tao

New religions are fragile. There is a limited audience for religious innovation and the more dramatic the innovation, the smaller the audience. Millennialist groups are also fragile. If they defer the events of the end indefinitely, they risk losing the power and immediacy of their message, but if they set a date for the imminent transformation of the world, they risk disconfirmation of their prophecies and the inevitable transformation or even dissolution that comes with it. Accordingly, millennialist new religions are doubly fragile, as Chen Tao ("True Way" or God's Salvation Church) shows.

Chen Tao developed out of a revelation experienced by Hon-Ming Chen (1955–) in Taiwan in 1992. Afterward, he immediately began to devote himself to the study of scriptures, such as the Bible, the Buddhist Sutras, and the Dao-De-Jing. Chen's eclectic background also included participation in a UFO religious group. By 1995, Chen had become convinced that North America was the "Pure Land of God." By 1997, he and some twenty-five followers had settled in Garland, Texas, chosen in part for the resemblance of its name to "God's land" and identified as one of the two holiest places on earth (along with Pei-pu, Taiwan, Chen's birthplace). A Chen Tao spokesperson even identified Garland as the place where the creation of the original humans had occurred.

From his direct communications with God, Teacher Chen, as he was known, became convinced of the imminent end of the world. He documented his beliefs in a self-published book, *God's Descending on Clouds (Flying Saucers) to Save People* (1997). Like others before him, including William Miller (1782–1849) whose prediction of the end on October 22, 1844, ushered in the Great Disappointment, Chen actually set a date for the reappearance of Jesus on earth. The scheme was twofold. On March 28, 1998, Jesus would make an announcement on the local TV channel 18; then on March 31, at precisely 10:00 a.m., he would appear in person at 3513 Ridgedale Drive in Garland.

Chen set his prediction of the imminent end into a vast cosmic drama that drew on Buddhist and Daoist ideas, UFO ideology, and biblical interpretation. Throughout the universe, he believed, there has been an eternal battle between the "heavenly devil kings," beings who fell from their original state as angels and individuals dedicated to practicing the "Right Way." In Chen's interpretation, the story about the mating of the "sons of God" with the "daughters of men" in Genesis 6 recounts the introduction into our world of the heavenly devil kings. But humankind in 1997 was supposed to enter a final three and a half year period of tribulation after which the heavenly devil kings will be vanquished and a loving God will offer salvation to all. Thus, humanity stood at the doorstep of the Kingdom of God.

Of course, Chen's specific predictions suffered the same unequivocal and devastating disconfirmation that every similar prediction had. Jesus did not show up as promised and Chen was left to pick up the pieces. At first, moments before the 10:00 a.m. deadline, Chen asked his assembled followers to turn to each other and shake each other's hands because God had already descended to earth and was inside them. But that internalization of the apocalypse did not convince many. Chen soon relocated to Lockport, New York, and tried to keep preaching that the millennial events would happen both externally, as he had originally promised, and internally, in a rationalization similar to the claim of the early Seventh-day Adventists that Miller's prediction was true but that the events of the end had begun to unfold in heaven and not on earth. Chen kept up his preaching until 2002, when a schism in the small group led to his departure. Since then, virtually nothing has been heard about the group.

Chen Tao experienced the fate that befalls many new religions. For a time it attracted followers, but it was unable to sustain itself after the decisive disconfirmation of prophecy.

See also: Chinese New Religious Movements; Millennialism; Millerites, The; UFO Religions.

Further Reading

Gallagher, Eugene V. 2014. *Reading and Writing Scripture in New Religious Movements: New Bibles and New Revelations*. New York: Palgrave.

Prather, Charles Houston. 1999. "God's Salvation Church: Past, Present and Future." *Marburg Journal of Religion* 4, no. 1. Available at: www.unimarburg.de/religionswissenschaft/journal/mjr/prather.html.

Saliba, John, & Amanda Telefsen 2011. "Chen Tao." *World Religions and Spirituality Project*. Available at: https://wrldrels.org/2016/10/08/chen-tao/.

Wessinger, Catherine 2000. *How the Millennium Comes Violently: From Jonestown to Heaven's Gate*. New York: Seven Bridges Press.

Children and New Religious Movements

Children are the future, the saying goes. The formative years of childhood, when children are at their most malleable, are consistently invoked in discussions ranging from education policy, nutrition, censorship, legislation, to religious practice. New religious movements are engaged in such debates about the proper shaping of children, as well as the subject of them. Children represent the next generation of these movements, which is why new religious movements and their opponents are invested in their upbringing.

There are new religious movements that seem particularly tailored to children or which focus exclusively on them as an object of study and worship. For example, many Marian apparitions have occurred in the presence of children, a fact, which appears to denote the spiritual purity and credulity of children to believe their senses and to be less likely to explain away magical or supernatural phenomena. Then there are the Indigo Children: a New Age assertion that there are children born with special, psychic abilities who represent the next level of human evolution. Though this movement has dwindled with increased knowledge of learning disabilities and autism-spectrum disorders (which some have argued manifested as extrasensory perception), there are those who still hold this belief.

Nonetheless, the conversation regarding the intersection between children/childhood and new religious movements revolves around two primary hubs: religions that place an emphasis on childbearing and childrearing as essential features of church belief and/or practice and accusations of child (sexual) abuse, endangerment, and brainwashing at the hands of insidious "cults."

CHILDBEARING AND CHILDREARING

Numerous new religious movements emphasize the importance of childbearing, not only as a means of ensuring numerical strength of stability but for theological and religious reasons. For the Church of Jesus Christ of Latter-day Saints (LDS Church), bearing children is a central rite in the Mormon system of "exaltation." Prior to their birth to earthly mothers, these children were born spiritually to a Mother and Father God in heaven; by entering physical bodies on earth, these "spiritual children" have the opportunity to become exalted like their divine parents, becoming Mother and Father Gods to a new generation of spiritual children (who will repeat the process). During several decades in the nineteenth century, childbearing was tied to the system of plural marriage advocated by the Church;

during that period, Mormon women had eight children on average and reared their families communally with their fellow sister-wives. Though the LDS Church has since done away with this practice, some fundamentalist Mormons—those who split off after the official end of plural marriage in 1890—continue to enter plural marriages and advocate for large families raised by multiple mothers. Some of these groups have come under scrutiny for abusive practices within plural marriage systems, including the marriage of underage, child brides to older (sometimes much older) men.

Not only childbearing but childrearing is essential to certain new religions. The Oneida Community, a nineteenth-century utopian community, practiced stirpiculture. Men and women were selected as mates based on certain ideal qualities they possessed—a fact which Oneidans believed would ensure the birth of perfect children. These children were then raised not by their parents but by the community. This level of detachment from parents and oversight by the community (though hard to achieve in reality) reflected the position of the Church that, since the Christian millennium had arrived, human beings must begin to live "perfectly," which meant divesting themselves of human attachments—including those of parent to child and vice versa. The Unification Church also placed a heavy emphasis on the matching of partners and the creation of children. Unificationists (often pejoratively called "Moonies") believe that children conceived from parents who are married in unions founded in total love of each other through love of God will be perfect themselves. This group would become the target of anticult activity when many young people during the 1970s converted to the faith.

On the other hand, are those religions that advocate for celibacy. Following a revelation that sex and its result, progeny, were the roots of sin, Mother Ann Lee (1736–1784) enjoined her group, the Shakers, to practice celibacy—a decision most likely influenced by her own devastating experience of multiple miscarriages. This has stymied the Shakers' ability to grow, however, given the lack of second-generation members to refill the depleting ranks as older members die. Centuries later and somewhat conversely, Bhagwan Shree Rajneesh (1931–1990) advocated for free love without procreation. At Rajneeshpuram, Rajneesh emphasized the importance of spiritual self-advancement, a process that would be disrupted, particularly for women (who he believed were spiritually superior), if childrearing became a priority.

CONCERN FOR MINORS: RUMORS AND REALITIES

New religious movements are generally suspected entities, but when children become involved, this suspicion is heightened exponentially. It is very often the plight of children around which many discussions of "dangerous cults" coalesce. For example, in 1978, tragedy struck Peoples Temple at their home in Jonestown, Guyana. Fueled in part by an ongoing custody battle between Jim Jones (1931–1978) and former members of Peoples Temple, external pressures reached a crescendo in November of that year and resulted in the mass revolutionary suicide of 918 members, including 300 children. The deaths of the children was particularly cruel, as they ostensibly had not consented to join Peoples Temple or to ingest cyanide. Peoples Temple became the rallying cry for those concerned with the welfare of children in the clutches of new religious movements. This focus would shift in the next decade during the height of the Satanic Panic. Following the reemergence of purportedly repressed memories, Michelle Smith reported experiencing abuse at the hands of Satanists when she was a child; the book *Michelle Remembers* (1990) recounted her alleged abuse and was coauthored with her therapist, and later husband, Lawrence Pazder (1936–2004). This book, coupled with accusations of Satanic ritual (and sexual) abuse against a California daycare provider (later disproven), led to a campaign against Satanism. Though the actual instances of such ritual abuse were almost nonexistent, the fear from parents was palpable, leading to a slew of accusations against these imagined, devilish antagonists.

Riding the wave of Jonestown, the Satanic Panic, and the boom of new religions during the 1960s, the anticult movement of the 1980s and 1990s was born from concerned parents whose children had converted to unfamiliar religions, particularly the International Society for Krishna Consciousness (ISKCON) and the Children of God (later "The Family"). Arguably the first organized anticult group was FREECOG, which was founded specifically to extricate young men and women from The Family. Children, as vulnerable individuals (even those of college age), were perceived as the natural targets of brainwashing, or the overriding of individuals' will and cognitive functioning with strict religious beliefs (a viewpoint since debunked by psychologists). As a countermeasure to cults' brainwashing methods, children from these movements were often kidnapped and subjected to "deprogramming," which involved attempts to strip away the cult's damaging rhetoric from the "victim." These methods led to the successful prosecution of certain prominent anticult leaders and the effective downfall of the movement by the mid-1990s.

At certain moments, the accusations leveled against new religious movements have skirted the line between free exercise violations and protection of children. In 1993, the Branch Davidians came under fire when accusations of child abuse emerged. These claims were disproven, though the leader of the Branch Davidians, David Koresh (1959–1993), was embarking in marital and sexual relationships with underage girls. On this basis and spurious illegal weapons charges, the Bureau of Alcohol Tobacco and Firearms and the Federal Bureau of Investigation served a warrant to arrest Koresh, which spurred a fifty-one-day siege ultimately resulting in a fire that killed most in the Waco, Texas, compound, including many children. Even more recently, Christian Scientists have been brought to task by the judicial system on accusations of child abuse and neglect. Christian Scientists eschew medical intervention, which can become tricky when children are involved; many have argued for their right to determine their children's treatment on free exercise grounds.

See also: Anticult Movement, The; Brainwashing; Branch Davidians; Christian Science; Church of Jesus Christ of Latter-day Saints; Cult; Deprogramming; FREECOG (Free the Children of God); Fundamentalist Mormons; Indigo Children; International Society for Krishna Consciousness (ISKCON); Jones, Rev. Jim (1931–1978); Koresh, David

(1959–1993); Lee, (Mother) Ann (1736–1784); Love Israel Family, The; Marian Apparitions; New Age, The; Oneida Community, The; Peoples Temple; Rajneesh, Shree Baghwan/Osho (1931–1990); Satanic Panic; Satanism; Sex, Sexuality, and New Religious Movements; Shakers, The; Unification Church, The.

Further Reading

Lewis, James R., & J. Gordon Melton, eds. 1994. *Sex, Slander and Salvation: Investigating the Children of God/The Family.* Stanford, CA: Center for Academic Publications.

Nilsson, Sanja. 2016. "Children in New Religions." In James R. Lewis & Inga B. Tøllefson, eds., *The Oxford Handbook of New Religious Movements.* New York: Oxford University Press.

Palmer, Susan J., & Charlotte E. Hardman, eds. 1999. *Children in New Religions.* New Brunswick, NJ: Rutgers University Press.

Rochford, E. Burke, Jr. 2014. "Children and Generational Issues." In George D. Chryssides & Benjamin E. Zeller, eds., *The Bloomsbury Companion to New Religious Movements.* London: Bloomsbury Academic.

Children of God (The Family International)

The encounters of members of the youth counterculture and representatives of Pentecostal and fundamentalist forms of Christianity during the "Summer of Love" of 1967 produced an array of groups known collectively as the Jesus People. One of the most notorious groups was first widely known as the Children of God, then as the Family of Love starting in 1978, and then as The Family beginning in 1982.

ORIGINS AND DEVELOPMENT

The Children of God had their origins in the career and experiences of David Brandt Berg (1919–1994). Berg was born into a family of evangelists. By 1944, he had committed himself to a full-time and largely itinerant Christian ministry and was ordained by the Christian and Missionary Alliance. For several years Berg worked with Rev. Fred Jordan (1909–1988) who had his own radio and television shows and a group of institutes called Soul Clinics.

In the 1960s, Berg had several religious experiences that he understood as giving him a special task. In early 1968, he moved to Huntington Beach, California, where he received a communication from God that gave him his true calling. He concluded that he was to bring the word of God to the growing, and sometimes disillusioned, "hippie" population in southern California and beyond. Since his ministry had already included an element of music, his small band of followers, then known as Teens for Christ, began to sing one night a week at a Christian coffeehouse. His ministry began to succeed when he instructed his young musicians to dress like the members of the youth culture they were trying to reach. Echoing the antiestablishment rhetoric of the counterculture, Berg was very critical of "Churchianity," which he saw as mired in bureaucracy and unable to bring the vital message of Jesus to young people. He offered instead a new kind of church.

At the outset Berg's brand of Christianity shared more with its Pentecostal and fundamentalist inspirations, especially in the matter of sexual ethics, than it did with the youth counterculture. His followers focused on reading the word of God in the scriptures, sometimes literally and sometimes not, and spreading it through missionary efforts. The virtually nonstop proselytizing quickly bore fruit and by 1972 there were more members of what was known as the Children of God outside the United States than within it.

As Berg's movement grew, so did his position within it. From the start, the Children of God had a distinctive millennial message, with Berg claiming that he was God's chosen prophet for the end-times and that the second coming would unfold in 1993. As the Children of God established their communal colonies throughout the world, it became more difficult for Berg, who was known within the movement as Moses David, Father David, or simply Dad, to remain in close contact with his followers. In the early 1970s, he began to communicate with his communities almost solely through letters. They quickly became known as "MO Letters" and gradually achieved the status of scripture within the Children of God. Berg's new church had a new message and the Bible now had to be read through the clarifying lenses provided by the MO Letters.

David Brandt Berg was an independent Christian missionary when he had the religious experiences that led him to begin the Children of God, an outreach ministry to members of the youth counterculture, in Huntington Beach, California, in 1968. (Special Collections, Davidson Library, University of California, Santa Barbara)

The group's communal houses were intended to reestablish the sharing of goods that characterized the primitive Christian communities described in Acts 2:44. The practice of communal living both connected with the developing ethos of the counterculture and provided a basis for further innovations.

CONTROVERSIES

The Children of God was controversial virtually from the beginning. The decisions of young adults to abandon more conventional lives for communal living and itinerant missionary work did not sit well with some of their families. Opposition from parents and other interested parties quickly developed and led to the formation in 1972 of the first organized contemporary anticult group in the United States, "The Parents Committee to Free Our Sons and Daughters From the Children of God," later shortened to "Free the Children of God" or FREECOG. FREECOG was intimately associated with Ted Patrick (1930–), one of the first to practice forced "deprogramming" in the United States.

Initially, the mere fact of conversion to the Children of God was sufficient to provoke opposition. But later developments within the group provided much more fuel for its opponents and inflamed public sentiment against the group. In 1974, Berg began to spell out what he called the Law of Love. He reasoned that since the Children of God were the final Church before the end would come, they had total freedom to express their love for others and for God. In practice, the Law of Love had troubling consequences that provoked government actions against the Children of God throughout the world.

One expression of the Law of Love was the practice of "flirty fishing," instituted in Berg's inner circle in 1974 and more broadly in 1977. Flirty fishing encouraged female members of the group to express their love for others, even to the point of physical intimacy, as a strategy of evangelization. The practice even led to members joining escort services to facilitate meeting more potential converts. Although the practice was discontinued in 1987 and forcefully condemned, it continued to taint public perceptions of the group.

Also problematic was the implementation of the Law of Love in communal living situations, where adults freely engaged in sexual relations with other adult members to whom they were not married but also sometimes in full view of children. In Mo Letters, Berg described children as sexual beings with their own rights to sexual pleasure. The most notorious example occurred with the adopted son of Karen Zerby (1946–), who had risen to a position of influence within the group as Berg's consort and then wife. Zerby's son, Ricky Rodriguez (1975–2005) known as Davidito, was initially portrayed as a model of childhood sexuality in a set of letters eventually published as *The Story of Davidito* in 1982. What the book showed, however, was a harrowing experience of childhood sexual abuse, which eventually contributed to Davidito's murder of one of the nannies who had molested him and his own suicide in 2005. Zerby did help to put an end to the practice of flirty fishing in 1987 and The Family renounced all adult sexual contact with children in 1986. The reputation for abuse stuck with the group, however. It led to a series of raids in several countries in the early 1990s that were designed to protect the children living in communal homes.

THE FAMILY AFTER DAVID BERG

When Berg died in 1994, his personal charisma had already been transferred to the MO Letters, the scriptures of his new church. In addition, Zerby, known within the group as Maria, Mama Maria, Maria Fontaine, and other names, had already gained a position of authority. Zerby married Peter Amsterdam (né Steven Kelly, 1951–) and together they have led The Family since 1994. As Berg did, they continue to issue letters that guide the group and are considered scripture. In addition, members claim to have communicated with Berg, who now resides in the spirit world.

Queen Maria and King Peter have done a lot to rein in the excesses that flourished under Berg and bring the group closer to the mainstream Christianity, of which Berg was initially so critical. But their most dramatic innovation has threatened the ability of The Family to continue as an identifiable group. In the summer of 2009, they announced a "reboot" of The Family, which was executed in 2010. Members were told that they no longer needed to live communally and that instead of forsaking the world, as the first members had been exhorted to do by Berg, they were now to integrate themselves into it. The Reboot came as a shock, particularly to the original members who had been part of the group for decades. They now faced the daunting prospects of finding work and sustaining themselves, tasks for which they had little preparation. Although Maria and Peter continued to provide religious guidance online (see https://karenzerby.org/), it is not clear that The Family will continue to have any other existence other than as an online community.

See also: Anticult Movement, The; Charisma and Leadership in New Religious Movements; Children and New Religious Movements; Deprogramming; FREECOG (Free the Children of God); Millennialism; New Scriptures and New Religious Movements; Patrick, Ted (1930–); Sex, Sexuality, and New Religious Movements.

Further Reading

Bainbridge, William Sims. 2002. *The Endtime Family: Children of God.* Albany: SUNY Press.

Borowik, Claire. 2017. "The Family International: The Emergence of a Virtual New Religious Community." In Eugene V. Gallagher, ed., *"Cult Wars" in Historical Perspective: New and Minority Religions*, pp. 108–120. New York: Routledge.

Chancellor, James D. 2000. *Life in the Family: An Oral History of the Children of God.* Syracuse, NY: Syracuse University Press.

Shepherd, Gary, & Gordon Shepherd. 2013. "Reboot of The Family International." *Nova Religio* 17: 74–98.

Van Zandt, David E. 1991. *Living in the Children of God.* Princeton, NJ: Princeton University Press.

Williams, Miriam. 1998. *Heaven's Harlots: My Fifteen Years as a Sacred Prostitute in the Children of God Cult.* New York: William Morrow.

Chinese New Religious Movements

In many ways, the religious world of East Asia derives from China, often through the transmission of Chinese texts. Many of the terms and ideas adapted by Japanese, Korean, and Vietnamese religions are Chinese in origin, though even within

China their meanings as well as the religious systems themselves have been applied depending upon the particular historical moment. For example, though Confucianism is a Chinese philosophical system, it is treated as a competing ideological system by the Chinese government; the only religions that are formally recognized in China are Buddhism, Daoism, Catholicism, (Protestant) Christianity, and Islam (though the position of the latter has becoming increasingly fragile in mainland China).

In a communist society, the political and legal status of religion inevitably impacts the growth and sustainability not only of new religions but of established traditions that find themselves living as minority traditions. However, it is important not to return to problematic tropes that paint China as areligious or antireligious (even though certain administrations may exhibit such tendencies). Religions exist, both imported and homegrown, and are vast in their diversity. Those who claim to be a member of a new "old" religion or a new "new" religion in China face many of the same challenges that all new religions face: how to sustain themselves over time, how to spread their message, and how to adapt when elements of their beliefs and practices become unsustainable. Though political and social culture may circumscribe these activities, they exist and are a testament to the possibility for religious innovation in all contexts.

NEW (OLD) RELIGIONS

Not all religious diversity in China is attributable to new religions but rather to the emergence of sects of traditional Chinese religions and to the processes of globalization that have brought major world traditions to East Asia.

Since the Ming dynasty (1368–1644), there have been records of sectarian movements, which many Chinese citizens would not consider to be new religious movements in a traditional sense. Some sectarian traditions in Taiwan and mainland China are centuries old and are viewed as natural variations of established religious traditions. Numerous sectarian traditions were founded this way in China; often they were lay-driven and involved an adaptation of a major tradition, such as the focus on a particular mantra, practice, or deity. For certain of these traditions, prohibitions against them may have existed but were lifted (and on occasion reissued); often those traditions that establish formally separate, rather than informal organizations, are those that experience government pushback.

The White Lotus movement, for example, was a sixteenth- and seventeenth-century Buddhist sect that believed that Maitreya Buddha would bring imminent change to the world. According to various reports, the group acted as a moral check on the current government. During a time when poverty was widespread, the existence of the movement showed that the needs of the people were not being met by those in power, requiring action on the part of authorities in case they wished to stem the tide of full-blown revolution. Nonetheless, the White Lotus movement, despite the policy changes it inspired, continued to be prohibited, since it was seen as potentially threatening to society.

Not all traditions were homegrown. Through various processes, including those that were economic as well as religious and cultural, religions such as Christianity and Islam came to China. Christianity appeared in China as early as the seventh century; however, it was through the work of Jesuits during sixteenth and seventeenth centuries that it established a true presence, specifically in the form of Catholicism. Though neither religion would achieve anything close to numerical supremacy, Protestants would arrive headway and achieve fewer gains in membership in proportion to Catholics, the exception being in Hong Kong, which was a British colony through much of the nineteenth and twentieth centuries. In 2018–2019, numerous protests broke out in Hong Kong over concerns that mainland China would eradicate the religious freedom protections enjoyed by Hong Kong's population, many of whom are Christian. As members of "minority" religions, even those that are formally recognized by the government, concerns abound that their status is only nominally protected.

Islam has existed in China almost since it was founded in the seventh century, though estimates show that Muslims comprise less than 2 percent of the population (most of whom are Sunni). Muslims, particularly Hui Muslims (ethnically Chinese adherents of Islam), have been enabled to practice in relative peace. Recently, however, Muslims have faced mounting persecution, from the defacement of mosques to outbursts of violence. In 2018–2019, reports arose that Chinese Muslims were being detained in "re-education" camps, where they were subject to torture and possibly even involuntary organ donation. This brought international scrutiny to China and its treatment of religious minorities, which revealed troubling patterns of religious and racial profiling and raised the specter of fears over "antireligious" communist China.

NEW (NEW) RELIGIONS

Not only new "old" religions but new "new" religions have grown in China as well as Taiwan, which for a time was a principality of China (and in the view of some, primarily Chinese officials, should remain as such). As noted, religious innovation has been a part of Chinese history for centuries. In the nineteenth century, the Taiping movement (or rebellion, 1850–1864), led by the God Worshipping Society and its founder Hong Xiuquan (1814–1864), the self-proclaimed son of God and brother of Jesus Christ, managed to stage a coup, overthrowing the Qing dynasty and ruling for over a decade. Based on his particular interpretation of the Bible, the Taiping movement represented a period of modernization for China, where gender equality reigned and certain addictive practices, such as the smoking of opium or consumption of alcohol, were prohibited. The movement was ultimately quashed and Xiuquan executed, but the popularity of its message along with the fact that it sustained rule for several years highlighted the ability of new religions to inspire support among the Chinese rank-and-file.

The establishment of China as a communist Republic made things more difficult for new religions, albeit not impossible by any means. One such religion that was allowed to grow despite its prohibited status was Falun Gong. Its founder Li Hongzhi (1951–), while arguing that it was not a religious movement, argued that the universe emanated from the Dharma Wheel, whose movement mirrors the growth, death, and rebirth of all life on earth. All life was interconnected. All practitioners of Falun Gong develop a "Falun," an entity that resides in their lower abdomen that mimics the movement of the Dharma Wheel: absorbing energy from the universe, and releasing it, keeping the two forces in constant balance. The movement lacks a formal institutional body, which is somewhat ironic given the amount of persecution it has experienced at the hands of the Chinese government and media.

Falun Gong made international headlines following a series of nonviolent protests it led outside communist headquarters in Beijing on April 25, 1999. Around ten thousand Falun Gong members sat for hours in condemnation of a media propaganda campaign against Falun Gong; the group also wished to be recognized as an accepted religion. The government responded by detaining members, imprisoning them for unspecified lengths of time and, as was rumored in 2008, potentially subjecting them to organ harvesting. Falun Gong represents one of the more extreme cases of the Chinese government's suppression of minority religions, a fact that is ironic given that Falun Gong claimed some one hundred million members in the 1990s and the numbers are believed to have grown since then.

Most Chinese new religious movements have never experienced the level of numerical significance and sustainability as Falun Gong; some, like Chen Tao, are decidedly short-lived. Also called God's Salvation Church or God Saves the Earth Flying Saucer Foundation, Chen Tao was founded in the 1990s in Taiwan by Hon-Ming Chen (1955–), a junior college instructor of social science, after he experienced a revelation from God telling him to redirect his focus to religious work. He had previously been a member of a Taiwanese UFO religion, and combined elements of Buddhism, millennialist Christianity, and belief in UFOs in Chen Tao. Known as Teacher Chen, he revealed, among other things, that illness was the result of past karma, and that the liberation from these bodies will cure them. In the process he wrote several major texts that detailed his millennialist message, namely, *The Practical Evidence and Study of the World of God and Buddha* (1996) and *God's Descending in Clouds (Flying Saucers) on Earth to Save People* (1997).

Ultimately, Chen moved the group to the United States in 1997, believing it to be the "Pure Land of God." From there, he issued a series of apocalyptic prophecies, including a series of natural and societal catastrophes, which would prompt God to appear on television in March 1998 and then again in human form three days later. When these events did not materialize, the movement lost a good degree of momentum, fizzling out over the next few years.

CHINESE NEW RELIGIOUS MOVEMENTS OUTSIDE OF CHINA

As evidenced by Teacher Chen's decision to move Chen Tao to the United States, many Chinese new religions have found viable homes outside of China or managed to spread their religious message outside of China. Li Hongzhi, the founder of Falun Gong, began traveling to spread his message in Europe, Australia, and the United States, among other destinations. Ultimately, he settled in the United States in 1996; during the 1999 protests, the Chinese government sought to extradite him for his role in encouraging the protests, but to no avail.

In other instances, Chinese new religions may flourish in the West, but in a different form than they did in China. Like yoga from India, the Chinese medical practices known as Qigong have taken hold in new cultures, particularly in the United States. The term means to "manipulate energy" and is linked to ancient Taoism. Qi (chi), the force that sustains life, thus, the aim of Qigong is to balance the yin and yang (dark-light, disorder-order) through meditation, physical mastery, and traditional methods of healing. The practice received a renewed boost in the 1950s when a doctor, Liu Guizhen (1920–1983), cured himself of various ailments, ultimately garnering some two hundred million practitioners by the 1980s. Those who practice Qigong in China are often reticent to describe it as religious, which may be one of the reasons that the practice is allowed to proliferate in China. The practice gained purchase across the globe during the late twentieth century, fueled by countercultural interest in alternative healing practices and Asian religions. Often, Qigong is combined with other practices rather than practiced on its own, adapted by religious New Age or modern "wellness" culture.

Whether sectarian, the result of innovation, or the result of global processes of cultural exchange and migration, new religions in China have a long history, one that defies the image of China as anemic when it comes to religious diversity or its people as faithless or unable to find paths to express their religiosity. Nonetheless, it is unclear how the Chinese political climate will impact the ability of these religions to thrive and new ones to emerge.

See also: Chen Tao; Falun Gong; Globalization and New Religious Movements; Media and New Religious Movements; New Age, The; Sect; UFO Religions.

Further Reading

Chou, Kai-Ti. 2008. *Contemporary Religious Movements in Taiwan: Rhetorics of Persuasion.* Lewiston: The Edwin Mellen Press.

Edelman, Bryan, & James T. Richardson. 2003. "Falun Gong and the Law: Development of Legal Social Control in China." *Nova Religio* 6, no. 2: 312–331.

Lang, Graeme, & Lars Ragvald. 1998. "Spirit Writing and the Development of Chinese Cults." *Sociology of Religion* 59, no. 4: 309–328.

Pye, Michael. 2004. "New Religions in East Asia." In James R. Lewis, ed., *The Oxford Handbook of New Religious Movements.* New York: Oxford Handbook of New Religious Movements.

Seiwert, Hubert Michael. 2003. *Popular Religious Movements and Heterodox Sects in Chinese History.* Leiden: Brill.

Walton, Jonathan. 2014. "Old-Time Religion in New New China: Alternative Religious Movements in the Post-Mao Era." *CrossCurrents* 64, no. 2: 262–281.

Christadelphians

Like many millennialist Christian sects, the Christadelphians maintain that their beliefs arise from an accurate reading of the Bible. Founder John Thomas (1805–1871), an English immigrant to the United States, aligned with the growing Restoration Movement, a diffuse Christian movement focused on restoring the "true" Church and seeking a pristine, original reading of the Bible. Thomas soon split with the broader movement over his belief that his views were the only beliefs that guaranteed salvation. Thomas returned to England in the late 1840s to lecture on his views, which sparked the beginning of the Christadelphian movement, formally, in England; the U.S. branch would incorporate in 1864. Nonetheless, Thomas rejected the idea of a formal movement or himself as the founder; he believed, firmly, that he was introducing people to the correct way of reading the Bible and nothing more.

Besides the belief that the Bible is the only inspired authority and rule of life, the Christadelphians most notable beliefs are their unitarianism and their millennialism. They reject the Trinity, or the belief that God, Jesus Christ, and the Holy Spirit make up one divine entity. Rather, they believe that God is the highest being and creator of the world. Jesus is both son of Man and son of God, but he was only elevated to an immortal being after his death. They believe that Christ will return soon and bring about the events predicted in the Bible, including the Apocalypse and the coming of the Kingdom of God (which will be centralized in Jerusalem, but will extend across the entire globe). Christadelphians do not believe that baptism and repentance of sins, though necessary for entrance into the community, guarantee one's salvation; rather they emphasize living "in Christ," throughout their lives. The name Christadelphian means "Brethren in Christ." In this way, they live their belief that salvation comes not through Christ's death, who was human when he died, but through emulating his sinless life.

Christadelphians are not centrally organized; each "ecclesia" (congregation) is governed autonomously, reflecting the anticreedalism and individualism of Restorationist Christianity. Thus, small variations may occur in belief. However, due to a set of documents created in the nineteenth century discussing proper governance, large deviations between ecclesiae are uncommon and most are relatively uniform in practice. Christadelphians are democratic in organization, with "brethren" elected to a governing committee. There are also no ordained clergy, but rather male members of the ecclesiae rotate preaching and teaching duties.

Though a relatively unknown religious movement, there are around fifty thousand Christadelphians around the globe today, spanning over one hundred countries.

See also: Millennialism; Sect; Unitarian Universalism.

Further Reading

Lippy, Charles H. 1989. *The Christadelphians in North America*. Lewiston, ME: Edwin Mellen Press.

Tennant, Harry. 1986. *The Christadelphians: What They Believe and Preach*. Birmingham, UK: Christadelphian Magazine & Publishing Association Ltd.

Wilson, Brian R. 1961. *Sects and Society: A Sociological Study of the Elim Tabernacle, Christian Science and Christadelphians*. Berkeley; Los Angeles: University of California Press.

Christian Identity

The "ten lost tribes of Israel" have long exercised the imaginations of readers of the Bible. Their disappearance traces to the conquering of the ancient northern kingdom of Israel by the Assyrian empire around 722 BCE and the subsequent deportation of many of its residents. Since that time, many groups, including the Pashtuns of Afghanistan and Pakistan and groups of Jews in Kurdish lands, Kashmir, India, Ethiopia, Nigeria, and Ghana, among other places, have claimed to be their descendants. Beyond that, since the late nineteenth century, others have claimed that Aryan groups, including the Anglo-Saxons, Celts, Germans, and Scandinavians, are the true descendants of the lost tribes, who migrated from the ancient Near East across the Caucasus mountains to northern Europe.

The Christian Identity movement, which began to flourish in the United States in the 1940s, derives from British Israelism. Taking shape in the late 1800s, British Israelism posited both that white Aryans are the descendants of the lost tribes of ancient Israel and that the Jews are actually the descendants of the Mongolian-Turkish Khazars. The movement continues the ancient debate between Jews and Christians about who constitutes the "true Israel."

The most prominent proponent of British Israelism in the United States was Herbert Armstrong (1892–1986), who founded what would become known as the Worldwide Church of God in 1933. While Armstrong, like the British figures who preceded him, held out the possibility of salvation for the Jews, others in the United States turned British Israelism in an increasingly anti-semitic direction.

In the 1920s, *The Dearborn Independent* newspaper, owned by Henry Ford (1863–1947) and edited by a Ford Motor Company executive, promulgated anti-semitic conspiracy theories and published the notorious fictional anti-Jewish polemic, *The Protocols of the Elders of Zion* (first published in Russian in 1903) among other scurrilous items. Such texts promoted the idea of a worldwide Jewish conspiracy of cosmic proportions and aimed to rally opposition to the Jews' insidious goals. Christian Identity both drew upon and amplified such existing anti-semitic ideas.

The minister and political organizer Gerald L. K. Smith (1898–1976), who founded both the Christian Nationalist Crusade and the America First Party, influenced several early prominent Christian Identity preachers. Among them was Wesley Swift (1919–1970) who founded what would become known as The Church of Jesus Christ–Christian in the 1940s. The organization that continues his ministry (see www.kingidentity.com) bills him as the single most important figure of the early days of the Christian Identity movement and offers more than thirty publications and more than 250 cassette tapes of his teachings for sale.

As Christian Identity took shape in the 1940s, it had several distinctive characteristics that set it apart from British Israelism. While retaining the notion that white Aryans were the true descendants of the lost tribes of Israel, it became explicitly anti-semitic and racist. It reinforced those attitudes with a "two seed theory" that offers a distinctive account of the creation of human beings. White people, it asserts, are the descendants of Adam, but Eve also mated with the serpent in the Garden of Eden and Cain is the offspring of that union. Cain, after killing his brother Abel, then mated with pre-Adamic people of color. Consequently, all people of color, including the Jews, are the descendants of Cain. That interpretation of the Bible is used to support the racial and religious superiority of white people over all others. Christian Identity also emphasizes a millennialist view that we are living in the end-times during which an apocalyptic battle will take place between white Aryans and the Jews and "mud peoples."

Christian Identity constitutes more of a subcultural strand or part of the cultic milieu than a single institution. Its beliefs appeal to a diverse array of white supremacists, antigovernment activists who style the current government as a Zionist Occupation Government, survivalists who withdraw from society in anticipation of Armageddon, and other extremists. But because it constitutes a diffuse ideology more than a set of institutions, it is difficult to assess to what degree individuals or groups hold Christian Identity ideas.

Christian Identity flourished again in the 1980s and 1990s when groups like Gordon Kahl's (1920–1983) Posse Comitatus engaged in a shootout with law enforcement officers; Robert Mathews's (1953–1984) The Order or Silent Brotherhood perpetrated a series of robberies to raise funds for white supremacist organizations until Mathews died in a shootout with federal agents; and the religious and white supremacist commune, The Covenant, The Sword, and The Arm of the Lord, founded by James Ellison (c. 1941–) engaged in a standoff in 1985 with federal authorities that ended with Ellison's imprisonment on weapons charges.

The 1992 clash between Randy Weaver and his family with U.S. marshals at Ruby Ridge, Idaho, which ended with the deaths of Weaver's wife and son and one marshal, and also the siege of the Mount Carmel Center of the Branch Davidians by agents of the Bureau of Alcohol, Tobacco, and Firearms and then the Federal Bureau of Investigation in 1993, contributed to the popularity of antigovernment ideas, which were also endorsed by Christian Identity.

Ideas nurtured in the milieu of Christian Identity continue to motivate anti-semitic and racist ideologies and also acts of violence by domestic terrorists, such as the murder of eleven congregants at the Tree of Life synagogue in Pittsburgh in 2018 by Robert Gregory Bowers and the shooting at the Poway, California, Chabad synagogue by John T. Earnest in 2019, which took the life of one congregant.

See also: Branch Davidians; Cultic Milieu; Millennialism; Race and New Religious Movements.

Further Reading

Aho, James A. 1990. *The Politics of Righteousness: Idaho Christian Patriotism.* Seattle: University of Washington Press.

Barkun, Michael. 1997. *Religion and the Racist Right: The Origins of the Christian Identity Movement*, rev. ed. Chapel Hill: University of North Carolina Press.

Lamy, Philip. "Christian Identity: An American Millennial Mythology." In Eugene V. Gallagher & W. Michael Ashcraft, eds., *Introduction to New and Alternative Religions*, vol. II, pp. 173–189. Westport, CT: Greenwood.

Christian Science

HISTORY

The Church of Christ, Scientist or Christian Science emerged at a moment of great experimentation regarding the powers of the human mind and will to shape both material and spiritual reality. During the late nineteenth century, Christian Science emerged alongside, albeit separate from, a broader religious movement known as "New Thought." Though the Church has been declining in membership and congregations of late, its cultural and popular presence still loom large, as a result of its particular views on health and healing.

These views arose from the religious experiences of Christian Science's founder, Mary Baker Eddy (1821–1910). Plagued by sickness throughout her life, Eddy eschewed the treatments of Western medicine (which had not worked for her) in favor of nontraditional approaches to healing, particularly those of Phineas Quimby. Quimby, a practitioner of magnetic healing, had determined by deduction that patients who improved under his care were those who believed themselves to be healed. In other words, their healing was the result of right thinking or belief that one's body was well. After studying under Quimby, Eddy experienced a near-fatal fall on ice in 1866, which temporarily paralyzed her. Believing that her death was near, Eddy began to read the Gospel accounts of Jesus's miraculous healings. Following her meditation on these passages and after a period of three days, Eddy arose, completely healed.

Over the next few years, Eddy would create the system that came to be called Christian Science. Grounded in the Bible and traditional Christian views on God, the saving and healing power of Christ, and the coming Kingdom of God, Eddy developed a new system of religious practice that emphasized the healing power of the human mind. Over their lifetimes and due to the hegemonic growth of Western medicine, Eddy believed humans had lost the ability to tap into their own divine, healing power, turning instead to external remedies or drugs, which treated the symptoms, but not the cause of illness. What Christian Science offered as a practice, then, was the means of channeling a practitioner's belief in God and Christ into tangible, bodily effects. Eddy would begin teaching these beliefs in 1870, but it was in 1875 that the turning point came with the publication of her text, *Science and Health* (later called *Science and Health with Key to the*

For more than a century, the First Church of Christ, Scientist in Boston has been the headquarters of Christian Science. Reflecting her suspicions about ordained clergy and church hierarchies, Mary Baker Eddy named her central work, *Science and Health with Key to the Scriptures*, the pastor of all Christian Science churches in 1895. (Library of Congress)

Scriptures). She intended for the text to be read alongside the Bible, with commentary in the former corresponding to passages in the latter. In this way, *Science and Health* served as a lens for revealing the healing potential of certain passages of the Bible.

The church continued to grow following Eddy's death in 1910, achieving its peak in 1936 with a reported membership of approximately 270,000, the vast majority of which were women. Abjuring standard missions and marred by critics such as Mark Twain and controversies regarding its position on medical care, the Church of Christ, Scientist gradually saw that number plateau and dwindle. At present the church claims around eighty-five thousand members worldwide. Notwithstanding its comparatively minor presence, the Church maintains a steady impact on journalistic and print culture, particularly through its periodical, *The Christian Science Monitor*, which has won seven Pulitzer prizes since 1950 (the journal itself was established by Eddy in 1908).

BELIEFS AND PRACTICES

Eddy balked at the idea of establishing a Christian Science "creed," or a set of specific doctrinal beliefs. Instead, she listed a set of six tenets (*Science and Health with Key to the Scriptures*, 496–7). The first tenet maintained that the Bible was all one needed to achieve eternal life—a belief that aligned Christian Scientists with most Protestants, as would the second tenet that established the supremacy of an infinite Father God, the reality that Jesus Christ was God's son, and the fact of humanity's creation in the image of the Father. After that, the tenets depart from traditional Christian theology, beginning with the idea that evil is "unreal." Therefore, sin is defined as the wrongful belief that evil exists; in fact, believing that evil exists can produce deleterious physical effects or illness. Further, all material existence is illusory: everything is spirit, everything is God. Once one acknowledges the idea that one's pain is a projection of the mind, then through prayer and proper focusing of mental and spiritual energies, a Christian Science practitioner can heal all physical ailments, just as Christ could. In fact, the prayers of Christian Scientists are specifically geared toward connecting with the "Mind" of Christ. Thus, the "science" of Christian Science is reflected in the idea that the mind and will can produce tangible or provable effects. In other words, one's mental faculties are the source of all salvation, both spiritual and physical.

Given the belief that external or physical elements such as pain, evil, and even matter are illusory, Christian Science is not heavy with outward ceremonies or rituals. Baptism and communion, for example, are practiced "spiritually," rather than ceremonially. Spiritual baptism refers to the daily act of spiritually purifying the mind and soul of wrong thinking, whereas spiritual communion is prayer, whereby a Christian Scientist invokes the mind of Christ (rather than his physical body, such as in Catholic understandings of communion). Perhaps more famous than their shunning of external ceremonies is Christian Scientists' eschewing of all external medical treatment, particularly that prescribed by Western medicine. It is these views that have made Christian Scientists the target of public ire and, occasionally, the defendant in courts, when Christian Scientist parents deny treatment for their ill children. Such controversies have plagued Christian Science since the 1880s, when Eddy proclaimed herself a "Professor of Obstetrics," even though she had no formal medical training in that or other medical disciplines. More serious charges of manslaughter or negligent homicide have arisen when an individual, often a child, dies under the care or advice of a Christian Scientist practitioner. Such cases raise questions regarding the protection of Christian Scientists under the free exercise clause of the First Amendment. In the fifty or so such cases brought against Christian Scientists since 1887, the courts have almost unanimously found in favor of the defendants on the grounds of religious freedom.

CHURCH AND CULTURE

In many ways, Eddy was the reluctant founder of a new religion, believing, as did many sectarian Protestants, that she was simply moving Christianity to its next logical stage. However, after amassing quite a following, it became clear that she had a formal movement on her hands, leading to the official founding of the Church of Christ, Scientist in 1875 and to the construction and opening of the First Church of Christ, Scientist in Boston in 1894 (now known as the Mother Church). However, reflecting her belief that the Bible was the only guide one needed to attain eternal life, Eddy named *Science and Health* the official pastor of the Church in 1895. In this way, the Church of Christ, Scientist is a lay church: Church officers are not ordained clergy, but those charged with carrying out Church bylaws. Each week a "Reader" who has been appointed by the board of directors of his or her congregation reads a sermon printed and disseminated in the *Christian Science Quarterly*—a system that ensures that the service is identical in each congregation around the globe.

There are, however, individuals known as "Christian Science practitioners," who have been accredited through the Church, having undergone a prescribed course of study. Practitioners see "patients" or Christian Scientists seeking an experienced healer to pray for them or to direct them in their own prayer to heal whatever ails them physically or spiritually. Individuals seeking personal guidance or simply a space for quiet meditation may seek instead to visit a Christian Science Reading Room. Not restricted to Christian Scientists, the Reading Rooms act as both bookstore and site of contemplation on passages of the Bible and Christian Science texts.

Though past its heyday as one of (if not the) most successful religions to arise from the New Thought movement, the Church of Christ, Scientist maintains an institutional, literary, cultural, and personal presence in the United States and over seventy countries worldwide. Though the Church itself has experienced many peaks and valleys, for their part, practicing Christian Scientists continue to experience the results of healing through prayer and to look forward to a time even death will be no more.

See also: Eddy, Mary Baker (1821–1910); New Thought.

Further Reading

Eddy, Mary Baker. 1934. *Science and Health with Key to the Scriptures.* Boston: Published by the First Church of Christ, Scientist.

Gottschalk, Stephen. 1973. *The Emergence of Christian Science in American Religious Life.* Berkeley: University of California Press.

Michell, Deidre. 2009. *Christian Science: Women, Healing, and the Church.* Lanham, MD: University Press of America.

Peel, Robert. 1988. *Health and Medicine in the Christian Science Tradition: Principle, Practice, and Challenge.* New York: Crossroad.

Ruetenik, Tadd. 2012. "The First Church of Christ, Pragmatist: Christian Science and Responsible Optimism." *Journal of Religion and Health,* 51, no. 4: 1397–1405.

Church of All Worlds, The

The history of the first Pagan church in the United States is intertwined with the life of one of its founders, the influential teacher Tim Zell (1942–). While at Westminster College in Fulton, Missouri, Zell and another student read Robert Heinlein's science fiction novel, *Stranger in a Strange Land.* Taken with the description of its Mars-born hero who returned to earth, they began, like him, to "share water" as a ritual act. They formed a Water-Brotherhood known as Atl, from the Aztec word for water. It soon had some one hundred participants. By 1967, Zell was identifying as a Pagan, and in 1968 Atl was incorporated as the Church of All Worlds (www.caw.org), named for the religion in Heinlein's novel. In 1970, the Church was officially recognized by the Internal Revenue Service as a religion.

Over time Zell's ideas have evolved, but at their core is a deep appreciation of earth as a single living being (Gaea), a belief in divinity as imminent in each individual, the desire to live in harmony with nature, and an emphasis on open, positive sexuality. Those convictions are shared by many other contemporary Pagans.

As an organization, the Church has gone through distinct periods, which are mirrored in its most influential publication. Along with its incorporation in 1968, the Church began to publish the periodical *Green Egg*. It lasted until 1976 and then was revived in 1988. By 1998, Zell had lost control of *Green Egg*, and his position as Primate of the Church was challenged, which prompted him to take a sabbatical from the Church for a year. In 2002, he disaffiliated from the Church. Financial and legal issues prompted the dissolution of the Church in 2004. In 2004, Zell founded the Grey School of Wizardry, and in 2006 he reestablished the Church of All Worlds under his leadership.

Throughout the organizational ups and downs, Zell continued to develop his Pagan teaching. From 1974 on, he was joined in his endeavors by his spouse Morning Glory Zell (née Diana Moore, 1948–2014). The Church secured fifty-five acres in Mendocino County in northern California, which continues to serve as the site for festivals and other events (see www.annwfn.org). Trying to awaken the wonder of traditional mythological tales, for a time the Zell-Ravenhearts bred "unicorns" by altering the horns of white goats into a single horn. They also searched for mermaids in the South Seas. Morning Glory herself set out a Pagan theology of sexuality, specifically polyamory, in several published pieces. She and Tim, who had adopted the first name of "Oberon" in 1994, participated in two successive triadic relationships. In the latter one, all three partners took the surname of Ravenheart.

Oberon Zell remains a respected Pagan elder and teacher and the Church continues his legacy.

See also: Neopaganism.

Further Reading
Sulak, John C. 2014. *The Wizard and the Witch: Seven Decades of Counterculture, Magick & Paganism: An Oral History of Oberon Zell and Morning Glory*. Woodbury, MN: Llewellyn Worldwide.

Church of Jesus Christ of Latter-day Saints, The
HISTORY

Hovering at around sixteen million members in 2019 and less than two hundred years old, the Church of Jesus Christ of Latter-day Saints (LDS Church) is arguably the most successful new religious movement of the modern era—and certainly the most successful new religion originating in the United States. For a time, its growth seemed exponential with little sign of slowing, leading to Rodney Stark's 1998 prediction that the Church would house 265 million members by

2080. Two decades later, this astounding figure no longer seems plausible as the growth rate has decelerated due to a variety of reasons (smaller family size and a shift in missionary protocol, among others). Notwithstanding the slackened pace, the sustainability of LDS Church, more colloquially known as the Mormon Church or Mormonism, in the face of persistent persecution and scrutiny is an extraordinary accomplishment that hints at the peculiar history of a peculiar people.

The success of the Church is due to multiple factors. Joseph Smith Jr., born to parents who we would now call "religious seekers," was barely a teenager in 1820 when his town of Palmyra, New York, was swept up in a wave of religious revivals, where itinerant preachers rode into town, converting masses of people at once in raucous tent meetings. Young Smith felt overwhelmed by the many Christian denominations all claiming to have the right path to salvation. After encountering a Bible passage (James 1:5) that enjoined him to "ask of God," he retreated to the woods and received what would be known as "The First Vision." God the Father and Jesus appeared to Smith and told him, not only that every church claiming his soul was false but that he would found the one true, restored Church. Three years later Smith received "The Second Vision." This time the angel Moroni appeared to him, alerting him to the existence of a set of golden plates, buried in a hill nearby, and his role as their translator. Another four years later, Moroni deemed Smith worthy to retrieve the plates and a set of seer stones to aid in their translation. Dictating to a variety of scribes as he translated the plates, Smith eventually produced a six-hundred-page manuscript that came to be titled *The Book of Mormon*. The book contained the lost history of an ancient civilization brought to the New World by tribes of Israel, whose constant warring ultimately led to their eradication.

The publication of *The Book of Mormon* in March 1830 was soon followed by the founding of the Church that following April. By this time, Smith and his new Bible had garnered much attention, some good and some bad. On the side of good were a cadre of devoted believers, who risked stigma and often their livelihoods to join the fledgling Church, even picking up and leaving their homes when a move became necessary because of sometimes violent opposition. Moving west, Smith and the "Saints" first settled in Kirtland, Ohio. This was a time of great innovation and industry, as it was here that Smith would receive most of the revelations regarding the theology, ritual, and structure of church. It was also the site of the first Mormon temple as well as the place where he would implement the economic system of "consecration," whereby every industry and business was under LDS control (the experiment failed, leading to the defection of several of his most trusted advisers). It was also here that he would have his revelation regarding the Church's most controversial doctrine: plural marriage or polygamy.

Even while at Kirtland, Smith had his sights set on a different location: Jackson County, Missouri, which had been revealed as the site of Zion, the "chosen land" where the Saints would gather in anticipation of the second coming of Christ. Though he would only live there briefly, from 1838 to 1839, Smith sent Saints ahead of him to construct the city of God. But as the number of Saints increased in the area, hostilities grew with outsiders. Tensions grew high enough that skirmishes broke out into what became known as "The Mormon War" in 1838, precipitating the infamous "extermination order" of Governor Lilburn Boggs, calling for the Saints to leave the state or risk extermination. Temporarily defeated, the Saints resettled in Commerce, Illinois—renamed Nauvoo—where construction of a Temple soon followed. However, the stigma had not left the Saints. In 1844, a series of events would occur that ultimately resulted in the death of Joseph Smith and his brother Hyrum Smith in a jail cell in Carthage, Illinois, at the hands of an angry mob.

Though there were a number of contenders for Smith's seat as prophet and president of the Church, the mantle fell on Brigham Young. It was Young who would lead the Saints to Utah (initially called "Deseret") in 1846/1847, and it was Young who would implement much of the work that Smith had introduced. As both prophet of the Church and later territorial governor of Utah, Young consolidated LDS power, while simultaneously expanding the Church in both geographic area and numbers. He reintroduced the practice of consecration and began to implement the practice of plural marriage in earnest. All of this occurred while the federal government ramped up its pressure to undercut the power of what its officers believed was a dangerously hierarchical, heretical, and with the practice of plural marriage, immoral religion. After years of such pressure and following a revelation, the fourth Prophet, Wilford Woodruff issued the "First Manifesto" in 1890, ending the practice of plural marriage. This gesture ultimately enabled Utah to gain statehood in 1896.

Once the Saints were fully incorporated into the United States, they experienced more than a century of slow, sometimes begrudging, acceptance characterized by their search for legitimacy. Still smarting from years of persecution, the Church and its members were buoyed by a unique institutional structure and theology that has enabled the Church and its people to adapt as needed.

BELIEFS AND PRACTICES

All Saints believe that Joseph Smith restored the gospel of Jesus Christ and that the LDS Church is the true, restored Church. Restorationist Christianities are built around the idea that they are returning to an earlier, pristine version of Christianity, the "true" Church as Christ intended. What distinguishes Saints from other such movements is that by restoring the gospel, Smith also reopened the biblical canon. From his first vision, the Church that Smith built was grounded in the idea that God was still speaking to his chosen, enabling the continued production of new scripture. Not stopping with *The Book of Mormon*, Smith produced other new scriptures. Furthermore, Smith opened the door for revelation to continue after he was gone. This would occur first through the figure of each new Prophet, who could produce new, binding scripture, which would be (and still are) published in the *Doctrine and Covenants*.

From the many revelations Smith and, to a lesser degree, later prophets received, arose the bulk of LDS belief and practice. Saints share many beliefs with fellow Christians: that humans are made in the image of God, that Christ is the savior of humanity and will return again, and that the soul is eternal. However, these beliefs are not without a certain LDS spin that often sparks debate as to whether Saints are Christian. Saints believe that God was once a man, who had been exalted to divine status, primarily by bearing many "spirit children" with a Mother God while in heaven. For these spirit children to be exalted like their father, God created the earth and human beings, so that these spirits could be born into the world and choose to be exalted by following the restored gospel. One of the primary means of achieving exaltation is through the institution of marriage and reproduction, whereby more spirits may be born into the world. This was the theological basis for the practice of plural marriage, though, as noted, the practice was officially ceased by the mainstream Mormon Church at the turn of the twentieth century. Further, as a millennialist version of Christianity (hence the name "Latter-day"), Saints believe that through the work of exaltation, they help to usher in Christ's second coming and the ensuing one thousand years of his reign on earth.

Much of this work of exaltation takes place through various Temple rituals, performed by those with the Aaronic (lower) or Melchizedek (higher) priesthood. As part of his restoration of the Church, Smith simultaneously reinstituted the rites of Temple worship and the priestly lineage of Aaron in his LDS Church. Once young men come of age and are proved Mormons in good standing, they are gifted the priesthood and are able to perform essential rituals in Mormon Temples. The most important of these rituals are: (1) endowment, where a Mormon is ceremonially incorporated into the eternal LDS community and given a celestial name, known only to them; (2) sealing, the sacred ceremony where two people are joined for eternity, thus guaranteeing that they will ascend to celestial heaven together; and (3) baptism for the dead, whereby people who died before accepting the restored gospel may be baptized vicariously by a living Saint. Temples themselves are distinctive buildings, not only for their size and generally impressive construction but also for highlighting the stereotype of Mormon secrecy. Non-Mormons (and Mormons who are not in good standing) are unable to enter the Temple or to observe essential Mormon rituals.

Beyond the stigma of secrecy, Mormons are also critiqued for their more open practices, such as those evolving from the Word of Wisdom, or the Mormon "health code." Prescriptions against the consumption of alcohol, coffee, and tea, for example, have given Saints the reputation of being straitlaced—an image that both sets them apart and often makes them the targets of ridicule.

INSTITUTION AND CULTURE

Adhering to codes such as the Word of Wisdom and generally living a good, moral life is essential to remaining a Mormon in good standing, which highlights the degree of influence that the institution of the Church has on Saints' daily existence. The Church itself bears both hierarchical and democratic strains within its structure. Authority and decisions move from the top—comprising the First Presidency and the Quorum of Twelve Apostles—down through the ranks of various church officials tasked with either preserving the spiritual governance of the Church or its financial and institutional needs. The hierarchy also reflects the fact that the Church is patriarchal in nature, as women are not permitted to hold most offices beyond those specifically related to charitable work, the nurturing of children, and the supporting of LDS women. The Relief Society, a branch of the Church traced back to its earliest days, is the most visible representation of women in the Church and is conceived as the women's "arm," helping women to be good Mormons as well as good wives and mothers. From a democratic standpoint, since all young men and, increasingly, young women, are expected to play a role in the running of the Church, authority is diffused among the Saints. This has the effect of creating a cohesive, motivated, and engaged religious community.

Perhaps the most visible symbol of these democratic efforts is the church's missionary program. Though not mandated, it is recommended that all young Mormon men serve on a two-year mission from the ages of eighteen to twenty—and most will, leading to an average of seventy thousand Mormon missionaries in 160 countries at any given time. Mormon women are also able to go, and with the recent lowering of the minimum age for female missionaries from twenty-one to nineteen, more have opted to go. Grueling and strenuous, with little downtime and recreation, these missions serve as testing grounds for faith—of the potential converts and of the missionaries themselves. Most missionaries cite their mission experiences as a pivotal moment for the cementing of their faith.

As the most visible members of the Church, Mormon missionaries are arguably the most easily parodied, as seen most recently in the groundbreaking musical, *The Book of Mormon*. The musical was the hallmark of a "Mormon moment" in contemporary culture, where Mormons found themselves in the spotlight as both media darlings and cultural curios. Seen also in the successful political careers of those like Mitt Romney and John Huntsman, Saints were becoming accepted in positions of leadership, even if they were still quizzed over the bizarre practices of the Mormon past and present. Much of this media attention kept the specter of Mormon "peculiarity" alive enough to keep the LDS Church just slightly outside of the mainstream in the United States. However, the exposure also worked to engage people who would otherwise have little to no familiarity with the Church.

From first visions to the contemporary stage and screen, the Church has evolved and adapted, shifting course when needed, but never straying from the central values and practices that make it distinctive. Though perhaps it will not achieve the hundreds of millions of followers predicted by Stark, the peculiar church and its people will undoubtedly be around in another one hundred years.

See also: Book of Mormon, The; Fundamentalist Mormons; Smith, Joseph (1805–1844).

Further Reading

Bowman, Matthew. 2012. *The Mormon People: The Making of an American Faith*. New York: Random House Trade Paperbacks.

Bushman, Claudia. 2008. *Contemporary Mormonism: Latter-day Saints in Modern America*. Lanham, MD: Rowman & Littlefield Publishers, Inc.

Bushman, Richard. 2008. *A Short History of Mormonism*. New York: Oxford University Press.

Shipps, Jan. 1987. *Mormonism: The Story of a New Religious Tradition*. Urbana: The University of Illinois Press.

Church of Satan, The

The Church of Satan was founded on April 30, 1966, by Anton Szandor LaVey (1930–1997) in San Francisco. LaVey intentionally aligned the establishment of his new religious group with the holiday of Walpurgisnacht, celebrated in northern Europe and Scandinavia as the time when witches would gather to welcome Spring. LaVey's choice of symbolism was designed to set his church in contrast to the Christianity that dominated his cultural milieu. Opposition to Christianity is a frequent theme in LaVey's writings.

LaVey was a colorful character who claimed a dramatic biography that included stints in the circus and carnivals, in bars and nightclubs as an organist, and as a photographer for the police, among other things. He had a real interest in magic and the occult and perhaps an even greater interest in flouting convention. LaVey's musical career made him a minor celebrity and he gradually developed a social circle whose interests mirrored his. He convened "magic circles" at his home in San Francisco for discussions of magic, the occult, and other subjects rarely brought up in polite society. That group provided the basis for the Order of the Trapezoid, which was the precursor of the Church of Satan.

DOCTRINES AND PRACTICES

LaVey's Satanism is rational rather than esoteric. For him, Satan is a metaphor rather than an actual being, let alone one with cloven hooves and a forked tail. LaVey's thinking centers on his understanding of human nature. For him, human beings are no different from other animals. Unfortunately, their desires to act on their instincts—for sexual pleasure, vengeance against enemies, and self-satisfaction, for example—have constantly been frustrated by the restrictions imposed on them by ethical systems. Religions, in LaVey's view, have been the major forces repressing human instincts.

In his major work, *The Satanic Bible*, Christianity is subjected to a particularly scathing critique. LaVey, for example, argues that all of the virtues recommended in the "beatitudes" found in the Gospel of Matthew's "Sermon on the Mount" need to be reversed. For example, he praises the strong instead of the weak, the bold instead of the humble, the iron-handed instead of the poor in spirit, and the victorious instead of the vanquished. Since there is no other world, he argues, individuals should feel free to indulge themselves in this one. The only restriction on self-indulgence that LaVey acknowledges is that the pursuit of personal desires should not cause harm to anyone else.

LaVey insisted that his ideas did not amount only to a philosophy because humans have a need for ritual as well. He staged several rituals, including the baptism of his daughter Zeena and the wedding of two of his followers, to attract public attention, and he conducted other rituals for his inner circle at the headquarters of the Church of Satan at 6114 California St. in San Francisco, which he had painted entirely black. One reflection of LaVey's idea that Satanism represented "controlled selfishness" is his assertion that the most important holiday in the Satanic religion should be the date of one's own birth.

ORGANIZATION

In part because of its emphasis on individualism, the Church of Satan never achieved a high degree of organization. From those who had participated in his "magic circle" gatherings, LaVey formally constituted an inner circle to guide the church, the Council of Nine. But in effect it had little influence. Also, LaVey himself was more interested in staging provocations and pursuing his own interests than in doing the work necessary to establish, guide, and expand a religious group.

Beginning in 1970, the Church experimented with setting up a network of affiliated groups, called "grottoes," but by 1975 this initiative had faded away. It was revived in the late 1980s, only to disappear again. LaVey had a difficult time identifying grotto leaders who could both manage their own groups effectively and maintain sufficient continuity with his teachings. In LaVey's estimation, the increase in revenue and membership that the grotto system offered was not worth the organizational headaches that it caused.

Although the Church of Satan was formally a membership organization, the broad dissemination of LaVey's writings essentially made membership optional. For those who did want to join, it was a straightforward process. One simply wrote to LaVey and paid a fee (originally $100, but by 2018 $225) and received confirmation of membership. At its height, the Church claimed a membership of some ten thousand, though that is surely an exaggeration.

LaVey had a cynical attitude toward fundraising, expressing a willingness to give people whatever they wanted in terms of titles and paraphernalia so long as they sent him cash in return. In the mid-1970s, LaVey developed a scheme to raise more money by selling initiations into the Satanic priesthood. That strategy had substantial consequences.

SCHISMS AND FURTHER DEVELOPMENTS

When LaVey decided to offer priesthoods for cash, Michael Aquino, who had been part of the inner circle of the Church of Satan and who had edited the church's bulletin *The Cloven Hoof,* strongly objected. Aquino eventually split with LaVey in 1975, stating his reasons in a formal letter. Aquino took the degrees of initiation into the Church of Satan very seriously and was appalled by LaVey's willingness to use them to raise funds. He accused LaVey of trying to turn the Church of Satan into a "Church of Anton" and asserted that LaVey's actions showed that he no longer wielded Satanic authority.

Although there had been other, short-lived schisms before 1975, Aquino's departure from LaVey's church to form The Temple of Set was the most significant. While claiming to be the rightful heir of the original Church of Satan, Aquino actually took Satanism in a markedly different direction. Where LaVey had emphasized the use of reason to critique conventional pieties and pretensions and saw Satan as a metaphor for his religious philosophy, Aquino claimed direct inspiration from the ancient Egyptian god, Set. Aquino recorded the revelations in a series of religious texts beginning with the *Diabolicon*, which he had received while still a member of LaVey's group. Despite its initial claims, then, the Temple of Set moved progressively further away from the Church of Satan, while still remaining in the Satanic milieu.

When LaVey died in 1997, his daughter Karla and Blanche Barton who was LaVey's companion and the mother of his son, Satan Xerxes, assumed joint leadership of the Church of Satan. That arrangement, however, did not last. Like Aquino, Karla LaVey asserted that the church under Barton's leadership had departed from the principles enunciated by her father. In an effort to preserve her father's legacy, Karla founded The First Satanic Church. One way that her church attempts to signal its continuity with LaVey is by requiring that all candidates for membership first read *The Satanic Bible*. Karla's church still maintains a minimal website.

John Dewey Allee, an early member of LaVey's Church of Satan, also founded a splinter group, the First Church of Satan. In the early 1990s, Allee produced a newsletter named *Brimstone* that described itself as the official publication of the Ancient Brotherhood of Satan. The Ancient Brotherhood of Satan appears to have mutated into the First Church of Satan, which retained its predecessor's criticism of LaVey's Church of Satan for having forsaken its roots. The website for the First Church of Satan now declares that membership is by invitation only. It directs readers to the public site of the Allee Shadow Tradition, which was founded in 2003. The FAQs on the site show that Allee has moved well beyond LaVeyan Satanism to his own idiosyncratic system.

One group that has gained substantial public attention in the second decade of the twenty-first century for public actions against groups like the Westboro Baptist Church and opposition to any official acts that appear to establish one particular religion is The Satanic Temple. Although that group shares with the Church of Satan a desire to question authority and conventional piety, it claims no affiliation with or descent from LaVey's group.

Despite defections and challenges from competing groups in the Satanic milieu, the Church of Satan founded by LaVey has retained a public presence after the death of its founder. In 2001, Peter H. Gilmore was appointed high priest of the church by Blanche Barton. His wife, Peggy Nadramia, serves as the High Priestess of the church, which is now headquartered in New York City's Hell's Kitchen area. Following in the tradition of LaVey, Gilmore has made multiple media appearances and published a collection of his own essays, *The Satanic Scriptures*.

See also: LaVey, Anton Szandor (1930–1997); Satanic Panic; Satanism.

Further Reading

Aquino, Michael. 2015. *The Church of Satan*, 8th ed. San Francisco: Self-published.

Dyrendal, Asbjørn, James R. Lewis, & Jesper A. Petersen. 2016. *The Invention of Satanism*. Oxford: Oxford University Press.

Gilmore, Peter H. 2016. *The Satanic Scriptures*, 10th anniversary ed. Baltimore, MD: Underworld Amusements.

Introvigne, Massimo. 2016. *Satanism: A Social History*. Leiden: E. J. Brill.

LaVey, Anton Szandor. 1969. *The Satanic Bible*. New York: Avon Books.

Church of the Lord (Aladura)

While Christianity was originally introduced into sub-Saharan Africa by Western missionaries, thousands of independent churches have been established by African leaders who claimed charismatic inspiration outside of the mainline Western denominations. In Nigeria, the most prominent African-Initiated Churches (AICs) have been described as "Aladura" churches, which can trace their origins to prayer groups formed during the 1918 flu epidemic. In the Yoruba language, Aladura refers to "one who prays," the "owners of prayer," or the "praying community." The Church of the Lord (Aladura) is one such group that has expanded from Nigeria to other African countries and even into Europe and the United States. Other groups include the Cherubim and Seraphim Society, the Christ Apostolic Church, and the Celestial Church of Christ.

The Church of the Lord (Aladura) Worldwide (see www.aladura.net) originated in the revelatory experiences of Josiah Olunowo Ositelu (1900–1966) in 1925. On May 19, Ositelu beheld a great light in which appeared a large eye. He then continued to receive visions and revelations. Later, in August, he heard a divine voice tell him that he had been appointed a prophet, just like the biblical Elijah and Elisha. Ositelu quickly gathered some followers but only formally inaugurated his church in 1930. From the beginning Ositelu's movement exhibited schismatic tendencies and observers have counted as many as eighteen breakaway groups throughout the history of the Church. Some, however, eventually reconciled and the schisms did little to inhibit the growth of the Church.

The Church emphasizes its orthodoxy, though elements of traditional Yoruba religion are evident in its practices. It claims to be Pentecostal, biblical, evangelical, and prophetic, with a social ministry and ecumenical outlook.

In addition to Baptism and Communion, the ritual life of the Church centers on the spiritual diagnosis and treatment of problems experienced by its members through prayer and the subsequent intervention of the Holy Spirit. For example, a prayer written during the early years directs members to confess their sins to God and beg for forgiveness and spiritual blessings. Those who pray faithfully are assured that they will be repaid with what is good for them and that they will prosper. Other prayers implore the Holy Spirit to give the petitioner power. A former head of the Church described prayer as the meeting place of heaven and earth, where petitioners receive a revitalization of spiritual strength.

Other rituals of the Church include an annual pilgrimage to a site called Mount Tabieorar, which is actually flat, near the town of Ogere. The pilgrimage takes place from August 10 to 22; members believe that God is particularly receptive to prayers from the site and provide testimonies of what God has done for them during their visits. On the 22nd, the head of the church reads divine messages to the assembled faithful. Connected by a footpath is the Victory Night Ground, more recently constructed as a site where services are held on the third Friday of every month. People of all religions are invited to attend, though the Church views those gatherings as an opportunity for recruitment. The "mercy ground" is another site where members can roll on the ground, either naked or wearing the white robes that are characteristic of many Aladura churches, to express their humility before God.

The Church of the Lord (Aladura) is organized hierarchically. The current primate is Dr. Rufus Okikiola Ositelu, who is the fourth to hold that office. The primate's office in Nigeria is the international headquarters of the group. Under it are various consultative groups that help run the affairs of the Church, which is divided into geographically organized provinces, headed by bishops and composed of at least five dioceses. A diocese is further broken down into zones, which include at least six local churches. The bureaucratic organization administers a worldwide flock that numbers as high as seven million.

See also: African New Religious Movements; Charisma and Leadership in New Religious Movements; Kimbangu, Simon (1887–1951); Movement for the Restoration of the Ten Commandments of God, The; Pentecostalism; Shembe, Isaiah (c. 1865–1935).

Further Reading

Baiyewu, Timothy Olu Wilson. 2014. *The Transformation of Aladura Christianity in Nigeria.* Ph.D. Thesis, University of Beyreuth, Germany. Available at: https://epub.uni-bayreuth.de/2588/1/Tim%27s%20PhD%20Dissertation%20to%20Prof%20Berner.pdf.

Peel, J. D. Y. 1968. *Aladura: A Religious Movement among the Yoruba.* London: Oxford University Press.

Ray, Benjamin. 1993. "Aladura Christianity: A Yoruba Religion." *Journal of Religion in Africa* 23: 266–291.

Turner, Harold W. 1967. *History of an African Independent Church, Vol. I, the Church of the Lord (Aladura).* Oxford: Clarendon Press.

Church Universal and Triumphant, The

The I AM Activity never recovered from its trial on charges of mail fraud in the 1940s. Although the group, founded in 1930 by Guy (1878–1939) and Edna Ballard (1886–1971), continues to spread the message of the Ascended Masters through the Saint Germain Foundation (www.saintgermainfoundation.org), other groups proclaiming similar messages have become more prominent.

In the early 1950s, a former member of the splinter Bridge to Freedom movement, Frances Ekey, started another religious enterprise in the "I AM" tradition, called Lighthouse of Freedom. Its newsletter featured more messages from Ascended Masters, communicated through an anonymous recipient. The anonymous messenger was Mark L. Prophet (1918–1973) who had been contacted by the messenger El Morya early in his life.

By 1958, at El Morya's urging, Prophet had split from Ekey to form the Summit Lighthouse in Washington, D.C. It was directly influenced by the I AM teachings and also by broader theosophical currents of thought. Prophet's group would become the Church Universal and Triumphant (CUT) in 1974. By 1964, Mark's wife Elizabeth (1939–2009), whom he had married in 1963, also began to serve as a messenger of the Ascended Masters. After Mark's sudden death, Elizabeth consolidated her position as the leader of the Church. She identified herself as the "Mother" of the Church and associated herself with Mary, the mother of Jesus, whom she divinized as the "Mother of the Flame" of the holy I AM.

The headquarters of the Church moved from Washington, D.C., where it began, to Colorado, to several sites in southern California in the late 1970s and early 1980s, and then to an expansive ranch in southwestern Montana, near Yellowstone National Park, in the mid-1980s. During the time at the ranch, the group intensified its apocalyptic expectations.

From the beginning the Summit Lighthouse/CUT had an extensive publishing program that brought the teachings of the Ascended Masters to audiences in the United States and beyond. The Prophets also conducted intensive courses, eventually organized under the auspices of Summit University.

BELIEFS AND PRACTICES

The Prophets presented their teachings as both continuing and completing those of the Ballards. They, too, received messages from the Ascended Masters, though from a much larger group that eventually included Mark himself, as the Master Lanello, after his death. The message was similar as well. The Masters teach that the "Mighty I AM Presence" is actually present in every person and that individuals can unite their "Holy Christ Self" with the great I AM through a process called ascension. Over time, the Prophets drew inspiration from various religious traditions, adapting, for example, ideas of karma and reincarnation from eastern religions and also attributing them to Jesus in a series of books on his "lost years" and "lost teachings."

CUT taught that individuals can cultivate the recognition of their true identities through the recitation of simple decrees, such as "I AM a being of violet fire! I AM the purity God desires!" Such statements are viewed as having the power to heal physical illnesses and to relieve mental and spiritual problems. Affirmations play a central role in the regular religious services of CUT, though ministers of the Church also administer sacraments, including baptism, communion, marriage, confession, and last rites.

The Prophets also inherited from the I AM movement an intense patriotism. Both movements saw the United States as playing a pivotal role in human history and embraced a fervent anti-communism. In CUT mythology, that dualistic view of the world was amplified by the belief that fallen angels, known as Nephilim, have long been opposing the Children of God and orchestrating efforts to enslave the human race.

Elizabeth emphasized that to escape the malevolent control of the Nephilim who controlled much of the world, individuals needed to separate themselves. Although CUT tried to effect such separation on one of its California campuses, dubbed Camelot, the most drastic effort occurred in the mid to late 1980s when followers were urged to give up everything and move to the safe haven of the Montana ranch, where they could take refuge from the imminent nuclear war. Some three to four thousand did.

CHALLENGES

After nuclear war did not break out on March 15, 1990, CUT suffered an immediate loss of members, and Elizabeth, like many others before her, had to devise an explanation for the failed prophecy. Her response had two prongs. First, Elizabeth assured her followers that their preparations had indeed forestalled the horror of nuclear war. But she also cautioned them that her warning would remain in effect until 2002. The Church would need to live with the ensuing tension for more than a decade.

Several other challenges to the movement occurred during the 1980s and 1990s. A 1986 lawsuit by a former member alleging various forms of misconduct by the Church resulted in a $1.5 million judgment against CUT. Between 1992 and 1994, the Church also temporarily lost its tax-exempt status because of issues concerning the purchase of weapons by Church members.

But the biggest challenge came with the withdrawal from active leadership by Elizabeth due to her 1998 diagnosis of Alzheimer's disease. Elizabeth formally retired in 2000 and then died in 2009. Although CUT has not identified a successor to Elizabeth as the messenger of the Ascended Masters, it maintains an active presence through its website (www.summitlighthouse.org) and through events held in major cities throughout the world.

See also: Ballard, Guy W. (1878–1939); I AM Activity, The; Millennialism; New Age, The; Prophet, Elizabeth Clare (1939–2009); Theosophy.

Further Reading

Abravanel, Michael. 2013. "The Summit Lighthouse: Its Worldview and Theosophical Heritage." In Olav Hammer & Mikael Rothstein, eds., *Handbook of the Theosophical Current*, pp. 173–191. Leiden: Brill.

Prophet, Elizabeth Clare. 1997. *Violet Flame to Heal Body, Mind, and Soul*. Corwin Springs, MT: Summit University Press.

Prophet, Erin. 2009. *Prophet's Daughter: My Life with Elizabeth Clare Prophet Inside the Church Universal and Triumphant*. Guilford, CT: The Lyons Press.

Whitsel, Bradley C. 2003. *The Church Universal and Triumphant: Elizabeth Clare Prophet's Apocalyptic Movement*. Syracuse, NY: Syracuse University Press.

Conspiracy Theories

Beyoncé and Jay-Z are members of the Illuminati, a global network of elites who secretly control every government. Someone shot JFK from the grassy knoll. The moon landing was faked. Whether a curious concept to entertain or a genuine belief that explanations given for various events are unsatisfactory at best or hiding something sinister at worst, conspiracy theories abound in the world today.

New religious movements are frequent subjects of conspiracy theories, both by members of these groups and by the public. Neither members of new religious movements nor members of the public are more or less likely to believe conspiracy theories: both employ them to make meaning out of events and the world around them.

CONSPIRACY THEORIES IN NEW RELIGIONS

Many conspiracy theories entertained by new religious movements involve some overarching global order or the government. Members of white supremacist religions like Christian Identity often believe that Jews, blacks, or people of color, among other foes, are secretly running the world and attempting to eradicate whites. Believing as they do that white people are the superior race, this conspiracy theory justifies defensive action for such groups. For parents of Indigo Children—children believed to have extraordinary, even supersensory or supernatural, abilities—the overdiagnosis of conditions such as autism and attention-deficit hyperactivity disorder is the result of a global effort by "Big Pharma" to deny the existence of Indigo Children and maintain the hegemony of the pharmaceutical industry.

In some cases, the belief in conspiracies may prompt a group to take action against their "enemies." In the last days of the Peoples Temple Agricultural Project in Guyana, Jim Jones (1931–1978) became increasingly convinced that there was a vast conspiracy of disgruntled ex-members, the media, and the U.S. government attempting to infiltrate and undermine him and his religion. This paranoia contributed directly to the mass murder-suicide in 1978, when, following the visit by U.S. Representative Leo Ryan and the defection of several members, Jones determined that the anticipated end was nigh. Similarly, Shoko Asahara (1955–2018) blamed a vast, global conspiracy on his inability to spread the message of Aum Shinrikyō, a millennialist group, precipitating the sarin gas attacks on the Tokyo Subway in 1995.

Though the mechanisms of Joseph Smith's (1805–1844) murder in a locked jail cell are undisputed, the events leading up to his death are shrouded in suspicion. To this day, members of the Church of Jesus Christ of Latter-day Saints believe their founder was the victim of a conspiracy by law enforcement, an angry mob, and the Illinois government. Why were Smith and his fellow captives left unguarded? Why were they placed in the second-floor jail cell, where there was less chance to escape? Years of persecution shaped the Mormon mentality that they were a religion under siege, a fact that extended to their belief that the prophet's death was not the tragic result of faulty oversight.

CONSPIRACY THEORIES ABOUT NEW RELIGIONS

During the nineteenth century, much of the persecution of Mormons stemmed from the public's belief that they were conspiring to take over the government and establish their Prophet as head of church and country. Following Smith's death, many believed that the remaining Mormons had signed a blood oath to avenge their martyred Prophet. These fears explain, in part, the persistent cultural suspicion that the public should be wary of Mormon "rule."

Notions that "cults" are, by their nature, out to manipulate, control, and provoke violence are consistently employed by the anticult movement. Playing on society's fears has enabled the anticult movement, during its heyday of the 1980s and 1990s and in a diminished capacity in the twenty-first century, to act with impunity against fringe religions. Such was the case during the Satanic Panic of the 1980s, when anticult activists, bolstered by media coverage, perpetuated the notion that there was a vast network of Satanists posing a threat to society and its children in particular. This led to arrests and trials of supposed "Satanists," most of whom were released and the charges against them eventually debunked.

On occasion, the ambiguity of a particular event allows conspiracy theories to linger years after the fact. Many still posit that the 1993 fire at the Mount Carmel Center, which killed over eighty Branch Davidians, was set by the Branch Davidians themselves. While it is certainly possible that, in facing their imminent demise, some Branch Davidians chose to take their own lives, most established accounts that cite the Federal Bureau of Investigation and Bureau of Alcohol, Tobacco, and Firearms as the catalysts counter this alternative narrative.

Rumors have surrounded Scientology since its inception, though more recently, they have involved the current President of the Church, David Miscavige (1960–). Speculation as to the whereabouts of Miscavage's wife has been featured in the media, exacerbated by the refusal to respond to these queries or to have her speak publicly. This rumor has led to defections by celebrities like Leah Remini (1970–) who has fueled this conspiracy with her tell-all book and HBO special.

Their tension with the outside world and "strange" beliefs make new religions ripe for conspiracy theories, both inside and outside. Though it is their very deviation from the norm that might prompt new religions to be proprietary about their beliefs and practices, their secrecy prompts further speculation by the public.

See also: Anticult Movement, The; Asahara, Shoko (1955–2018); Aum Shinrikyō; Branch Davidians; Christian Identity; Church of Jesus Christ of Latter-day Saints, The; Cult; Indigo Children; Jones, Rev. Jim (1931–1978); Peoples Temple; Satanic Panic; Satanism; Scientology; Smith, Joseph (1805–1844).

Further Reading
Barkun, Michael. 2013. *A Culture of Conspiracy: Apocalyptic Visions in Contemporary America*, 2nd ed. Berkeley: University of California Press.
Dyrendal, Asbjørn. 2016. "Conspiracy Theories and New Religious Movements." In James R. Lewis & Inga B. Tollefsen, eds., *The Oxford Handbook of New Religious Movements,* 2nd ed. New York: Oxford University Press.
Robertson, David G. 2015. "Conspiracy Theories and the Study of Alternative and Emergent Religions." *Nova Religio* 19, no. 2: 5–16.
Singler, Beth. 2015. "Big Bad Pharma: The Indigo Child Concept and Biomedical Conspiracy Theories." *Nova Religio* 19, no. 2: 17–29.

Conversion

The linguistic root of the term "conversion" refers to a "turning," both away from something and toward something else. Conversion is a prominent phenomenon in many religions, particularly those that seek converts through missionary outreach. For many, the biblical narratives about Saul of Tarsus who became known as the Christian missionary Paul after a series of dramatic events (see Gal. 1:11–16; Acts 9:1–22; 22:3–21; 26:2–23) have served as a model for understanding conversion.

But the reading of Saul's conversion as sudden, complete, and irreversible simplifies the data in the biblical texts and, hence, the phenomenon they describe. As various studies have shown, conversion is a much more complicated and variable process than it is a single moment. That is certainly the case for new religions.

New religions, particularly in their earliest phases, must attract members to secure their continued existence. In new religions that develop from sectarian conflicts, however, such as the Shakers in the eighteenth century, the Ahmadiyya Muslims in the nineteenth century, or the Branch Davidians in the twentieth century, members may not claim that they have left their former religious group for another, new one. Instead, they may argue or imply that their religions have left them by failing to uphold founding truths, compromising with the world around them, or some other process. Such claims highlight the fact that, although it may have a specific theological meaning within religious traditions, conversion is a scholarly category that is used to classify, analyze, and compare religious phenomena. As such, it is used for different purposes by different scholars, and generalizations about conversion need to be carefully evaluated.

The simplified understanding of conversion as sudden, complete, and irreversible may also obscure the complexity of individuals' religious lives. Some individuals, sometimes identified as seekers, may cobble together idiosyncratic mixes of beliefs and practices from multiple sources; that personal "spirituality" may also be in a continual flux as individuals try out and discard new elements. Many participants in the so-called New Age movement of the late twentieth century, for example, drew on multiple, even conflicting, sources for their own religious purposes. Similarly, many who profess not to practice any religion but instead to have a personal spirituality draw on eclectic sources. Some individuals have extensive "conversion careers" during which they move in and out of religious affiliations.

On their part, some religious groups offer at least some of their benefits without demanding full membership or abandonment of individuals' religious affiliations. The Church of Scientology, for example, provides its spiritual "technology" to anyone who is willing to sign up, and pay, for one of its courses. It also claims that the practice of Scientology is compatible with any religion. Under its founder, Anton LaVey, the Church of Satan exercised only a fitful and rudimentary control over its members and they accordingly constituted a self-designated audience for LaVey's teachings rather than a recognizable social unit.

On the other hand, some new religions exert much more social control over their membership. Scientologists who decide to join the elite "Sea Org" must sign a billion-year contract that signals a decisive break from their former lives. Peoples Temple, particularly in its later phase at the Peoples Temple Agricultural Project in Jonestown, Guyana, sought to serve all the needs of its members, from basic sustenance to social action and religious worldview. Without the dramatic removal of its members to a remote location, the Nation of Islam has also sought to provide for its members' religious, social, material, and educational needs by sponsoring a variety of businesses and other institutions.

Conversion, therefore, is a complex process that can take many forms. It depends not just on the experiences of individuals but also on the ways that religious groups present themselves and what they demand of their adherents; the historical, social, religious, and material contexts in which both individuals and groups are located; and the interactions among those diverse factors.

CHOICE OR BRAINWASHING?

Understanding conversion to new religions has been complicated not only by the complexity of the phenomenon itself and the various ways in which it has been treated by scholars but also by a concerted effort of cultural opponents of new religions to deny any legitimacy to the processes by which people have become members. Beginning in the early 1970s, a loose coalition of parents and others began to raise alarms about their, often adult, children who had joined groups like the Unification Church or The Children of God (now The Family International). Unwilling to believe that individuals could have joined such groups of their own volition, the opponents of "cults" developed the idea that members had somehow been duped into joining.

A variety of images were used to describe the process of "unwillingly" becoming a member of a new religious group, including "on-the-spot hypnosis" or "programming," but they all focused on the passivity of susceptible individuals and their exploitation by unscrupulous leaders. On such a basis, many anticult activists decided that individuals needed to be rescued from these groups. In the early 1970s, Ted Patrick (1930–) became one of the most widely known exponents of the process of "deconversion" or "deprogramming."

Deprogramming rested on a series of assumptions about membership in new religions that were easy to grasp. Young, vulnerable "children" had been hoodwinked into membership by wily manipulators. Their very decisions showed that they were not in their right minds. Consequently, they needed to be returned to their former status. Deprogramming, which often involved kidnapping, the use of force, and other questionable practices, was what could return them to "normal" life. Capitalizing on fears about brainwashing conducted in prisoners of war camps during the Korean War, deprogramming and related concepts found a receptive audience in the general public.

Much more a delegitimizing tactic than a description and analysis of the process of conversion, brainwashing has nonetheless secured a hold on the public imagination that it has yet to relinquish. For a time, the brainwashing theory was even taken seriously by courts. Eventually, thanks both to its repudiation by organizations like the American Psychological Association and the efforts of scholars who subjected the brainwashing hypothesis to empirical examination, it lost substantial influence in some quarters even as it continued to shape popular understandings of new religions.

The most devastating refutation of the brainwashing hypothesis came from sociologist Eileen Barker's meticulous study of the Unification Church in Great Britain. Ultimately, Barker found that among those who even went so far as to visit a Unification Church center, only about half of 1 percent would be associated in any way with the movement in two years, and by no means all of them as full-time members. Barker showed decisively that nearly all who came into contact with the Unification Church were quite capable of resisting its attraction. If the Church had been practicing brainwashing, it was certainly not any good at it. There are multiple indications that other new religions have success rates that are much more similar to the Unification Church than they are to the inflated fears of anticult activists.

MODELS OF CONVERSION

Since brainwashing cannot explain conversion to new religions, this provides openings for other explanations. Scholars have developed both general models of conversion and ones specifically concerning new religions. Two of the most prominent focus on the stages through which individuals typically move toward conversion.

Lewis Rambo, for example, charts a path from the general context, which can either promote or restrict religious change, to the experience of crisis by an individual, which can, in turn, spur a quest to seek new ways of understanding one's life. The stage of interaction is when searching individuals encounter representatives of a specific group; if those interactions are positive, they can prompt commitment to a new religious perspective and group. Multiple consequences then follow, often including a revaluation of the recent convert's past, including religious commitments and social relationships and movement into a new identity, social group, and religious perspective.

That general model of conversion fits with empirical observations of new religions. The emphasis on context, and particularly the constraints it may exercise, suggests that not everyone is a potential convert, despite some of the more irresponsible claims of the contemporary anticult movement. The focus on an individual's quest for new meanings and new social situations emphasizes the active roles that individuals play in "converting themselves" rather than their passivity in the face of overwhelming, persuasive forces. The focus on the consequences of conversion directs attention to the ways in which converts are, or are not, integrated into the new groups that they join, how groups strive to maintain and increase the commitments of converts, and how a lack of ongoing alignment between what individuals are looking for and what groups actually provide can contain the seeds of further crises that can lead to new episodes in individuals' conversion careers.

Based on fieldwork with the early Unification Church in California, John Lofland and Rodney Stark developed a theory of conversion to a "deviant perspective," which Lofland modified in a later essay based on new information about the same group. The original essay directs its attention to both predisposing conditions that characterize someone before contact with the group and situational contingencies that lead to a successful recruitment/conversion. Succinctly put, they argue that for conversion to occur a person must experience acute tension within a religious problem-solving perspective: that is, people who are satisfied with their lives and people who are not religious are less likely to convert. Moreover, the perceived tension leads someone to self-define as a religious seeker. Like Rambo, Lofland and Stark emphasize that a potential convert must encounter the group at a turning point in her or his life. They also stress that an affective bond must be reaffirmed or created and attachments outside of the group must be rejected or neutralized through intensive interactions if one is to become a "deployable agent" of the group. Lofland adds both more detail and nuance in his later essay, and he specifically urges reconsideration of the image of the convert as a passive actor through whom social forces operate. Instead, he commends a more interactionist approach in which potential converts play active roles in bringing about and maintaining or abandoning their conversions.

As scholars of religion in general and scholars of new religions in particular have increasingly turned their attention to the phenomenon of conversion, an increasingly complex account of it has developed. Many Neopagans, for example, eschew the language of conversion and prefer to describe their participation in contemporary Paganism as a "coming home" or realization of what they had implicitly known all along. Others, including many in New Age circles, prefer a language of self-discovery or realization to one of conversion, which is associated with coercive missionary efforts. But many analysts would still include such phenomena under the category of conversion.

The advent of the internet and the presence of many new religions, sometimes solely, on the worldwide web has also made matters of association or affiliation much more evidently complex. As the contexts in which new religions originate and grow have changed, so have the ways in which people engage with them. And scholars continue to refine the ways in which they describe and analyze membership in new religions.

See also: Anticult Movement, The; Brainwashing; Children of God (The Family International); Church of Satan, The; Disaffiliation and Ex-membership in New Religious Movements; Insider/Outsider Problem, The; Nation of Islam, The; Patrick, Ted (1930–); Peoples Temple; Scientology; Seekers; Unification Church, The.

Further Reading
Barker, Eileen. 1984. *The Making of a Moonie: Choice or Brainwashing?* Oxford: Basil Blackwell.
Lofland, John. 1977. "'Becoming a World-Saver' Revisited." *American Behavioral Scientist* 20: 805–818.
Lofland, John, & Rodney Stark. 1965. "On Becoming a World-Saver: A Theory of Conversion to a Deviant Perspective." *American Sociological Review* 30: 862–875.
Rambo, Lewis R. 1993. *Understanding Religious Conversion.* New Haven, CT: Yale University Press.
Rambo, Lewis R., & Charles E. Farhadian, eds. 2014. *The Oxford Handbook of Religious Conversion.* New York: Oxford University Press.
Richardson, James T., ed. 1978. *Conversion Careers: In and Out of the New Religions.* Beverly Hills, CA: Sage.

Cosmotheism

After Timothy McVeigh executed the devastating bombing of the Alfred P. Murrah Federal Building in Oklahoma City in 1995, in which 168 people died and more than 500 were injured, the sources of his inspiration quickly came to light. McVeigh was deeply troubled by what he saw as the unjustified government actions against the Branch Davidians near Waco, Texas, two years earlier. But his specific actions were modeled on the opening scene in a previously obscure novel, *The Turner Diaries*, published by the far right ideologue, William Pierce (1933–2002) under the pseudonym Andrew MacDonald. The novel is told in retrospect from the perspective of the one hundredth anniversary of the "Great Revolution" that was inaugurated by a truck bombing of the Federal Bureau of Investigation's headquarters in the Hoover Building in Washington, D.C.

Pierce held a PhD in Physics and briefly taught at a state university but he devoted most of his life to radical political causes. He was associated with George Lincoln Rockwell's American Nazi party, George Wallace's bid for the presidency, and Willis Carto's anti-semitic National Youth Alliance before founding his own white nationalist organization, the National Alliance, in 1974.

Pierce's racist and anti-semitic views permeate *The Turner Diaries*. The immediate trigger for the novel's fictional action is the passing of the "Cohen Act," which outlawed all private ownership of guns in the United States. In response, a group of revolutionaries, fueled by indignation at the government's threats to personal liberties and its imposition of a liberal policy of racial equality, undertakes to overthrow the system. The novel is permeated with religious imagery. The titular character, Earl Turner, is hailed as a martyr; after his initiation into "The Order," he feels born again. The revolutionaries see themselves as fulfilling God's grand design for racial purity and a secure homeland, and understand their beliefs as constituting a living faith.

Though the novel uses language that clearly connects to various Christian concepts, it renounces connections to all established religions. In fact, Pierce developed his own religious worldview of "Cosmotheism" beginning in the 1970s. Drawing on diverse sources, including Nietzsche, Cosmotheism expresses a millennialist vision. In contrast to *The Turner Diaries*, it seeks a progressive evolution of the white race in accordance with nature that will secure its survival, protect its uniqueness, and improve its distinct characteristics, and would include the racial purification of vast swaths of Europe, the Americas, Australia, New Zealand, and even southern Africa. All would become all-white societies once again animated by Aryan social and spiritual values (https://natall.com/). The National Alliance promotes "a New Consciousness, a New Order; a New People."

Pierce's ideology has inspired multiple other violent actions, including those of Robert Matthews of the white supremacist group The Order in the early 1980s.

See also: Branch Davidians; Christian Identity; Millennialism; Violence and New Religious Movements.

Further Reading

Gallagher, Eugene V. 1997. "God and Country: Revolution as a Religious Imperative on the Radical Right." *Terrorism and Political Violence* 9: 63–79.

Macdonald, Andrew (William Pierce). 1978. *The Turner Diaries*, 2nd ed. Fort Lee, NJ: Barricade Books.

Course in Miracles, A

HISTORY

A Course in Miracles records a collection of revelations received by Helen Schucman (1909–1981) over seven years from a disembodied "Voice" that she identified as Jesus Christ. The course was published in 1976 in three volumes: the *Text*, the *Workbook*, and a *Manual for Teachers*. Schucman received other material from the Voice, but neither she nor readers of the *Course* have accorded it the same authority as the *Course* itself.

When she received the *Course*, Schucman was working as a research psychologist at Columbia University's College of Physicians and Surgeons under the direction of William Thetford (1923–1988). She and Thetford had a fractious relationship from the beginning. In June of 1965 during a personal meeting, Thetford told Schucman that "there must be another way" for them to relate to each other. They came to see the *Course* as outlining the principles of that other way.

Although Schucman was the scribe for the *Course*, others played important roles in its reception, editing, and dissemination. From the beginning, Thetford served as a crucial sounding board and supporter; in addition, he typed the first manuscripts from Schucman's notes. Early on, Kenneth Wapnick (1942–2013) worked closely with Schucman and Thetford on editing the manuscript. In 1975, Judith Skutch and her husband Robert established the Foundation for Inner Peace, which became the publisher and the holder of the trademark for *A Course in Miracles*. It maintains a website (www.acim.org) of digital resources related to the *Course*, including a list of study groups throughout the world.

The *Course* continues to have a broad audience. But since there is no central organization that controls the dissemination and reception of the *Course*, many individuals have positioned themselves as teachers of its principles. Despite some efforts to enforce orthodoxy, diverse understandings have proliferated.

BELIEFS AND PRACTICES

The *Course* describes itself as "a course in mind training" (*Text*: 13). The reader is admonished to "seek not to change the world but choose to change your mind about the world" (*Text*: 415). It emphasizes that each individual is a Son of God. Humans, however, remain asleep about their true identities. Jesus is important in the *Course* because he awoke to awareness of his true nature; he therefore constitutes a role model for what anyone can achieve.

The gnostic perspective of the *Course*, which declares this world to be illusory and without meaning; pain, suffering, and evil to be parts of a self-generated dream; human beings to be ignorant of their true nature; and Jesus's suffering and death to be figments of a guilty imagination, also determines the way in which Jesus's resurrection is depicted. In the *Text*, the Voice asserts that "Your resurrection is your reawakening. I am the model for rebirth, but rebirth itself is merely the dawning on your mind of what is already in it" (*Text*: 86). Rather than being the unique agent of human salvation, Jesus is the example of what every individual can accomplish.

In the *Course*, "miracles" are understood "as an expression of an inner awareness of Christ and the acceptance of His Atonement" (*Text*: 4). The *Text* further emphasizes that "Miracles are everyone's right" and that they can be received through prayer, in which individuals receive God's love and then express it to others (*Text*: 1). Miracles involve accepting God's forgiveness and then extending it to others (see *Text*: 2). Miracles, however, are a temporary need, given the condition in which humans find themselves. The *Course* assures its readers that "When you return to your original form of communication with God by direct revelation, the need for miracles is over" (*Text*: 4).

The central ritual for the audience of *A Course in Miracles* is detailed in the *Workbook*. That text provides a set of 365 exercises that are to be undertaken one a day over the course of a year. The *Workbook* aims to make the theoretical framework of the *Text* meaningful by aligning the individual's mind and perception with the fundamental ideas of the *Course*. Every lesson is arranged in a similar fashion, beginning with a simple affirmation, followed by directions about how to apply the idea it expresses. Lesson 40, for example, focuses on cultivating a positive personal identity as one "blessed as a Son of God" (*Workbook*, 62). The reader is directed to make that affirmation frequently throughout the day, adding whatever attributes the reader thinks a Son of God would have.

Practitioners reverently refer to *A Course in Miracles* as "the Course" and spend considerable time studying the books of the Course for the wisdom they are held to possess. (Philip Sermanni/Dreamstime.com)

The *Workbook* ritualizes an individual's encounter with the *Course* but it also allows substantial flexibility in how any individual will enact the daily lessons. It does not require that the lessons be practiced in a community setting. The loose guidance built into the *Course* itself virtually guarantees that there will be substantial variation in how its principles will be put into practice.

RECEPTION AND CONTROVERSIES

Since Schucman and Thetford declined to exercise control over the fate of the *Course*, the leadership vacuum was filled by individuals who claimed to teach the principles of the *Course*. Kenneth Wapnick and Gerald Jampolosky were early interpreters who gained audiences; in the 1990s, Marianne Williams reached a wide audience with *A Return to Love*. New teachers continue to appear.

The *Course* also received harsh critiques from a variety of psychologists and other secular figures. Some, who generally resonate with the direction to find one's own inner teacher, find the Christian language of the *Course* off-putting. Others find that the *Course* promotes passivity in the face of urgent political challenges. From another angle, evangelical Christians have found its teaching about Jesus to be heretical. Nonetheless, the *Course* continues to inspire readers throughout the world.

See also: New Age, The.

Further Reading

Anonymous. 1975. *A Course in Miracles* (*Volume One: Text*; *Volume Two: Workbook*; *Volume Three: Manual for Teachers*). Tiburon, CA: Foundation for Inner Peace.

Miller, D. Patrick. 1997. *The Complete Story of the Course: The History, the People, and the Controversies behind a Course in Miracles*. Berkeley, CA: Fearless Books.

Wapnick, Kenneth. 1991. *Absence from Felicity: The Story of Helen Schucman and her Scribing of a Course in Miracles*. Roscoe, NY: Foundation for "A Course in Miracles."

PRIMARY SOURCE DOCUMENT

Preface to *A Course in Miracles* (1977)

This Preface was written in 1977, in response to many requests for a brief introduction to A Course in Miracles. The first two parts—"How It Came" and "What It Is"—Helen Schucman wrote herself; the final part—"What It Says"—was written by the process of inner dictation described in the Preface.

How It Came

A Course in Miracles began with the sudden decision of two people to join in a common goal. Their names were Helen Schucman and William Thetford, Professors of Medical Psychology at Columbia University's College of Physicians and Surgeons in New York City. It does not matter who they were, except that the story shows that with God all things are possible. They were anything but spiritual. Their relationship with each other was difficult and often strained, and they were concerned with personal and professional acceptance and status. In general, they had considerable investment in the values of the world. Their lives were hardly in accord with anything that the Course advocates. Helen, the one who received the material, describes herself:

Psychologist, educator, conservative in theory and atheistic in belief, I was working in a prestigious and highly academic setting. And then something happened that triggered a chain of events I could never have predicted. The head of my department unexpectedly announced that he was tired of the angry and aggressive feelings our attitudes reflected, and concluded that "there must be another way." As if on cue, I agreed to help him find it. Apparently this Course is the other way.

Although their intention was serious, they had great difficulty in starting out on their joint venture. But they had given the Holy Spirit the "little willingness" that, as the Course itself was to emphasize again and again, is sufficient to enable Him to use any situation for His purposes and provide it with His power.

To continue Helen's first-person account:

Three startling months preceded the actual writing, during which time Bill suggested that I write down the highly symbolic dreams and descriptions of the strange images that were coming to me. Although I had grown more accustomed to the unexpected by that time, I was still very surprised when I wrote, "This is a course in miracles." That was my introduction to the Voice. It made no sound, but seemed to be giving me a kind of rapid, inner dictation which I took down in a shorthand notebook. The writing was never automatic. It could be interrupted at any time and later picked up again. It made me very uncomfortable, but it never seriously occurred to me to stop. It seemed to be a special assignment I had somehow, somewhere agreed to complete. It represented a truly collaborative venture between Bill and myself, and much of its significance, I am sure, lies in that. I would take down what the Voice "said" and read it to him the next day, and he typed it from my dictation. I expect he had his special assignment, too. Without his encouragement and support I would never have been able to fulfil mine. The whole process took about seven years. The Text came first, then the Workbook for Students, and finally the Manual for Teachers. Only a few minor changes have been made. Chapter titles and subheadings have been inserted in the Text, and some of the more personal references that occurred at the beginning have been omitted. Otherwise the material is substantially unchanged.

The names of the collaborators in the recording of the Course do not appear on the cover because the Course can and should stand on its own. It is not intended to become the basis for another cult. Its only purpose is to provide a way in which some people will be able to find their own Internal Teacher. . . .

In-1. This is a course in miracles. *2 It is a required course. 3 Only the time you take it is voluntary. 4 Free will does not mean that you can establish the curriculum. 5 It means only that you can elect what you want to take at a given time. 6 The course does not aim at teaching the meaning of love, for that is beyond what can be taught. 7 It does aim, however, at removing the blocks to the awareness of love's presence, which is your natural inheritance. 8 The opposite of love is fear, but what is all-encompassing can have no opposite.*

In-2. This course can therefore be summed up very simply in this way:
2 Nothing real can be threatened.
3 Nothing unreal exists.
4 Herein lies the peace of God. . . .

T-1.I.1. There is no order of difficulty in miracles. 2 One is not "harder" or "bigger" than another. 3 They are all the same. 4 All expressions of love are maximal.

T-1.I.2. Miracles as such do not matter. 2 The only thing that matters is their Source, which is far beyond evaluation.

T-1.I.3. Miracles occur naturally as expressions of love. 2 The real miracle is the love that inspires them. 3 In this sense everything that comes from love is a miracle.

T-1.I.4. All miracles mean life, and God is the Giver of life. 2 His Voice will direct you very specifically. 3 You will be told all you need to know.

T-1.I.5. Miracles are habits, and should be involuntary. 2 They should not be under conscious control. 3 Consciously selected miracles can be misguided.

T-1.I.6. Miracles are natural. 2 When they do not occur something has gone wrong.

T-1.I.7. Miracles are everyone's right, but purification is necessary first.

T-1.I.8. Miracles are healing because they supply a lack; they are performed by those who temporarily have more for those who temporarily have less.

T-1.I.9. Miracles are a kind of exchange. 2 Like all expressions of love, which are always miraculous in the true sense, the exchange reverses the physical laws. 3 They bring more love both to the giver and the receiver.

T-1.I.10. The use of miracles as spectacles to induce belief is a misunderstanding of their purpose.

T-1.I.11. Prayer is the medium of miracles. 2 It is a means of communication of the created with the Creator. 3 Through prayer love is received, and through miracles love is expressed.

T-1.I.12. Miracles are thoughts. 2 Thoughts can represent the lower or bodily level of experience, or the higher or spiritual level of experience. 3 One makes the physical, and the other creates the spiritual. . . .

T-1.III.1. I am in charge of the process of Atonement, which I undertook to begin. 2 When you offer a miracle to any of my brothers, you do it to *yourself* and me. 3 The reason you come before me is that I do not need miracles for my own Atonement, but I stand at the end in case you fail temporarily. 4

My part in the Atonement is the cancelling out of all errors that you could not otherwise correct. 5 When you have been restored to the recognition of your original state, you naturally become part of the Atonement yourself. 6 As you share my unwillingness to accept error in yourself and others, you must join the great crusade to correct it; listen to my voice, learn to undo error and act to correct it. 7 The power to work miracles belongs to you. 8 I will provide the opportunities to do them, but you must be ready and willing. 9 Doing them will bring conviction in the ability, because conviction comes through accomplishment. 10 The ability is the potential, the achievement is its expression, and the Atonement, which is the natural profession of the children of God, is the purpose.

Source: *A Course in Miracles*, copyright ©1992, 1999, 2007 by the Foundation for Inner Peace, 448 Ignacio Blvd., #306, Novato, CA 94949, www.acim.org and info@acim.org, used with permission. Available at: https://acourseinmiraclesnow.com/read-acim-online/.

Courts and New Religious Movements

In many countries, courts have the ability to determine what qualifies as a religion. Such is the case in the United States because of certain constitutional (the First Amendment) and legislative (such as the Johnson Amendment) standards related to religious freedom. Seemingly, it is the job of the court (and perhaps the Internal Revenue Service) to simply allow all religions to practice unmolested; however, this has rarely been the case. At their best, courts prosecute genuine wrongdoing of predatory religions and religious practitioners and respect the right to free exercise of even the most fringe religious groups. At their worse, courts act as arbiters of "true" versus "false" religious practices. In other words, courts have the power to write into law those groups that some would qualify as "cults," a pejorative label that is hard to shed and usually says much more about the person, or system, using it than the group to which it applies.

NEW RELIGIOUS MOVEMENTS AND RELIGIOUS LIBERTY

Unsurprisingly, new religious movements have served as test cases for religious liberty, particularly in the United States, often setting legal precedent for future cases of religious practice. Whenever practitioners of a new religious movement are brought to court, it is very often the religion itself that is on trial, thus raising the questions: how free *is* the free exercise of religion and for whom is it free?

Such was certainly the case for members of the Church of Jesus Christ of Latter-day Saints who, throughout the nineteenth century, were the frequent target of judicial censure primarily for their most controversial practice: plural marriage. Despite the often vigorous defenses mounted by both polygamist men and plural wives at the sacred importance of the practice, most Mormon polygamists tried were convicted. In the process of prosecuting alleged polygamists, court precedent was changed, seemingly to ensure conviction: the Morrill Anti-Bigamy Act (1862) made bigamy illegal; juries in trials of polygamists were to be selected by the federal, not state officials; and spousal privilege (where one spouse cannot be asked to testify against another) was waived to ensure that plural wives could be put on the stand. Eventually, George Reynolds, who had been convicted under the Morrill Act, appealed his conviction on First Amendment grounds, reaching the Supreme Court in 1879; in a unanimous decision, the court decided against Reynolds, arguing that a law banning polygamy was constitutional, though commuting his sentence of hard labor.

The Supreme Court was equally unfriendly to pleas made on behalf of two members of the Native American Church in 1989. Alfred Leo Smith and Galen Black were fired from their jobs at an Oregon drug rehabilitation clinic and denied unemployment benefits because they had ingested peyote, an hallucinogenic substance derived from cacti, as part of a religious ritual. Peyote was illegal under Oregon law, but the American Indian Religious Freedom Act (1978) had been passed to protect the religious use of the substance. *Employment Division v. Smith* reached the Supreme Court in 1990; in a 5–4 decision, the court decided against Smith and Black, arguing that First Amendment rights did not inoculate the plaintiffs from complying with state law. The majority opinion stated that while the First Amendment forbade the government from prohibiting the free exercise of religion, Oregon's ban against peyote was not targeted at a specific religion, but was a general rule for all and thus not a violation of free exercise. Since that time, legal measures have been taken to further protect peyote use for (quite literally) card-carrying members of the Native American Church.

Three years later, the Supreme Court set precedent in favor of a new religious movement's religious liberty in the case, *Church of the Lukumi Babalu Aye v. Hialeah*. The Church of Babalu, whose members practiced Santería, an Afro-Caribbean religion derived from Cuba, practiced animal sacrifice as part of their rituals. After establishing their presence in Hialeah, Florida, the City Council issued a ban on such practices. The Supreme Court heard the case in 1993 and ruled unanimously for the Church of Babalu, citing the clearly discriminatory nature of the ban (no commercial slaughterhouses were forced to stop operations, and their practices were arguably less humane than those of the Church). The win was perceived as a watershed by members of new religious movements, who feared that their ability to practice their religions unmolested would always be contested, simply for going against the norm.

However, acknowledgment of discriminatory practices does not necessarily equate to acceptance of all new religious practices and traditions. Bias persists, as scholars have argued it did in the trial of Branch Davidians following the deadly fire in 1993 at the Mount Carmel Center in Waco, Texas. Over the course of the fifty-one-day siege, four members of the Bureau of Alcohol, Tobacco, and Firearms and eighty-two members of the Branch Davidians were killed; however, criminal proceedings were only brought against Branch Davidians, a number of whom served prison sentences. In the civil trials that ensued, members of law enforcement were granted immunity and exculpatory evidence was often ignored;

ultimately no civil charges were effectively sought against the Federal Bureau of Investigation.

Fear also persists that First Amendment protections could be abused and lead to the creation of inauthentic religions. Such is the case for the Church of the Flying Spaghetti Monster (Pastafarianism), whose members have sought recognition as a real religion under the law in various countries, including the United States; as of 2019, judges in New Zealand and the United States have ruled it satiric religion. (Its members can perform marriages, however.) The Church of Scientology has also experienced its share of legal battles—most related to silencing the voices of its accusers but also related to its status as a legitimate religion; it has won and lost and won again its tax-exempt status over the years. Scientology is often viewed askance by the courts of law and public opinion for its secrecy and targeting of ex-members and critics with lawsuits—a view that has led to a belief that the Church exploits the legal system and its constitutional protection to protect potentially criminal practices. The Church staunchly denies such claims and insists that it is simply exercising its rights, under the law, to defend itself and to ensure its sustainability as an institution.

LEGAL ISSUES AND CRIMINAL PROCEEDINGS

The question of religious liberty is always a factor when court cases against new religious movements arise; the more "accepted" a person's religion, the less likely his or her beliefs will be tried for their legitimacy if standing trial. This does not mean that cases involving new religious movements are always void of criminality on the part of the practitioner or the religion. Though the reasons for prosecuting new religious movements, as well as their leaders and members, are various, there are several primary "hubs," around which such cases coalesce: child abuse, sexual deviance, and violence.

Christian Scientists, who eschew medical intervention in favor of prayer and a focus on "right thinking," have been tried numerous times for child neglect. In instances when a child's life is at stake, Christian Scientists who choose to eschew medical treatment may be considered liable under the law if the child dies or serious medical harm occurs. The majority of cases brought against Christian Scientist parents in such cases have favored the view that the child's right to life trumps the parents' right to free exercise; this is seen as particularly true in cases where a child is too young to assent to their parents' religious beliefs. In other instances, false accusations of child abuse led to the prosecution of innocent parties. At the height of the Satanic Panic in the 1980s, when fears abounded that Satanists were performing rituals on children, daycare workers at the McMartin Preschool in Manhattan Beach, California, were indicted on accusations of Satanic sexual abuse. The trial lasted for six years, ultimately resulting in the dismissal of all charges when the accusations brought by parents were revealed to be unfounded.

Sexual abuse of minors was at the heart of the trial of Warren Jeffs (1955–), leader of the Fundamentalist Latter-day Saints (FLDS)—though in this instance, the accusations were well founded. Following the discontinuation of plural marriage by the Church of Jesus Christ of Latter-day Saints in the late nineteenth century, some Mormons split from the Church, and some founded their own groups to continue practicing polygamous marriages. The FLDS is one such group, though its system of plural marriage is by no means that of other Fundamentalist Mormon sects. Jeffs oversaw all marriages, often between underage girls and (much) older men. Following a raid of the Yearning for Zion Ranch in 2008, Jeffs was tried and ultimately convicted of sexual assault of a minor and aggravated sexual assault against a child, both of whom were his wives (aged 12 and 15); other members of FLDS were convicted of similar charges.

In 2019, NXIVM, specifically its founder Keith Raniere (1960–), supposed "recruiter" Alison Mack (1982–), and other executives, were brought to trial on accusations of kidnapping and sex trafficking (not of minors). Allegations of sexual abuse and unlawful imprisonment were raised following several exposés by former female members of NXIVM who were recruited and compelled to perform sexual acts on prospective clients.

Occasionally, acts of violence have led to the prosecution of new religious groups. During the 1980s, members of the Osho movement, who for a brief time operated their own city, Rajneeshpuram in Oregon, were accused of bioterrorism, namely, by poisoning locals who were antagonistic to the group. However, it was their illegal wiretapping operation, which ultimately led to criminal charges and convictions of several high-ranking members of the group and the deportation of its leader, Shree Bhagwan Rajneesh (1931–1990). Following the deadly sarin gas attack in a Tokyo subway in 1995, several members of the Japanese new religious group, Aum Shinrikyō, were brought to trial. Its founder, Shoko Asahara (1955–2018), was tried, convicted, and ultimately executed in 2018 for his role in the attack.

It is not only new religious movements but their opponents who have seen the inside of a courtroom for potentially criminal actions. The anticult movement came to prominence during the 1980s and 1990s, beginning as a diffuse group of parents concerned for their children who had joined new religious movements and growing into a well-oiled system of activists and professional "deprogrammers," who would extricate people from these groups for a fee. However, the actions of certain deprogrammers, such as founder of FREECOG (Free the Children of God) Ted Patrick (1930–), were ultimately deemed equally dangerous as the tactics employed by alleged "cults." Patrick was tried and convicted for conspiracy and kidnapping, leading to a prison sentence and fines, and a subsequent backlash against the methods of deprogramming and the anticult movement in general.

See also: Anticult Movement, The; Asahara, Shoko (1955–2018); Aum Shinrikyō; Branch Davidians; Children and New Religious Movements; Christian Science; Church of Jesus Christ of Latter-day Saints, The; Cult; Deprogramming; FREECOG (Free the Children of God); Fundamentalist Mormons; Law Enforcement and New Religious Movements; Marriage and Relationships in New Religious Movements; Native American Church, The; NXIVM; Pastafarianism (Church of the Flying Spaghetti Monster); Patrick, Ted (1930–);Rajneesh, Shree Bhagwan/Osho (1931–1990); Rajneesh/Osho Movement, The; Santería; Satanic Panic; Satanism; Scientology; Sex, Sexuality, and New Religious Movements; Violence and New Religious Movements.

Further Reading

Bradney, Anthony. 2014. "Legal Issues." In George D. Chyrssides & Benjamin E. Zeller, eds., *The Bloomsbury Companion to New Religious Movements*. London: Bloomsbury Academic.

Davis, Derek H., & Barry Hankins, eds. 2003. *New Religious Movements and Religious Liberty in America*. Waco, TX: Baylor University Press.

Lucas, Phillip Charles, & Thomas Robbins, eds. 2004. *New Religious Movements in the Twenty-First Century: Legal, Political, and Social Challenges in Global Perspective*. London: Routledge Press.

Richardson, James T. 1998. "Law and Minority Religions: 'Positive' and 'Negative' Uses of the Legal System." *Nova Religio* 2, no. 1: 93–107.

Richardson, James T. 2004. "Legal Dimensions of New Religious Movements." In *The Oxford Handbook of New Religious Movements*. New York: Oxford University Press.

Crowley, Aleister (1875–1947)

BEGINNINGS

Once called "the Wickedest Man in the World," Aleister Crowley has enjoyed pop cultural relevance and infamy beyond his years. He has been known more for his decadent lifestyle and persona than for his religious innovations and writings. But Crowley was prolific in writing, publishing consistently on Western esotericism and occult subjects throughout his life, including the very scriptures that would form the basis of his religious movement, Thelema.

Born Edward Alexander Crowley II, son of the heir to a lucrative brewing business, Crowley tested boundaries at an early age. Following the death of his devoutly Christian father (a member of the Plymouth Brethren, a conservative evangelical Christian movement), when he was eleven, Crowley began to question the strict Christian moralism of his upbringing and the historical truth of the Bible. Rebellious in behavior, as well as action, his mother dubbed him "the Beast," a name he would eventually appropriate, calling himself "Beast 666," in reference to the demonic creature of the same name in Revelation 13. Crowley also formally adopted the name Aleister while at Cambridge University

WESTERN OCCULTIST

It was after university and in the midst of his travels—he was an accomplished mountaineer—that Crowley formally encountered occult religious circles and ideas. In 1898, he was initiated into the Hermetic Order of the Golden Dawn. His time in the religious group was fraught with conflict, particularly with fellow member, poet William Yeats, who criticized his lavish lifestyle, alleged drug use, and burgeoning bisexuality. Finding himself edged out of the central leadership of the group, Crowley embarked on travels once again, which yielded significant results.

While in Egypt in 1904, Crowley reported having a mystical experience, wherein a being named Aiwass, who claimed to be the messenger of the god

Horus, revealed a message that Crowley would transcribe into *The Book of Law*. The text contains his most famous phrase, "Do what thou wilt shall be the whole of the law," which implied that the individual Will was the ultimate in the universe. That came to be the founding principle of Thelema. Reflecting his eclectic esoteric influences, Thelema placed emphasis on magical and mystical practices, neopagan notions of imminent divinity, spiritualist beliefs in the possibility of communion with higher planes, and Hindu and Buddhist meditative practices. Scholars typically find Crowley's theology difficult to pin down, a fact that reflects his absorption of the various cultures that surrounded him.

Over the years, Crowley continued to add to the Thelemic sacred canon and spread his message through his writings and his eventual creation of the A.A. (not to be confused with Alcoholics Anonymous), which was an occult order focused on the eternal advancement of humanity. Placing himself in direct competition with other occult groups, including the Golden Dawn and the Ordo Templi Orientis, the establishment of the A.A. led to a period of grappling for authority during the 1910s. Since it was the newest of the occult groups, Crowley, once again, found himself pushed out by those more established in esoteric circles. In response, Crowley continued to travel, beginning in the United States, then later to Tunisia, Paris, and Berlin. While he faced a seemingly entrenched power structure in England, Crowley felt freer to spread his particular brand of Thelemic occultism in other areas of the globe.

LEGACY

Plagued by ill health and geographically circumscribed by the outbreak of World War II, Crowley returned to England, where he lived a quieter existence than before. He was still writing until the end. Having wiled away his fortunes and eluded permanent success as an established religious figure, Crowley died in poverty and obscurity in 1947. However, his influence seemed to wax after his death. Brought into the mainstream by popular figures like the Beatles, who put his picture on their album, *Sargent Pepper's Lonely Hearts Club Band* and referred to him in song, Crowley has experienced a renaissance of sorts among modern occultists, who view him as a founding father not only of Thelema but of many New Age and occult religious groups, such as Gerald Gardner's Wicca and L. Ron Hubbard's Scientology. By his own estimation, he was larger than life; it seems in his death that this is true.

See also: Hermetic Order of the Golden Dawn, The; Magic and New Religious Movements; Occultism and Esotericism; Ordo Templi Orientis; Satanism; Scientology.

Further Reading
Crowley, Aleister. 1938. *The Book of the Law*. York Beach, Maine: Samuel Weiser, Incorporated. Originally published in 1904.
Crowley, Aleister. 1962. *The Book of Lies*. Ilfracombe, Devon: The Hayden Press. Originally published in 1912.
Lachman, Gary. 2014. *Aleister Crowley: Magick, Rock and Roll, and the Wickedest Man in the World*. New York: TarcherPerigree.

Crystals

The use of crystals and other stones in healing has a long history reaching back to ancient Egypt and continuing through Greco-Roman antiquity to the Middle Ages. In the modern era, their use became prominent during the New Age movement of the 1970s and 1980s. One of the forerunners of the New Age, the clairvoyant Edgar Cayce (1877–1945), developed the idea that the ancient, mythical continent of Atlantis was powered by crystals. Frank Alper (1930–2007), who served as a channel for both Moses and "the Christos" and founded the Arizona Metaphysical Society in 1974, channeled three volumes of material on Atlantis (see *Exploring Atlantis*, 1982). He developed the idea that Atlantean civilization widely and readily used crystals, especially in healing rituals in its temples (see www.adamis.ch).

The basic idea is that crystals can absorb energy, amplify it, and discharge healing power. In healing practices crystals can be placed on the body, aligned with the seven chakras or energy centers of the body, or they can be arranged around a person's body. In either case, they are supposed to convey healing energy. Underlying the use of crystals is the conception that the individual is a microcosm of the universe, sometimes expressed in the image of the individual as a spark of the divine. Consequently, becoming attuned with the macrocosm will promote health. Along with channeling, the use of crystals is one of the two most distinctive features of New Age practices.

Marcel Vogel (1917–1991), a research scientist with IBM for twenty-seven years, did much to popularize the use of crystals. In the second phase of his career, he focused on the possibility of communication between humans and plants and on the capacity of crystals to store, amplify, and transmit thought energy. Vogel claimed that he became aware of the healing power of crystals virtually by accident. While he was working at IBM, a coworker told him that he had hurt his back while skiing. Acting on intuition, Vogel reached into his pocket for a crystal he happened to have there, pulsed his breath onto it, and applied it to his colleague's back. The coworker immediately entered an altered state of consciousness and fell to the ground. He quickly recovered and reported that his pain was gone. Although Vogel was reluctant to take seriously what happened, he soon began decades of intense study of what crystals could accomplish.

Vogel quickly became convinced of the healing power of crystals and shared his knowledge in demonstrations and workshops that garnered a large audience of New Age practitioners. He eventually developed a trademarked crystal shape for use in healing. The Vogel crystal is four-sided with double pyramidal terminations where one set of angles is more acute. Vogel also claimed that his crystal form reproduced in its shape the Kabbalistic tree of life (see www.vogelcrystals.net and www.marcelvogel.org).

Vogel developed a simple protocol for using crystals that has been widely adopted among those who work with them. He stressed that crystals have no inherent power but are rather tools that when used properly can amplify the bioenergetic fields that surround individuals. Vogel also believed that many individuals would intuitively choose crystals that best fit their own energy fields. He also argued that

Among devotees of the New Age and the associated circles of alternative therapies and wellness, crystals are believed to have healing properties. Precisely which crystals possess which properties and how they should be used have become matters of discussion in those overlapping parts of the cultic milieu. (Nikki Zalewski/Dreamstime.com)

six-sided crystals were capable of stronger effects than four-sided ones and that eight-sided ones were stronger yet. Other practitioners of crystal healing have developed elaborate systems of classification, linking specific stones, specific healing functions, sounds, and colors.

Before use, crystals need to be cleansed, either by rinsing them in water, leaving them out in the moonlight or sunlight, or smudging them with burning herbs (e.g., sage) or incense. Since they are neutral tools, they then need to be charged. Vogel recommends drawing in the breath, focusing on the crystal, and then quickly exhaling the breath through the nose onto the crystal. He claims that the user will then be able to perceive a faint, but distinct vibration from the crystal. Once charged, the crystal is ready to be put to work.

Crystal healers have typically made very strong claims for their effectiveness, though standard scientific methods have yet to confirm them. Vogel, for example, claimed that the body stored vibrations or "programs" that keep it from normal function. He gave the example of a broken bone, claiming that even after the physical injury had healed there remained a disturbing vibration at the site of the injury. The use of a crystal, however, could remove the lasting negative effects.

The New Age as a movement has faded into the cultural background. But many of its practices and ideas, including the use of crystals, have been diffused into the overlapping contemporary alternative and holistic medicine, wellness, and healthy lifestyle movements. Scores of books have been published instructing individuals how to work with crystals and a variety of workshops are offered both online and in face-to-face settings. Work with crystals is often combined with therapeutic massage and other therapies like Reiki. In many instances, crystal healing is still presented as a scientific pursuit. Crystals have also been embraced by the fashion industry, with fashion designer and former Spice Girl Victoria Beckham (1974–) having lined the catwalk for her shows with black obsidian to stave off negative energy and carrying a collection of crystals in her handbags. Beyond their prominence in New Age practices, crystals continue to influence contemporary culture in various ways.

See also: Cayce, Edgar (1877–1945); Channeling; Healing, Health, and New Religious Movements; Kabbalah; New Age, The.

Further Reading
Frazier, Karen. 2017. *Crystals for Beginners: The Guide to Getting Started with the Healing Power of Crystals.* Berkeley, CA: Althea Press.
Kemp, Daren, & James R. Lewis, eds. 2007. *Handbook of New Age.* Leiden: E. J. Brill.
Melton, J. Gordon. 2013. "Revisionism in the New Age Movement: The Case of Healing Crystals." In Eileen Barker, ed., *Revisionism and Diversification in New Religious Movements*, pp. 201–211. Burlington, VT: Ashgate Publishing Company.
Van Doren, Yulia. 2017. *Crystals: The Modern Guide to Crystal Healing.* London: Quadrille Publishing.

Cult

Few categories in the study of religion have as great a divergence between their scholarly and popular usages as "cult." In the news and entertainment media, "cult" is almost always used as a pejorative term to stigmatize a particular group, usually religious, as illegitimate and likely dangerous. Among scholars, the term has had technical uses, often in typologies designed to distinguish one kind of religious group from another. The dramatic difference in what it means to call a group a "cult" has produced many misunderstandings and even conflicts among commentators at the same time that it has threatened the ongoing viability of small, alternative religious groups.

SCHOLARLY UNDERSTANDINGS

Although the use of the Latin term "cultus" to refer to an organized system of religious worship has a long history, the roots of the scholarly understanding of "cult" go back to the efforts of the German sociologist Max Weber (1864–1920) and his student Ernst Troeltsch (1865–1923), to distinguish churches and sects. Focusing on European Christianity, Troeltsch identified as churches the state-supported religious bodies of most European countries. They consisted primarily of individuals who had been born into them, had relatively inclusive social structures, and accepted and compromised with the values and institutions of the surrounding society. On the other hand, sects were schismatic movements that broke off from their parent bodies, sought members through conversion, and opposed the dominant values and institutions of the surrounding society.

Over time, other scholars proposed refinements, corrections, and elaborations of the developing church-sect theory. H. Richard Niebuhr (1894–1962), for example, envisaged a process in which breakaway sects themselves began to compromise with the surrounding society, which in turn prompted more schisms, followed by schismatic groups again compromising with dominant values and

The attraction of the Children of God for young members of the counterculture of the 1960s and later led to the formation of the first anticult organization in the United States and the popularization of the term "cult" as a pejorative description of new religions. (Davidson Library, University of California, Santa Barbara)

institutions, in a continuing cycle of reform and accommodation. Since church-sect theory was based on the analysis of European and American Christian groups, it generally worked effectively as a system of classification for them. But a growing awareness of religious diversity beyond Christianity revealed its limitations. There were forms of religious groups that eluded classification as churches or sects, even within Christianity.

The American sociologist J. Milton Yinger (1916–2011) introduced a more complex set of categories—established church, ecclesia, denomination, sect, established sect, and cult—in which the final category, cult, functioned mainly as a catch-all for groups that could not be classified under any of the other five categories. Others proposed typologies of sects and groups that would in other typologies be identified as cults. The British sociologist Bryan Wilson (1926–2004), for example, classified groups according to their proposed path to salvation. Over time, such typologies proliferated, and church-sect-cult theories consequently had diverse analytical language.

HISTORICAL DEVELOPMENTS

At the same time that sociologists of religion were striving to refine categorizations of religious groups, religious diversity was becoming greater and more evident. The repeal of the Asian Exclusion Act in 1965 paved the way for an influx of Asian gurus and teachers into the United States. The rise of the counterculture of the 1960s provided these religious figures, as well as homegrown ones, with an audience that was eager to seek wisdom in whatever form it might take. Also, postwar Japan saw a proliferation of new, and then "new new" religions. Beyond that, the diversity of innovative religious movements inspired by Christianity and Islam in Africa, for example, also attracted scholarly attention. Both the general public and scholars were challenged to make sense of the apparent explosion of new religious movements throughout the world.

Several observers reached to the past, specifically the late nineteenth and early to mid-twentieth centuries, for a descriptive category that could adequately describe at least some of the new religious developments. Independent of, but eventually intersecting with, the scholarly use of the term, some commentators seized upon the term "cult." Since the late nineteenth century, it had been used to describe groups like the Mormons, Jehovah's Witnesses, and Christian Scientists, which were perceived by some to have sufficiently departed from appropriate (orthodox, conservative, evangelical) Christian doctrine as to merit classification as something other than churches or sects.

In that usage, "cult" is clearly a term of derogation; it indicates an unacceptable degree of theological deviation. It was used to mark the boundaries between legitimate and illegitimate forms of Christianity. Of course, it was wielded by individuals who took their own orthodoxy and possession of the truth for granted. The term was never used by individuals to describe their own religious convictions and practices; it was always used against others whose beliefs and practices were viewed as erroneous, if not outright heretical for some reason. It conveyed a theological judgment that carried with it social repercussions.

Christian polemicists developed the concept of a "cult" in great detail. Among the influential books were Reformed Protestant J. K. Van Baalen's (1890–1968) *The Chaos of the Cults: A Study in Present-Day Isms* (1938), which went through multiple editions, and Walter Martin's (1928–1989) *The Kingdom of the Cults* (1965), which also went through several editions. Those books, and others like them, became the foundational texts for a vigorous Christian anticult movement devoted to identifying which groups counted as cults and cataloging their errors from a conservative, evangelical Protestant point of view.

Thus, when, in the early 1970s, some parents whose adult children had joined new religious groups became alarmed by their children's willingness to turn their back on their conventional social and religious upbringings, they had a well-honed social weapon at hand. The earliest anticult movement outside of Christian countercult circles, began with the formation of a loose coalition (Free the Children of God) dedicated to "freeing" members of the new, millennialist Christian group, the Children of God. Those activists quickly seized upon the term "cult" to describe the groups they were worried about. In the hands of the burgeoning anticult movement, however, the category was loosened from its religious moorings, including its association with doctrinal error, and given a new powerful meaning.

THE ANTICULT MOVEMENT

Though it was only loosely organized, the early anticult movement developed a cluster of concepts that proved attractive both to aggrieved parents and a general public wary of religious innovation. Building on parents' convictions that their children could not possibly have willingly joined groups like the Children of God, the "Hare Krishnas," or the "Moonies," anticult activists developed an alternative explanation for the conversion of young adults. Instead of deciding for themselves to adopt new religious identities, cult opponents argued, young adults had somehow been deceived, or even coerced, into membership in alternative religions. Activists quickly seized upon the concept of brainwashing, developed to describe efforts at indoctrination of captives in prisoners of war camps during the Korean War, as an explanation for conversion.

A related image implicitly posited that converts to new religions had been "programmed" and that to leave the groups they needed to be subjected to a process of "deprogramming," which in its early days often included violent kidnappings of members of alternative religions and holding them against their will while haranguing them to abandon their religious commitments. The brainwashing-deprogramming nexus of concepts conveyed the dominant perception that "cults" were led by manipulative and deceitful leaders who were only acting for personal gain and that members of "cults" had not joined of their own volition but were deceived by wily recruiters. Although it had been present all along, the third part of the opponents' characterization of "cults," that they do harm to both members and society, was cemented by the murder-suicides at Peoples Temple's Agricultural Mission in Guyana in 1978. The negative understanding of "cults" as being led by deranged and deceitful leaders, who prey on vulnerable individuals and who will lead them inevitably to harm or even death, continues to exert substantial influence in public discussions of alternative religious groups.

"CULT" AS A USEFUL SCHOLARLY CONCEPT

In response to the widespread and firmly embedded public perception of "cults" as illegitimate and dangerous, many scholars have proposed abandoning the term entirely in favor of "new religious movement" and analogous terms. Some have fought a, so far, losing battle to change the public perception of new religions as "cults." Some have also tried to cut through the welter of competing typologies and impose order on scholarly classifications of religious groups.

One noteworthy attempt has been undertaken by sociologists of religion Rodney Stark and William Sims Bainbridge. They have proposed an interrelated set of concepts that characterize the dynamism of any given "religious economy," or the total amount of religion in a given social environment. At the outset, they propose a simple distinction. In their system of classification, a church is a religious group that accepts the social environment in which it exists, while a sect is a religious group that rejects its social environment. Sects split off from parent groups that sect leaders and members find to have compromised too much with the societies in which they are located. The Davidian Adventists, for example, split from The Seventh-Day Adventists in the 1930s after their attempts at reform were rebuffed. Later, the Branch Davidians developed out of that initial schism. Sects present themselves as returning to and reinvigorating the original intentions and early practices of their parent bodies. In sectarian logic, it is the parent bodies that have succumbed to innovation and the sect itself that preserves valued tradition. Sects, then, are one element of dynamism in any religious economy.

But sects are not the only source of innovation. Religious innovation also comes from other sources. Groups that enter a religious economy from abroad are generally perceived as innovative. The International Society for Krishna Consciousness appeared in the United States, where it was founded by Swami Prabhupada in the 1960s, as a religious innovation even though it had deep roots in Hindu traditions in India. But new religions can also come about through sheer innovation, as with L. Ron Hubbard's creation of the Church of Scientology or Anton LaVey's establishment of the Church of Satan. Stark and Bainbridge categorize both imported and innovated new religions as cults.

In the same scheme, cults can be broken down into three main types. Audience cults consist of a shifting and diffuse group of people interested in various alternative, esoteric, or emergent forms of wisdom, but they do not form an identifiable social group. Client cults focus on the exchange of services for fees but do not form lasting social groups. Only cult movements sufficiently mobilize their membership to constitute ongoing social groups.

The Stark and Bainbridge model offers both a much more objective alternative to the public image of dangerous cults and an effective way of categorizing religious groups for analytical purposes.

See also: Anticult Movement, The; Brainwashing; Branch Davidians; Children of God (The Family International); Church of Satan, The; Conversion; Deprogramming; FREECOG (Free the Children of God); International Society for Krishna Consciousness (ISKCON); Peoples Temple; Scientology; Unification Church, The.

Further Reading

Bromley, David G. 2008. "Categorizing Religious Organizations: In Search of a Theoretically Meaningful Strategy." In James R. Lewis & Inga B. Tøllefsen, eds., *The Oxford Handbook of New Religious Movements*, Vol. II, pp. 17–24. Oxford: Oxford University Press.

Chryssides, George D. 2017. "From Deviance to Devotion: The Evolution of NRM Studies." In Eugene V. Gallagher, ed., *"Cult Wars" in Historical Perspective: New and Minority Religions*, pp. 43–54. New York: Routledge.

Melton, J. Gordon. 2004. "An Introduction to New Religions." In James R. Lewis, ed., *The Oxford Handbook of New Religious Movements*, pp. 16–35. Oxford: Oxford University Press.

Miller, Timothy. 2017. "Are the Cult Wars Over? And, If So, Who Won?" In Eugene V. Gallagher, ed., *"Cult Wars" in Historical Perspective: New and Minority Religions*, pp. 33–42. New York: Routledge.

Richardson, James T. 1993. "Definitions of Cult: From Sociological-Technical to Popular-Negative." *Review of Religious Research* 34: 348–356.

Ross, Rick. 2014. *Cults Inside Out: How People Get In and Can Get Out*. North Charleston, SC: CreateSpace.

Singer, Margaret, with Janja Lalich. 1995. *Cults in Our Midst: The Hidden Menace in Our Everyday Lives*. San Francisco: Jossey-Bass.

Stark, Rodney, & William Sims Bainbridge. 1985. *The Future of Religion: Secularization, Revival, and Cult Formation*. Berkeley: University of California Press.

Cult Awareness Network

Although it only lasted ten years (1986–1996) in its original form, the Cult Awareness Network (CAN) has played an important role in the conflicts about new religious movements or "cults" both in the United States and abroad. CAN served initially as a clearing house of information about new religions, and it referred parents and other interested parties to freelance individuals who specialized in the deprogramming, or forcible, involuntary extrication, of cult members. CAN was also instrumental in promulgating the image of the "dangerous cult" through the popular media.

ORIGINS

The contemporary anticult movement began in the early 1970s when parents who were distraught that their young adult children had joined new and exotic religious groups began to meet together with other sympathizers. The first organization, FREECOG (Free the Children of God), began in 1972 and focused on the Christian sectarian group founded in Huntington Beach, California, by David Brandt Berg. Like other early anticult groups, it drew a local membership, even when it expanded its focus to other groups. Participants in the anticult movement, however, soon concluded that the perceived cult problem far exceeded their own personal experiences. By 1974, members of FREECOG helped to found the Citizens Freedom Foundation (CFF) to become the organizational home of a national movement.

CFF, and other anticult organizations that cropped up around the same time, continued to struggle to establish a lasting presence in the 1970s. But a turning point came at the end of the decade when CFF was granted tax-exempt status for an educational trust called the Citizens Freedom Foundation–Information Services. Still, CFF strained to establish a national footprint. It appointed its first national director in 1980 and gradually developed a full organization. In September of 1986, CFF changed its name to the CAN and incorporated in California.

SERVICES

From its origins, the anticult movement was inextricably associated with the practice of deprogramming and the assumptions that authorized it. CAN was no different. Although CAN attempted to maintain an arm's-length relationship with deprogrammers, one of its primary services was to refer families to individuals who would undertake aggressive and often violent deprogrammings for a fee. In most cases, a portion of that fee was then returned to CAN in the form of a donation. As the abusive excesses of deprogrammings became more widely known, CAN attempted to distance itself further from the practice.

CAN also served as a source of information about groups identified as cults, a category that it continued to expand. CAN essentially repackaged public information about individual groups, making sure to include only what was derogatory and to exclude any statements from the group itself. That process created a feedback loop that amplified parents' concerns and moved them to take action. Since individuals only contacted CAN when they had misgivings about a particular new religion, when they received packets of negative information about the group, they became more willing to intervene in the religious lives of cult members. CAN officials and volunteers then stood ready to provide referrals to individuals who could help concerned families "recover" their "lost" loved ones.

CAN also actively courted media attention. In addition to holding conferences and providing references to speakers, CAN was always ready to provide succinct and easily understood expressions of its position to reporters seeking to understand the "cult problem." From CAN's perspective the problem was simple. Deceptive cults maliciously used brainwashing or thought control to attract vulnerable young people and exploit them for their own purposes. Cult members were powerless to disentangle themselves and needed to be rescued. Unlike mental health professionals and the courts, deprogrammers had an effective, if illegal, solution to families' problems. Successful retrievals of cult members earned CAN more supporters, volunteers, and donors.

CAN'S DEMISE

Despite its substantial influence on the public perception of new religions, CAN rested on a fragile foundation. When Cynthia Kisser (1949–) assumed the position of Executive Director in 1987, she moved to centralize the organization and finances of CAN in her Chicago area office. CAN was never on a sound financial footing since it depended on donations and the sales of packages of information on individual groups. Careful examination of its files has also revealed that CAN suffered from some definitely sloppy bookkeeping and probably some financial irregularities. In addition, it had also been sued by as many as fifty members of the Church of Scientology, a religion that CAN identified as a dangerous cult. The suits tied CAN up in litigation that eventually cost nearly two million dollars.

CAN's financial weakness was exposed when it was named as a defendant in a court case about a failed deprogramming. In the early 1990s, along with his mother, Cathy Tonkin, Jason Scott and several siblings attended the Life Tabernacle Church, a branch of the evangelical United Pentecostal Church, in Seattle, Washington. When Tonkin withdrew from the church, Jason (then eighteen) and his brothers Thysen (sixteen) and Matthew (thirteen) decided to stay. Tonkin soon contacted CAN and was referred to a deprogrammer, Rick Ross (1952–), who agreed to get the three boys out of the group. Jason's deprogramming, however, went badly.

Ross's attempt to pry Jason Scott from the Life Tabernacle Church followed an established pattern. Scott was violently kidnapped from his grandmother's home, physically detained in a remote location, and berated about his beliefs for nearly a week. After learning that he would be transferred to an Ohio cult rehabilitation facility called Wellspring, Jason decided to play along with his captors in hope of escaping. When he was able to slip away, Jason called the police and Ross and his helpers were arrested.

Although a 1995 trial on criminal charges ended with a hung jury, a subsequent 1995 civil trial ended with the conclusion that Ross's and his helpers' negligence had led to Jason's injuries. The jury awarded nearly five million dollars in compensatory and punitive damages to Jason, including a million dollars assessed against CAN. CAN's appeal of the verdict was unsuccessful, and it filed for bankruptcy in 1996. The Jason Scott case effectively destroyed the CAN and dealt the broader anticult movement a serious blow.

THE NEW CAN

The setbacks for the anticult movement were compounded when CAN's name, logo, phone number, and other assets were purchased at auction by attorney Steven L. Hayes, a Scientologist, for $20,000. Hayes represented a group of individuals who supported religious freedom, including some members of the Church of Scientology. CAN's files in some 150 boxes eventually ended up in the hands of another Scientologist, Gary Beeny, who donated them to the Foundation for Religious Freedom, which also had support from the Church of Scientology. Those files were subsequently donated to the special collections of the University of California, Santa Barbara.

The new CAN set itself up as a referral service, just like the old CAN. But instead of purveying only negative information about groups identified as cults, it focused on a message of religious freedom and tolerance for new and alternative religious groups, not least of which was the Church of Scientology.

The fate of the original CAN was particularly galling to those who worked for and supported it. Many feared that sensitive personal information that was now in the hands of CAN's staunchest opponent could be used to devastating effect. Moreover, they worried that those seeking help from CAN, using its established hotline, would now receive information diametrically opposed to what the old CAN would have dispensed. Cynthia Kisser was particularly vocal in sounding the alarm about the new CAN, especially after she failed to secure its assets after its bankruptcy.

In many ways, the history of CAN offers a compressed version of the "cult wars" that have lasted from the 1970s into the twenty-first century. As the first successful national anticult organization in the United States, CAN decisively shaped the public understanding of cults and the process of conversion to new and alternative groups. Though its reputation was definitely tarnished in some circles by its association with abusive practices of deprogramming, it could count enough successes to continue to attract approval and support from individuals who agreed with its portrayal of the menace of cults. It also, however, earned the wrath of many of the religious groups that it singled out for opprobrium. In the Church of Scientology, it encountered an adversary that could call on more volunteers and superior financial resources. CAN's collapse resulted in its name being co-opted in support of causes it had passionately opposed.

See also: Anticult Movement, The; Brainwashing; Courts and New Religious Movements; Cult; Deprogramming; FREECOG (Free the Children of God); Media and New Religious Movements; Ross, Rick (1952–); Scientology.

Further Reading

Gallagher, Eugene V., ed. 2017. *"Cult Wars" in Historical Perspective.* London: Routledge.

Shupe, Anson, & Susan E. Darnell. 2006. *Agents of Discord: Deprogramming, Pseudo-Science, and the American Anticult Movement.* New Brunswick, NJ: Transaction Publishers.

Shupe, Anson D., Jr., & David G. Bromley. 1980. *The New Vigilantes: Deprogrammers, Anti-Cultists, and the New Religions.* Beverly Hills, CA: Sage.

Cultic Milieu

Observers of new, alternative, and emergent religions have frequently noted that many groups seem to be short lived and that many individuals move from one group to another in search of religious nourishment. The diversity and fluidity of the broad field of new religious movements has long attracted individuals who are dissatisfied with the status quo. In fact, individuals have drawn on the resources offered by new religions to express their opposition to the dominant culture.

In 1972, British sociologist Colin Campbell (1940–) introduced the concept of the "cultic milieu" to encompass the diverse elements of what he called the cultural underground of society. Campbell notes that groups within the cultic milieu are subject to continual formation and collapse, that despite their diverse ideas they all deviate from the mainstream of a given society, that individuals who enter the cultic milieu can get involved with many different groups, and that participants in the cultic milieu will likely identify themselves as religious or spiritual seekers. Campbell also notes that the constantly shifting contours of the cultic milieu facilitate the formation of groups but also hinder efforts to maintain them. Campbell also anticipated that elements of the cultic milieu could enter the mainstream but emphasized the oppositional stance of those within the cultic milieu.

Scholars of new religions have found Campbell's concept helpful in describing and analyzing contemporary religious diversity outside the mainstream and have set about applying and modifying it. One notable contribution came from Christopher Partridge in 2004. Surveying the religious scene in the West, Partridge found that Christianity in many instances was deteriorating and being eroded by secularization. But at the same time a vigorous "occulture" was coming to inform the religious lives of many.

Like Campbell's concept of the cultic milieu, Partridge's occulture refers to a repertoire of oppositional, hidden, stigmatized, and rejected beliefs and practices. It runs the gamut from theosophical, mystical, Pagan, and New Age ideas to conspiracy theories about reptilians who actually control the earth and millennialist speculations about the Mayan calendar, among many other things. Partridge emphasizes, as did Campbell, that occulture does not constitute a single thing, but rather a constantly changing array of resources from which individuals can draw as they craft worldviews and practices that they find meaningful.

Concepts like Campbell's cultic milieu and Partridge's occulture can help observers make sense of the constantly shifting character of new religions in any given religious economy and the highly eclectic approach that many individuals take toward forming their own worldviews and religious or spiritual practices. They also suggest that new religious groups, ideas, and practices will continually be produced through processes of creative combination.

See also: Conversion; Cult; Sect.

Further Reading

Kaplan, Jeffrey, & Heléne Lööw, eds. 2002. *The Cultic Milieu: Oppositional Subcultures in an Age of Globalization.* Walnut Creek, CA: AltaMira Press.

Partridge, Christopher, 2004. *The Re-Enchantment of the West: Alternative Spiritualities, Sacralization, Popular Culture, and Occulture*, Vol. I. London: T & T Clark.

Damanhur

The communal and spiritually esoteric community, the Federation of Damanhur or, simply, Damanhur rose to prominence in the early 1990s when it was discovered they had been excavating an elaborate underground temple (known as the "Temples of Humankind") in secret in the foothills of the Alps in Italy. Construction was initially halted by the Italian government, though retroactive permission was granted, enabling completion of the Temple.

Oberto Airaudi (1950–2013), later called Falco Tarassaco, founded the community in the mid-1970s, an outgrowth of his interests in occult religious knowledge, his participation in magical ritual, and his work as a Spiritualist medium and healer. Airaudi had developed a following in Turin, but began to advocate for the idea of communal living as crucial to spiritual development, necessitating the move from an unincorporated group to an intentional, formal religious institution. The site of the community was chosen because Airaudi believed it sat at the intersection of the spiritual and natural worlds as well as served as a center point for global "energy" lines, making the land around them "alive." By the 1980s, Damanhur was operating as a *de facto* state, with its own currency, government, and school system. This autonomy was met with resistance by the local authorities, but those who lived at Damanhur were enabled to live and operate relatively unmolested.

Though communal living is advocated, not all members of Damanhur live on site. Members have varying levels of involvement, from those who wish to visit and study on site to those who choose to live communally and share all resources. Those who live in the community form groups called "nucleos," comprising fifteen to twenty people who reside in a single home. Unlike some religious utopias where marital and familial relationships are dissolved, families remain intact, and married couples may remain committed (though their marriage is periodically "renewed," to ensure that their commitment to one another is intact and that it is not preventing their spiritual advancement).

Members of Damanhur believe in God, but that God is unknowable and can only be approached through avatars or intermediaries. They believe that at one point in history, human beings were themselves spiritual entities, but over time, they became more attached to material reality, thus forgetting their spiritual origins. Thus, the aim of practice at Damanhur is to return to this earlier state through various practices, some, though by no means all, of which invoke magic. Among the paths one can take to renew this earlier spiritual essence are meditation, social activism, art, music, family life, or food production. All human actions are believed to awaken energies that tune the practitioner into the divine that exists within and around them. Relatedly, one of the aims of communal living is to create an environment where members can realize their divine spark by remembering that they share this essence with others, often referred to as "con te" or "I am with you."

The underground facility, the Temples of Humankind, was begun out of a desire to combine both secular and sacred art as a means of inspiring spiritual awakening for community members and visitors. It is often referred to as the "Eighth Wonder of the World," though primarily by members of Damanhur themselves. The Temple has eight halls, each dedicated to a different theme or spiritual principle, reflecting the eclectic esoteric origins of the group. For example, the Hall of Water, is dedicated to celebrating the feminine principle, thereby connecting it to the modern Goddess movement, which advocates for worship of the divine feminine alongside (and occasionally over against) the divine masculine. (The Hall of Earth is dedicated to worship of the divine masculine.)

The road sign at the entrance to the community of Damanhur provides glimpses of its Temples of Humankind as well as the landscape occupied by the community. (Lorenzo Pegoraro/Dreamstime.com)

More recently, the community has focused on environmentalism, earning it accolades from the United Nations as a model of sustainable living. Members of Damanhur have always maintained a sympathy with the animal world—often taking animal names or personas that are used alongside their given names. However, focus on respect of and sympathy with the plant world increased over time, leading to organic farming practices and a focus on green building, renewable energy, and homeopathic medicine.

See also: Art and New Religious Movements; Environmentalism and New Religious Movements; Goddess Worship; Magic and New Religious Movements; Mediums; Occultism and Esotericism; Spiritualism; Utopianism in New Religious Movements.

Further Reading

Airaudi, Oberto. 1997. *Tales from Damanhur.* Canavese, Italy: Damanhur Editrice.

Introvigne, Massimo. 1996. "Damanhur: A Magical Community in Italy." *Communal Studies* 16: 71–84.

Merrifield, Jeff. 2006. *Damanhur: The Story of the Extraordinary Italian Artistic Community.* Santa Cruz: Hanford Mead Publishers.

Deprogramming

At the heart of the concept of deprogramming is a powerful metaphor. The idea implies that, somehow, an individual has been subjected to influence that has effectively reprogrammed that person's mind to new, and unacceptable, ways of thinking and acting. In some instances, the equally powerful metaphor of brainwashing can be used to describe the cause of the perceived negative changes in an individual. For the person to return to her or his previous state, therefore, the effects of that programming or brainwashing need to be eradicated. According to those who endorse deprogramming, the goal is simply to return to individuals their free will rather than to impose on them any specific set of beliefs.

ORIGINS

The practice of deprogramming developed in the early 1970s as a way of combating what parents and others saw as the negative impact of various new religions on their young adult children. Those who joined new religions often gave up promising careers and abandoned their education, which appalled parents who had envisioned very different lives for them. Parents who believed that they had "lost" their children searched for a way to "rescue" them from entanglement in new religious groups.

Ted Patrick (1930–), a former state official in the San Diego area, claims to have developed the practice as a way of extricating individuals from the Children of God, a Christian sect under the leadership of David Brandt Berg (1919–1994) that had begun in Huntington Beach, California, in 1968. He soon extended his concern to other groups, such as the Unification Church and the International Society for Krishna Consciousness or "Hare Krishnas."

RATIONALE

In Patrick's hands, deprogramming was a blunt instrument. Despite his lack of psychological expertise and on the basis of relatively few encounters with "cult" members, Patrick concluded that members of groups like the Children of God had been seduced into joining through "on-the-spot hypnosis." Individuals were viewed as being virtually powerless to resist deceptive and manipulative cult leaders. Deprogrammers emphasized that everyone was vulnerable to the deceptive cults and that standard psychiatric or psychological treatments were incapable of getting individuals out.

When individuals did renounce their former affiliations with groups defined as cults, they reinforced the value of deprogramming, irrespective of the substantial human and financial costs. Some who had been deprogrammed even took up the practice themselves, basing their credibility on their status as former cult members. Even when they did not become deprogrammers, former members' dramatic stories of their rescues from cult life fueled the anticult movement and contributed to the negative portrayals of new religions in public discourse.

In the logic of deprogramming, since cult members had lost their free will and were thus unable to decide to leave a group on their own, they needed to be forcibly removed. The involuntary and coercive form of deprogramming pioneered by Patrick thus involved kidnapping individuals, imprisoning them against their will in often remote locations, and intensive, often belligerent, persuasive efforts to get the targeted individuals to abandon their new beliefs and commitments. Deprogramming did not always work, and some members returned to their groups only to be subjected to subsequent deprogramming attempts.

Early deprogrammers worked as freelance entrepreneurs but also maintained close relationships with various anticult groups that began to form in the 1970s. The deprogrammers would frequently receive referrals from the anticult organizations and, in turn, kick back parts of their fees. The arm's-length relationship gave deprogrammers unchecked freedom to operate and also allowed the anticult organizations to distance themselves from the violent, abusive, and illegal practices of some deprogrammers. Although deprogrammers professed altruistic motives for their actions, some were able to earn enough to make anticult work a full-time profession. A few deprogramming centers were also set up in the 1970s, including the Freedom of Thought Foundation ranch in Tucson, Arizona.

Deprogramming provided a simple, and frightening, explanation for the attraction of young people to what some perceived as a bewildering variety of exotic new religions. It also provided readymade dramatic stories to the news media, which, in turn, elevated the reputations of deprogrammers and the broader anticult network. Simplistic explanations of cult membership, influenced by the early deprogramming concept, still dominate media accounts of new religions.

Deprogramming, however, has been less successful in the courts. In the 1970s, for example, the logic of deprogramming informed parents' attempts to act as temporary conservatorships over their children in stigmatized new religions. By the early 1980s, however, judges became much less willing to grant conservatorships over children who were legal adults. In addition, some deprogrammers were convicted of abduction and false imprisonment. Ted Patrick, for example, was found guilty in 1980 and charged again in 1990, though those charges were dropped.

FROM DEPROGRAMMING TO EXIT COUNSELING

By the mid-1980s deprogramming was in disrepute. Charges of violence, drug use, and even sexual abuse by individual deprogrammers irrevocably tarnished individual reputations and the practice in general. At the same time, an influx of professionals into the anticult movement sparked efforts to develop standards and a code of conduct for deprogrammers. For a time, there was an attempt to distinguish voluntary from the notorious involuntary deprogrammings, but the term deprogramming remained indelibly associated with coercion. Adopting a different model, several former deprogrammers began to describe themselves as "exit counselors." Though the name had changed, exit counseling has the same goal as deprogramming: the departure of the targeted individual from the cultic group. The logic of deprogramming still informs the work of various sectors of the anticult movement, even after the practice has been disavowed.

See also: Anticult Movement, The; Brainwashing; Exit Counseling; FREECOG (Free the Children of God); Hassan, Steven (1954–); Love Israel Family, The; Patrick, Ted (1930–).

Further Reading

Richardson, James T., & David G. Bromley, eds. 1983. *The Brainwashing/Deprogramming Controversy.* Lewiston, NY: Edwin T. Mellen Press.

Shupe, Anson, & Susan E. Darnell. 2006. *Agents of Discord: Deprogramming, Pseudo-Science, and the American Anticult Movement.* New Brunswick, NJ: Transaction Publishers.

Zablocki, Benjamin, & Thomas Robbins, eds. 2001. *Misunderstanding Cults: Searching for Objectivity in a Controversial Field.* Toronto: University of Toronto Press.

Diamond Mountain Center

The diffusion of Buddhism in the West has been accomplished not only by emissaries from Buddhist lands but also by homegrown Western Buddhist teachers. Those teachers typically claim some authorizing connection to Buddhist teachers widely recognized as legitimate, even as they adapt and transform Buddhist teachings for different audiences. Michael Roach (1952–), an Arizona native and Princeton graduate, is linked to the Gelugpa lineage of Tibetan Buddhism. He was ordained as a monk in 1983 and received the title of Geshe, roughly equivalent to a doctorate in Buddhist philosophy, from the Sera monastery in Tibet in 1995.

Roach moved from being a student of Buddhism to becoming the founder of an American Buddhist institution as the result of a three-year, three-month, three-day silent meditative retreat that he began with a handful of others in 2000 in the desert in southeastern Arizona. Roach emerged from his retreat to found the Diamond Mountain University and Retreat Center in 2004. The Center would offer three five-week semesters of study on various Buddhist topics and other services. Roach also became a prolific writer and lecturer, drawing on the time that, at the direction of his own Tibetan teacher, he spent in the diamond industry to provide Buddhist insights on how to succeed in business.

But Roach also came out of his retreat making innovative claims. Despite his monastic ordination, he spent the retreat in the intimate company of another American, Christie McNally (1973–), whom he married in 1998. Although he was not formally qualified to do so, Roach declared that McNally should be recognized as a lama or teacher of the Buddhist Dharma by his few hundred followers. More dramatically, he declared that McNally was the reincarnation of the female deity Vajrayogini. Roach's unorthodox actions disturbed the Tibetan Buddhist community, earning a rebuke from the Dalai Lama and criticism from the influential American scholar and practitioner Robert Thurman (1941–). Some of his former students fell away, but Roach and McNally maintained an international following in the low hundreds.

Roach and McNally split up sometime before the three-year retreat scheduled to begin in late 2010. During the retreat, McNally began to behave erratically and she and her new husband Ian Thorson (1974–2012) were banished from the center in 2012 by the Diamond Mountain Board, in part, because of suspected domestic abuse. They relocated to a remote site near the Center, where Thorson died of dehydration and exposure in 2012.

Though the Thorson incident sullied Roach's reputation, both he and McNally continue to operate as Buddhist teachers and the Diamond Mountain Center continues to host retreats (www.diamondmountain.org) for people of diverse religions.

See also: Charisma and Leadership in New Religious Movements; Diamond Way, The.

Further Reading

Immergut, Matthew. 2013. "Death at Diamond Mountain: Research Dilemmas When a New Religious Movement Becomes a Cult." *Nova Religio* 17: 24–37.

Roach, Geshe Michael, & Lama Christie McNally. 2009. *The Diamond Cutter: The Buddha on Managing Your Business and Your Life*, rev. ed. New York: Doubleday.

Diamond Way, The

As part of the ongoing process of globalization over more than two thousand years, Buddhism has come to the West through multiple channels. Buddhist immigrants have brought their native practices with them and have inevitably changed them in their new contexts. Traveling Buddhist merchants have contributed to the spread of their religion. Buddhist teachers have either visited the West or relocated there to bring the dharma, the body of practice and doctrine that leads to awakening, to a new audience. In the later twentieth and early twenty-first centuries, Westerners have visited Buddhist countries as spiritual tourists, and some have remained to become serious students of Buddhism.

The Dane, Ole Nydahl (1941–), and his wife Hannah (1946–2007) visited Nepal on their honeymoon in 1968. There they began to study with the Tibetan Buddhist teacher Lapsong Tsechu Rinpoche (1918–2003). In the following year, they encountered Ranjung Rigpe Dorje (1924–1981), the sixteenth Karmapa or spiritual leader of the Karma Kagyu lineage of Tibetan or Vajrayana (Sanskrit for "Diamond Way") Buddhism. The Karma Kagyu lineage is one of four schools of Tibetan Buddhism and itself has four branches. The Nydahls became the Karmapa's students; accepted refuge in the Buddha, dharma, and sangha; and took their bodhisattva vows. In Nydahl's own telling, it was a remarkable transformation. He had abandoned his hippie life of the pursuit of thrills and pleasure, which included a stint of drug smuggling, for the life of a Buddhist.

By 1972, Nydahl was commissioned by the Karmapa to return to Europe as a formally recognized teacher to spread the message of Buddhism. Nydahl proved to be particularly adept at that task. In Denmark and Germany, he quickly established centers for the study of Buddhism. The centers teach Diamond Way's particular form of meditation on the guru. As the group's website puts it, the purpose of meditation is enlightenment, and it can be pursued by meditating on the Buddha or the Buddha-like characteristics of one's teacher (see www.diamondway-buddhism.org/buddhist-meditation).

Nydahl has worked assiduously to spread the Diamond Way teachings, and there are now more than 650 centers throughout the world. In the early 2000s, Nydahl appointed a group of "travelling teachers" to support the various centers, and by 2010 there were more than 230 of them. That, in turn, created a need for Nydahl to exercise more organizational control and to diminish tolerance for diversity among the centers. Few of those teachers, however, had anything like Nydahl's intensive Buddhist education.

As a European teaching Tibetan Buddhism, Nydahl has continually striven to establish his legitimacy. His autobiographical statements, for example, have emphasized the similarities between his own life and that of Milarepa (1052–1135), the renowned Tibetan yogi who also had turned from a life of sorcery and murder to Buddhism. Nydahl's formal recognition as a *lama*, or chief priest of the dharma in Tibetan Buddhism, in the early 1990s helped to shore up his status as an authoritative teacher.

Although he insists that he represents the orthodox Tibetan teachings of the Karma Kagyu lineage, Nydahl has streamlined and translated those practices to appeal to audiences outside of Tibet. Nydahl's presentation of Tibetan Buddhism, then, can be characterized as a neo-orthodox representation of Buddhism for a contemporary lay audience. Some Buddhists have criticized Diamond Way for watering down Buddhism and characterized it as providing only a basic introduction to Buddhism or a "lifestyle" Buddhism. Such criticisms illustrate the dilemmas faced by global traditions as they endeavor to adapt to contexts different from the ones in which they developed.

Despite the criticisms, however, Nydahl and the Diamond Way organization have played an important role in shaping Tibetan Buddhism both internationally and in its homeland. When the sixteenth Karmapa died, for example, a succession crisis developed over who could be considered the next reincarnation of the Karmapa and the continuator of his work. Nydahl was one of a minority who acknowledged Trinley Thaye Dorje (1983–) as the seventeenth Karmapa, and most of the centers supporting him are associated with the Diamond Way. But a schism has nonetheless developed over the question of succession.

See also: Conversion; Globalization and New Religious Movements; Soka Gakkai.

Further Reading

Nydahl, Ole. 1999. *Entering the Diamond Way: Tibetan Buddhism Meets the West*, rev. ed. Grass Valley, CA: Blue Dolphin Press.

Scherer, Bee. 2017. "A Neo-Orthodox Buddhism Movement in Transition: The Diamond Way." In Eugene V. Gallagher, ed., *Visioning New and Minority Religions: Projecting the Future*. New York: Routledge.

Scherer, Bee. 2010. "Interpreting the Diamond Way: Contemporary Convert Buddhism in Transition." *Journal of Global Buddhism* 10: 17–48.

Dianetics

During a period of intense reflection while recuperating from injuries suffered in World War II, Lafayette Ron Hubbard (1911–1986) devised what he viewed as a revolutionary therapeutic system. He called it Dianetics, from the Greek *dia*, "through," and *nous*, "soul." Hubbard was convinced that his insights into the human mind and the practices based on them could dramatically improve the lives of individuals and positively address any social problem.

Before he published his ideas, Hubbard had lived an extraordinary life. Official accounts from the Church of Scientology describe his initiation at age six as a blood brother in the Blackfoot tribe, his early travels to Asia, his part in expeditions to Alaska and the Caribbean, and other dramatic events. He was also a prolific writer of short stories, screenplays, and novels. In the official account, Hubbard's diverse experiences put him in an ideal position to investigate the human mind.

Hubbard first shared his thoughts in an unpublished manuscript in 1948, which was later published as *Dianetics: The Original Thesis*. The first published account of Dianetics appeared in 1950 in *Astounding Science Fiction*, a magazine to which he was a frequent contributor. Also in May 1950, *Dianetics: The Modern Science of Mental Health* appeared and quickly spent six months on the *New York Times* best-sellers list.

At the heart of Hubbard's therapy is his concept of the reactive mind, which exists below the level of the conscious, analytic mind. Complex images of traumatic events, called "engrams," are stored in the "bank" of the reactive mind. Those engrams can be reactivated when any element of the past trauma recurs, engendering both physical and psychological illnesses and compromising an individual's ability to function optimally.

Hubbard concluded that the negative effect of stored engrams could be dissipated through a process he called auditing, which restored an individual to a state of being "clear." Auditing involved a careful questioning of the client by a trained practitioner, which would bring the traumatic experience to the surface and then gradually dissolve its effects.

Hubbard's "new science" quickly found an eager audience and many engaged in the auditing processes that he outlined. Several challenges soon occurred. One was that there was an inevitable variation in the practice of Dianetics, which prompted Hubbard to strive to impose some order on an increasingly diverse set of practitioners. Another was that some began to report that they recovered traumatic experiences from not only their own lifespans but from past lives. Also, Hubbard's attempts to interest the American Medical Association and the American Psychiatric Association in his new therapy received no response. All of those factors helped to spur the transition from Dianetics as a therapy to Dianetics as the core practice of a new religious movement, Scientology.

See also: Freezone Scientology; Hubbard, L. Ron (1911–1986); Scientology.

Further Reading

Hubbard, L. Ron. 2007 [1950]. *Dianetics: The Modern Science of Mental Health*. Commerce, CA: Bridge Publications.

Urban, Hugh B. 2011. *The Church of Scientology: A History of a New Religion.* Princeton, NJ: Princeton University Press.

Disaffiliation and Ex-membership in New Religious Movements

People move into and out of religious groups virtually every day. In most cases, those changes in affiliation draw the attention of only a limited few. In some instances, however, the departures or arrivals are so dramatic and well publicized that they attract substantial attention. That has particularly been the case for new religious movements. Because of their novelty and their departure from cultural norms, new religions have long attracted public scrutiny, much of it hostile. In the public debates about the legitimacy of new religions, the testimonies of former members have played a significant role, even though such "noisy" apostates are definitely in the minority since most people who leave new religions simply continue their lives and make no effort to publicize widely why they left.

APOSTASY AND ATROCITY TALES

At first glance, the reports of former members would appear to be unimpeachable in their accuracy. After all, they can claim to know from first-hand experience intimate details of the groups of which they were once members. The situation, however, is much more complicated. Not every member of a group has the same access to its inner workings; neophytes and average members, for example, may not be fully aware of the decision-making processes of the leadership. Also, certain teachings may be reserved, as in the Church of Scientology, for those who have progressed along a carefully graded process of deepening awareness. Some ritual practices may only be undertaken by members in good standing or at an advanced stage of their participation. The knowledge and experiences of members may vary according to the time they have spent with the group, their position in any hierarchy within the group, their age and/or gender, or other factors. What ex-members have to say about a group, therefore, is necessarily a partial account that reflects the particularities of their own history with the group.

Beyond their particularity, statements made by former members are frequently not disinterested accounts, even when they are presented as such. Many defectors who publicize their reasons for leaving portray themselves as being selflessly interested in the public good. They depict their time within the group as personally damaging, morally suspect, religiously misguided, and a threat to the broader social order. They offer their own stories as cautionary atrocity tales.

As early as 1780, for example, Valentine Rathbun, who had left the Shakers after spending a brief period as a member, published a highly critical pamphlet that even included accusations that the Shakers practiced witchcraft and murder. As Rathbun put it, he only wanted to warn the public about such a dangerous group based on his experience. Rathbun's broadside clearly laid out the themes that have continued to appear in accounts of vocal ex-members. The leaders, he asserted, were deceptive and manipulative; their followers were virtually powerless to resist the enticements of a loving community and the prospect of salvation, but, in fact, were suffering real harm at the hands of a "new and strange" religious group.

Clearly, reports from former members like Rathbun are not neutral in their point of view. They aim to shape public perception of the group as illegitimate and dangerous and even move some outsiders to act against it. The same motivations are evident in a raft of exposés devoted to the Church of Scientology in the early twenty-first century. Leah Remini, for example, leveraged her memoir *Troublemaker*, into a multiseason documentary television series, *Leah Remini: Scientology and the Aftermath*, which gave a public platform to critical former Scientologists. Such clashes between new or alternative religious movements and disgruntled former members have been a persistent feature of American religious history since colonial days, and they show no signs of abating.

While the clashes between vocal former members and the groups that they have left have dominated the public discussion of new religions, some ex-members' exaggerations and proclivities for sketching dramatic, black and white images of despicable groups, on one side, and selfless public servants, on the other, have obscured the complicated processes of conversion, membership, and disaffiliation. A more nuanced understanding of both insiders and outsiders is needed.

VARIETIES OF DISAFFILIATION

In fact, very few members who leave new religions become dedicated opponents of their former groups. Nor do all members who join a new religion immediately express total commitment and leave all doubts permanently behind. Both members and ex-members have dynamic, complex, and varying relationships to their present and former religious communities.

Just as there are different kinds of insiders to religious groups, including those who have been born into them, those who have converted at one point or another in their lives, those who are at different points of initiation into the group, those who occupy different positions within a group's hierarchy, and those who remain members despite serious questions about one or another aspect of a group' theology or practice, among others, so also are there different kinds of outsiders. They include those who have encountered a group and perhaps even considered affiliation but have stopped short of commitment; those who have joined a parent group but then affiliated with a schismatic sect, such as the Fundamentalist Latter-day Saints (FLDS); those who simply fade away from their membership; those who take their leave while retaining a commitment to some aspects of a group's ideology or practice; those who have been excommunicated from a group in which they would have preferred to maintain membership; those seekers who move from one group to another without ever settling into sustained membership; and those, like Rathbun and Remini, who make something of a career of their opposition to the groups in which they once participated; among others. Every process of affiliation or disaffiliation has distinctive elements.

Observers need to take seriously the variety of ways in which disaffiliation can occur, the different roles that group leaders and members can play in the departure of any member, and the inevitably partial and tendentious nature of reports on their experience by ex-members and members alike. That should alter both the scholarly, and, perhaps more importantly, the public understanding of new religions. One reason that the pejorative label "cult" has achieved such broad acceptance and power in public discourse is that the images of manipulative leaders, deceived members, and imminent personal and social harm that it conveys have been anchored in the dramatic and often spectacular stories of personal suffering and disappointment promulgated by a handful of aggrieved former members.

The stories of former members have brought unquestionable abuses to light, as with the one-time practice of "flirty fishing" or religious prostitution practiced by some female members of the Children of God in the 1970s and 1980s or the practice under the FLDS prophet Warren Jeffs of promoting marriages between very young girls and much older men. Sometimes, as with the Children of God, such revelations have led directly to reform efforts within the groups that have been criticized. The question remains, however, of whether the testimony of a few former members, no matter how damaging and spectacular, provides a sufficiently broad and accurate characterization of a movement as a whole.

This is a particularly pressing problem for new religions, especially in their earliest phases. Established religions generally have been able to weather many different kinds of scandalous reports about, for example, financial malfeasance or widespread sexual abuse. But new religions have a much more precarious purchase on social legitimacy. As with the trial and conviction of Keith Raniere, the leader of NXIVM, in 2019, the exposure of the inner workings of a new, small religious group can effectively end its existence.

There are multiple reasons, then, to study carefully both what former members have to say about their groups and the processes by which they became ex-members. Vocal or "noisy" ex-members represent only a small sampling of those who leave new religions, and their sentiments may not be widely shared.

See also: Brainwashing; Children of God (The Family International); Conversion; Fundamentalist Latter-day Saints; Insider/Outsider Problem, The; NXIVM; Scientology; Seekers; Shakers, The.

Further Reading
Bromley, David G., ed. 1998. *The Politics of Religious Apostasy: The Role of Apostates in the Transformation of Religious Movements.* Westport, CT: Praeger Publishers.

Chryssides, George D. 2014. "The Insider/Outsider Problem in the Study of NRMs." In George D. Chryssides & Benjamin E. Zeller, eds., *The Bloomsbury Companion to New Religious Movements.* London: Bloomsbury.

Chryssides, George D., & Stephen E. Gregg 2017. "'The Silent Majority?': Understanding Apostate Testimony Beyond 'Insider/Outsider Binaries' in the Study of New Religions." In Eugene V. Gallagher, ed., *Visioning New and Minority Religions: Projecting the Future,* pp. 20–32. London: Routledge Press.

Jacobs, Janet Liebman. 1989. *Divine Disenchantment: Deconverting from New Religions.* Bloomington: Indiana University Press.

Rathbun, Valentine. 1781. *An Account of the Matter, Form, and Manner of a New and Strange Religion.* Providence, RI: Bennett Wheeler.

Remini, Leah 2015. *Troublemaker: Surviving Hollywood and Scientology.* New York: Ballantine Books.

Wright, Stuart A. 1987. *Leaving Cults: The Dynamics of Defection.* Washington, DC: Society for the Social Scientific Study of Religion.

Divine Principle

Although other religions may discuss a "Divine Principle," the focus here is on the Unification Church or Movement in which the term has two important references. The broadest concerns the divine principle that animates human history. More narrowly, it refers to the central scriptural text of the religious movement begun by the Rev. Sun Myung Moon (1920–2012) as the Holy Spirit Association for the Unification of World Christianity.

Like many other new religions, the Unification Church originated in the religious experience of its founder. On Easter morning in 1936, Jesus appeared to Moon and told him that he had a special mission on earth. Moon refined his understanding of his task throughout the 1940s, coming to believe that God, as a loving father, wanted this world to be a peaceful and happy place for his children. Unfortunately, as the Bible attests, things went awry virtually from the beginning. Because of Eve's seduction by the serpent or Satan in the Garden of Eden, she and Adam were not able to have perfect, sinless children and establish the Kingdom of God on earth. In a dramatic theological innovation, Moon claimed that although he was supposed to strive toward human perfection, marry, and establish a sanctified family, neither was Jesus able to restore humanity to the state that God originally intended. Consequently, the world is still waiting for a third Adam or the second advent of the Messiah.

Moon's understanding of salvation history is codified in *Divine Principle* (Unificationists do not use the definite pronoun with the title), whose first draft was produced in 1952. It is understood within the movement as both a commentary on the Christian Old and New Testaments and as a supplement to them. As such it plays a role within Unificationism that is similar to the role that *Science and Health with Key to the Scriptures* plays in Christian Science. In the late 1990s, *Divine Principle* was joined to a collection of the works of Moon to form the "Completed Testament Age" canon.

Although the lengthy text provides a comprehensive view of salvation history, its new message hinges on a reinterpretation of the familiar creation stories from Genesis. Like the Raëlians and other new religions, *Divine Principle* cautions against reading the Bible literally. For Moon, the Bible itself does not convey the truth; he likens it to a textbook that teaches the truth, but is in need of correct interpretation. Moon sets up a reciprocal dynamic; readers will know that they have understood the Bible accurately when their reading accords with what they learn from *Divine Principle*.

Reading the Bible accurately is crucial for Unificationists since the current world is entering its last days. The Second Advent of the Lord is imminent, as the work of the Rev. Moon testifies. *Divine Principle* asserts that at the time of the Second Advent the Lord will not simply repeat the words of the New Testament, but will provide new teachings that will establish the new heaven and new earth mentioned in Revelation 21:1. The new teachings will come from Rev. Moon. Although Moon was for a long time reticent about claiming any other role than prophet of the Second Advent, in speeches in the 1990s and 2000s, he fully embraced his identity as the Lord of the Second Advent. He proclaimed that he and his wife, Hak Ja Han Moon (1943–) were the True Parents of all humanity and that they functioned as the Savior and Messiah. Accordingly, *Divine Principle* has to be read as a scripture that prophesies the coming of the Rev. Moon to fulfill, at last, the plans that God has always had for the world.

In many ways, *Divine Principle* is at the center of life for Unificationists. It is preached about, taught, illustrated, summarized, and expanded upon in various contexts; it determines both the way group members view the world and the vocabulary they use to describe it. In their accounts of what drew them to the movement, many Unificationists cite their first encounter with *Divine Principle*.

See also: Christian Science; Millennialism; Moon, Rev. Sun Myung (1920–2012); New Scriptures and New Religious Movements; Raëlians, The; Unification Church, The.

Further Reading

Chryssides, George D. 1991. *The Advent of Sun Myung Moon: The Origins, Beliefs and Practices of the Unification Church*. London: Macmillan.

Gallagher, Eugene V. 2014. *Reading and Writing Scripture in New Religious Movements: New Bibles and New Revelations*. New York: Palgrave.

Moon Sun Myung. 1973. *Divine Principle*. New York: Holy Spirit Association for the Unification of World Christianity.

Druidry

As one of the strands of contemporary Neopaganism, Druidry is practiced by a cluster of groups that find their inspiration in ancient Celtic religion. As with Neopaganism, in general, there is some tension between Druid groups that claim to represent an unbroken tradition that reaches back to pre-Christian times and those who acknowledge that theirs is an imaginative reconstruction that makes use of ancient symbols, ideas, and practices. Some Druid groups that focus on connections to ancient ethnic wisdom see themselves as compatible with any religious affiliation, but many of the most prominent are Neopagan in orientation.

Although a Druid revival can be traced to the later eighteenth century in Britain, with the foundation of the Ancient Order of Druids in 1781, The Druid Order was established in its contemporary form in 1909 or 1912 by George MacGregor-Reid (?1862–1946). The group observed the Autumn and Spring Equinoxes and the Winter and Summer Solstices. In 1964, after a leadership dispute, Ross Nichols (1902–1975) left the group to found The Order of Bards, Ovates, and Druids (see www.druidry.org/).

Relying on both partial historical data about ancient Druids and his own fanciful reconstructions, Nichols understood the Bards to be the custodians of traditional wisdom expressed in stories and songs. In ritual situations, they are inspired by Awen, a spirit that comes from the Goddess. A central Druid ritual is the *Eisteddfod* or "session," which includes performances by musicians and poets. Where the Bards focus on the past, Ovates focus on wisdom from other worlds, including nature. Ovates practice divination and perform healing work for individual illnesses, social problems, and relations with nature. Druids, strictly speaking, organize rituals and represent Druidic groups locally and nationally. Although the three categories of Bards, Ovates, and Druids can be understood as initiatory ranks within some groups, "Druid" is also used as a general term for all who follow this Pagan path.

Local groups of Druids are generally known as groves and may be parts of broader associations called orders. There are multiple Druid organizations throughout Europe and in North America.

In the United States, the beginnings of Druidry can be traced to an act of student rebellion in 1963 at Carleton College in Northfield, Minnesota. At the same time that Tim Zell (1942–) and other students at Westminster College in Missouri were developing the Pagan Church of All Worlds, a group of students bridling at Carleton's mandatory worship requirement established the Reformed Druids of North America (RDNA) as a way of avoiding chapel attendance. The Carleton Druids' original rituals were a pastiche of general "religious" statements and some vague Pagan sentiments. But over time the immersion of some members grew more serious.

The greatest impact of the RDNA, however, came after the Berkeley grove ordained Isaac Bonewits (1949–2010) as a priest in 1969. Though he had been born into a Roman Catholic home, Bonewits had become interested in various alternative religions from an early age. He even devised an individualized major in magic and thaumaturgy at the University of California, Berkeley, becoming the first person to graduate with such a college degree. He quickly published his undergraduate thesis as *Real Magic* (1971). Bonewits eventually established a splinter group, the Schismatic Druids of North America, that focused more on Paganism. In 1983, he established Ár nDraíocht Féin (from the Irish "Our Own Druidism"), also known as A Druid Fellowship (ADF), which became the largest Pagan Druid group in the United States. Influenced by his academic work, Bonewits took a wider view of Druid origins. In particular, Bonewits followed the French scholar Georges Dumézil (1898–1986) in trying to discover the common pre-Christian Indo-European religious practices. Throughout his career as a Pagan teacher and writer, Bonewits worked to establish Druidry on a firm intellectual footing. As indicated in the introduction to what he called the "Classic ADF Liturgical Design," Bonewits aimed for a religious experience that was "esthetically pleasing, historically plausible, magically powerful, and spiritually satisfying" (see http://www.neopagan.net/NeoDruidismRiteOutline.html). As a scholarly practitioner, Bonewits gave his form of Paganism richness and depth that have continued to attract others.

In all its forms, Druidry remains a vital part of worldwide contemporary Paganism.

See also: Church of All Worlds, The; Neopaganism; Wicca.

Further Reading

Bonewits, Isaac. 1989. *Real Magic*. York Beach, ME: Samuel Weiser.

Clifton, Chas S. 2006. *Her Hidden Children: The Rise of Wicca and Paganism in America*. Lanham, MD: AltaMira Press.

Harvey, Graham. 1997. *Contemporary Paganism: Listening People, Speaking Earth*. New York: New York University Press.

Hutton, Ronald. 2007. *The Druids: A History*. New York: Continuum.

Dudeism

New religious movements have often been perceived to test the line between what counts as religious and what doesn't. The discourse about "cults," for example, has been devoted to distinguishing acceptable from unacceptable religions or even religion from nonreligion.

The challenges that religious innovations pose to the status quo are particularly evident in new religious movements that find their inspiration in elements of popular culture. Such groups, identified variously as invented, hyperreal, or fiction-based religions, have frequently made effective use of the worldwide web as a means of storing and widely disseminating information and of creating at least virtual communities. In several instances, religious groups have developed out of dedicated groups of fans of TV shows or films, as with religions based on *Star Trek*, Jediism (focused on the universe of the *Star Wars* films) or Matrixism (focused on the *Matrix* trilogy). Such is the case with Dudeism.

Dudeism derives from Ethan and Joel Coen's film, *The Big Lebowski*. The central character, the Dude, has simple desires: he wants to get high, listen to music, and go bowling. He wants simply to take it easy and "abide." While the film initially received negative reviews, it quickly built a devoted following. While watching the film again after an afternoon spent at a bar the future "Dudely Lama," American journalist Oliver Benjamin (1968–), decided to enshrine the outlook of the Dude in the Church of the Latter-day Dude.

As the church's name suggests, there is a hefty dose of parody included in Dudeism, which is reminiscent of other new religions, such as the Church of Satan and the Church of the Flying Spaghetti Monster. Dudeism professes to take nothing very seriously, including itself. Nonetheless, it bills itself as the "religion for its time and place" and takes its un-seriousness seriously, even as it admits to having only a "semi-organized worldview." The church does not emphasize doctrine, as the *Take it Easy Manifesto* puts it, "we prefer direct experience of takin'er easy" (https://dudeism.com/takeiteasymanifesto/).

Dudeism presents itself as an "open source" religion that welcomes members' perceptions about what is "dude" or "undude." Nonetheless, the church sees its dominant ethos of the "rebel shrug" manifested in ancient Daoism, and many other religious traditions.

Dudeism takes a similarly relaxed attitude toward ritual, though it does offer a "fast, free, and easy" process of ordination online. It claims nearly half a million ordained Dudeist priests, who can, among other things, officiate at weddings. The recommended final words to the wedding ceremony aptly capture Dudeism's ethos, "Dude and Dude, you may now seal it with a kiss, or what have you. Bar's over there."

See also: Anamadim; Cult; Jediism; New Religions on/and the Internet.

Further Reading

Coen, Ethan, & Joel Coen, dirs. 1998. *The Big Lebowski*. Gramercy Pictures.

Kosnáč, Pavel. 2017. "Pop Culture—A New Source of Spirituality?" In Eugene V. Gallagher, ed., *Visioning New and Minority Religions: Projecting the Future*, pp. 145–155. New York: Routledge.

Possamai, Adam, ed. 2012. *Handbook of Hyper-Real Religion*. Leiden: E. J. Brill.

E

Eckankar

A rich array of Indian religious traditions has inspired many new religious movements in the West. Some, like the International Society for Krishna Consciousness and the Self-Realization Fellowship, were brought to the West by Indian teachers, but others, like Theosophy and Diamond Way Tibetan Buddhism, were begun by Westerners who either had, or claimed to have had, direct contact with Indian Spiritual Teachers. Eckankar, which was formally established in the United States in 1965, falls into the latter category.

Paul Twitchell (1909–1971) was responsible for bringing Eckankar to light. He denied, however, that it was in any way a new religion. Instead, he portrayed it as the oldest religion on earth. Twitchell claimed to have experienced "God-realization" in 1956 and to have been tutored by a group of spiritual masters, including fictional individuals Twitchell identified as Sudar Singh and Rebazar Tarzs, who were part of the Vairagi order. Consequently, Twitchell presented himself as the 971st living Eck master in a lineage that went back to the God Rama, an incarnation of Vishnu, or, in

The founder of Eckankar claimed to be the 971st living Eck master. The stylized "Eck" in the symbol of the religion can mean Life Force or Holy Spirit or the source of everything. Individuals are believed to have a small spark of that Life Force, and Eckankar aims to help them achieve that realization. (Fidan Babayeva/Dreamstime.com)

other tellings, to a spiritual being named Gakko from the planet Venus. As the Eck master, he was the oracle of God for his time and the "Mahanta" who embodied the essence of God. The same titles would be held by Twitchell's successors, including Harold Klemp (1942–), the current living Eck master.

The origins of Eckankar are difficult to establish on some points, at least in part because Twitchell was prone to self-mythologization, even to the point of claiming multiple dates for his birth. It is clear, however, that Twitchell was a spiritual seeker. In 1950, he joined the Self Revelation Church of Absolute Monism, a subgroup of the Self-Realization Fellowship begun by Paramahansa Yogananda (1893–1952) led by Swami Premananda (1903–1995). In that group, Twitchell learned Kriya yoga. After being expelled from that group for personal misconduct, he became associated with Kripal Singh's (1894–1974) Ruhani Satsang, which was part of the Indian Radhasaomi tradition. Groups in that tradition blend elements of Sikhism and Hinduism in their beliefs and practices. Some scholars identify Singh as one of the greatest influences on Twitchell and his conception of Eckankar. Twitchell was also influenced by Theosophy, another new religion that claims to represent Eastern wisdom.

For a time, Twitchell also participated in Scientology, even attaining the status of "clear" on Scientology's Bridge to Total Freedom. Although Twitchell claimed originality for his religious teachings, careful scholarly detective work has shown that he was deeply influenced by the various religious associations before founding Eckankar, even to the point of borrowing wholesale from several sources in the books that he wrote. While he did arrange the sources that he borrowed into a distinctive new pattern, Twitchell's new presentation of an ancient religion owed those sources a substantial debt.

The goal of Eckankar is to lead practitioners to self-realization and then to God-realization, just as Twitchell himself had accomplished. Like the Radhasoami tradition, Eckankar imagines a universe consisting of a dozen different planes or levels and developed a growing group of spiritual exercises that an individual could undertake to approach the source of everything, called the "ECK" or the "Light and Sound of God." The teachings of Eckankar take a gnostic overtone when they portray the individual soul as a spark of Eck or Soul itself. Thus, self-realization leads to God-realization. Twitchell was particularly interested in the process of "bilocation" or soul travel, which could be achieved in a dream state or through meditation and visualization. That practice may have drawn on Scientology's concept of "exteriorization." One of the rituals that Twitchell developed consisted of chanting "Hu," a name for God or Eck. The Eckankar website (www.eckankar.org) contains links to audio and video recordings of the chanting and descriptions of other spiritual exercises.

When Twitchell died suddenly in 1971, the Board of Eckankar, possibly in collaboration with Twitchell's widow, appointed Darwin Gross (1928–2008) as the new Mahanta and 972nd living Eck master. As is fairly common in such moments of transition, Gross's leadership was not accepted by all Eckists and several left the group, despite the growth of the organization under his leadership. Through a complex set of maneuverings, Gross was ousted in 1984 by Harold Klemp, whom Gross had appointed as his successor in 1981.

Making it less culturally dissonant, Klemp has gradually emphasized the similarities between Eckankar and ancient Western wisdom traditions and diminished Twitchell's emphasis on technical Indian vocabulary. In the late 1980s, he moved the headquarters of Eckankar to Chanhassen, Minnesota, a suburb of Minneapolis. On 174 acres there he built the Temple of Eck, which is described as the worldwide center for the teachings of the Light and Sound of God, and two miles of "contemplation trails."

Although Eckankar does not release public membership figures, estimates of adherents number in the tens of thousands worldwide. Beyond that, Eckankar has nurtured a number of teachers who have gone on to found their own new religious movements. For example, John-Roger Hinkins (1934–2014) left the group to establish the Movement of Spiritual Inner Awareness. Darwin Gross, after being pushed out of the group by the man he recognized as the 973rd living Eck master, founded The Ancient Teachings of the Masters. The parent group and its offshoots continue to keep Twitchell's distinctive teachings alive and attract religious seekers.

See also: Diamond Way, The; Elan Vital (Divine Light Mission); International Society for Krishna Consciousness (ISKCON); Movement of Spiritual Inner Awareness; Scientology; Seekers; Self-Realization Fellowship (Yogananda); Theosophy; 3HO.

Further Reading

Lane, David Christopher. 2006. "Eckankar." In Eugene V. Gallagher & W. Michael Ashcraft, eds., *Introduction to New and Alternative Religions in America*, Vol. 3, pp. 113–131. Westport, CT: Greenwood Press.

Lane, David Christopher. 2017. *The Making of a Spiritual Movement: The Untold Story of Paul Twitchell and Eckankar*, 6th ed. Walnut, CA: MSAC Philosophy Group.

Olson, Roger E. 1995. "ECKANAR: From Ancient Science of Soul Travel to New Age Religion." In Timothy Miller, ed. *America's Alternative Religions*, pp. 363–370. Albany: SUNY Press.

Eco-Paganism

Many religions engage the idea that the natural world is sacred and should be preserved at all costs. Christianity argues that God is the creator of the world, thus to violate nature is a sin. Hinduism emphasizes the practice of vegetarianism, which is rooted in the principle of karma, and avoiding harmful deeds such as killing; eating no meat has the added effects of preserving animal life and preventing deforestation. Though ancient, in many ways, the concept of "Ecospirituality" has taken on new life in the twentieth century for a variety of reasons, not the least of which are movements like Eco-Paganism that link religious and ecological practices.

ROOTS AND EVOLUTION

Neopaganism descends from Paganism—with some claiming that the "newer" form is a direct continuation of the old and others perceiving the former as its own phenomenon built from ancient Pagan practices and modern, eclectic New Age spirituality. In antiquity, "Pagan" was a term used to describe non-Christians, particularly those who worshipped a pantheon of deities rather than one God. Thus, the term itself is difficult to define in any holistic sense. However, Neopagans often trace their roots to English Pagans, who were notable for their worship of nature and their pantheism (the belief that the divine is imminent in the world around them). Neopaganism emerged in earnest in England in the early to mid-twentieth century and in the United States in the 1960s and 1970s. The more recent U.S. movement, in particular, seemed to align itself with the growing environmentalist movement.

Neopagans often self-consciously focus on nature. Their holy days are often centered around natural events, such as the seasons, and their rituals often employ natural objects, such as plants and herbs, and even (though not always) take place outside in nature. Since they believe that the divine exists around, not simply above them, there is a natural commitment to loving and worshipping nature in its own right, not simply as a creation over which human beings may hold dominion. Those who consider themselves to be Eco-Pagans, however, take their love of nature to the level of +activism: fighting for the environment as a religious act.

ECOLOGICAL PRACTICES AND IDEOLOGY

In fact, many Eco-Pagans were environmental activists first, becoming drawn to Neopaganism for its naturalism. Eco-Pagans see their purpose as rooted in a fundamental interconnectedness with nature, meaning that they cannot exist in the world unless they are actively protecting it. In this way, commitment to the environment is as political as it is spiritual. Some Pagans maintain that Pagan activism is a synonym for Eco-Paganism. Very often their rituals involve some kind of protest or act of resistance. Eco-Pagans may hail from a variety of Pagan groups, including Wicca, Druidry, and Chaos Magick. In this way, Eco-Paganism cuts across "denominational" lines within Paganism: there is no singular sect of Eco-Pagans. However, some of the most notable names in Neopaganism are Eco-Pagans, such as Starhawk (née Miriam Simos, 1951–) who has been quite vocal of the need for recommitting spiritual, financial, and political resources to preserve the environment.

Outside of political activism, Eco-Pagans are often concerned with the process of healing, both of the earth and the earth as a source of healing. Rituals that are directed at healing the earth from the harm being done to it are many and often derive from indigenous spiritualties. Further, Neopaganism and alternative medicine have been traditionally aligned, and natural substances are often at the root of this connection. Thus, there exists a religious need among Eco-Pagans to preserve the earth to retain good physical and spiritual health. Additionally, Eco-Paganism is often connected to Ecofeminism. Ecofeminists argue that the oppression of women and the destruction of the environment are the result of the patriarchal systems of Western civilization, including major religious (namely Christian) and economic systems. Men in power perceived women as those closer to nature and therefore necessary to be controlled, lest they disrupt the forward advance of Western conquest and dominion of the natural world. Neopaganism is often viewed as a women-centered and feminist religion: the Goddess is worshipped equally if not more than male deities; women play central roles in leadership; and the female body is celebrated for its life-giving and nurturing abilities. Thus, it is quite natural that a nature-centered, women-focused religion would align with a nature-focused, feminist ideology.

IN THE AGE OF CLIMATE CHANGE

The environmentalist movement has been around for decades, but in the era of climate change, its aims have taken on a new sense of urgency. Unsurprisingly, Eco-Pagans have been at the forefront of those calling for change as global warming becomes a greater and more dangerous reality. For example, the Pagan Federation issued a "Statement on the Environment" in 2015, seeking signatures for those willing to commit their efforts to combating climate change and saving the environment. The statement argues that the earth has the capacity to heal itself if only people would stop harming it, thus efforts to end damaging practices such as fracking are necessary. Other Eco-Pagans are even more active in their resistance—protesting pipelines or performing pagan rituals on natural sites slated for demolition.

It is unclear how many Eco-Pagans there are in the world, since they often identify with a particular Neopagan sect. However, their message of religious environmentalism has been taken up in many quarters as the movement for action on climate change grows. In this way, Eco-Paganism has an impact larger than its numbers of members might suggest.

See also: Chaos Magick; Druidry; Healing, Health, and New Religious Movements; Neopaganism; New Age, The; Starhawk (1951–); Wicca; Women in New Religious Movements.

Further Reading
Gottlieb, Roger S. 2010. *The Oxford Handbook of Religion and Ecology*. Oxford: Oxford University Press.
Pike, Sarah. 2017. *For the Wild: Ritual and Commitment in Radical Eco-Activism*. Berkeley: University of California Press.
Taylor, Bron. 2009. *Dark Green Religion: Nature Spirituality and the Planetary Future*. Berkeley: University of California Press.
Tucker, Mary Evelyn, & John Grim, eds. 2017. "Nature Spiritualitis." In Mary Evelyn Tucker & John Grim, eds., *Routledge Handbook of Religion and Ecology*. New York: Routledge Press.

Eddy, Mary Baker (1821–1910)
EARLY LIFE AND DISCOVERIES

Mary Baker Eddy (née Mary Morse Baker) was born on July 16, 1821, in New Hampshire. Her parents, Mark and Abigail Baker, were both devout Congregationalists, though their daughter would later reject their Reformed Calvinist

The founder of Christian Science, Mary Baker Eddy, came to her conclusions about the unreality of matter and the ability of the mind to effect cures after suffering a near-fatal fall in 1866. She claimed that her method of healing followed the principles established in the miracles of Jesus. (Library of Congress)

doctrines, such as predestination, deeming them to be too severe. Eddy was a sickly child and adult, suffering nearly constant ailments or physical blights. Western medicine did little to alleviate her distress, leading her to consult those outside of the medical mainstream—specifically homeopathic doctors or healers. In 1862, she met Phineas Parkhurst Quimby, who was a practitioner of magnetic healing (whereby magnets were placed on pressure points on the body to draw out toxins) and a believer in mesmerism, or the idea that there is an invisible natural force connecting and possessed by all living things, which can be manipulated to help or harm the body. Quimby's work led him to the conclusion that many ailments were rooted in the mind. Accordingly, those who believed they were better actually felt better. It was Quimby who may have turned Eddy onto the idea that an individual could channel Christ's healing power by focused prayer and right thinking (which later caused controversy as to the originality of her views).

In 1866, came a turning point in Eddy's spiritual and physical journey. She experienced a near-fatal fall on ice, resulting in near paralysis. Despairing of recovery, Eddy turned to the Bible, specifically accounts of Christ's miraculous healings. After three days she rose, completely healed and on a journey of spiritual discovery that would lead to the founding of Christian Science a few years later.

FROM MIND CURE TO CHRISTIAN SCIENCE

After several years of Bible study coupled with a burgeoning mind-centered healing practice, Eddy became convinced that all humans possessed the ability to heal themselves, being gifted that capacity by God. However, years of wrong thinking or "sin" made them incapable of accessing such ability. Contributing to this clouded thought was modern, especially Western, medicine, which had created a monopoly on wellness: convincing people that they needed external remedies to become well. Defying these conventions, Eddy emphasized a new sort of practice that combined scientific methods tested through her healing practice and beliefs in God, Christ, and the truth of the Bible. Eddy intended this practice, which she called Christian Science, to supplement traditional Christian worship, even to work within other Christian denominations. However, her proposal was popular enough (or strange enough) to warrant its own denomination, leading to her founding of the Church of Christ, Scientist in 1875.

Arguably her greatest accomplishment was the publication of *Science and Health with Key to the Scriptures* five years earlier in 1870. Though Eddy was a prolific writer, it was *Science and Health* for which she was best known and which had the widest reach (selling in the tens of millions by the early twenty-first century). In the text, Eddy provides commentary meant to correspond to the Bible and unpack its hidden scientific meaning, and offers insight upon topics ranging from creation, to the apocalypse and marriage, to more scientific questions about medicine, "being," and physiology. In addition, the book explained how to practice Christian Science as well as how to teach it—a feature that would ensure the perseverance of the movement after she died. Eddy considered it her life's work to perfect *Science and Health*, spending the majority of her life editing and revising the text.

LATER LIFE AND LEGACY

Though her personal and family life was anything but stable—thrice married, twice widowed, and once divorced, bearing one son with whom she would have a markedly strained relationship—Eddy saw her Church continue to grow and her role in it expand accordingly. Following her third husband's (Asa Eddy's) death, Eddy settled in Boston, which became the hub of the Christian Science universe. In the last several decades of her life, Eddy experienced a series of incredible highs and lows. In 1894, the home of the First Church of Christ (known as the Mother Church) was completed in Boston; she would serve briefly as its pastor, but the experience along with her belief that the sacred texts should stand on their own, led her to declare *Science and Health* as the pastor the following year. During the ensuing decades, she founded the Christian Science Publishing Society and *The Christian Science Monitor*, launching the Church of Christ, Scientist as a juggernaut of the religious publishing world.

However, despite her steady stream of successes, Eddy was a controversial figure. The fact of her multiple marriages led to salacious gossip, but it was the accusations by former students that brought the greatest public scrutiny. Eddy was accused of practicing dangerous and misleading methods of healing—an accusation that would ultimately land her in court, though she would ultimately be acquitted of wrongdoing. Eddy also came under fire for her theory of "malicious animal magnetism," namely, the use of one's mental powers to "mentally assassinate" someone. Several Christian Scientists ultimately committed suicide for fear of becoming targets of malicious animal magnetism. Eddy reportedly became increasingly paranoid that mental assassins would seek to kill her. Psychiatrists from Eddy's time to the present have used this fact among others to pathologize Eddy, some going so far as to describe her behaviors as those of a schizophrenic. However, such analyses do little to explain the measure of her accomplishments, the depth of her religious thought, or the success of her religious movement.

On December 3, 1910, Eddy succumbed to pneumonia (though some Christian Scientists believed that she was not dead, but peacefully sleeping, reflecting the belief that material death was illusory and her true self—her spirit—lived on). Her death was announced in newspapers around the globe, remarking on her extraordinary life, how she had overcome her bodily foibles to found a religious movement that reimagined human ability and material reality.

See also: Christian Science; New Thought.

Further Reading

Eddy, Mary Baker. 1934. *Science and Health with Key to the Scriptures.* Boston: Published by the First Church of Christ, Scientist.

Eddy, Mary Baker. 2002. *Mary Baker Eddy: Speaking for Herself.* Boston: The Mary Baker Eddy Collection.

Gill, Gillian. 1998. *Mary Baker Eddy.* Reading, Mass.: Perseus Books.

Peel, Robert. 1966. *Mary Baker Eddy.* 3 volumes. New York: Holt, Rinehart and Winston.

PRIMARY SOURCE DOCUMENTS

Excerpt from Mary Baker Eddy's Autobiography *Retrospection and Introspection* (1875) and *Science and Health with Key to the Scriptures* (1891)

Mary Baker Eddy first founded The Church of Christ, Scientist in New England in 1879. The religious framework that followed came to be known as Christian Science. These excerpts from her autobiography and her foundational text, both of which illustrate the views that led up to the establishment of Christian Science and then sustained a robust following, focusing specifically on the role of the individual in relation to the divine.

Excerpt from *Retrospection and Introspection* (1875)

No person can take the individual place of the Virgin Mary. No person can compass or fulfil the individual mission of Jesus of Nazareth. No person can take the place of the author of Science and Health, the

Discoverer and Founder of Christian Science. Each individual must fill his own niche in time and eternity. The second appearing of Jesus is, unquestionably, the spiritual advent of the advancing idea of God, as in Christian Science.

Source: Eddy, Mary Baker. *Retrospection and Introspection.* Boston: Trustees under the Will of Mary Baker G. Eddy, 1891, p. 70.

Excerpts from *Science and Health with Key to the Scriptures* (1891)

The prayer that reforms the sinner and heals the sick is an absolute faith that all things are possible to God,—a spiritual understanding of Him, an unselfed love. Regardless of what another may say or think on this subject, I speak from experience. Prayer, watching, and working, combined with self-immolation, are God's gracious means for accomplishing whatever has been successfully done for the Christianization and health of mankind. . . .

Prayer cannot change the Science of being, but it tends to bring us into harmony with it. Goodness attains the demonstration of Truth. A request that God will save us is not all that is required. The mere habit of pleading with the divine Mind, as one pleads with a human being, perpetuates the belief in God as humanly circumscribed,—an error which impedes spiritual growth. . . .

The world must grow to the spiritual understanding of prayer. If good enough to profit by Jesus' cup of earthly sorrows, God will sustain us under these sorrows. Until we are thus divinely qualified and are willing to drink his cup, millions of vain repetitions will never pour into prayer the unction of Spirit in demonstration of power and "with signs following." Christian Science reveals a necessity for overcoming the world, the flesh, and evil, and thus destroying all error. . . .

Become conscious for a single moment that Life and intelligence are purely spiritual,—neither in nor of Spiritualized consciousness matter,—and the body will then utter no complaints. If suffering from a belief in sickness, you will find yourself suddenly well. Sorrow is turned into joy when the body is controlled by spiritual Life, Truth, and Love. Hence the hope of the promise Jesus bestows: "He that believeth on me, the works that I do shall he do also; . . . because I go unto my Father,"—[because the Ego is absent from the body, and present with Truth and Love.] The Lord's Prayer is the prayer of Soul, not of material sense. . . .

Our Father which art in heaven,
Our Father-Mother God, all-harmonious,
Hallowed be Thy name.
Adorable One.

Thy kingdom come.
Thy kingdom is come; Thou are ever-present.
Thy will be done in earth, as it is in heaven.
Enable us to know,—as in heaven, so on earth,—God is omnipotent, supreme.
Give us this day our daily bread;
Give us grace for to-day; feed the famished affections;
And forgive us our debts, as we forgive our debtors.
And love is reflected in love;
And lead us not into temptation, but deliver us from evil,
And God leadeth us not into temptation, but delivereth us from sin, disease, and death.
For Thine is the kingdom, and the power, and the glory, forever.
For God is infinite, all-power, all Life, Truth, Love, over all, and All. . . .

St. John writes, in the tenth chapter of his book of Revelation:—
And I saw another mighty angel come down from heaven, clothed with a cloud: and a rainbow was upon his head, and his face was as it were the sun, and his feet as pillars of fire: and he had in his hand a little book open: and he set his right foot upon the sea, and his left foot on the earth.
This angel or message which comes from God, clothed with a cloud, prefigures divine Science. To mortal sense Science seems at first obscure, abstract, and dark; but a bright promise crowns its brow. When understood, it is Truth's prism and praise. When you look it fairly in the face, you can heal by its means, and it has for you a light above the sun, for God "is the light thereof." Its feet are pillars of fire, foundations of Truth and Love. It brings the baptism of the Holy Ghost, whose flames of Truth were prophetically described by John the Baptist as consuming error. . . .

Human sense may well marvel at discord, while, to a diviner sense, harmony is the real and discord the unreal. We may well be astonished at sin, sickness, and death. We may well be perplexed at human fear; and still more astounded at hatred, which lifts its hydra head, showing its horns in the many inventions of evil. But why should we stand aghast at nothingness? The great red dragon symbolizes a lie,—the belief that substance, life, and intelligence can be material. This dragon stands for the sum total of human error. The ten horns of the dragon typify the belief that matter has power of its own, and that by means of an evil mind in matter the Ten Commandments can be broken. . . .
Love fulfils the law of Christian Science, and nothing short of this divine Principle, understood and demonstrated, can ever furnish the vision of the Apocalypse, open the seven seals of error with Truth, or uncover the myriad

illusions of sin, sickness, and death. Under the supremacy of Spirit, it will be seen and acknowledged that matter must disappear.

Source: Eddy, Mary Baker. *Science and Health with Key to the Scriptures.* Boston: The First Church of Christ, Scientist, 1906, copyright renewed 1934. Available at: http://christiansciencemedia.org/files/2010/03/Science-and-Health-with-Key-to-the-Scriptures.pdf.

Elan Vital (Divine Light Mission)

Elan Vital, or Divine Light Mission, experienced many iterations over its history, but its primary purpose has always been the dissemination of the teachings of Prem Rawat (1957–). Some of the organizational shifts were the direct result of Rawat's threading the line between the secular and religious implications of his thought.

It was Rawat's father, Shri Hans Ji Maharaj (1900–1966) whose stature as an Indian guru prompted the original creation of Divine Light Mission during the 1960s. After his father's death, then nine-year-old Rawat became his father's successor, over the protestations of his older brothers. Rawat spent his childhood attending school and touring India to spread his father's teachings, then going by the name Guru Maharaj Ji. He attracted the attention of a growing group of Western followers—particularly seekers associated with the ongoing countercultural movement—leading to extended travel in England and the United States during the 1970s. Divine Light Mission reached its height during the 1970s and 1980s, attracting over fifty thousand followers and drawing extensive media attention (due in great part to the youth of its guru). After decline in membership during the early 1980s, most ashrams were closed and the Divine Light Mission dissolved, but was reborn as Elan Vital. The administrative and charitable arm of the movement continued to operate from 1983 to 2010. In 2003, Rawat founded the Prem Rawat Foundation, and then in 2008, the Words of Peace Global, both of which are charged with the maintenance and dissemination of Rawat's discourses and message, much of which exists in digital, streaming form.

The movement of Elan Vital toward a more secular organization was foreshadowed by Rawat's repeated public insistences that his teachings not be narrowly defined as religious, but universal in their applicability. Throughout his tenure as the leader of Elan Vital, Rawat has sought to avoid transformation into an organized religion and has dropped much of the distinctive Indian and Hindu culture that characterized the earlier movement under his father. In fact, the name "Elan Vital," traditionally a French philosophical term translated as "vital force," was chosen specifically because it lacked Indian associations; it was around this time that Rawat also dropped the moniker Maharaji and stated a preference for his given name.

The primary aim of Elan Vital was self-knowledge or the realization that total inner peace was inherent in every person and simply needed to be unlocked through practice. To achieve this inner knowledge, practitioners engage in a teacher-student relationship, often with Rawat himself. The practitioner must approach the practice with a promise to engage in the techniques, known as "Knowledge," for at least one hour a day. The techniques themselves are intended to be secret (though descriptions of the practices have leaked and appear to involve a combination of meditation, chanting of mantras, and facial and bodily positioning), but were originally known under the names "Light," "Sound," "Name/Word," and "Nectar"; they came to be known as the First, Second, Third, and Fourth techniques.

During the era of the Divine Light Mission, practitioners would gather at ashrams to partake in the four meditative techniques and to hear "mahatmas" (renunciants or those who lived a life of asceticism and celibacy on site) discourse on Maharaji's teachings. *Darshan* (worship) of Maharaji occurred as would communal chanting. However, as Rawat began to move the movement away from its Hindu origins, these practices were discontinued. Today practice is undertaken on a primarily individual basis, and the teacher-student relationship most often exists virtually (students learn of the path of "Knowledge" through distance-learning courses).

Institutionally, the movement was always diffuse. At first, this reflected the fact that ashrams emerged somewhat haphazardly—the result of concentrated interest by local practitioners rather than institutional determination. Then, as Rawat continually avoided the trappings of organized religion, the ashram network fell apart. Today, Elan Vital exists in two organizations—the Prem Rawat Foundation and the Words of Global Peace—which maintain a strong online presence, but have successfully voided themselves of specifically religious intent and focus on the universality of Rawat's words.

See also: Charisma and Leadership in New Religious Movements; Hindu New Religious Movements; Seekers; Yoga.

Further Reading
Geaves, Ron A. 2004. "From Divine Light Mission to Elan Vital and Beyond: An Exploration of Change and Adaptation." *Nova Religio* 7: 45–62.
Geaves, Ron A. 2008. "Forget Transmitted Memory: The De-Traditionalized 'Religion' of Prem Rawat." *Journal of Contemporary Religion* 24, no. 1: 19–33.
Roof, Wade Clark. 2000. "Divine Light Mission." In *Contemporary American Religion*. New York: Macmillan Reference.

Environmentalism and New Religious Movements

Many date the beginning of the modern environmental movement to the publication of Rachel Carson's groundbreaking book, *Silent Spring* (1962), which targeted the harmful effects of pesticides. However, care for the environment has long been the purview of various religious traditions, including new religious movements. Even those born in the aftermath of Carson's book often claimed to be revitalizing ancient traditions that made care for the environment a religious act. These new religious movements must balance otherworldliness with this-worldliness and individual spiritual advancement with ethical commitment to community and planet. Some argue, however, environmentalism has become its own new religious movement.

ROOTS AND FORMS

Religions have engaged with nature long before religious environmentalism developed in the twentieth century. In South Asia, Hindus advocated for care of the earth, which often manifested in a focus on vegetarianism and an emphasis on the importance of respecting all living things (practices often reflected and further emphasized in Hindu new religious movements). Pagan traditions in Europe treated the natural world as the site of spiritual connection with the divine. Deities often corresponded to different earthly elements or phenomena. Religions in Africa and the Americas did not separate the natural from the supernatural realm. In African traditional religions, a pantheon of deities or spiritual beings had care of various natural elements, and much of the focus of different tribal and kinship groups was on mastering, and occasionally, appeasing these elements to create balance in their communities. In the South and North American context, various civilizations arose in tandem with their environmental and natural surroundings, prompting tribes with spiritual focus on agriculture, hunting, or the excavation of minerals.

As European colonial conquest increased and both religious and natural resources were threatened, a number of new religious movements arose in response to this infringement. Nativist millennial movements appeared throughout the nineteenth century among indigenous populations in Oceania, Africa, and North and South America. For example, the Ghost Dance movement, led by the prophet Wovoka, mixed Christian millennialism with Lakota practice and belief in response to Western expansion of the frontier. Wovoka promoted the idea that if the Lakota and other indigenous peoples danced the Ghost Dance, then Christ would return, ushering in a new world where the buffalo had returned and the earth-destroying Wasichus (white people) were gone. Though the movement ended in tragedy at Wounded Knee (1890), the Native American Church, which promotes a similar mix of Christianity, indigenous traditions, and environmental activism, has taken up the mantle in the twentieth and twenty-first centuries.

At the turn of the twentieth century, a number of new religious movements arose with an environmental focus. An offshoot of Theosophy, Anthroposophy, founded by Rudolf Steiner (1861–1925) merged scientific discovery with religious innovation, which led to a number of initiatives, including advocacy of biodynamic farming. Steiner, who argued for the unity of humanity alongside care for community and the earth, proposed a system of sustainable farming that employed various esoteric methods intended to invest the soil with both physical and spiritual fertilizer. Though the practice has been critiqued by those who argue for the pseudoscientific nature of these practices, overall its results and methods are aligned with those of organic farming practices throughout the globe.

Also emerging at the beginning of the twentieth century and in the occult religious milieu was Neopaganism. Neopaganism, whose members often claimed to be descendants of early Pagan traditions while combining these traditions with occult religious practices and knowledge, focused much of its ritual and belief on connection with the natural world. There are many forms of Neopaganism, some of which are more forward with their environmentalism, such as Druidry. Druids actively promote harmony and worship of nature, arguing that the earth is itself the site of the divine, and partake of nearly all rituals and festivals outside (and often at major Pagan sites throughout the United Kingdom). Druids are commonly engaged in critique of practices such as fracking or economic exploitation of land, arguing that such activities violate the landscape, which is inherently divine.

Though active in the first half of the twentieth century, Neopaganism became far more prominent, particularly in the United States, during the 1960s and 1970s, as a part of the general Zeitgeist of New Age religions. For New Age religions in general, many have taken environmentalism or increased awareness of the natural world as an element of spiritual practice.

THE IMPACT OF CLIMATE CHANGE

Now that climate change is an assured fact, those new religious movements that ground themselves in care for the earth have felt a greater urgency to disseminate their views. Additionally, environmentalism itself has spawned its own religious movements. Perhaps most notable is Eco-Paganism. Though Eco-Pagans, like Neopagans, derive much of their ritual and belief from ancient Paganism, many Eco-Pagans were environmental activists or ecofeminists before they tied their environmentalism with religious views. Eco-Paganism is an inherently political religious movement that considers protest or acts of resistance religious, ritual acts. Others have argued that several new traditions, called new religious environmental movements, have emerged since the 1990s from the desire of certain environmental interest groups to tie their activities to theological and religious concerns. They make care for "God's creation" central to their efforts at effecting social and political change.

See also: Anthroposophy; Druidry; Eco-Paganism; Ghost Dance Movement (Wovoka); Hindu New Religious Movements; Millennialism; Native American Church, The; Neopaganism; New Age, The; Steiner, Rudolf (1861–1925); Theosophy.

Further Reading

Ellingson, Stephen, Anthony Paik, & Vernon A. Woodley. 2012. "The Structure of Religious Environmentalism: Movement Organizations, Interorganizational Networks, and Collective Action." *Journal for the Scientific Study of Religion* 51, no. 2: 266–285.

Pike, Sarah M. 2017. *For the Wild: Ritual and Commitment in Radical Eco-Activism.* Berkeley: University of California Press.

Shibley, Mark A. 2011. "Sacred Nature: Earth-based Spirituality as Popular Religion in the Pacific Northwest." *Journal for the Study of Religion, Nature, and Culture* 5, no. 2: 164–185.

Urban, Hugh B. 2015. *New Age, Neopagan, and New Religious Movements: Alternative Spirituality in Contemporary America.* Berkeley: University of California Press.

Essene Groups

Claiming a connection to an authoritative past helps new religions temper their innovative character, establish cultural continuity with the dominant religions in a given religious economy, and chart a path for converts to follow as they leave old commitments and move to embrace new ones. Consequently, many new religions offer new understandings of prior scriptural texts. The Church of Jesus Christ of Latter-day Saints, for example, describes *The Book of Mormon* as "another testament of Jesus Christ." Swami Prabhupada, the founder of the International Society for Krishna Consciousness claimed to present the Bhagavad Gita "as it is." A similar dynamic can be seen in many other groups.

Drawing on ancient sources, popular accounts of the discovery and content of the Dead Sea Scrolls, and esoteric traditions, several contemporary groups that trace their origins to the ancient Jewish sect of the Essenes developed in the late

The location of the Dead Sea Scrolls and caves, and Qumran Excavations of Essene Monastery. Several contemporary groups claim that they are continuing the religious practices of the ancient Jewish sectarian group that was located by the Dead Sea and produced the Dead Sea Scrolls, which were found in late 1946 and early 1947. (Library of Congress)

twentieth century. They are independent, and often critical, of each other. The degree to which they make use of the texts of the ancient Qumran community varies. Their theologies are diverse and often quite eclectic, as are their practices. Virtually all of the contemporary Essene groups, however, identify as Christian. The see the ancient Essenes as the first Christians, whose religion has been repressed throughout history and is only now reemerging.

Among the contemporary Essene groups is the Vero Essene Yahad (the ancient Essene term for community), headquartered in Vero Beach, Florida, with a secondary office in Cleveland, Tennessee (www.jacksonsnyder.com/vero-yahad/). It focuses on the study of ancient texts, including the Dead Sea Scrolls. Others, like the Essene Church of Christ (www.essene.org), which maintains a farm outside of Elmira, Oregon, focus less on ancient texts and more on their own scriptures, while retaining the claim to be direct descendants of the ancient Essenes. The Essene Church of Christ advocates a vegetarian diet and recognizes both a male and female Christ. Another group, the Brotherhood of Christ Church (www.brotherhoodofchristchurch.org), an intentional community of sectarian Mormons located in rural south-central Iowa, claims to live in accordance with the Community Rule of the Dead Sea Scrolls, which it has adapted to the current time. It, too, has produced its own set of scriptures.

The diversity of contemporary Essene groups mirrors the diversity of the broader field of new religions. But each of them constitutes a creative attempt to appropriate an authoritative past while simultaneously making it respond to contemporary interests.

See also: Church of Jesus Christ of Latter-day Saints, The; International Society for Krishna Consciousness (ISKCON); New Scriptures and New Religious Movements; Theosophy.

Further Reading
Hammer, Olav, & Jan A. M. Snoek. 2006. "Essenes, Esoteric Legends about." In Wouter J. Hanegraff, ed., in collaboration with Antoine Faivre, Roelof van den Broek, & Jean-Pierre Brach, *Dictionary of Gnosis and Western Esotericism*, pp. 340–343. Leiden: Brill.
Kreps, Anne E. 2018. "Reading History with the Essenes of Elmira." In Dylan Burns & Almut-Barbara Ranger, eds., *New Antiquities: Transformations of Antiquity in the New Age and Beyond*, pp. 149–174. Sheffield, UK: Equinox.

Exclusive (Plymouth) Brethren

The Exclusive Brethren, along with the Open Brethren, represent the two broad sects of the Plymouth Brethren, an evangelical Christian sect born in Ireland under the leadership of John Nelson Darby (1800–1882). Darby was a devoted Bible teacher and believed the Bible was the only true authority one needed. Though an Anglican, he grew increasingly critical of the clergy, believing that there should be no mediator between believers and the Holy Spirit or believers and the Bible. He developed his own system for reading the Bible known as "Dispensationalism," since he divided up the Bible's, and therefore the world's, history, into "dispensations" or eras that corresponded to certain time periods or events in biblical and postbiblical history. Dispensationalist readings of the Bible are inherently millennialist as they look forward to the Second Coming of Christ and the establishment of the Kingdom of God as the seventh and final dispensation. (Currently, we are living in the "Church" Age, which has been ongoing since the establishment of the Christian Church.) They are also specifically "premillennial" meaning that the event known as the rapture, when all true Christians will be raised to heaven, will occur prior to the millennium.

Out of Darby's particular millennialist and evangelical worldview grew the Plymouth Brethren, founded in the late 1820s. Reflective of Darby's aversion to institutional oversight, early adherents refused to adopt a denominational name, preferring simply "the Brethren." From the initial group, the Open and Exclusive Brethren split in 1848 over questions of discipline. While both maintain a network of loosely networked churches, the Open Brethren maintain that if a member faces discipline in one congregation, he or she would not have to face discipline in another; the Exclusive Brethren maintain that he or she would. Those who identified as Exclusive Brethren also identify as "Darbyites," "Connexional Brethren," or, simply, "Plymouth Brethren." Under each branch of Plymouth Brethren there are also several denominations or churches, reflective of further splits in later years.

Despite the variety of Exclusive Brethren sects, all have in common the commitment to the Bible as the source of saving knowledge and the model for how to live on earth. Darby's translation of the Bible in accordance with his Dispensationalist view remains central to the Brethren's interpretation of the text. Unlike many evangelical Protestant groups, Exclusive Brethren partake of the Lord's Supper every week, which they see as the most important aspect of Christian ritual practice. Some of the more stringent Exclusive Brethren churches will refuse communion to Christians who are not members of the church or to members who are not in good standing with the church.

Worship, referred to as "Meetings," usually takes place in "Halls," rather than churches. There is also no formal clergy. A member of the church in good standing, almost exclusively a man, will serve communion and preach from the Bible. Women wear head coverings while praying in accordance with the Apostle Paul's pronouncement that "every woman that prayeth or prophesieth with her head uncovered dishonoureth her head" (1 Cor. 11:3). Music is also a central aspect of Brethren worship, since all share the same hymnbook, which was mandated and updated by Darby. More exclusive meetings may be called if a church issue requires discussion, wherein only the men would attend. But also, more inclusive daily Bible studies are often open to those who are not members of the church.

In many ways, the Exclusive Brethren represent just another sect of Christianity. However, it is their commitment to exclusivity and, in some more extreme instances, isolation from Christianity as a whole that casts suspicion over the group as well as critique. The actual number of Exclusive Brethren is difficult to calculate given the variety of sects. What is known is that it has members spanning the United Kingdom, North America, Australia, and continental Europe. Its website (http://www.plymouthbrethrenchristianchurch.org) highlights the humanitarian focus of the modern movement with its "Rapid Relief Team," which has sent members to help in the aftermath of natural or human-made disasters. Though exclusive in membership, the Exclusive Brethren have managed to maintain a global presence in a modernizing world.

See also: Millennialism.

Further Reading
Bachelard, Michael. 2008. *Behind the Exclusive Brethren.* Victoria, Australia: Scribe Publications.
Hardy, Ann. 2011. "Destiny, the Exclusive Brethren, and Mediated Politics in New Zealand." In Guy Redden & Michael Bailey, eds, *Mediating Faiths: Religion and Socio-Cultural Change in the Twenty-First Century,* pp. 189–202. London: Routledge Press.
Introvigne, Massimo. 2018. *The Plymouth Brethren.* New York: Oxford University Press.

Exit Counseling

When the contemporary anticult movement began to coalesce in the early 1970s, it depended on a set of interlocking assumptions. The young adults who joined various new religions, their parents and others claimed, could not have been in their right minds. In fact, they must have been coerced or duped by persuasive powers that they could not resist. They must, therefore, have been "programmed" by the group to abandon their former lives and adopt new ways of thinking and acting. Consequently, parents and other concerned parties felt justified in taking drastic steps to "rescue" cult members from a fate they did not intend.

From such thinking was the practice of deprogramming born. Ted Patrick (1930–), a state official in the San Diego area, became alarmed by the missionary activities of the Children of God, a new Christian sectarian group, and determined to oppose it. He concluded that its members somehow clouded the minds of their recruits and coerced them to reject their former lives in favor of new ones in the group. The solution, he thought, was clear. Cult members needed to be deprogrammed and returned to their freedom of will.

In the hands of Patrick and other early exponents, deprogramming was hardly subtle. Often it involved kidnapping individuals, holding them in isolation against their will, and badgering them until they abandoned their cultic beliefs and commitments. While deprogramming had some early successes, it also had some notorious failures and its abusive nature eventually gained it more disapproval than support.

Some who still wanted to combat the perceived dangers of cults sought another way. In the 1980s, practitioners like Carol Giambalvo and Steven Hassan moved toward a different model for extricating cult members. They abandoned the coercive practices that had put deprogrammers like Patrick into legal trouble and focused on therapeutic interventions that involved both family members and the cult member. In contrast to the sometimes questionable practices of early deprogrammers, they tried to professionalize the field and establish codes of ethics.

The move toward an "exit counseling" model was reinforced by psychologists' general rejection of the brainwashing hypothesis as applied to cult membership and a growing unwillingness of the courts to accept brainwashing as an explanation for cult membership. Today, some form of exit counseling is the predominant means by which concerned families try to promote their children's departures from stigmatized groups.

Despite its move toward alignment with standard counseling practices, however, exit counseling, unlike other forms of counseling, still presumes a single result: leaving the group is the only acceptable outcome.

See also: Anticult Movement, The; Brainwashing; Cult; Deprogramming; Hassan, Steven (1954–); Patrick, Ted (1930–).

Further Reading

Giambalvo, Carol. 1992. *Exit Counseling: A Family Intervention: How to Respond to Cult-Affected Loved Ones*, 2nd ed. Bonita Springs, FL: American Family Foundation.

Hassan, Steven. 2000. *Releasing the Bonds: Empowering People to Think for Themselves*. Somerville, MA: Freedom of Mind Press.

Shupe, Anson, & Susan E. Darnell. 2006. *Agents of Discord: Deprogramming, Pseudo-Science, and the American Anticult Movement*. New Brunswick, NJ: Transaction Publishers.

Falun Gong

Falun Gong or Falun Dafa, which translates to the "practice" or "teachings" of the Dharma Wheel, respectively, is a Chinese new religious movement that rose to global prominence in the late 1990s due to their nonviolent demonstration against the Chinese Communist government and the government's subsequent campaign of suppression against the religion. Outside communist headquarters in Beijing on April 25, 1999, ten thousand members of the movement sat in silent protest of state-sponsored propaganda. Falun Gong, which at that time had reportedly reached nearly one hundred million members, petitioned for a cessation of negative media coverage and legal recognition as an accepted religion. In response, the government declared Falun Gong illicit and began detaining and imprisoning members of the movement in forced labor camps or psychiatric institutions. Most members who were not detained went underground, though a few succeeded in a brief takeover of Chinese media outlets in 2002.

As a result of the Chinese government's actions, there was an international outcry against the suppression of Falun Gong and other minority religious groups in China. However, global events in the early 2000s, such as the war on terror, eventually overshadowed the plight of Falun Gong, which faded from view leaving the Chinese government to continue suppressing the movement out of the public eye. Beginning in 2008, however, reports of organ harvesting from imprisoned Falun Gong members came to light (with some estimating that 1.5 million Falun Gong members have been killed for their organs). This has led to a new spate of accusations against the Chinese government's mistreatment of religious practitioners.

Yet, even when it has been the focus of media attention, few have understood or known much about Falun Gong beyond what was reported, often erroneously.

ORIGINS AND FOUNDER

Falun Gong was founded by Li Hongzhi (1951–). Despite its cosmological, moral, and spiritual elements, Li maintained that it was not a religious movement, but rather a philosophy of interconnectedness between everyone and everything in the universe. Li, as the teacher who brought this knowledge to the world is revered in a way very similar to Confucian reverence for elders. From a very early age he trained under a variety of spiritual masters from various traditions, including Daoism and Buddhism, which explains the eclectic nature of Falun Gong's belief system. By the 1980s, Li was developing what he had learned into a

Members of the Chinese new religious movement Falun Gong participate in the widespread practice of coordinated movement, body postures, and meditation that is designed to cultivate qi (chi) or life energy. Practitioners are directed to cultivate their own Falun, which mimics the Great Wheel of Dharma by absorbing energy from the universe and releasing energy into it. (Charlotte Leaper/Dreamstime.com)

cohesive system, which he would eventually introduce by formally founding Falun Gong in 1992.

The movement took hold rapidly in China and in Chinese communities across the globe, counting members in the millions by its first few years. By 1995, Li deemed it necessary to spread his message further, traveling to Europe, Australia, Oceania, and the United States. He would ultimately settle in the United States with his family in 1996. During the demonstrations and ensuing persecution of Falun Gong in the late 1990s, the Chinese government sought to extradite Li for encouraging the protests and disrupting the peace. Their request was denied and Li remained in the United States, where he lives today, earning accolades for his work on peace initiatives, particularly for marginalized religious communities.

BELIEFS AND PRACTICES

Foundational to Falun Gong is the belief that the universe, often called "the Great Ultimate," (or *Tai Chi*) emanates from the Dharma Wheel. The movement of the great wheel is mirrored by all life in the universe: when the wheel turns in one direction, it takes in energy (*qi*) from the cosmos, and when it moves in the other direction, it releases energy. All of this energy moving in and out of everyone and everything highlights their interconnectedness. Practitioners of Falun Gong first must develop a "Falun," which Li located in their lower abdomen, which is an entity that rotates constantly, mimicking the great Dharma Wheel, either absorbing energy from the universe or releasing it, with the aim to maintain a consistent state of flow or balance between the two. Once established, the Falun constantly turns (since it is synchronized with the universe), which is a departure from other traditions that maintain that qi is maintained, gained, or released through active practice. Poor health or bad luck are believed to be the effects of karma, which will eventually become eliminated by the constant rotation of the Falun; thus Falun Gong members generally refuse medical intervention.

Practitioners often emphasize the "scientific" versus the "religious" nature of their practices, noting their attunement to the universe as something quantifiable. For this reason, there is little formal and religious ritual associated with Falun Gong, with the exception of personal study of Li's message and often participation in breathing exercises. However, there is a great deal of emphasis on developing *xinxing*, which means "heart nature" and often maps onto what other religious systems consider a moral or ethical compass. Xinxing is characterized by three virtues: truthfulness (*zhen*), benevolence (*shan*), and forbearance (*ren*). Every Falun Gong member cultivates these traits to determine what is a good and moral action and what is an evil course.

Ironically given the degree of persecution leveled at Falun Gong, the movement lacks formal institutions. It organized, in many respects, *because* of the degree of state suppression it experienced; prior to that, Falun Gong was numerically significant, but organizationally diffuse. Nonetheless, the movement has suffered mightily at the hands of the Chinese government, making it difficult to know how many members there are and the state of the movement more generally.

See also: Chinese New Religious Movements; Healing, Health, and New Religious Movements; Media and New Religious Movements; Millennialism.

Further Reading
Chang, Maria Hsia. 2004. *Falun Gong: The End of Days*. New Haven, CT: Yale University Press.
Lu, Yunfeng, Yuxin Su, & Na Zhou. 2018. "Doctrinal Innovation, Resistance, and Falun Gong's Politicization." *The China Review: An Interdisciplinary Journal on Greater China* 18, no. 4: 41–62.
Ownby, David. 2008. *Falun Gong and the Future of China*. New York: Oxford University Press.
Penny, Benjamin. 2012. *The Religion of Falun Gong*. Chicago: The University of Chicago Press.

Farm, The

Of the many intentional communities that arose from the countercultural movement of the 1960s and 1970s, The Farm Community is arguably the most successful. Established in 1971 by Stephen (1935–2014) and Ina May Gaskin (1940–), The Farm combines communal living, vegetarianism, avoidance of Western medicine particularly in relation to childbirth, and a commitment to achieve the highest levels of spiritual consciousness. Those who come to live at the Farm are often spiritual seekers, though over time, The Farm came to encompass corporate, educational, and humanitarian ventures, thus expanding its influence to those with more secular interests.

In 1970, Stephen Gaskin left San Francisco and embarked on an extended speaking tour on his particular religious and social views, accompanied by Ina May and many friends. Over the course of the tour, the group determined that they were a community without a home. To remedy this, the group bought one thousand acres of farmland in Lewis County, Tennessee, and formally established The Farm. Three hundred people moved from California to Tennessee and took voluntary vows of poverty and chastity outside of marriage. These monastic features of The Farm led to Stephen Gaskin's dubbing as "the abbot," even though his role was eventually transferred to a council of elders charged with the administration of the community—a model that remains today.

The Farm began to grow in popularity, aided both by Gaskin's published teachings and Ina May's midwife institute, and the number of members soon ballooned to over sixteen hundred. This caused a tremendous amount of stress to the community's resources and finances and eventually led to a mandate that all residents must support themselves. Unsurprisingly, many left the community after that, shrinking the number significantly and making it possible for the group to get back on its feet financially and to grow and administer the many programs of social and spiritual advancement that reflected its initial charter.

BELIEFS AND AIMS

The Farm's belief system is ecumenical in tone; members subscribe to a particular set of outlooks, though The Farm's website acknowledges that this list is not exclusive. Among those established beliefs is the belief in higher, nonmaterial planes of consciousness, culminating in the spiritual plane, which introduces the reality that ultimately all matter and spirit are one. Achieving consciousness of the spiritual plane is the primary goal of all religious practice at the Farm and reflects the Asian origins of its religious thought. The group practices pacifism and vegetarianism, though they emphasize that one's diet will not impact spiritual growth. They also highlight their ecological and humanitarian aims, noting their beliefs that the earth is sacred and that compassion is a central virtue. Given its renown as a center for midwifery, it is unsurprising that childbirth and childrearing are considered holy endeavors. Additionally, marriage is considered a sacrament—most members are married—and premarital sex is discouraged.

Reflecting its birth from the surrounding counterculture, at its outset Farm members smoked marijuana, though they regarded its use as sacramental and for the purpose of contacting higher dimensions of existence. The Farm's website now disavows the abuse of any substance, combating critiques that the community is a shelter for drug users, without formally disavowing the practice (though its significance dimmed over the years). (http://www.thefarm.org/about-our-community/basic-beliefs-agreements/)

IN PRESENT DAY

The Farm currently counts two hundred resident members, most of whom are original, (and four thousand former members who maintain contact with the group), though its broader significance is belied by that number. Ina May is considered the mother of modern midwifery and her books on childbirth are best-sellers; women come from around the country to give birth at the Farm. Outside of its own publishing company, The Book Publishing Company, The Farm has founded numerous nonprofit organizations, such as Plenty International, which acts as a relief and humanitarian aid program, and the Swan Conservation Trust, which focuses on restorative ecological projects in the face of climate change, among several others.

The Farm began as a countercultural project, a fact still reflected in its eclectic spiritual aims and focus on intentional living. However, it has transformed into a thoroughly modern icon of a thriving utopia.

See also: Findhorn Foundation, The; Love Israel Family, The; Seekers; Utopianism in New Religious Movements.

Further Reading

Gaskin, Stephen. 1974. *Hey Beatnik! This is the Farm Book*. Summertown, TN: The Book Publishing Company.

Gaskin, Stephen. 1976. *This Season's People: A Book of Spiritual Teachings*. Summertown, TN: The Book Publishing Company.

Stevenson, Douglas. 2014. *Out to Change the World: The Evolution of the Farm Community*. Summertown, TN: The Book Publishing Company.

Farrakhan, Louis (1933–)

Louis Farrakhan has been a central figure in the Nation of Islam virtually since he joined in 1955. Born Louis Eugene Walcott to Caribbean immigrant parents in the Bronx in 1933, he was a talented musician who eventually made a career as a calypso singer. Walcott had met Malcolm X (1925–1965) before he attended the Nation's Savior's Day celebrations in 1955, but he was initially frightened by Malcolm's fierce condemnation of white people. After his conversion in 1955, however, Louis X formed a close bond with Malcolm and became an assistant minister at the Boston Temple. Elijah Muhammad (1897–1975) eventually gave him the last name of Farrakhan, "The Criterion."

Farrakhan's rise within the Nation was rapid. He learned well from his mentor Malcolm and became a powerful and tireless proponent of Elijah Muhammad's teachings. When Malcolm was silenced and suspended by the Nation in 1964, Farrakhan replaced him as the minister of the Harlem Temple No. 7. Farrakhan and Malcolm eventually split over Malcolm's revulsion at Elijah's multiple extramarital affairs. Farrakhan defended Elijah and thereby further ingratiated himself with the prophet.

Farrakhan enjoyed such approval from Elijah that he was viewed, with trepidation by some, as a potential successor to the Messenger. But before Elijah died in

1975, he established his son, Wallace Dean Muhammad, as his successor. When Wallace Dean quickly moved to bring the teachings of the Nation closer to Sunni Islam, Farrakhan resisted. By 1977, he had split from Wallace Dean and announced his intention to restore the Nation on the principles preached by Elijah.

Farrakhan buttressed his claim to leadership in multiple ways. He reminded his audiences of his closeness to Elijah and of all the positive things Elijah had said about him. He even claimed to be the spiritual son of Elijah. Moreover, Farrakhan supported his position with claims to charismatic authority. Along with other members of the Nation who declined to follow Wallace Dean, Farrakhan endorsed the assertion that Elijah Muhammad had, in fact, not died. His most elaborate endorsement of that idea came in his account of an experience in 1985 when he was taken into the heavens to board the Mother Ship or Mother Wheel (see Ezek. 1:15–18). There he received a direct verbal commission from Elijah himself and also obtained full knowledge of God's message to humanity.

Over Farrakhan's long tenure as the head of the Nation, he has been involved in multiple controversies. For example, his role in the assassination of Malcolm X remains to be fully clarified. He has frequently been accused of anti-semitism. And in 2010, he urged members of the Nation to receive auditing from the Church of Scientology. Nonetheless, the Nation remains a vital religious organization under his leadership.

See also: Charisma and Leadership in New Religious Movements; Malcolm X (1925–1965); Muhammad, Elijah (1897–1975); Nation of Islam, The.

Further Reading
Gardell, Mattias. 1996. *In the Name of Elijah Muhammad: Louis Farrakhan and the Nation of Islam.* Durham, NC: Duke University Press.
Marable, Manning. 2011. *Malcolm X: A Life of Reinvention.* New York: Penguin Books.

Father Divine (1876–1965)

Despite his diminutive stature, Father Divine was larger than life. Beyond the revelation that he was God, his charisma, magnetism, and message of universal brotherhood captivated an interracial audience, at the same time that he perturbed the suppressive forces of white supremacy. He melded activism with evangelism, and bore a signature style and flair for preaching that would brand him a religious icon of the twentieth century

EARLY LIFE AND INFLUENCES

Born George Baker—though his original name is a subject of speculation—in 1876 in Rockville, Maryland, the future religious leader came of age at the height of Jim Crow and segregation. In fact, few details from his early life remain; this is due in part to the lack of record-keeping by the Peace Mission Movement and in part to Divine's staunch refusal to describe the history of God in mortal terms. Nonetheless, there is a high likelihood that he was born of former slaves, a fact that grounds his later civil rights activism in a family history shaped by subjugation and racism.

Divine bounced around the country through the turn of the twentieth century, working as a gardener, among other professions. While working in California in 1906, he came across the works of Charles Fillmore (1854–1948), one of the primary figures of the New Thought movement. New Thought was premised on the idea that through "right thinking," often joined with prayer in Christian-leaning New Thought groups, such as Fillmore's Unity School of Christianity, people could achieve both this and otherworldly salvation. Also around this time, Baker met Samuel Morris, an itinerant Baptist preacher known for proclaiming himself God during church services. Father Divine soon attached himself to Morris as the "Messenger" to Morris's God (similar to Nation of Islam founder Elijah Muhammad's relationship to W. D. Fard, the latter who claimed to be Allah). Eventually, however, Father Divine rejected Morris (who had been calling himself "Father Jehovia") as God and took that mantle upon himself.

By 1912, Father Divine had traveled South, where he experienced hardship in the form of arrests but also triumphs as his movement grew, particularly among women. Father Divine had begun teaching that gender categories should be rejected and celibacy adopted; both were the result of his belief that he brought heaven on earth, where such divisions were moot.

NEW YORK AND THE INTERNATIONAL PEACE MISSION MOVEMENT

By 1914, Father Divine had relocated to Brooklyn, where his small, all-black denomination lived communally and abstained from sex, alcohol, and tobacco. While in Brooklyn, he formally adopted the name "Rev. Major Jealous Divine," though he became better known as Father Divine. He also had a brief marriage with disciple, Penninah Jones, though the two would often live apart.

In 1919, he and his growing group of followers moved to Sayville, New York, on Long Island. There Father Divine and the Peace Mission Movement endured a similar roller-coaster of highs and lows. His following continued to grow and now attracted both black and white devotees. His wealth also grew, and with it, his ability to help his followers find housing and jobs. Nonetheless, this period was punctuated by Father Divine's arrest for disturbing the peace, a charge brought on by repeated run-ins with his white neighbors who disliked the large, interracial gatherings on their street. He was tried and eventually convicted of the crime for which he served a sentence of less than a year. This event catapulted Father Divine into the public eye and, conversely, only increased his popularity. Soon he spoke to sell-out crowds in Harlem's Rockland Palace, which could hold ten thousand spectators; this would become the regular site of his Peace Mission Movement's meetings.

After moving to Harlem, Father Divine witnessed his Peace Mission Movement grow and establish branches in the Western United States and outposts in Europe and Australia. As his fame and notoriety grew, Father Divine was called upon to speak on political issues of the day, though, at first, he aimed to stay politically neutral. As God, he believed he must lead people to salvation through his message of positive thinking, not broad-scale political activism. Nonetheless, outbursts of racism compelled him to take a more stalwart political stance on occasion, leading to the creation of the "Divine Righteous Government Coalition," among other initiatives, to combat discrimination of all kinds.

Father Divine's time in Harlem became increasingly plagued with trial and misfortune due to schisms, persistent legal issues and threats of extradition, and the illness of his wife Penninah (who was older than Father Divine by some decades). He eventually opted to move the headquarters of the Peace Mission Movement to Philadelphia, Pennsylvania. Following Penninah's death, he married Edna Rose Ritchings (1925–2017) in 1946, a white woman who thereafter would be known as Mother Divine (and whom he later claimed was the reincarnation of Penninah).

LEGACY

Father Divine's time in Philadelphia enjoyed neither the highs of publicity and popularity nor the lows of indictments and suppression. He lived quietly on a large estate called Woodmont outside of Philadelphia, and continued to agitate for civil rights, particularly integration. He died of natural causes on September 10, 1965, though Mother Divine, who served as figurehead of the Peace Mission Movement until her death in 2017, and other followers argue that his spirit lives on. They continue to refer to Father Divine in the present tense and keep his rooms as Woodmont perfectly pristine for him.

See also: Charisma and Leadership in New Religious Movements; International Peace Mission Movement; Law Enforcement and New Religious Movements; Muhammad, Elijah (1897–1975); Nation of Islam, The; New Thought; Race and New Religious Movements; Unity School of Christianity.

Further Reading

Lindsey, Rachel Mcbride. 2014. "'Seen and Read by Men': Biblical Text and the Living Epistles of Father Divine's Peace Mission Movement." *Journal of Africana Studies* 2, no. 3: 347–378.

Watts, Jill. 1992. *God, Harlem U.S.A.: The Father Divine Story*. Berkeley: University of California Press.

Weisbrot, Robert. 1983. *Father Divine and the Struggle for Racial Equality*. Urbana: University of Illinois Press.

Findhorn Foundation, The

Since 1962 a small colony in Northeast Scotland, near the Moray Firth, has played an important role among those interested in alternative spiritualties and ways of life. The Findhorn Foundation now maintains not only the original settlement known as The Park, which can house several hundred people at any one time. It also manages the nearby Cluny hotel as well as a retreat house on the island of

Iona and a satellite community on the neighboring island of Erraid. In many ways, it remains the most successful and enduring New Age community.

The development of Findhorn is rooted in the lives of Peter (1917–1994) and Eileen Caddy (1917–2006) and also Dorothy Maclean (1920–2020), who would become deeply involved with Findhorn's famously productive garden. Each of them was associated for some time with the spiritual teacher Sheena Govan (1912–1967). Maclean met her in the early 1940s and Peter Caddy met her in the later 1940s. He eventually married her, before leaving her for Eileen, who, an inner voice told him, was his "other half."

Govan was the conduit through which many esoteric influences reached the founders of Findhorn, but Eileen quickly became the group's focal point. The generative event for Findhorn occurred in 1953 when, on a visit to Glastonbury with Peter and Govan, Eileen received what she understood as a direct communication from God. That initiated a prophetic career for Eileen that would continue through her life and eventually have an international impact.

Although Peter urged Eileen to accept Sheena as her teacher, it was Eileen's ongoing communications from God that provided the teachings around which a group would eventually cohere. In 1957, Peter and Eileen took over the management of the Cluny Hill Hotel, near Forres, Scotland, where Maclean also worked. When their employment with the hotel ended in late 1962, the Caddys moved to a caravan, or trailer, park near the village of Findhorn. Maclean soon joined them in 1963. Eileen continued to receive messages from God, which she relayed to Peter and recorded in writing. The voice Eileen heard even identified her as Mary, the mother of the Christ, or at least as the bearer of the Mary principle, which can nourish Christ energies and help them meld with human nature. But despite the Christian inflections of Eileen's messages, Findhorn is associated with no specific religious tradition.

In the early days of the settlement, the Caddys and Maclean eked out a basic existence, but they were buoyed by the extraordinary bounty produced by a garden planted in unpromising, sandy soil. Maclean reported that she was in touch with the nature spirits, or "devas," and it was through their cooperation that the garden produced such an impressive yield. Consequently, one of the central premises of Findhorn, along with the inner listening epitomized by Eileen's faithful recording of what she heard from the voice that communicated with her, became cocreation with nature. The third pillar, in part arising from the hardscrabble early days, was that work is love in action. Those principles continue to guide all activities at Findhorn, from the continued tending of the remarkable garden, through the dissemination of the messages received by Eileen, to the provision of services to visitors, such as the intensive Experience Week, which is offered frequently.

Gradually, through their participation in overlapping social networks, others came to live, at least temporarily, in the caravan park by the shore. The initial publication in 1967 of a selection of Eileen's received messages, *God Spoke to Me*, attracted more interest and more visitors. One of those who came to Findhorn in 1970 was the American New Age thinker David Spangler (1945–). Spangler quickly assumed a position of authority alongside Peter Caddy in the small group, emphasizing its role in educating people about the potential for transformation of human consciousness. Spangler stayed until 1973 and left a lasting mark on Findhorn.

By 1972, Findhorn was formally registered as a Scottish charity. In 1997, as a nongovernmental organization, it became associated with the United Nations' Department of Public information (now the Department of Global Communications) through which it continues to promote its ecological principles. It purchased the Cluny Hill Hotel in 1975 and finally purchased the original caravan park in 1983.

The growth and longevity of Findhorn are remarkable in a cultural milieu marked by shifting allegiances of individuals and the ephemerality of such groups. Eileen Caddy's teachings have provided a solid foundation and continue to be marketed in various forms, including one that provides a devotional reading for each day of the year. Findhorn today offers a substantial array of workshops, conferences, special events, and long-term guest programs. Some three thousand individuals participate in Findhorn programs every year. Between its hosting of visitors and its publishing and other businesses, Findhorn's influence extends well beyond the comparatively small number of people who are in residence at any given time.

Presenting itself since the end of the 1980s as an ecovillage, Findhorn participates in a variety of networks with other ecologically minded and intentional spiritual communities. In addition to its garden, it has developed innovative approaches to construction and waste management.

Throughout its lifespan Findhorn has been remarkably free of scandal and controversy. Peter and Eileen's early divorces from their spouses and marriage to each other raised eyebrows, and many visitors to Findhorn have decided that it was not the place for them, but Findhorn's key figures have remained free of the kinds of accusations that are frequently made of leaders of alternative religious groups.

See also: Caddy, Eileen (1917–2006); Environmentalism and New Religious Movements; New Age, The.

Further Reading

Bogliolo, Karin, & Carly Newfeld. 2002. *In Search of the Magic of Findhorn*. Forres, Scotland: Findhorn Press.

Caddy, Eileen. 1992. *God Spoke to Me*, 3rd ed. Forres, Scotland: Findhorn Press.

Caddy, Eileen. 2007. *Flight into Freedom and Beyond: The Autobiography of the Co-Founder of the Findhorn Community*, rev. ed. Forres, Scotland: Findhorn Press.

Sutcliffe, Steven J. 2003. *Children of the New Age: A History of Spiritual Practices*. New York: Routledge.

PRIMARY SOURCE DOCUMENT

Excerpts from Eileen Caddy's *God Spoke to Me* (1992)

Eileen Caddy was one of the three founders of the spiritual Findhorn Foundation in Scotland. She authored a number of books that have inspired her community, and have increased the number of Findhorn followers. An excerpt from her 1992 publication, God Spoke to Me, *follows below.*

Open your eyes

Open your eyes. Raise your consciousness. Behold the signs and wonders of the times.

Be surprised at nothing—this is important. Be shocked at nothing. My ways are strange and wonderful. I have much to reveal when you are ready to receive. Prepare yourself now and know that My kingdom is come, My will is being done. Recognise it. (p. 19)

The living force

I AM always there, like the breath that keeps your body alive. Become aware of Me all the time.

I AM the living force within your being.

I AM life. (p. 25)

Let Me use you

Let Me use you as you are. You are My creation. Through the years you have been trained and tested and you have drawn nearer to Me. You realise that of yourself you are nothing, but with Me you are everything. Nothing is impossible when your life is hid in Me. Let Me use you.

Never waste time praying for material needs. I know your needs and will meet them one by one. Raise your consciousness and become aware of Me until I become all that matters and I AM your all in all. (pp. 41–42)

"Now are ye the sons of God"

"Now are ye the sons of God." Not yesterday or even tomorrow but *now*. Now are things opening up as never before. Now are hidden truths and secrets being revealed.

This is happening *now*. The time of waiting and wondering is over. The time of action is upon you.

Live fully in the moment. Time will be as nothing and there will be time for everything.

You will be guided by Me—in the *now*. (p. 46)

This is My gift to you

Accept this day as a special day, a day of rebirth. This is my gift to you. You are being reborn in Spirit and in truth. This is the biggest turning point in your life—from this day on, all is new.

I want you to become aware of this and accept it as a fact now. You are to witness tremendous changes in your life and living. They may be gradual, but they will gather in momentum, and nothing will stop these changes, this transformation, from taking place. You will grow in stature; the old will pass away and *all* will be made new.

You are now moving into the most glorious epoch of your life, for you now know the truth. You know that I AM life, that I AM love, that I AM your consciousness and that I AM within you.

This is something no one can take from you, that nothing can change. This is reality. This is something which you have been seeking and have now found. It is the greatest treasure, the greatest truth, for it brings you to that conscious oneness with Me. Then you *know* that all I AM is yours and all I have is yours, and you are Mine.

Let these truths become a part of you; absorb them as you breathe. They are the breath of life. (pp. 57–58)

The three commandments for the New Age

See love	See light
Speak love	Send light
Be love	Be light

See truth
Speak truth
Be truth

These three commandments for the New Age have been conceived at this specific time to help all those seekers on the path to aim high.

Behold perfection in its great wonder and glory. (p. 61)

Bring down my heaven

These commandments must be passed to those who are ready to see, to speak, to be My word.

"As a man thinketh in his heart so is he." As you think those commandments, live them, and as they become a part of you, a new world is waiting to open for you.

Concentrate fully on my wonders; they are around you. Start from the foundation of your being and build My temple of light, love, and wisdom. See it grow day by day, see it flourish. See the beauty of it and let your heart sing at all you behold. Treasure My word and make it live. Accept nothing but the perfect.

Plant the seed of love in every heart; nurture it and watch it grow into perfection. Bring down My heaven upon this earth. (p. 61)

Know what you are doing

You must know what you are doing. You must know where you are going. This conscious awareness is vitally important to your advancement along the spiritual path—there is nothing vague about it. You may not know where the next step is going to take you, but nevertheless the next step has to be taken in complete faith and confidence and in the assurance that by taking it you will eventually reach the goal.

Do what has to be done in utter confidence, without wavering. Be not swayed by any outside influence. Seek the answer from within, find it and act upon it. Learn to act only from that "withinness"—this is where you will always find Me. Inner awareness, inner conviction, is all you need act upon.

When you place yourself in My hands to use as I will, you cannot hold a part of yourself back. I ask for all, for only in this way can I use My channel. There cannot be two parts of you, for we are one and you have to become aware of the oneness until you see the two melt into one and know the meaning of the words, "I and my Father are one; I am in Him and He is in me." There is no longer any separateness.

This is a new life and this life is perfect. Walk it in joy and confidence. (pp. 93–94)

Revelation

This is an historic and momentous time in the progress of humanity. At this time the veil is being rent in two and that which has been hidden through the ages is now to be revealed. (p. 96)

Source: Caddy, Eileen. *God Spoke to Me*, 3rd ed. Rochester, VT: Findhorn Press, 1992.

Food and New Religious Movements

"You are what you eat." Such an adage is employed as a reminder that if you eat "junk" your body will become "junk." However, for some, this is true not only from a physiological, but from a spiritual standpoint. The body, as the home of the soul, must be fueled with an eye to a person's spiritual well-being. The notion that food—or the abstention therefrom—can be salvific can both ally and conflict with dietary practices recommended for health or healing.

Particular foods can also become imbued with religious meaning or salvific properties. Bread and wine become the body of Christ; the foods on the Seder plate represent various stages of the Passover story, returning whoever eats them to the biblical Exodus moment; specific foods are prepared and consumed to petition or appease the various Orishas central to practice in Santería; and the pouring of ghee (clarified butter) into fire reenacts the Hindu deity Prajapati's creation of all living creatures. Foods bear sacred properties and, whether eaten or not, enjoy ritual significance.

Many new religious movements are founded on or experiment with the very notion that food and its consumption are linked to sacred, often salvific ends.

PREPARING HOLY VESSELS

Numerous millennialist groups have proffered guidance on proper eating practices in the hope of better preparing the individual for the coming Kingdom of Heaven. Besides its brief foray into plural marriage, the Church of Jesus Christ of Latter-day Saints is perhaps best known for its prohibition of certain substances, such as alcohol, tobacco, and "hot drinks" (which has been interpreted to mean caffeine). Historians have noted that the language of the Word of Wisdom—the source of these proscriptions—is rather vague and most likely reflected its nineteenth-century context (e.g., only wine made by non-Mormons is prohibited, highlighting the Mormon fear of being poisoned by opponents). As a result, the precise adherence to the Word of Wisdom has varied over time, often depending upon who the prophet is at a given time. Nonetheless, the Word of Wisdom is still viewed by many Latter-day Saints as a guide for consumption. Along with abstention from certain substances, the Word of Wisdom also advocates for semivegetarianism, recommending meat only during colder months or moments of famine. Mormons have long been known to store food, often food they have grown or raised themselves, reflecting their earlier history when food was often scarce but also a sense of preparedness as the Kingdom of God approached.

Similar to the Latter-day Saints, Seventh-day Adventists also approached food with an eye to the end-times. An offshoot of the nineteenth-century Millerites, Seventh-day Adventists believe that the world is no longer living during a period of probation; now, every action is being judged by God. Thus, it is important that all people are living as though the last days are nigh, which means avoiding sin of all kinds and seeking purity, both spiritually and bodily. Seventh-day Adventists adhere to many Jewish kosher laws, including abstention from unclean foods such as pork and shellfish. Like the Latter-day Saints, they avoid alcohol and tobacco, though unlike them, they advocate for total vegetarianism. John Harvey Kellogg (1852–1943), founder of Kellogg's foods, was a Seventh-day Adventist who created foods (grain-based cereals, mostly) that aligned with this biblical diet.

Equally interested in consuming based on a plant-based, biblical diet are Rastafari. Rastafarianism arose in Jamaica as a religious resistance movement among poor blacks, who believed that salvation came through self-actualization and avoidance of anything related to Babylon (white culture and institutions), including food. Rastafari emulate the basic diet of the Old Testament and often grow their own food. Seeking autonomy and self-empowerment through food is also found in the practices of the Nation of Islam. Keeping halal (Islamic dietary laws) became a means of differentiating Nation of Islam members from both non-Muslims and other African American religious groups. The greatest strictures, however, were focused on the avoidance of "soul food," or food associated with black culture in the South. Much of this food was unhealthy and had been created out of necessity during the era of slavery, since slaves were denied the choicer foods and cuts of meat. For the Nation of Islam, food became a source of both spiritual and racial redemption.

Though he would eventually disclaim the reality of racial lines, Father Divine (1876–1965) and his International Peace Mission Movement sought the uplift of the poor and downgraded, most of whom were racial minorities. Divine, who claimed to be God incarnate, led massive interracial gatherings and emphasized outreach for those who were struggling. One of the primary means of gathering his community together and serving the needy simultaneously was through Holy Communion Banquets. Often thousands attended, creating a supersized reenactment of the Last Supper. Additionally, by breaking bread as a blended racial group during the height of Jim Crow in the 1930s, Father Divine broke taboos regarding segregated eating. Hunger, of both a physical and spiritual variety, knew no race in his view.

SPIRITUALIZING FOOD

Food, as something that binds humans firmly to their bodily needs, can also be perceived as an anchor to spiritual advancement. In the New Thought tradition, which typically elevated mind over matter (which in certain cases led to the belief that matter itself was illusory), the Unity School of Christianity brought things down to earth with its focus on proper eating. Its founder, Charles Fillmore (1854–1948), had originally held to the view that food was of little consequence to salvation. However, he became increasingly convinced that the manner in which food was managed and prepared could have direct bearing on a person's mind and soul. For example, consuming too much meat meant that a person was absorbing the trauma of animal slaughter. He began to advocate for a vegetarian diet so as to avoid absorbing such spiritually debilitating effects.

In the late twentieth century, Heaven's Gate, a Christian UFO religion, aimed to progress to The Evolutionary Level Above Human. Its members adapted traditionally millennialist ideas of a new world order to a modern context: it would not be Christ and angels, but aliens and spacecraft that would usher those who were ready to the next stage of their evolution. Part of the preparation for this evolutionary step came through bodily preparedness, which for those members of Heaven's Gate meant eating a prescribed and somewhat ascetic diet. Food, as a necessary feature of human survival, would cease to have relevance following their evolution, thus, in their abstention they could simulate this new level and separate themselves from the rest of humanity.

Fasting is common to many religions. Some fast on a given day or period in time to show humility toward God, to repent for sins, or to focus the mind and body on achieving an advanced spiritual state. Certain new religious movements employ fasting in a similar way, particularly those that stem directly from Abrahamic religions, Hinduism, and Buddhism. Numerous new religious movements, particularly those that hail from Hindu backgrounds, also employ periods of sustained meditation that can encompass fasting. The Breatharians, however, take fasting to the next level of devotion, believing that food is unnecessary for survival. All that one needs is breath ("spirit") to sustain oneself. This practice has been roundly criticized by the medical community as a dangerous and potentially life-threatening practice.

FOOD, NEW RELIGIONS, AND THE ENVIRONMENT

In the era of climate change, it is unsurprising that certain new religious movements have linked the production and consumption of food to ethical and spiritual imperatives for conservationism. Sustainable farming and eating practices have become major features of religious movements, such as Anthroposophy and Eco-Paganism. Such movements tend to advocate not only for a plant-based diet but connect care for the earth to eating and spiritual practice. As religions are increasingly required to account for the perils of climate change, it will be interesting to see whether new religions will emerge whose focus is on the practice of eating responsibly.

See also: Anthroposophy; Breatharianism; Church of Jesus Christ of Latter-day Saints, The; Eco-Paganism; Environmentalism and New Religious Movements; Father Divine (1876–1965); Fillmore, Charles (1854–1948) and Myrtle (1845–1931); Healing, Health, and New Religious Movements; Heaven's Gate; Hindu New Religious Movements; International Peace Mission Movement; Millennialism; Millerites, The; Nation of Islam, The; New Thought; Rastafari; Santería; Seventh-day Adventism; Unity School of Christianity.

Further Reading

Cimino, Richard. 2014. "New Religious Movements Shaping American Eating Habits." *Religion Watch* 30, no. 2 (Dec): 7–8.

Griffith, R. Marie. 2004. *Born Again Bodies: Flesh and Spirit in American Christianity.* Berkeley: University of California Press.

Rapport, Jeremy. 2011. "Corresponding to the Rational World: Scientific Rationales and Language in Christian Science and the Unity School of Christianity." *Nova Religio* 14, no. 4 (May): 11–29.

Sack, Daniel. 1999. "Food and Eating in American Religious Cultures." In Peter W. Williams, ed., *Perspectives on American Religion and Culture.* Malden, MA: Blackwell.

Zeller, Benjamin, Marie Dallam, Reid L. Neilson, & Nora Rubel. 2014. *Religion, Food, and Eating in North America.* New York: Columbia University Press.

Fortune, Dion (1890–1946)

Dion Fortune, born Violet Mary Firth in Wales in 1890, can be counted among the golden generation of British occultists, which includes Aleister Crowley (1875–1947) and Gerald Gardner (1884–1964). Like her famous peers, Fortune injected her own personal religious interests and aims into her brand of occult religion, which influenced burgeoning new religious movements such as Wicca.

Following a traumatic experience while at school, in 1913, Fortune began studying psychotherapy as a means of curing her own mental woes. By 1914, she was working as a mental health counselor for those with "sexual dysfunction." It was during this time that she became interested in occult religious ideas, primarily by reading about and attending lectures by the Theosophical Society. As she became more convinced about Theosophy's belief in the Ascended Masters, she grew disillusioned by psychotherapy and left her practice.

Over the next decade, Fortune would experience varying levels of involvement in several occult religious movements, including Theosophy, Freemasonry, and, eventually, the Hermetic Order of the Golden Dawn into which she was initiated in 1919. Though the Order would not become her permanent religious home, it was here that she developed an interest in Kabbalah, a mystical strain of Judaism, also adopted by Hermetic and Christian occult groups. In 1924, she founded the Society of the Inner Light to differentiate her growing occult knowledge from the various other groups with which she affiliated. As a result of her earlier experience in the Theosophical Society, Fortune started to dabble in trance mediumship, which ultimately spurred her most significant contributions to British occultism: her prolific publications.

From 1922 until her death in 1946, Fortune wrote the equivalent of a book a year (plus half a dozen texts published posthumously). Her earliest texts reflect her interests in psychotherapy, but as her magical and mediumistic abilities grew, her texts began to reflect the special, sacred knowledge she received through her ritual practices. Most of the books were nonfiction, such as *Psychic Self-Defense* (1930), *The Mystical Qabalah* (1935), and *The Cosmic Doctrine* (1949), and served to cement her as a celebrity within British occultism. She also wrote a series of novels, reflecting themes of esotericism and romance, which Fortune saw as an extension of her occult work.

Fortune died of leukemia in the months following the end of World War II. During the crisis, she had gathered fellow magical practitioners and occultists in an effort to psychically protect as well as to visualize a glorious outcome for England.

See also: Crowley, Aleister (1875–1947); Gardner, Gerald (1884–1964); Hermetic Order of the Golden Dawn, The; Kabbalah; Magic and New Religious Movements; Neopaganism; Occultism and Esotericism; Theosophical Society, The; Theosophy; Wicca.

Further Reading

Fortune, Dion. 1930. *Psychic Self-Defense*. London: Rider & Company.

Fortune, Dion. 1935. *The Mystical Qabalah*. London: Williams and Norgate.

Knight, Gareth. 2000. *Dion Fortune and the Inner Light*. Loughborough, UK: Thoth Publications.

Sadovsky, Sonja. 2014. *The Priestess and the Pen: Marion Zimmer Bradley, Dion Fortune and Diana Paxton's Influence on Modern Paganism*. Woodbury, UK: Llewellyn Press.

Fourth Way, The

During the late nineteenth century, a number of new religious movements arose that claimed access to theretofore hidden information about the nature of the universe, the abilities of human beings, and the reality of unseen, spiritual dimensions. Often these movements claimed to absorb wisdom of Eastern religious traditions, translated for a Western audience. Arguably, the most well known was Theosophy, founded by Helena Petrovna Blavatsky (1831–1891) and Henry Steel Olcott (1832–1907), which created a strong institutional structure that formalized the wisdom of its founders. Less prominent, more diffuse, but equally significant in terms of its contribution to the world of occult religious movements, was the Fourth Way, a practice created by G. I. Gurdjieff (c. 1866–1949) and disseminated by P. D. Ouspensky (1878–1947).

Gurdjieff, who was born in then Russian-controlled Armenia, traveled to India after encountering Theosophy and met a series of teachers and gurus over a number of years. Though he refused to reveal their identities or the specifics of what they had told him, Gurdjieff began to build his own understanding of the sacred knowledge he reportedly gleaned. Most important among his discoveries was that most human beings exist in a state of "waking sleep," unaware of their capacity to achieve higher levels of consciousness, awareness of ultimate truth, and even advanced physical ability. At one point, long ago, human beings were aware of these innate abilities, but over time, and with the advent of exclusive, institutionalized religions, people eventually lost this awareness. Gurdjieff's teachings focused on awakening students through a process of self-development known as "The Work," and later, advertised by his student Ouspensky under the name "The Fourth Way."

Contrary to most world religions, which Gurdjieff argued only focused on one or two aspects of human nature, his program of self-development focused on nurturing the whole person. There were three traditional ways or "schools" for human advancement: the Way of Fakir, which aims to master the body; the Way of the Monk, which seeks to control the emotions; and the Way of the Yogi, which focuses attention and mastery of the mind. The Fourth Way combined all of these paths into one, believing that to achieve higher knowledge and total self-mastery, all components of the person must be engaged at once.

To achieve this focus, the Fourth Way proposes a number of methods. Most important is the principle of mindfulness or "conscious labor," whereby a practitioner learns to block distractions, to avoid daydreaming, and to prevent the mind from wandering. By being completely attentive to a particular task, the person is able to perform that task more efficiently and with greater awareness of the person's abilities. This mindfulness engages the practice of "intentional suffering," which promotes the idea that people should ward against those activities that are most distracting (and often enjoyable), such as oversleeping, eating rich food, and even sex. Though abstention from any of these is not intended to be permanent (Gurdjieff was adamant that no one needs to adopt the life of an ascetic), awareness of what causes distractions is important for the practitioner to know as he or she proceeds on the path to self-development. Knowing one's behavior, including one's weaknesses, is part of the process of "self-observation" recommended by Gurdjieff.

Most practitioners of the Fourth Way are initiated by a teacher, though often communal practice is encouraged. Gurdjieff employed dance and music to enable students to enter a meditative and focused state. However, emphasis was laid on each individual developing, in day-to-day life, a means of focusing attention and attaining higher levels of self and universal knowledge. Organizationally, the movement has failed to coalesce into a singular group. At the outset, Gurdjieff failed to establish a central institution, a fact exacerbated when his most famous student, Ouspensky, began teaching his own interpretation of Gurdjieff's teachings. A variety of claimants to Gurdjieff's and Ouspensky's work and legacy have emerged, including the Gurdjieff Foundation, and, today, an Online School of the Fourth Way. Most encounter the Fourth Way through its various publications, particularly those of Ouspensky, who was the most prolific disseminator of the practice.

See also: Blavatsky, Helena Petrovna (1831–1891); Gurdjieff, G. I. (c. 1866–1949); Occultism and Esotericism; Olcott, Henry Steel (1832–1907); Ouspensky, P. D. (1878–1947); Theosophy.

Further Reading
Gurdjieff, G. I. 2013. *In Search of Being: The Fourth Way to Consciousness*. Boston: Shambhala Publications.

Ouspensky, P. D. 1947. *In Search of the Miraculous: Fragments of an Unknown Teaching.* London: Routledge Press.

Ouspensky, P. D. 1957. *The Fourth Way: A Record of Talks and Answers Based on the Teachings of G. I. Gurdjieff.* New York: Knopf Press.

Fox, Kate (1837–1892), and Margaret (1833–1893)

EARLY YEARS AND HYDESVILLE

Kate's and Maggie's path toward religious authority and celebrity began early. At eleven and fourteen, respectively, the sisters began to hear what they described as "rappings" in their home in Hydesville, New York, in 1848. Curious about the source of these strange noises, the girls began to interrogate the source, asking "it" to perform certain acts, such as snap its fingers, and answer questions about itself (with a different number of raps signifying either "yes" or "no"). They determined that the noisemaker was a spirit and dubbed it (or him) "Mr. Splitfoot." As rumors began to swirl around these events, Kate and Maggie went to stay with their sister Leah Fox Fish (1831–1890) in Rochester, New York, but the phenomena followed.

At that time, upstate New York was a hotbed of religious innovation and activity. Thus, it was not long before the girls began to collect a cadre of religious seekers interested in supernatural phenomena, beginning with radical Quakers Amy and Isaac Post. Soon thereafter, Kate and Maggie began to conduct séances, emerging as mediums who could speak to, and even channel, the deceased. Thus, the religious movement known as Spiritualism was born.

SPIRITUALIST CELEBRITIES AND BEYOND

Only a year after their experiments with Mr. Splitfoot, Kate and Maggie were demonstrating their abilities in front of packed audiences at lecture halls. Their tender age and gender certainly added to the novelty of their exhibitions, drawing viewers with ranging levels of voyeuristic curiosity and genuine interest. Their status as religious celebrities helped to bolster ties between Spiritualism and the broader women's rights movement—a reform effort with which many initial and future Spiritualists were involved. The girls emerged as social and cultural figures even before they were conceived as religious leaders.

The religious significance of Kate and Maggie's burgeoning movement became apparent quickly. Since the girls claimed contact with the deceased, they could learn about what happened after death. Challenging their historical context and the predominant Christian views regarding heaven, hell, and salvation, the girls could offer definitive proof about what eternity looked like. Soon, prophetic figures such as Andrew Jackson Davis (1826–1910) began to tout the sisters' authority and findings. They also began to hold mass séances, which often included notable figures of their day, such as William Lloyd Garrison (1805–1879), Horace Greeley (1811–1872; Greeley became something of a guardian to Kate and Maggie), and Sojourner Truth (1797–1883).

Though Leah would join her sisters, leading séances in New York, Kate and Maggie earned true celebrity status as they embarked on a national, and later international, tour, organized to highlight their abilities and spread Spiritualism further. By the 1850s, Spiritualism counted practitioners in the millions due in great part to the culture of séances emphasized by the sisters. Along the way, Maggie enjoyed a brief marriage to Elisha Kane (1820–1857), who was convinced that the sisters were involved with fraud and ultimately convinced Maggie to convert to Roman Catholicism; she would resume her Spiritualist practices after his death. Kate married a London Spiritualist, H. D. Jencken (1828–1881), with whom she would have two children.

The sisters' fame brought fortune and renown, on the one hand, and vice and skepticism on the other. Both sisters were heavy drinkers, and it became clear over time that Maggie was an alcoholic. This and the unrelenting pressure of the spotlight led to the rapid unraveling of their reign as Spiritualism's most celebrated duo. In 1888, Maggie issued a confession stating, in some detail, how the girls had manufactured the various supernatural phenomena experienced at their séances. Though they had been under suspicion from the start, Maggie's admission that they had performed most of the rappings themselves, knocking under the table with their feet or knuckles, sent shockwaves through the Spiritualist community. That year, both sisters formally denounced Spiritualism, the religious movement to which they had given birth.

Kate and Maggie would die in relative poverty within a year of each other. Notwithstanding their renunciation of the movement, Spiritualism would live on in various forms, both secular and religious, as future generations continued to hope for word from the beyond.

See also: Fraud and Deception in New Religions; Ghosts, the Paranormal, and New Religious Movements; Spiritualism; Women in New Religious Movements.

Further Reading
Braude, Ann. 2001. *Radical Spirits: Spiritualism and Women's Rights in the Nineteenth Century*. Second Edition. Bloomington: Indiana University Press.
Weisberg, Barbara. 2009. *Talking to the Dead: Kate and Maggie Fox and the Rise of Spiritualism*. New York: HarperCollins.

Fraud and Deception in New Religions

Accusations that religions are involved in defrauding their members have been around as long as religions have. For example, a second-century broadside against Christianity, written by the philosopher Celsus (c. 178 CE), attributes the miracles of Jesus to magic, rather than divine intervention. Celsus asserts that Jesus could only bamboozle foolish old women and other credulous rubes. The idea that new religions are deceiving their members, a pillar of the stereotype of "dangerous cults," is nothing new.

Claims about unseen forces at work in human life, as Celsus's critique shows, are difficult to prove on grounds that satisfy both believers and skeptics. Where the believer may see the Holy Spirit at work, suspicious observers may see subterfuge. The same dynamic that characterizes Celsus's work recurs in all contexts where religious movements claim to improve the physical and mental health of individuals. Claims to faith healing in contemporary Pentecostal groups, Scientology's claims to have improved the mental health of participants moving along the Bridge to Total Freedom toward and beyond the state of clear, and Christian Science's claims to effect healing through prayer have all been subjected to corrosive questioning. In some cases, scientific proof had been adduced to undermine religious claims. Even in these cases, such proof has proven incapable of shaking the faith of religious participants.

One pillar of the stereotype of "dangerous cults" is that the leaders are definitely not who they claim to be. Simply put, they are frauds. It is difficult, however, to find neutral standards by which, for example, Ann Lee (1736–1784) could be shown not to be the Second Coming of Christ in female form or the Rev. Sun Myung Moon (1920–2012) and his wife could be determined not to be the True Parents of humankind. Leadership claims justified by appeal to charismatic authority portray the claimant as being commissioned by powerful unseen forces. Although leaders have to maintain their charismatic status in the eyes of their followers by mutually agreed-upon means, as long as they do they are relatively impervious to external criticism.

But in some cases the unmasking of a leader has been accomplished with decisive results. The statements of some members of the Theosophical Society that they had helped Madame Blavatsky (1831–1891) fabricate appearances of the Mahatmas severely damaged Blavatsky's credibility, even though some Theosophists rejected the charges. Malcolm X (1925–1965) recounts that finding out about Elijah Muhammad's (1897–1975) infidelities undermined his acceptance of Elijah's authority and paved the way for his exit from the Nation of Islam. Those who stayed with Elijah blamed Malcolm for insubordination and some out of loyalty eventually participated in his assassination.

In some cases, the results are more ambiguous. In 1978, it became clear that Peoples Temple's utopian experiment at Jonestown was failing, which threatened the status of Jim Jones as the leader and embodiment of apostolic socialism. Behind the scenes, the inner circle tried to shore up Jones's authority, even as his deteriorating health and drug dependence reduced his capacity to lead. The convulsive end to Peoples Temple in the murder-suicides of the "White Night" in November 1978 rendered moot whether the group could make a transition to a new form of leadership in which Jones played a lesser role.

Opponents of new religions have frequently called upon government bodies to "do something" about "dangerous cults." Such pleas have produced much more talk than action. When actions have been taken, the results have often been unsatisfactory for all involved. For example, alarmed by the widespread positive reception of the prophet Simon Kimbangu's (1887–1951) miracle-working ministry in the Belgian Congo in 1921, the colonial authorities incarcerated him. His lifelong detention, however, did nothing to stop the spread of the Church of Jesus Christ on Earth through the Prophet Simon Kimbangu, which continues to this day.

The prosecution in 1942 of members of the "I AM" Activity, founded by Guy (1878–1939) and Edna Ballard (1886–1971), was based on accusations of fraud.

Former members of the group, spurred on by the exposé *Psychic Dictatorship in America* (1940), claimed that Ballard's books contained eighteen "false representations." Since the movement had knowingly sent books containing its teachings through the mail, it had committed mail fraud. Despite attempts to deny it, the case put the U.S. courts in the position of adjudicating the truth of religious claims, something for which they were ill-suited. The case dragged on for years until the guilty verdict was vacated in 1946, though it had irreparably damaged the movement.

From a materialist perspective, all religions that claim interaction with unseen forces are frauds because the existence of such forces cannot be demonstrated. From the perspective of believing insiders, however, such claims are meaningless and show only that materialists have not had the religious experiences that would convince them. In between there is a vast gray area. Social interactions between claimants, such as charismatic leaders and their followers, can maintain and reinforce worldviews in which interactions with gods, spirits, or other unseen forces make sense and have real impacts. The temptation on the part of leaders to take advantage of followers' credulity, however, is ever present. Jim Jones and his inner circle, for example, knew that his displays of spiritual healing were a sham, but they rationalized his performances as a way of capturing the attention of his audience. Fraud may be difficult to prove, especially in the realm of religion, but it does happen.

See also: Anticult Movement, The; Charisma and Leadership in New Religious Movements; I AM Activity, The; Kimbangu, Simon (1887–1951); Lee, Mother Ann (1736–1784); Muhammad, Elijah (1897–1975); Scientology; Spiritualism; Theosophy.

Further Reading

Long, Carolyn Morrow. 2002. "Perceptions of New Orleans Voodoo: Sin, Fraud, Entertainment, and Religion." *Nova Religio* 6: 86–101.

Van Eck Duyaer van Twist, Amanda, ed. 2016. *Minority Religions and Fraud: In Good Faith*. New York: Routledge.

Whitehead, Deborah. 2015. "The Evidence of Things Unseen: Authenticity and Fraud in the Christian Mommy Blogosphere." *Journal of the American Academy of Religion* 83: 120–150.

FREECOG (Free the Children of God)

One of the most prominent groups of "Jesus people" to emerge in the late 1960s was the Children of God (COG). Founded by David Brandt Berg (1919–1994) in Huntington Beach, California, in 1968, the group sought members among young adults searching for meaning. Virtually as soon as the group achieved any success, however, it also elicited strong opposition from families who thought that they had "lost" loved ones to a "cult."

Among the worried parents was William Rambur, whose twenty-two-year-old daughter had joined COG and moved to their commune in Texas. Frustrated in their inability to extricate their daughter from the group, in 1972, the Ramburs made common cause with other worried families and formed "The Parents Committee to Free Our Sons and Daughters From the Children of God," later shortened to "Free the Children of God" or FREECOG. The organizers were aided by Ted Patrick (1930–), who had recently had his own encounters with COG and would soon become a well-known deprogrammer who expanded his efforts to many other groups.

As the first dedicated contemporary anticult group, FREECOG offered its members important social support as they learned that their experiences were not unique. It disseminated information about Berg's group and attempted to warn others about the danger posed by it. It also provided referrals to other parents who were wrestling with similar issues and to former COG members. It could put individuals into contact with the growing group of deprogrammers who promised to get members out of groups for a price. Members shared the conviction that the young people who joined COG could not have done so willingly and must have been subjected to undue influence.

Over time, FREECOG widened its focus to include other new religious groups such as the International Society for Krishna Consciousness (the "Hare Krishnas") and the Unification Church. As the scope of FREECOG's interests widened, efforts were also made to make it a national organization. A reorganization as the Volunteer Parents of America only lasted a short time. In 1974, however, the Citizens Freedom Foundation (CFF) was established with William Rambur as its president. That group had national representation on its board, including a member from Canada, and became the most prominent anticult organization in the western United States.

Despite attempts to engage local, state, and federal governments in the anticult effort, FREECOG and its successor organizations remained volunteer organizations with very little infrastructure and a constant need for donations to sustain their work. Only when the Cult Awareness Network developed out of the CFF in 1979, did FREECOG's original vision of a nation-wide united front against cults take shape.

See also: Anticult Movement, The; Brainwashing; Cult; Cult Awareness Network, The; Deprogramming; Love Israel Family, The; Patrick, Ted (1930–).

Further Reading
Patrick, Ted, & Tom Dulack. 1976. *Let Our Children Go!* New York: E. P. Dutton.
Shupe, Anson D., Jr., & David G. Bromley. 1980. *The New Vigilantes: Deprogrammers, Anti-Cultists, and the New Religions.* Beverly Hills, CA: Sage.

Freemasonry

Careening through the National Mall, hell bent on discovering treasure hidden by the founding fathers, Nicholas Cage has become the pop cultural touchstone of an ancient, secret society known as the Freemasons. In the film *National Treasure* (2004), Cage follows the trail of masonic signs to riches untold—using a map that appears on the U.S. Constitution. Fodder for film and conspiracy theories alike, Freemasonry, with its web of gnostic symbols and secret rituals, is still an enigma to the casual observer, even if it has become tacitly accepted as a component of European and American history.

ORIGINS AND HISTORY

The precise date of origin of Freemasonry is difficult to pinpoint. The name "Freemason" originates from the loose organization of stonemason fraternities in the fourteenth century; nonetheless, precisely when it adopted religious and esoteric significance varies according to the continent and source. Sometime during the seventeenth and eighteenth centuries, rituals began to develop among the fraternities and membership became an increasingly drawn out process that began with an invitation from an initiated member.

Lodges developed in the United Kingdom, with the first Grand Lodge founded in 1717 in London. In the British colonies (later the United States), the earliest lodges appeared in Pennsylvania around the same time. Prior to the Revolutionary War, the colonial lodges operated under the jurisdiction of their parent chapters in the United Kingdom. However, lodges proliferated in the colonies without British authorization, leading to theories of their involvement with the outbreak of Revolution in the late eighteenth century. Following the Revolution, Grand Lodges were established in each state.

Freemasonry developed differently in its various contexts, often prompting schisms within the broader movement or simply variations in practice. Freemasonry developed on the European continent, specifically France, in the eighteenth century among English expatriates; the English and French branches ultimately split over issues of jurisdiction and practice. In Italy, Masonic lodges developed later and were often aligned with particular political parties and interests. In the United States, following western expansion, Native Americans were encouraged to join Masonic lodges as a means of "civilizing" them;

When Freemasonry developed in the American colonies, it attracted many elite members of society. George Washington, who joined a Masonic lodge at age twenty, is depicted here with some of the symbols of Freemasonary, many of which derived from groups of stone masons in the fourteenth century. (Library of Congress)

however, just the converse occurred when western American lodges began to appropriate the rituals of various Native American tribes into their practices. Thus, the eastern and western chapters of Freemasonry often reflected a completely different style of Masonic practice.

BELIEFS AND PRACTICES

Freemasonry is a movement of symbols and rites. The symbol of the Freemasons derives its components from the tools of stonemasons: namely, the square ruler and the metal compass as well as various symbols meant to represent various biblical or religious themes, such as King Solomon's Temple. Each symbolic component bears a secret meaning and often a morality lesson. This knowledge is revealed to initiates over time and during the various rituals of the society. While visual symbols represent pieces of knowledge or designate Masonic sites of worship, certain gestures or signs are used to identify true Masons (which, unsurprisingly, are closely kept secrets by those who have been initiated).

Since membership is historically exclusive and marked with distinction, central to Freemasonic practice are those rituals that bring a new member gradually into the society. There are three degrees of "craft," which is the name given to Masonic practice and belief. The three degrees correspond to different stages in the novice Freemason's journey, namely, Entered Apprentice, Fellowcraft, and Master Mason. At each stage, the novice is taught trade secrets, such as identifying gestures and the meaning behind certain symbols, and introduced to the sacred history known only to initiated Freemasons. Despite the sacred nature of these rituals, there is no standard version of each rite, meaning that multiple variations exist. Some of this results from the secret and autonomous nature of each lodge. Reflecting this secrecy, at each stage of initiation, the Freemason must swear on one sacred text—often the Bible, Qur'an, or Bhagavad Gita—known in that moment as the "Volume of Sacred Law," never to reveal the secrets of the Freemasons or risk expulsion.

Freemasons organize themselves into "lodges," which comprise the institutional and communal center of religious practice. Lodges refer not to the building itself but to the members of a particular jurisdiction. Freemasons are said to meet "as" a lodge, not "in" a lodge. Thus, when a Freemason is initiated into the society, he or she is initiated into a specific lodge. With some exceptions, Freemasons are able to visit any Masonic lodge outside of their usual jurisdiction. Masonic Temples, or the physical sites of worship, are easily identifiable by their symbols, though the structures themselves vary from the stately architecture required by Grand Lodges to storefront rentals. Though concentrated in the United States and, now to a lesser degree, in the United Kingdom, Masonic lodges exist throughout Europe, Australia and New Zealand, Southeast Asia, and South America.

Prince Hall Freemasonry is an offshoot of Freemasonry that exists specifically for African American Masons. So named for Prince Hall, an African American who was refused entry into colonial lodges prior to the Revolution. Prince Hall and several other African Americans were initiated into a British-affiliated

Masonic chapter, but following the end of the Revolutionary War, they were forced to create their own Masonic lodge, since they were not formally recognized as Masons. Such segregation persisted throughout the nineteenth and much of the twentieth centuries. Though such discrimination is now abolished in Masonic lodges, Prince Hall lodges still operate (though, they also open their doors to members of all races).

Women have been historically prevented from formally joining Masonic lodges. Those who were able to enter into these groups were often unable to move up the ranks nor hold positions of any great power. This has not prevented women from establishing parallel institutions nor even from claiming the title of Freemason for themselves or their societies. For the most part, Masonic lodges are still segregated by gender, even though there is a greater number of Freemasonic women today. More recently, questions have arisen regarding Transgender Freemasons about which the response has been to accept both male and female Transgender members. For those who transition after their initiation, they are allowed to remain a member of their respective lodge.

RELIGIOUS LEGACY AND CULTURAL INFLUENCE

The reach of Freemasonry is extensive. Beyond the persistence of Masonic lodges and the mythos of its underlying influence in American society, Freemasonry has also impacted the growth of other new religious movements. For example, prior to the leadership of Aleister Crowley (1875–1947), Ordo Templi Orientis, a German occult religious group, modeled many of its rituals on Freemasonry, particularly those involving initiation. Contemporaneously, though in the American context, Timothy Drew, later Noble Drew Ali (1886–1929) founded the Moorish Science Temple and argued that African Americans were descended from the Moors (Muslims of the Iberian peninsula), while borrowing much of the symbolism and distinguishing garb of Masonic lodges.

Freemasons have had their critics as well. As an esoteric religion that claims secret, occult knowledge, Freemasonry has been critiqued by a variety of Christian denominations, including the Catholic Church. The Catholic Church and Masonic lodges share a high ceremonialism, devotion to religious symbols, and mysterious knowledge, thus making them competitors in certain ways. As an alternative religious group, Freemasons were also targets of the Nazis during World War II. Prior to the war, German Freemasons wore forget-me-not flower pins as a sign of membership in the Freemasons; coincidentally, Nazis involved in the charitable branch of the party began wearing similar forget-me-not pins. For a time, German Freemasons were able to wear these secret symbols of Masonic membership without detection. In commemoration of the thousands of Freemasons murdered during the Holocaust, Freemasons now wear a forget-me-not pin.

Additionally, as evidenced by films like *National Treasure*, theories abound as to the far-reaching influence of Freemasonry and secret societies in general. The notion of an institution within American society working to direct or control the government of the country is still popular and has led to bans on secret societies in

England in the late eighteenth century, American political parties running on "anti-Masonic" propaganda in the nineteenth century, and political corruption scandals in various European nations such as Italy. More recently, conspiracy theorists have linked the Freemasons with the Illuminati, a mysterious, global group of individuals supposedly bent on world domination. Unlike the Freemasons, for whom evidence abounds, the existence of the Illuminati—or at least the degree of their influence—has not been definitively proven.

See also: Ali, Noble Drew (1886–1929); Conspiracy Theories; Crowley, Aleister (1875–1947); Hermeticism; Membership and New Religious Movements; Moorish Science Temple of America, The; Occultism and Esotericism; Ordo Templi Orientis.

Further Reading

Albanese, Catherine. 2007. *A Republic of Mind and Spirit: A Cultural History of American Metaphysical Religion.* New Haven, CT: Yale University Press.

Hackett, David. 2014. *That Religion in Which All Men Agree: Freemasonry in American Culture.* Berkeley: University of California Press.

Önnerfors, Andreas. 2018. *Freemasonry: A Very Short Introduction.* Oxford: Oxford University Press.

Stavish, Mark. 2007. *Freemasonry: Rituals, Symbols & History of the Secret Society.* Woodbury, MN: Llewellyn Publishing Worldwide.

Freezone Scientology

In 1950 L. Ron Hubbard (1911–1986) published the results of his investigations into the human mind, first in the pulp magazine *Astounding Science Fiction* and then as *Dianetics: The Modern Science of Mental Health.* Soon individuals began to adapt his ideas and therapeutic exercises to their own purposes, sometimes forming separate groups. Hubbard initially accepted such uses of his insights as potentially helpful research, but soon realized that virtually none of those experiments were producing what he saw as useful information. His ideas, he concluded, only achieved their power when enacted exactly as he had developed them. From the beginning, then, even before the therapeutic practice of Dianetics was incorporated into the new religion of Scientology, Hubbard faced the challenge of imposing order on divergent understandings of his message.

Dianetics and Scientology have continued to be practiced outside of the structure of the Church of Scientology since those early days, most recently by those who identify themselves as independent, "open source," or "Freezone" Scientologists. Those individuals typically assert that Hubbard's teaching, in its original form, can be a powerful tool even outside of the Church's control. They often assert that the bureaucratic structure of the Church has consistently frustrated the spirit of open inquiry and experimentation that characterized Hubbard's early work. They are particularly critical of the Church's efforts under David Miscavige (1960–) to maintain strict control over the practice of Scientology. For its part, the contemporary Church argues that it is completely necessary to safeguard the purity of Hubbard's original teachings and to combat unauthorized uses of them that threaten to compromise their effectiveness and undermine their authority.

By 1965, Hubbard issued a policy letter, "Keep Scientology Working," that reasserted the Church's control over Scientology's spiritual technology or "tech" and identified any unapproved uses of that tech as high crimes against the Church. Hubbard's concern with enforcing both orthodoxy and orthopraxy indicates that there continued to be individuals who were practicing the principles of Scientology independent of the control of the Church.

By 1982, Scientology had formed the Religious Technology Center (RTC), which controls and governs the use of all trademarks, symbols, and texts of Scientology to ensure the precise application of Hubbard's teachings. The RTC, though not involved in the daily administration of the Church of Scientology, is its highest ecclesiastical authority and Miscavige currently serves as the Chairman of its Board. Under Miscavige the RTC has taken extraordinary measures to preserve Hubbard's "applied religious philosophy" exactly as he delivered it. It has, for example, deposited copies of Hubbard's original teachings in a remote underground vault. In 2007, the RTC published new editions of Hubbard's foundational teachings that it claimed removed any editorial mistakes that had crept into the texts and returned Hubbard's powerful "tech" to its pristine form.

The efforts of the RTC indicate two things. First, as in many other religions, there is considerable interest in identifying and maintaining the original message of the founder in scriptural form. Second, because Scientology asserts that its tech always works when it is applied precisely as Hubbard instructed, it is vigilant about improper or unauthorized uses of that tech.

Beyond taking positive steps to preserve Hubbard's teaching in pristine form, Scientology has also developed defensive measures designed to stigmatize anyone who attempts to practice Scientology outside of the Church. Such individuals are identified by the Church as "suppressive persons," or "SPs," antisocial individuals who stand in the way of others realizing the benefits of Scientology. They are also known as "squirrels," who have a distorted understanding of Scientology. SPs can be subject to disciplinary actions, including excommunication if they are unable to reform their behavior. Such actions on the part of the Church have propelled some former members into the Freezone.

The independent practice of Scientology, then, carries with it a potentially heavy price, particularly in the years since Miscavige has consolidated his power within the Church. But the Church's often strenuous efforts to eradicate unauthorized uses of Scientology have not always succeeded.

For example, "Ron's Orgs" (Ron's Organization and Network for Standard Technology) were founded in 1984 by a former executive in the Church of Scientology, Bill Robertson (1936–2016), who is credited with originating the term "Freezone." Robertson claimed that he had been told by Hubbard that if he could no longer contact Hubbard directly he should start Scientology anew and reestablish Hubbard's original "tech." Ron's Orgs can now be found throughout Europe, Russia, and the former Soviet States.

One well-known independent Scientologist in the United States is Mark "Marty" Rathbun (1957–), who, before he left the Church in 2004, served as Inspector General of the RTC and was responsible for auditing celebrity Tom Cruise. After leaving, Rathbun has delivered counseling and auditing services independent of the Church; he has also provided damning information about the Church to media outlets. The complexity of Rathbun's relationship to Scientology is suggested by his clashes with other critics of the Church, including actress Leah Remini (1970–), who has published a memoir critical of the Church and a documentary series.

Although their numbers remain small, independent Scientologists nonetheless challenge the Church's understanding of itself as the guardian of Hubbard's legacy, while they strive in their own ways to benefit from it.

See also: Dianetics; Disaffiliation and Ex-Membership in New Religious Movements; Hubbard, L. Ron (1911–1986); Scientology.

Further Reading

Cusack, Carole M. 2017. "'Squirrels' and Unauthorized Uses of Scientology: Werner Erhard and Est, Ken Dyers and Kenja, and Harvey Jackins and Re-Evaluation Counselling." In James R. Lewis & Kjersti Hellesøy, eds., *Handbook of Scientology*, pp. 485–506. Leiden: E. J. Brill.

Park, Terril. 2017. "From the Church of Scientology to the Freezone." In Eugene V. Gallagher, ed., *"Cult Wars" in Historical Perspective*, pp. 152–164. New York: Routledge.

Rathbun, Mark. 2012. *The Scientology Revolution: What Every Scientologist Should Know*. N.p.: self-published.

Fundamentalist Mormons

HISTORY

In the public mind, Mormons—mainstream and fundamentalist alike—are affiliated with the practice of plural marriage or polygamy. However, it is only fundamentalist Mormons who still consider the practice a central tenet of their religious lives. Though mainstream Mormons eschew plural marriage and those who practice it, fundamentalist Mormons, in their many varieties, believe they represent the true Church as conceived by Joseph Smith.

Joseph Smith, the first Prophet of the Church of Jesus Christ of Latter-day Saints (LDS Church), reportedly received the revelation regarding plural marriage as early as 1831. Smith began revealing the revelation to a select few and implementing the practice in secret during the mid-1830s. However, the practice itself was not formally canonized as a part of Mormon scripture until 1843. Following Smith's assassination in 1844 and the Mormons' settlement in the territory that would become modern-day Utah, the next Prophet, Brigham Young, formalized the practice in 1852. The next forty years witnessed the heyday of plural marriage and the escalation of anti-Mormon ideology and legislation in response to the rollout of "the Principle," as it is known among Latter-day Saints.

In 1887, the Edmunds-Tucker Act was passed by Congress; it was a piece of legislation that formally disincorporated the LDS Church, enabled the seizure of church assets, and prompted the raiding of Mormon households to arrest suspected polygamists. Mormon officials now faced an impossible choice between the church's revival and the retention of a scriptural doctrine of the church. In

1890, it appeared the choice had been made when the fourth prophet, Wilford Woodruff, issued what came to be known as the "First Manifesto," formally discontinuing the practice of plural marriage. Still, the practice persisted for some years, necessitating the issuance of a "Second Manifesto" in 1904 by Joseph F. Smith (Joseph Smith's nephew), which made the practice of the Principle an excommunicable offense.

The vast majority of Latter-day Saints ceased the practice. However, there were those who felt the 1890 Manifesto was an act of great apostasy, leading a series of schismatic groups to break off and form their own sects of Mormonism, most of whom elected their own prophets.

VARIETIES OF BELIEF AND PRACTICE

The practice of plural marriage, as originally conceived, was a product of Mormon cosmology and historical circumstances. Joseph Smith revealed that all human beings had previously existed as the spiritual children of a Father and Mother God. These spiritual children came to earth and gained bodies to become "exalted." Exaltation is a long, multistage process occurring on earth and in the afterlife, whereby a person is ultimately divinized, becoming like the original Father and Mother God. While on earth, progress toward exaltation is achieved through performance of various sacred rituals, which occur in consecrated Temples, including "sealing." Heterosexual marriage is the most common sealing ritual (though people can be sealed to children, relatives, and even to those already dead, such as Joseph Smith). Bonded for "time and eternity," those sealed are able to live together in the afterlife; those who are not sealed, face an eternity alone. Plural marriage arose from the idea that community in the presence of God is the true mark of heaven; the more people sealed together, the more "celestial" the heavenly experience. Further, at the time the sealing ritual was developed in the mid-nineteenth century, there were far more female than male Mormon converts, thus marriage into a polygamous household immediately strengthened new members' bonds to fellow Mormons and the faith.

Today, both mainstream and fundamentalist Mormons believe sealing to be a sacred rite, however, the former have separated the practice from its polygamous origins. Yet, it is also not fair to paint all fundamentalist Mormons with the same brush. Though most fundamentalist sects practice some form of plural marriage (preferring that term or "the principle," to polygamy), for most, the practice is not compulsory. Further, not all fundamentalists belong to official "groups," such as the United Apostolic Brethren or the Fundamentalist Latter-day Saints (FLDS); many are called "independents," practicing plural marriage without belonging to an official sect. Most groups and independents trace their origins to Lorin C. Woolley, who was the primary proponent of plural marriage during the early twentieth century and who founded the Council of Friends (made up of those excommunicated for continued practice of the Principle) in 1929. Woolley claimed that in 1886, then-Prophet Woodruff granted him special authority to perform plural marriages. This solved the central dilemma for those who broke off—namely, how to claim succession from the prophetic authority of the Church. Though, now that Woolley claimed special priesthood abilities outside of the church, this enabled others to do the same, meaning that schism would continue as different men claimed status as prophets.

Marriage or courtship among fundamentalist Mormons ranges from traditional (but highly regulated) dating among young people to marriages arranged by the prophet. For those in the Allred Group, for example, young people participate in a variety of coeducational activities, such as dances, sporting events, or socials. Dating proceeds according to conventional standards for a young man and woman, and the young woman's consent is essential to both courtship and marriage. However, in the FLDS under Prophet Warren Jeffs, marriages were arranged by the church hierarchy, which could lead to marriages between underage girls with much older men. Contrary to popular perception, there are fundamentalist Mormons who practice monogamy, while still remaining devoted to their particular sect. Overall, however, plural marriage appears to be a practice continued only by a dwindling, but stalwart minority. Still, even for those sects where the vast majority practice monogamy, most show little interest in being resorbed into the mainstream LDS Church. Many of these sects, which are concentrated in the southwestern United States, are over a hundred years old, with their own established institutions, practices, and histories. For them, the goal is acceptance by their parent church and the surrounding society, not absorption and the potential loss of their distinctiveness.

CONTROVERSY AND CULTURE

The LDS Church has expended great effort to distance itself from its polygamous past with varying degrees of success. Similarly, many fundamentalist Mormons have sought to mitigate misunderstandings of the nature and lived reality of plural marriage. These processes have been complicated by two overlapping phenomena: first, certain high profile arrests and raids on fundamentalist compounds, particularly that of the Yearning for Zion (YFZ) Ranch in El Dorado, Texas, and, second, numerous pop cultural portrayals of fundamentalist Mormons.

Suspicions over instances of statutory rape, child abuse, and polygamy have persistently plagued FLDS, fair or not. In 2008, suspicions became reality following the raid of the YFZ Ranch, the primary home of the FLDS Church led by Warren Jeffs. Following a hotline call by a young woman who claimed to be the victim of physical and sexual abuse, a large-scale operation involving local police and a SWAT team ensued, leading to the arrest and eventual trial of many members of its male hierarchy, most notably Jeffs (who received a life sentence), on accusations of rape, underage marriage, and child abuse. During the process, families were broken up and women were often parted from their children for extended periods of time. The raid and subsequent trials made headlines for months. Images of women in conservative dress, uniform hairstyles, and multiple children firmly etched into the public imagination the depraved practices of fundamentalist Mormons. Thus, the LDS Church and non-FLDS fundamentalists were compelled to define themselves and their beliefs over against those perpetuated by Jeffs at the YFZ Ranch.

Yet, the persistent coverage of the YFZ raid also highlighted the public's fascination with Mormons, particularly its supposedly strange practices of polygamy. In the last decades, this fascination has transformed into a veritable pop culture phenomenon, with FLDS serving as the subject matter for shows like HBO's *Big Love* and TLC's *Sister Wives*. Such shows have sought to highlight the "normalcy" of "good" polygamous relationships (as well as the deviance of "bad" plural marriages) and the authentic beliefs of those involved; however, they have also served to perpetuate the stereotype that most, if not all, Mormons practice plural marriage. Latter-day Saints, both mainstream and fundamentalist, have had mixed reactions to such portrayals; they are encouraged by the general interest in Mormonism, but often argue against the accuracy of the practices and relationships as they are shown. The long-term impact of such shows and (un)sympathetic media attention on the public's perception of the LDS Church, fundamentalist Mormons, and the Principle is yet unknown.

See also: Book of Mormon, The; Church of Jesus Christ of Latter-day Saints, The; Smith, Joseph (1805–1844).

Further Reading

Bennion, Janet. 2012. *Polygamy in Primetime: Media, Gender, and Politics in Mormon Fundamentalism*. Waltham, MA: Brandeis University Press.

Quinn, D. Michael. 1998. "Plural Marriage and Mormon Fundamentalism." *Dialogue: A Journal of Mormon Thought* 31, no. 2: 19–86.

Wright, Stuart, & James T. Richardson. 2011. *Saints under Siege: The Texas State Raid on the Fundamentalist Latter Day Saints*. New York University Press.

G

Gardner, Gerald (1884–1964)

Viewed by many as the father of modern witchcraft, Gerald Gardner built on the foundation laid by fellow British occultist, Aleister Crowley (1875–1947), while making his own mark on the religious movement that would often bear his name, Gardnerian Wicca or Wicca. Despite this characterization, Gardner maintained that his involvement in Wicca involved the revival of an ancient religion, not the foundation of something new.

Gardner was born in Lancashire, England, but due to familial and, later, professional circumstances, he primarily lived abroad until his early fifties, when he returned to England and began his engagement with witchcraft. Having already dabbled with Spiritualism and Freemasonry, Gardner was initiated into another reputedly occult religious group, the Rosicrucian Order Crotona Fellowship. He left the Order soon thereafter, however, for the New Forest Coven. The story goes that Gardner was brought to a large manor house in 1939, told to strip naked, and initiated into the ancient coven. It was at this time that he first encountered the word Wicca and learned of its connections to witchcraft.

Gardner remained in the New Forest Coven until 1944; from 1945 to 1950, he founded and operated a nudist colony called Four Acres. During the 1940s, Gardner dabbled in various branches of Neopaganism and occult religion, such as Druidry, and, after meeting Crowley, the Ordo Templi Orientis, which he would join in 1947. Then in 1951, Gardner took up residence as the "resident witch," on the Isle of Man, where there would soon be a museum devoted to folk magic and witchcraft. The 1950s were foundational for the development of Gardner's own understanding of Wicca, which he began to share prolifically in a variety of texts, including his own version of *The Book of Shadows*, a traditional book of spells and rituals possessed by most witches. Gardner was instrumental in forwarding the idea of Goddess Worship, arguing that fealty was due to both a male "Horned God" and a "Mother Goddess." His publishing career slowed in the 1960s due to ill health; he died from a heart attack while sailing home from Lebanon in 1964.

Critics have scrutinized Gardner's claims of expertise and his showmanship, viewing his religious persona as performative, rather than authentically religious. Scholars have challenged Gardner's claims to initiation into one of the oldest English covens, the New Forest coven in 1939, arguing that he founded a new religion in the 1940s. Nonetheless, most Wiccans maintain that their religion is an ancient religion in new guise, echoing Gardner's conclusions and aligning themselves indelibly with Gardnerian witchcraft.

See also: Crowley, Aleister (1875–1947); Druidry; Goddess Worship; Magic and New Religious Movements; Neopaganism; Occultism and Esotericism; Ordo Templi Orientis; Rosicrucianism; Wicca.

Further Reading

Davies, Owen, ed. 2017. *The Oxford Illustrated History of Witchcraft and Magic.* Oxford: Oxford University Press.

Gardner, Gerald. 1959. *The Meaning of Witchcraft.* London: Aquarian.

Gardner, Gerald. 2015 [1950]. *The Gardnerian Book of Shadows.* London: Forgotten Books.

Heselton, Philip. 2012. *Witchfather: A Life of Gerald Gardner.* 2 Volumes. Loughborough, UK: Thoth Publications.

Gender and New Religious Movements

Gender, as distinct from sex, refers to cultural norms that explain and affirm biological or bodily differences. In other words, gender is not tied solely to anatomy, but to understandings of and prescriptions for how to act, talk, feel about oneself, and think. While one's "sex" is characterized as male or female (or intersex, for those whose anatomy does not conform to one gender or another), one's gender is characterized by words like "masculine," "feminine," and "androgynous," and more recently "cis" and "trans" to denote those whose gender matches their biological sex and those whose gender does not or is more fluid, respectively. The implication of the variety of gendered characteristics and identification is that many now deny the binary nature of gender, viewing it instead as a spectrum.

Religions have long partaken in discourse about and the construction of gender characteristics and norms. In the Hindu tradition, deities often bear both masculine and feminine traits and appear as male or female avatars; until recently, however, most rituals were performed by male priests. In many African traditional religions, deities also manifest as male or female, a fluidity that is mirrored in the parity between male priests and female priestesses. Christianity, on the other hand, describes God as a Father and employs the pronoun "He" in the Bible, which serves as the source text for the clear differentiation—and often the subsequent ranking—of men and women, masculinity and femininity. Thus, traditions vary. New religious movements, as sites of innovation and experimentation, have both challenged and reaffirmed gender norms depending upon the traditions they draw from or the religious lineages they seek to correct.

DISSOLVING GENDER BINARIES

Numerous new religions did away with gender boundaries or enabled easy crossing between genders as well as the creation of entirely new genders. Spiritualism, the nineteenth-century religious movement based on communication between human beings and spirits, allowed women to achieve a certain degree of authority not typically awarded to them. In general, women were perceived as particularly sensitive to the supernatural, which made them natural mediums—those who communicate with or channel spirits. Not only did they gain social authority, but Spiritualist mediums were often possessed by male spirits, which enabled them to exist as both man and woman in a single body. Theosophy, an offshoot of Spiritualism founded by Helena Petrovna Blavatsky (1831–1891), grew from the idea that a series of Great Masters—both male and female—had been guiding humanity toward spiritual advancement for millennia. Blavatsky, as the spiritual figurehead of the movement, spoke with, channeled, and published the messages of these Masters in the process becoming one of the most renowned female religious leaders of her time. In the late twentieth century, channeling would emerge as a New Age form of Spiritualism and Theosophy. Among its famous channels is JZ Knight (1946–) who channels Ramtha, a male, divine entity who is thirty-five thousand years old and hails from Atlantis; she has founded the Ramtha School of Enlightenment based on her presentations of Ramtha's teachings.

Millennialist Christians also experimented with gender norms. Certain groups of Pentecostals, who believe spiritual gifts such as tongues and healing are signs of the "latter rain" or the last days, are notable for their racial progressivism as well as their simultaneously traditional and progressive gender norms. At its inception in the early twentieth century, Pentecostalism affirmed traditional gender roles, while also witnessing a rash of renowned female preachers, such as Aimee Semple McPherson (1890–1944) and Maria Woodworth-Etter (1844–1924). The ecstatic nature of worship and a democratic belief in the power of the Spirit enabled these charismatic women to traverse gender boundaries and become bona fide religious celebrities.

Postmillennialist movements argued that since gender would cease to exist when Christ returned (see Gal. 3:28), gender distinctions were moot. Quite often, these groups bore a utopian or communalist bent. The Shakers are famously celibate, believing as they do that sex is the root of sin and that sex will cease when the Kingdom of God arrives; they live communally and men and women are perceived as equals. These beliefs are rooted in unconventional ideas about gender revealed by Mother Ann Lee (1736–1784). Mother Ann explained that God was both male and female, a fact that would be mirrored in the Christ's first and second advents. Jesus represented the first, male incarnation, and the second incarnation would manifest the female side of God (many have believed that Mother Ann was this second incarnation). A few decades later, The Oneida Community, founded by John Humphrey Noyes (1811–1886), dispensed with traditional genders and gender roles: women wore special garments that allowed for more mobility (i.e., pants), communal tasks were divided without recourse to gender, and romantic attachments were prohibited. Believing that Christ had already returned in AD 70, Noyes attempted to replicate the Kingdom of God, wherein he believed gender would cease to be relevant.

Contemporary religious movements have also witnessed the rejection of gender by both men and women. Marshall Applewhite (1931–1997) and Bonnie Lu Nettles (1927–1985), better known as "Do" and "Ti," eschewed traditional genders, revealing to the members of their religious group, Heaven's Gate, that they were aliens come to earth to guide humanity toward "the evolutionary level above human" or TELAH. Members of Heaven's Gate took on different names, wore the same monochromatic uniform, and dispensed with traditional relationships, thus, readying their "vessels" for transformation to the next level where gender, among other things, would cease to exist. Though the members would ultimately determine to leave their vessels through ritual suicide in 1997, they did so having prepared their souls and minds for their genderless forms at the next level.

In a variation of this trend of dissolving gender boundaries, there are also a number of new religious movements that, while denying that gender is important in any ultimate or immediate sense, tend to subvert traditional hierarchies of men and women by placing women on top. After Claude Vorilhon's (1946–) encounter with the Elohim, an extraterrestrial race of beings who claimed credit for the creation of humanity (in laboratories) and all feats traditionally associated with God in the Bible, he encouraged women to stop reproducing. Since reproduction was rendered moot with these new revelations about human origins, women's traditional roles as mothers was negated, freeing them to pursue spiritual advancement. Raël, as Vorilhon would come to be called, believed that women were inherently superior to men, in part, because they were more capable than men of subjugating their human, sexual desires into religious pursuits. Similarly, Shree Bhagwan Rajneesh (1931–1990) or "Osho" revealed that women were more spiritually advanced than men—a fact that he mirrored in the almost entirely female staff he kept at his religious compound, Rajneeshpuram in Oregon. Osho himself was "genderless," having transcended beyond simplistic human categories, and thus representing what all of his followers should aspire to become. Finally, Neopaganism, though an extraordinarily broad movement, is known for empowering women and pursuing equality of the sexes. Nonetheless, Goddess Worship, is a form of Neopaganism that advocates for worship of the goddess, either as an entity that bears both male and female attributes or as an entirely female divinity. The Goddess movement was heavily influenced by feminist critiques of religion and reflects a dual desire to pursue equality for men and women, while simultaneously raising women up.

REINFORCING GENDER NORMS

Religions that reinforce specific gender identities and norms can do so consciously or inadvertently. The Church of Jesus Christ of Latter-day Saints bears both democratic and authoritarian impulses—most Mormons serve some role in the Church, even though it is governed by a strict hierarchy. However, it is men who hold the vast majority of the official roles in the LDS Church and the Church does reinforce certain patriarchal tropes: an emphasis placed on women as mothers and wives with men serving as breadwinners and heads of household. Nonetheless, Mormon women do enter the workforce, with many choosing to do so after their children are in school. In certain instances, Fundamentalist or Schismatic Mormons—those who broke from the LDS Church over the practice of plural marriage—often take gender norms and hierarchies to an extreme. The Fundamentalist Church of Latter-day Saints led by Warren Jeffs (1955–), for example, enforces strict gender codes—specific dress, specific jobs, prescribed amounts of mobility—and oversaw the marriage of women, many of whom were underage, to elders and authorities in the Church.

Some Islamic new religious movements also strengthen traditional gender roles. The Nation of Islam reinforces the idea of men as protectors and women as the protected, a fact replicated in recommendations for dress (modest) and the advocacy for women to focus much of their time at home. However, female members of the Nation of Islam are not prevented from seeking personal and professional lives outside of the home—they are simply expected to present themselves in a particular way when they do. ISIS, or the Islamic State of Iraq and Syria, has taken a particularly regressive view of women, choosing to interpret the Qur'an and Sunnah to enforce the dominion of men over women.

In other cases, not only gender norms but strict gender divisions occur. Dianic Wiccans, a Neopagan group, often exclude men from their rituals and deny the need for men in personal or romantic relationships. Rastafarianism has been critiqued for shutting women out of religious rituals, such as "reasoning" sessions, and, on occasion, for overt misogyny. Rastafarianism arose as a resistance movement against the hegemony of white, European culture or "Babylon" in Jamaica, and reinterpreted the Bible to advocate for the redemption of black people. However, the movement also adopted a somewhat negative view of women—as potential sources of impurity during Rasta ceremonies—and a traditional view of gender roles. Feminist critiques have emerged within the movement recently, however.

Some religions attract those of particular genders, even without making gender a constitutive focus of their belief or practice. For example, Satanism and Scientology reportedly attract more men than women. Scholars have posited that Satanism, which exists primarily through virtual communities, appeals to young men with more anarchistic tendencies who desire an individualistic religious philosophy. Scientology, which also promotes individual evolution and advancement, appeals to "geek culture" primarily through its founder L. Ron Hubbard's (1911–1986) background as a science fiction writer, and the focus on evidence-based, "scientific" results in its practice. Nonetheless, neither of these religions precludes women nor relegates women to traditional roles—they simply tend to skew male.

In all of these instances, whether gender roles are negated, dissolved, or reaffirmed, new religions highlight the dynamic nature of gender and the discourse around what gender is and should be.

See also: Applewhite, Marshall (1932–1997), and Bonnie Lu Nettles (1927–1985); Blavatsky, Helena Petrovna (1831–1891); Channeling; Church of Jesus Christ of Latter-day Saints, The; Fundamentalist Mormons; Goddess Worship; Heaven's Gate; Hubbard, L. Ron (1911–1986); ISIS; Knight, JZ (Ramtha) (1946–); Lee, Mother Ann (1736–1784); Mediums; Nation of Islam, The; Neopaganism; Noyes, John Humphrey (1811–1886); Oneida Community, The; Pentecostalism; Raëlians, The; Rajneesh, Shree Bhagwan/Osho (1931–1990); Ramtha's School of Enlightenment; Rastafari; Satanism; Scientology;

Shakers, The; Spiritualism; Theosophy; Utopianism in New Religious Movements; Vorilhon, Claude (Raël) (1946–); Wicca; Women in New Religious Movements.

Further Reading

Fedele, Anna, & Kim Knibbe, eds. 2013. *Gender and Power in Contemporary Spirituality: Ethnographic Approaches.* London: Routledge Press.

Goodwin, Megan. 2016. "Gender." In George D. Chyrssides & Benjamin E. Zeller, eds., *The Bloomsbury Companion to New Religious Movements.* London: Bloomsbury Publishing.

Hunt, Steven. 2013. "'Laboratories' of Gender? Masculinities, Spirituality and New Religious Movements in Late Twentieth-Century Britain." In Lucy Delap & Sue Morgan, eds., *Men, Masculinities and Religious Change in Twentieth-Century Britain.* Basingstoke, UK: Palgrave Macmillan.

Palmer, Susan J. 1994. *Moon Sisters, Krishna Mothers, Rajneesh Lovers: Women's Roles in New Religions.* New York: Syracuse University Press.

Tøllefsen, Inga B. 2016. "Gender and Religious Movements." In James R. Lewis & Inga B. Tøllefsen, eds., *The Oxford Handbook of New Religious Movements*, Volume II. New York: Oxford University Press.

Ghost Dance Movement (Wovoka)

BACKGROUND AND HISTORY

Though the Ghost Dance movement existed in earnest only from 1889 to 1890, it represented the culmination of decades of discord between white settlers and Lakota Sioux Indians, which was itself one among many conflicts born from centuries of conquest in the "new world." Best described as a religious revitalization movement, the Ghost Dance mixed Christian millennialism with Native American, specifically Paiute, religious ideas. Having witnessed their land and its resources, particularly their precious buffalo, dwindle at the hands of white settlers, those who practiced the Ghost Dance believed that they could return the world to its precontact origins, and in the process, bring back those who had died at the hands of the "Wasichus" (white people).

The Ghost Dance originated in the prophetic visions of the Messiah, Wovoka or Jack Wilson (1856–1932). Born Quoitze Ow, Wovoka was a Paiute Indian who worked under Nevadan farmer, David Wilson, from the ages of eight to thirty. From Wilson, a devout Christian, Wovoka learned to read and understand the Bible. From the time he left the Wilson farm to the time of his visions related to the Ghost Dance, Wovoka gained a reputation as someone with mystical power. Reportedly, he could control the weather and heal the sick. Then on January 1, 1889, during a solar eclipse, Wovoka claimed to receive a vision, which foresaw the resurrection of the dead and the removal of all white settlers from the land. According to his "Messiah Letter," Wovoka explained that to bring about this outcome, all indigenous peoples must dance a Ghost Dance for five days. His message spread through tribes, having a particular impact among Lakota Sioux Indians, who like most Plains Indians, had experienced recent defeats at the hands of whites.

Although it was short lived (1889–1890), the Ghost Dance revitalization movement that originated among the Lakota Sioux, instigated by the prophet Wovoka, continues to have resonance for Native Americans. This image shows Arapaho Indians participating in the traditional "round dance" that formed the basis of the Ghost Dance ritual. (National Archives)

As the Ghost Dance spread throughout the West during 1890, in South Dakota, the Bureau of Indian Affairs (BIA) had set about implementing assimilation procedures for neighboring Lakota Sioux. Traditional subsistence practices were replaced with farming; Lakota children were taken off-site to boarding schools, where they were instructed in the merits of Western, Christian civilization. With some exceptions, these efforts failed. This, coupled with the fact that Lakota were turning increasingly to the Ghost Dance, led the BIA to grow frustrated and alarmed at Indian "intransigence." Hostilities continued to escalate, particularly as witness reports began to emerge of massive groups of Native Americans performing the Ghost Dance. From the outside, it appeared that the Lakota were preparing for battle.

The tensions burst forth into tragedy in December 1890. Following appeals made by white settlers alarmed at the spread of the Ghost Dance, the federal government issued a call to gather various tribal chiefs to seek their help in quelling the growing fervor. Defying this more diplomatic goal, the BIA agent at Standing Rock (which straddles North and South Dakota) ordered the arrest of Hunkpapa Lakota chief, Sitting Bull; a protest ensued, which resulted in the death of Sitting Bull. Fearing reprisals, the military was called in to remove all Lakota from the area, which ultimately resulted in the Massacre at Wounded Knee, located on the Lakota Pine Ridge Reservation in South Dakota, on December 29, 1890. Though the specific trigger for the massacre is unknown (the Lakota had been disarmed previously), the army fired on the Lakota, killing hundreds and marking the de facto end of the Ghost Dance movement.

BELIEFS AND PRACTICES

Echoing his Christian upbringing, Wovoka's central religious claim was that the Second Coming of Jesus had occurred and that the Messiah now walked the earth. Some speculated that Wovoka was actually the manifestation of Jesus in the flesh; however, though he was called "Messiah" (which simply means "anointed one"), Wovoka maintained that Christ himself would be reincarnated on earth in 1892 and that he was merely a prophet of the savior's return. For this reason, the end-times predicted in the Book of Revelation were at hand. However, diverging from traditionally white Christian readings of how the events would proceed, Wovoka gave the end-times a decidedly Paiute spin. In his vision, Wovoka saw all deceased Paiute and those of other tribal nations surrounding God ("the Great Spirit") on his throne; God promised that all would be returned to their ancient tribal lands and all resources would be restored. The specific means of bringing this about was by dancing a Ghost Dance for five days on end, which would induce trances, enabling practitioners to see their deceased ancestors and to aid in their passage back to earth.

Though the performance of the Ghost Dance formed the central rite of this new religious movement, there was a great deal of spiritual and ritual preparation that went into its practice. Most important was the necessity to live a good and moral life, to "do right always," as Wovoka wrote in the Messiah Letter. A major component of such moral rectitude was the avoidance of harm. Though the BIA and neighboring white settlers would interpret the growing movement and its rhetoric around the removal of the white man as bearing hostile, potentially violent overtones, the movement could be classified as a nonviolent protest. Ghost dancers were to remain unarmed when performing the dance; their trances were not meant to induce blood lust, but to return the world to original, sacred time *without* shedding blood.

Eyewitness accounts of the Ghost Dance often depicted a rather frenzied array of dancers who jerked about and fell into trances. While these more ecstatic outcomes accompanied successful practice of the rite, the Ghost Dance, itself, was quite ordered in its practice. Based on traditional practices of the "round dance," Ghost dancers would often hold hands in a large circle and move in a slow, shuffling cycle around an individual (often the prophet himself) who would be exhorting them in prayer or song. The dance generally proceeded with the accompaniment of drummers who may have also been singing. The repetition of the movements, the rhythmic accompaniment, and the words of the dance leader would often mix leading practitioners into states of trance—where they would often exhort or prophesy themselves—or faint. The dance would last for hours, sometimes all night.

While performing the Ghost Dance, practitioners were to don "ghost shirts." These garments were said to be imbued with sacred power, making the wearer impervious to bullets. It was the presence of these shirts and the belief that they were "bullet-proof" that seemed to confirm the notion that the movement was militant in intent. During the massacre at Wounded Knee, many of those killed wore the ghost shirts.

CULTURAL LEGACY

At first, the public response to Wounded Knee was favorable, viewing the outcome, while tragic, as an act of justifiable violence against a dangerous and revolutionary "cult." Newspaper accounts touted the actions of soldiers. Colonel James W. Forsyth, who had charge at the time of the Massacre, was relieved of his command, but eventually exonerated and returned to his post. Twenty Medals of Honor—the country's highest military honor—were awarded to soldiers for their involvement in the campaign against the Ghost dancers (In 2001, the National Congress of American Indians formally condemned these Medals and asked the U.S. government to rescind them; the U.S. government did not). Over time, the shape of public opinion shifted and both the Ghost Dance and its violent end at Wounded Knee became symbols of indigenous resistance against the oppressive powers of white, Christian civilization.

More specifically, the Ghost Dance movement experienced a cultural renaissance with the publication of *Black Elk Speaks* by John Neihardt in 1932. Neihardt related the experiences of Black Elk, an Oglala Sioux healer and holy man, who had survived Wounded Knee. Similar to Wovoka, Black Elk experienced prophetic visions, many of which aligned him with the Messiah and drew him to the Ghost Dance movement. Though Black Elk had converted to Catholicism by the time of the book's publication, the account of his religious and personal experience would form a part of a greater push for Native American rights.

In 1973, Wounded Knee was chosen as the site of a sustained seventy-one-day protest by the American Indian Movement (AIM) against the U.S. government's repeated violations of treaties with various tribes across history. The outbreak of hostilities was catalyzed by a specific instance of political corruption in the hierarchy of the Lakota nation. Protesters were comprised primarily of Oglala Lakota Sioux, marking another point of symmetry between the 1890 massacre and the 1973 standoff between the AIM and federal agents. While this protest did not achieve its ultimate ends, similar to the original Ghost Dance, it revived the specter of Wounded Knee, which still serves as a monument to Native American resistance.

See also: Millennialism.

Further Reading

Hittman, Michael. 1997. *Wovoka and the Ghost Dance*. Lincoln; London: University of Nebraska Press.

Neihardt, John, Philip J. Deloria, & Vine Deloria, Jr. 2014. *Black Elk Speaks: The Complete Edition*. Lincoln: University of Nebraska Press.

Niezen, Ronald. 2000. *Spirit Wars: Native North American Religions in the Age of Nation Building*. Berkeley: University of California Press.

PRIMARY SOURCE DOCUMENT

Wovoka's Messiah Letter (1891)

In 1891, enthnologist James Mooney was dispatched by the Bureau of American Ethnology to report on the Ghost Dance movement. During the course of his research, he came across a copy of Wovoka's Messiah message, provided by a Cheyenne named Black Short Nose. Wovoka (or, Jack Wilson) delivered his message as a speech. A transcription of the speech, taken down by a member who attended the Carlisle Indian School, follows below.

Wovoka's Messiah Letter (1891)

When you get home you must make a dance to continue five days. Dance four successive nights, and the last night keep up the dance until the morning of the fifth day, when all must bathe in the river and then disperse to their homes. You must all do in the same way.

I, Jack Wilson, love you all, and my heart is full of gladness for the gifts you have brought me. When you get home I shall give you a good cloud [rain?] which will make you feel good. I give you a good spirit and give you all good paint. I want you to come again in three months, some from each tribe there [the Indian Territory].

There will be a good deal of snow this year and some rain. In the fall there will be such a rain as I have never given you before.

Grandfather [a universal title of reverence among Indians and here meaning the messiah] says, when your friends die you must not cry. You must not hurt anybody or do harm to anyone. You must not fight. Do right always. It will give you satisfaction in life. This young man has a good father and mother. [Possibly this refers to Casper Edson, the young Arapaho who wrote down this message of Wovoka for the delegation.]

Do not tell the white people about this. Jesus is now upon the earth. He appears like a cloud. The dead are all alive again. I do not know when they will be here; maybe this fall or in the spring. When the time comes there will be no more sickness and everyone will be young again.

Do not refuse to work for the whites and do not make any trouble with them until you leave them. When the earth shakes [at the coming of the new world] do not be afraid. It will not hurt you.

I want you to dance every six weeks. Make a feast at the dance and have food that everybody may eat. Then bathe in the water. That is all. You will receive good words again from me some time. Do not tell lies.

Source: Mooney, James, trans. *The Ghost-dance Religion and the Sioux Outbreak of 1890.* 14th Annual Report of the Bureau of American Ethnology, Part 2. Washington, D.C., 1896.

PRIMARY SOURCE DOCUMENT

Mrs. Z. A. Parker, Description of a Lakota Ghost Dance at Pine Ridge, South Dakota (June 20, 1890)

The following is Mrs. Z. A. Parker's description of a Ghost Dance observed on White Clay creek at Pine Ridge Reservation, Dakota Territory, June 20, 1890.

. . . The ceremonies had just begun. In the center, around the tree, were gathered their medicine-men; also those who had been so fortunate as to have had visions and in them had seen and talked with friends who had died. A company of fifteen had started a chant and were marching abreast, others coming in behind as they marched. After marching around the circle of tents they turned to the center, where many had gathered and were seated on the ground.

I think they wore the ghost shirt or ghost dress for the first time that day. I noticed that these were all new and were worn by about seventy men and forty women. The wife of a man called Return-from-scout had seen in a vision that her friends all wore a similar robe, and on reviving from her trance she called the women together and they made a great number of the sacred garments. They were of white cotton cloth. The women's dress was cut like their ordinary dress, a loose robe with wide, flowing sleeves, painted blue in the neck, in the shape of a three-cornered handkerchief, with moon, stars, birds, etc., interspersed with real feathers, painted on the waists, letting them fall to within 3 inches of the ground, the fringe at the bottom. In the hair, near the crown, a feather was tied. I noticed an absence of any manner of head ornaments, and, as I knew their vanity and fondness for them, wondered why it was. Upon making inquiries I found they discarded everything they could which was made by white men. . . .

As the crowd gathered about the tree the high priest, or master of ceremonies, began his address, giving them directions as to the chant and other matters. After he had spoken for about fifteen minutes they arose and formed in a circle. As nearly as I could count, there were between three and four hundred persons. One stood directly behind another, each with his hands on his neighbor's shoulders. After walking about a few times, chanting, "Father, I come," they stopped marching, but remained in the circle, and set up the most fearful, heart-piercing wails I ever heard-crying, moaning, groaning, and shrieking out their grief, and naming over their departed friends and relatives, at the same time taking up handfuls of dust at their feet, washing their hands in it, and throwing it over their heads. Finally, they raised their eyes to heaven, their hands clasped high above their heads, and stood straight and perfectly still, invoking the power of the Great Spirit to allow them to see and talk with their people who had died. This ceremony lasted about fifteen minutes, when they all sat down where they were and listened to another address, which I did not understand, but which I afterwards learned were words of encouragement and assurance of the coming messiah.

When they arose again, they enlarged the circle by facing toward the center, taking hold of hands, and moving around in the manner of school children in their play of "needle's eye." And now the most intense excitement began. They would go as fast as they could, their hands moving from side to side, their bodies swaying, their arms, with hands gripped tightly in their neighbors', swinging back and forth with all their might. If one, more weak and frail, came near falling, he would be jerked up and into position until tired nature gave way. The ground had been worked and worn by many feet, until the fine, flour-like dust lay light and loose to the depth of two or three inches. The wind, which had increased, would sometimes take it up, enveloping the dancers and hiding them from view. In the ring were men, women, and children; the strong and the robust, the weak consumptive, and those near to death's door. They believed those who were sick would be cured by joining in the dance and losing consciousness. From the beginning they chanted, to a monotonous tune, the words—

Father, I come;
Mother, I come;
Brother, I come;
Father, give us back our arrows.

They kept up dancing until fully 100 persons were lying unconscious. Then they stopped and seated themselves in a circle, and as each recovered from his trance he was brought to the center of the ring to relate his experience.

Source: Mooney, James, trans. *The Ghost-dance Religion and the Sioux Outbreak of 1890.* 14th Annual Report of the Bureau of American Ethnology, Part 2. Washington, D.C.: Government Printing Office, 1896.

Ghosts, the Paranormal, and New Religious Movements

Film and popular media have generally cast human encounters with ghosts, the paranormal, and the supernatural as sites of danger and horror (and occasionally humor). However, there are numerous occasions, often among new religious movements, where ghosts, aliens, or the undead serve a religious, and potentially salvific, function.

DEALING WITH THE DECEASED

In Hydesville, New York, in 1848, Kate (1837–1892) and Margaret Fox (1833–1893) reported hearing strange sounds in their home. They began to engage with the source, which revealed itself to be a spirit named Mr. Splitfoot, asking it/him to perform or answer particular questions. From these initial "rappings," Spiritualism was born. Spiritualism posits that human beings are capable, usually through the skill of a trained medium, of contacting the deceased and the spiritual world which they inhabit. During the nineteenth century, Spiritualism exploded in popularity, counting in the tens of million those who participated in its practices, from the one-time attendee at a séance to the devoted member. Some of the enthusiasm for Spiritualism would diminish when it was revealed that some mediums manufactured certain effects (the Fox sisters eventually admitted as much); though this was certainly not the case for all.

Kardecism and Spiritism, the European and South American versions of Spiritualism, respectively, would have their own lives apart from their American counterparts. In Brazil and various Caribbean nations, specifically, Spiritist practice continues to maintain a robust practice, often merging with other indigenous and imported religions through ritual. Though not affiliated with nineteenth-century Spiritism, the Ghost Dance movement proceeded on the belief that the performance of certain rituals could raise the dead. Wovoka (né Jack Wilson; c. 1856–1932), a Paiute Indian, had a vision during a solar eclipse in 1889; in it, he saw the return of the ancestors and buffalo, whose deaths had been precipitated by the actions of white settlers in the American west. To bring about their return, native peoples needed to perform the "ghost dance," a communal ritual that often lasted days and induced trances in its participants. Though the movement was ultimately cut short by the massacre of over two hundred peaceful ghost dancers at Wounded Knee by the U.S. army, the belief that a return was possible to a lost world along with its people and animals would persist in American Indian mythology and practice.

In some cases, the line between ghost and divine entity is impossibly thin, even potentially interchangeable. Theosophy was the child of Spiritualism and the esoteric interests of founders Helena Petrovna Blavatsky (1831–1891) and Henry Steel Olcott (1832–1907). Before founding Theosophy, Blavatsky served as a Spiritualist medium and Olcott attended séances; it was in Spiritualist circles that the two would meet. Theosophy took the notion that a spiritual plain existed with which human beings could make contact and proposed that some of the entities who made contact were "Mahatmas" or "Masters"—those who were spiritually advanced and had been sent to earth to aid humanity toward spiritual enlightenment. The I AM Activity, an offshoot of Theosophy, emerged when its founder Guy Ballard (1878–1939) was contacted by Saint Germain—once the Count of St. Germain (1710–1784) and now an "Ascended Master" there to guide Ballard and all of humanity toward knowledge of their essential, divine nature.

One finds parallels in the appearances of Ascended Masters with the appearances of the Virgin Mary throughout the world. There are countless reports of Marian apparitions, some of which have spawned their own sects or cultus. Often Mary appears to children.

It is not surprising that it is often children who see—and believe in their ability to see—ghosts and supernatural beings. Children, who are less skeptical and more open to the possibility of the paranormal than incredulous adults, are likely targets and sources of spirit or supernatural contact. Indigo Children, or those believed to have special or supersensory abilities, are believed to attract mythical beings such as faeries and to bear the ability to see and speak to ghosts. Though rarely included under the umbrella of Indigo Children, it is not surprising that Kate and Margaret were children (eleven and fourteen, respectively) when Mr. Splitfoot first came calling.

FROM VAMPIRES TO E.T.

Ghosts are not the only supernatural creatures engaged by religious groups. In the twentieth century, a number of UFO religions arose, founded variously on the belief that extraterrestrials played some role in the creation, maintenance, and future (or demise) of the earth and its inhabitants. Raëlism, for example, believe that a race of aliens, known as the Elohim, created human beings in laboratories.

Mythical creatures such as vampires and faeries have also found religious homes. Otherkin are those who believe that they are half-human and half-something else, such as alien, faery, shapeshifter, angel, among other possibilities. Though many Otherkin resist the notion that they are a religion, certain religious beliefs, such as the notion that their advanced evolutionary state is the product of reincarnation, undergird their self-understanding. Vampirism, either in the form of devotion to vampires or the belief that one is a vampire, has also coalesced into religious circles, predominantly online. The Temple of the Vampire, which boasts its own *Vampire Bible* (1989), is one such group that, while prohibiting the consumption of blood, seeks to invoke the power of the Vampire Gods through its rites.

See also: Ballard, Guy W. (1878–1939); Blavatsky, Helena Petrovna (1831–1891); Children and New Religious Movements; Fox, Kate (1837–1892), and Margaret (1833–1893); Ghost Dance Movement (Wovoka); I AM Activity, The; Indigo Children; Kardecism (Spiritism); Marian Apparitions; Mediums; Olcott, Henry Steel (1832–1907); Otherkin; Spiritualism; Theosophy; UFO Religions; Vampirism.

Further Reading

Bader, Christopher. 2011. *Paranormal America: Ghost Encounters, UFO Sightings, Bigfoot Hunts, and Other Curiosities in Religion*. New York: New York University Press.

Braudy, Leo. 2018. *Haunted: On Ghosts, Witches, Vampire, Zombies, and Other Monsters of the Natural and Supernatural Worlds*. New Haven, CT: Yale University Press.

Gutierrez, Cathy. 2009. *Plato's Ghost: Spiritualism in the American Renaissance*. New York: Oxford University Press.

Laycock, Joe. 2014. "Approaching the Paranormal." *Nova Religio* 18, no. 1: 5–15.

Globalization and New Religious Movements

Globalization involves the flows of capital, goods, technology, people, ideas, and culture throughout the world. Although the pace and character of globalization have changed in the contemporary world, especially with the virtually instantaneous accessibility of news, entertainment, and opinion through the internet, globalizing forces have been at work throughout history.

Religion has frequently played a role in both promoting and resisting globalization. For example, the commission given by the resurrected Jesus to his remaining eleven disciples at the end of the gospel according to Matthew to "go therefore and make disciples of all nations" (Matt. 28:19) indicates the global ambitions of Matthew's form of the early Christian movement. But religion has also aided the attempts of indigenous peoples, such as the Saami of northern Scandinavia, to resist the homogenizing processes of globalization.

The same technologies and other processes that enable the rapid global spread of news and popular entertainment also help religions spread their messages and those who are curious find such messages. But even before internet technology, the global flow of religious actors promoted the establishment and spread of new religious movements.

THE EIGHTEENTH AND NINETEENTH CENTURIES

Although Ann Lee (1736–1784) joined the sectarian "Shaking Quakers" in England in 1758 and then assumed a leadership role, she was prompted by a vision in 1774 to set sail for America with eight of her followers. The United Society of Believers in Christ's Second Appearing, known colloquially as the Shakers for their enthusiastic worship style, prospered in the colonial United States, spreading from the Northeast into the Midwest. The initially successful missionary efforts of the Shakers show again how Jesus's commission to his disciples promoted the globalizing of Christianity in its various forms.

Although the Church of Jesus Christ of Latter-day Saints is a new religion that was founded in the United States by Joseph Smith (1805–1844), its foundational text, *The Book of Mormon*, recounts the story of the global processes that led to the book itself being buried on the hill Cumorah by the angel Moroni. Among its narratives is the account of how Lehi, his family, and others were guided by God to leave Jerusalem before its destruction by the Babylonians in 586 BCE; they eventually sailed to North America. The text also reveals a post-resurrection visit of Jesus to the Americas. Eventually, the records of such travels were engraved on gold plates and buried, only to be recovered by Joseph Smith, translated from their original "reformed Egyptian," and published in 1830. Mormons have since focused on spreading their message throughout the world.

The founding of the Theosophical Society in the late nineteenth century reveals a complex pattern of global influences. Helena Petrovna Blavatsky (1831–1891) grew up in a well-to-do Russian family and traveled widely. She claimed that while in India she met a group of "Masters of Ancient Wisdom" and then went to Tibet for extensive training in the occult sciences. While in the United States in 1874 she visited the farm of the Eddy brothers in Vermont, which had gained a reputation as the site of spiritualist séances. While there, Blavatsky met Colonel Henry Steel Olcott (1832–1937), a soldier, lawyer, journalist, and American convert to Buddhism. With William Quan Judge (1851–1896), they established the

Theosophical Society in New York City in 1875. In 1890, Blavatsky and Olcott moved to India, where they set up a headquarters for the Society in Adyar.

Those vignettes from the eighteenth and nineteenth centuries show how new religions can both spring from and contribute to the processes of globalization. Ann Lee brought a distinctive form of Quaker sectarianism from England to the United States; the Mormons understand themselves as the products of a flow of emigrants out of ancient Israel and into the New World; and the distinctive ideology of Theosophy draws on influences from around the globe.

THE TWENTIETH AND TWENTY-FIRST CENTURIES

In the past two centuries, processes of religious globalization have continued and increased their reach. For example, after World War II, returning soldiers and their spouses brought to the United States a form of the Nichiren (1222–1282) Buddhism known as Soka Gakkai whose adherents focus on chanting praise of the Lotus Sutra and believe that we are in the last days of the Buddhist dharma. The group places a strong emphasis on evangelization and claims members in nearly two hundred countries and territories throughout the world (see https://www.sgi.org/snapshot/).

The Immigration and Nationality Act of 1965, which finally put an end to the quota system that had governed immigration from Asian countries to the United States, contributed to an influx of Asian gurus and teachers in the United States. Among them was A. C. Bhaktivedanta Swami Prabhupada (born Abhay Charan De; 1896–1977). After taking a vow of renunciation in 1959, he lived as a monk and composed commentaries on the scriptures of Vaishnava Hinduism. Prabhupada undertook a solitary missionary voyage to the United States in 1965, and in New York City in 1966 founded the International Society for Krishna Consciousness (ISKCON), colloquially known as the "Hare Krishnas" for their repetitive public chanting.

From Prabhupada's perspective, he was not founding a new religion, but in the United States his particular form of Hinduism appeared as something new indeed. The Krishna Consciousness movement shows that globalized religions can be apprehended very differently when dispersed to new contexts. What was recognized as a sectarian form of Hinduism in India was perceived as a new religion or "cult" in the United States and other Western countries. The transplanting of religions from their native soil into other regions can transform both how they are perceived and how they function.

The Unification Church was transplanted to the United States in the 1950s and 1960s. Building on the charismatic experiences of its founder, the Rev. Sun Myung Moon (1920–2012), the Church was founded in Korea in 1954 as the Holy Spirit Association for the Unification of World Christianity. Moon's movement quickly achieved missionary success in Japan. In the late 1950s and early 1960s, the first missionaries came to the West Coast of the United States. They brought with them an idiosyncratic version of Christianity, leavened with elements from indigenous Korean religions. It emphasized the millennial hope for a third Adam who would reestablish the perfect family that God originally desired. The Unificationists' desire to bring together all of Christianity and their missionary activities throughout the world demonstrate their global scope. Their notorious mass wedding ceremonies, which frequently bring together people of different races, also express the homogenizing goals of their religion.

The movement of religious traditions, borne by immigrants and missionaries, throughout the world inevitably leads to changes as religious communities adapt to their new social and cultural contexts and welcome converts from their host societies. Diasporic communities have long raised the question expressed in Psalm 137 referring to the Babylonian captivity: "how can we sing the Lord's song in a foreign land?" (Ps. 137:4). The proliferation of Christian groups in sub-Saharan Africa shows the diversity of answers that such a question can receive. In addition to the churches founded by missionaries of mainline Christian denominations, Africa has seen an ongoing explosion of Independent or African-Initiated Churches. They are often tied to individual prophetic figures such as Simon Kimbangu (1887–1951), founder of the Church of Jesus Christ on Earth Through the Prophet Simon Kimbangu, and Isaiah Shembe (1865–1935), founder of the South African Nazarite Church. Such groups aim to practice a religion that is both truly Christian and truly African.

Individuals forcibly removed from Africa to the Caribbean and North America in the Atlantic slave trade also faced the dilemma of practicing their traditional religions in a new, oppressive context. New religions such as Candomblé, Santería, and Vodou developed in part as ways of combining traditional forms of worship, with the new ones imposed on vulnerable populations by slaveowners. In Jamaica, the Rastafari explicitly engage in a discourse about how they have suffered from the forces of globalization. They have adopted the plaintive question of Psalm 137 as their own. They identify themselves as living in a new "Babylon" and, adopting another biblical metaphor, seeking a new "Exodus," out of their now postcolonial situation, either internally through their sacramental ingestion of marijuana (*ganja*) or externally by returning to the Ethiopia that they see as "the land of their fathers."

In some cases, diasporic religious groups make accommodations in either their practices or message or both, as when ISKCON temples welcome Hindus from other traditions who have nowhere else to worship. In other cases, new adherents transform the inherited tradition, as with some of the American appropriations of Zen Buddhism by the Beats and others in the 1950s. Also, the Western embrace of yoga as part of the general wellness movement in some instances goes beyond accommodating an Indian practice to new contexts and toward a complete erasure of its religious roots and meanings.

Accommodations are not always sufficient to fend off opposition. Often both homegrown and transplanted traditions face criticism and resistance. In fact, the negative characterizations of groups like the Unificationists or Hare Krishnas as "cults" (United States) or "sectes" (Europe) stem in part from their very foreignness in the new contexts in which they find themselves. Such backlash against imported new religions can be understood in part as a local reaction against the social and cultural diversity promoted by globalization. In some cases, cultural opposition to new religions can cause them to shift their geographical centers, as with the reaction of The Family/The Children of God to exposés of their questionable sexual practices in the 1970s and 1980s.

New religions that are founded through innovation rather than importation also participate in the processes of globalization. The Church of Scientology, for example, declares its goal to be nothing less than "clearing" the entire planet. Through its training and technology programs it aims to remove the negative effects of stored traumatic experiences so that all individuals can flourish and reach their full potential. Scientology's goals, therefore, are no different than those of the "Great Commission" in the gospel according to Matthew; it intends to go and make disciples of all nations.

Even religious groups that are not dedicated to proselytization with the vigor evinced by the Unificationists, Scientologists, and others can have a global impact. Anton LaVey (1930–1997), the founder of the Church of Satan, was notoriously lax in his organizational efforts. Nonetheless, his most important work, *The Satanic Bible*, especially once it became available through the internet, became the primary means by which individuals throughout the world came into contact with his form of Satanism. Without much effort, he nonetheless attracted adherents and converts, even when he could not offer them a lasting structure in which they could locate themselves.

The internet even has the capability of establishing border-spanning virtual communities of like-minded individuals. Some Neopagans, especially those who may be geographically or socially isolated from others, use the internet as a way of forming religious communities and engaging in practices. Some religious groups even seem to exist solely or primarily on the internet with a global clientele, such as Jediism.

See also: Blavatsky, Helena Petrovna (1831–1891); Candomblé; Church of Satan, The; Children of God (The Family International); International Society for Krishna Consciousness (ISKCON); Jediism; Kimbangu, Simon (1887–1951); Rastafari; Santería; Scientology; Shakers, The; Shembe, Isaiah (c. 1865–1935); Soka Gakkai; Theosophical Society, The; Unification Church, The; Vodou; Yoga.

Further Reading

Beyer, Peter. 1994. *Religion and Globalization*. Thousand Oaks, CA: Sage.

Cowan, Douglas E. 2005. *Cyberhenge: Modern Pagans on the Internet*. New York: Routledge.

Hexham, Irving, & Karla O. Poewe. 1997. *New Religions as Global Cultures: Making the Human Sacred*. Boulder, CO: Westview Press.

Jenkins, Phillip. 2011. *The Next Christendom: The Coming of Global Christianity*. New York: Oxford University Press.

Kaplan, Jeffrey. 2006. "New Religious Movements and Globalization." In Eugene V. Gallagher & W. Michael Ashcraft, eds., *Introduction to New and Alternative Religions in the United States*, 5 volumes, vol. I, pp. 84–124. Westport, CT: Greenwood.

Lucas, Phillip Charles, & Thomas Robbins, eds. 2004. *New Religious Movements in the 21st Century: Legal, Political, and Social Challenges in Global Perspective*. New York: Routledge.

Gnostic Groups

The word "gnosis" means "knowledge" in Greek. At base, Gnosticism, a loosely affiliated tradition often associated with early Christian mystics, is the search for special or esoteric ("hidden") knowledge of God. Gnostics generally emphasize the importance of spirit over matter, believing that the individual soul must progress through various stages of spiritual knowledge to achieve total oneness with God. The notion that one could not only have special knowledge of God but could achieve salvation and actually unite with God was banned as heretical by the early Christian Church. Nonetheless, the Gnostic tradition persisted throughout the centuries.

Though this tradition has ancient, specifically Christian, origins, elements of Gnosticism, as well as groups that have self-labeled or been labeled as gnostic, are found among new religious movements. Such groups are very often eclectic in nature, drawing inspiration, beliefs, and practices from a variety of traditions. For example, Samael Aun Weor (born Victor Manuel Gómez Rodriguez; 1917–1977) who founded the Universal Christian Gnostic Church in Mexico in 1949, combined Christian theology, Tantric Buddhism, Rosicrucianism, and Theosophy, among other traditions to spark a "Revolution of Consciousness." This Revolution of Consciousness meant the death of one's individual consciousness and the birth of "objective" consciousness; the transformation into a being that could act as a bridge to higher dimensions; and personal sacrifice in pursuit of spreading this wisdom.

Groups that have formed out of the Theosophical tradition are often described as gnostic. Theosophy arose during the late nineteenth century; its basic principle was that throughout history, Mahatmas or "Great Masters" had been guiding humanity along a path of spiritual evolution. Not only that, but people could communicate with these Great Masters via mediums and the writings that often emerged through the Master-medium connection. Several twentieth-century groups arose out of the Theosophical tradition, such as I AM Activity and the Church Universal and Triumphant, whose leaders claimed special relationships with particular Great (or in the case of I AM Activity, "Ascended") Masters.

There have also been several Gnostic new religious movements born during the counterculture, several of which reflected the broader New Age milieu. The Church of Scientology was built on its founder L. Ron Hubbard's (1911–1986) discovery that people were actually immortal beings called Thetans who, over successive lifetimes, had become weighted down by the memory of past trauma, called engrams. The bulk of Scientology's practice is focused on ridding oneself of these engrams and realizing one's innate divinity. For those who achieved higher levels of mental and spiritual advancement, they could become privy to esoteric knowledge regarding the origins of the universe and the world, which involved extraterrestrial beings. Scientology is not typically cast as such, but several so-called UFO religions bear elements of Gnosticism in their belief and practice. Heaven's Gate, for example, was built upon the notion that human beings' spiritual advancement depends upon their acceptance that their physical bodies are simply "vessels" for a more potent spiritual and intellectual power. In the

1990s, the group prepared themselves for graduation to the Evolutionary Level of Above Human (TELAH), which would occur when supernatural, extraterrestrial beings would bring them to a spaceship. And not explicitly New Age, though attractive to many who dabbled in that world, Elan Vital (earlier the Divine Light Mission) has also been cast as Gnostic by scholars. While explicitly denying that this is a religious group, Elan Vital emphasizes the reality that inner peace exists within every person and only requires realization through practice. The techniques for doing so are referred to simply as "Knowledge," and are held as secrets, revealed only from teacher to student.

There are numerous other examples one could cite regarding contemporary Gnostic groups. And given the diversity of the Gnostic tradition and the fact that there are groups that bear the markers of Gnosticism without actually employing the word to describe themselves, it is difficult to know how many "Gnostics" there are in the world.

See also: Church Universal and Triumphant, The; Elan Vital; Heaven's Gate; Hubbard, L. Ron (1911–1986); I AM Activity, The; Mediums; Mysticism; New Age, The; Scientology; Theosophical Society, The; Theosophy; UFO Religions.

Further Reading

Clasquin, Michel. 1992. "Gnosticism in Contemporary Religious Movements: Some Terminological and Paradigmatic Considerations." *Journal for the Study of Religion* 5, no. 1: 41–55.

DeConick, April D. 2016. *The Gnostic New Age: How a Countercultural Spirituality Revolutionized Religion from Antiquity to Today.* New York: Columbia University Press.

Zoccatelli, Pierluigi. 2006. "Gnostic Movement." In Peter Clarke, ed., *The Encyclopedia of New Religious Movements.* London: Routledge Press.

Goddess Worship

Goddess worship has a long history. Hindus have worshipped goddesses alongside gods since the inception of the religion (additionally, multiple deities often manifest as either male or female or as both genders at once). Greek and Roman religious systems host a pantheon of goddesses, whose involvement in global history dates to the beginning of the world. Thus, when those who identify as Goddess acolytes, Goddess feminists, or Goddess Pagans claim descent from an ancient history of Goddess worship, they are not wrong. However, the twentieth-century Goddess movement as a predominantly Western phenomenon also acts as a foil to religious (primarily Judeo-Christian) systems that have been historically patriarchal and goddess-less.

ORIGINS AND HISTORY

The Goddess movement emerged as one of many sects of Neopaganism that found root in England and the United States in the twentieth century. Broadly conceived, Neopaganism claims derivation from European Paganism, which predated Christianity and thus is the "oldest" Western religion. Modern Neopagans share with ancient Pagans an ecocentric focus, a belief that the divine exists in the natural world, and a focus on human agency, particularly that of women, to engage with these various divine forces and extract power from them. However, modern Neopagans are also heavily influenced by twentieth-century British occult and magical religion, which incorporated a variety of sacred rituals and secret knowledge into ancient Paganism. Wicca was perhaps the most recognizable sect to exhibit this amalgam of ancient practices and new knowledge and techniques. In that sense, most Neopaganisms are new "old" religions—an identity that the Goddess movement mirrors.

During the 1960s, several Wiccan feminists developed the Goddess movement, influenced by the writings of feminist authors then critiquing the damaging effects of patriarchal religion (particularly Judeo-Christianity) and Wiccan practices. Starhawk (1951–; née Miriam Simos) and Zsuzsanna Budapest (1940–) were chief among those who believed that worship of the Goddess represented a separate strain of Neopagan practice and identity—one that specifically focused on the divine feminine. Since that time, the Goddess movement has grown in number, reaching more than half a million members in the United States and nearly 150,000 members in the United Kingdom.

BELIEFS AND VARIETIES

Goddess worshippers highlight the centrality of the Goddess (sometimes, though not exclusively, called Gaia) to pre-Christian religious rituals, particularly in areas related to the sustaining and nurturing of life: agriculture and childrearing. In fact, some argue that the earth is the body of the Goddess. As a result of this ancient focus on the Goddess, human women were also revered for their perceived closeness to the life-giving powers of earth and were awarded the same power as men (this is akin to shamanic religious cultures throughout the world). For this reason, Goddess worship is often synonymous with Goddess feminism, because of the devout focus on women in both ritual and belief. In contrast to other Neopagan traditions, where the concept of "God" or a God and Goddess is present, in the Goddess movement, the male deity is given little to no attention; however, most Goddess worshippers deny strict distinctions between genders, arguing that male and female exist as points on a spectrum and that most people exhibit aspects of both.

Most Goddess Neopagans believe that devotion to the Goddess declined due to persecution and the hegemony of Christian institutions, which also served to relegate women to a supplemental and servile position to men. However, many agree that the advent of the New Age, the rise of feminism, and the burgeoning environmentalism movement prompted a renewal of Goddess worship. For this reason, most Goddess rituals and beliefs revolve around the reawakening of women to their own divine power and the resacralization of the earth, with which women have a sacred connection. Starhawk wrote in her seminal book on the Goddess, *The Spiral Dance* (1989), that the three central principles of Goddess worship are immanence (referring to the divinity inherent in nature and in all living things, especially women); interconnectedness (between the natural world and the greater universe and all living things); and community (among all beings, but particularly women).

Beyond these central principles, however, the Goddess movement is quite diffuse and eclectic in its practices and even in the particular version of the Goddess worshipped. Some worship traditionally Pagan deities, similar to Wiccans and other British Neopagans, whereas others worship Hindu goddesses, or goddesses from indigenous religions (e.g., Maori). Some worship one goddess, whereas others worship multiple goddesses, believing this reflects more accurately the socially inclined nature of women. There are also those that argue that the goddess is a metaphor for women's internal divinity, rather than an actual deity or set of deities. There are practitioners who identify as Goddess Neopagans as well as another type of Neopagan and others who refuse to self-label and choose to practice on their own, without belonging to a coven or religious group. Temples or worship sites focused on various goddesses have been opened throughout the globe, most often in the United States and the United Kingdom. Rituals are also derived from a variety of sources and traditions: magic, shamanic healing, channeling, divination, among other practices, are employed in the practice of worshipping and connecting to a goddess.

Though there is little centralization when it comes to the Goddess movement, both ritually and institutionally, there are certain beliefs that Goddess Neopagans hold in common with other Neopagans. For example, the Wiccan Rede—"An' it harm none, do what ye will"—is often held by those who identify with the Goddess movement, alongside the Rule of Three, or the belief that "what you send, returns three times over," a rule that requires practitioners to weigh carefully the result of their actions. Most Goddess Neopagans are eco-conscious as well and much of Goddess worship occurs outdoors, often at festivals or at well-known Pagan sites. In fact, over the last few decades as climate science has increasingly proclaimed the dire state of the earth, Goddess Neopagans (particularly those who view the earth as Goddess, not just as a site to worship her) are Eco-Pagans.

THE GODDESS AND CONTEMPORARY CULTURE

"Discover the Goddess within." This mantra has become a common trope not only of New Age religion but of a broader wellness culture, which merges spirituality and health. "Goddess" has become a term tied to particular fitness practices, foods, beauty products, and self-help books. Thus, the Goddess movement has spawned a cultural movement, one that is divorced in many ways from its religious roots. Goddess culture promotes the image that women can achieve wholeness through certain regimens that balance mental and physical well-being. That these regimens are often accompanied with price tags has given Goddess Neopagans, particularly those who also identify as Eco-Pagan, pause, since their aim is to deemphasize the need for individual advancement and material accumulation in favor of community advancement and ecocentrism. This appropriation of the term "Goddess" to sell a particular lifestyle is a natural extension of the movement's female consciousness, to some, and a diluting of the religious message of the movement, for others.

Ironically, the Goddess movement has come under criticism for cultural appropriation, particularly of indigenous rituals. Eclectic by nature but also reflecting New Age religious culture that allows for "bricolage" religion—or the practice of gathering a variety of beliefs and practices to serve a particular religious group or individual—Goddess worship has absorbed many rituals that emphasize the earth or women, including rites of Native American groups. Already protective of their practices after years of suppression and cultural borrowing, indigenous religious people have resisted the idea that their practices can be absorbed by (primarily white) religious practitioners.

Nonetheless, the Goddess movement has provided a vital and sustainable form of Neopaganism that makes women central. Goddess worship has also transcended religious practice and become a vital part of modern environmentalism as well as all movements that seek to subvert power structures built on the subjugation of a particular group and seek equality. Many Goddess Neopagans are also political activists, some of whom are involved in the movement called "Reclaiming Witchcraft," which seeks to combine the principles of Goddess worship with direct political action. As a lobbying force and a religious body, the Goddess movement continues to make its mark.

See also: Eco-Paganism; Environmentalism and New Religious Movements; Gender and New Religious Movements; Healing, Health, and New Religious Movements; Magic and New Religious Movements; Neopaganism; New Age, The; Occultism and Esotericism; Shamanism; Starhawk (1951–); Wicca; Women in New Religious Movements.

Further Reading
Christ, Carole P. 1997. *Rebirth of the Goddess: Finding Meaning in Feminist Spirituality.* New York: Routledge Press.

Eilberg-Schwartz, Howard. 1989. "Witches of the West: Neopaganism and Goddess Worship as Enlightenment Religions." *Journal of Feminist Studies in Religion* 5, no. 1: 77–95.

Eller, Cynthia. 1995. *Living in the Lap of the Goddess: The Feminist Spirituality Movement in America.* Boston: Beacon Press.

Ruether, Rosemary Radford. 2005. *Goddesses and the Divine Feminine: A Western Religious History.* Berkeley: University of California Press.

Starhawk. 1989. *The Spiral Dance: A Rebirth of the Ancient Religion of the Great Goddess.* San Francisco: Harper & Row Publishers.

Grant, Kenneth (1924–2011)

In esoteric and occultist circles in twentieth-century England, Kenneth Grant bridged generations. He assimilated the influences of major figures like Aleister Crowley (1875–1947), helped others like the artist and occultist Austin Osman Spare (1886–1956) reach a broader audience, and melded his various influences into an esoteric system of his own.

Grant first encountered Crowley's writing as a teenager, and he claimed that reading Crowley on magick had changed his life. Around the same time, in 1939, he claimed to have had a dream in which he was given his own magical symbol, identified as "Aossic" and in several variant spellings. Grant sought out Crowley and served as his secretary and personal assistant for a brief time in 1944. His association with Crowley gave him access to Crowley's collection of esoteric writings and the opportunity for personal tutorials. For the rest of his life, Grant studied Crowley's works and considered himself part of the new religion of Thelema that Crowley had started.

In 1948, Grant was formally recognized as a ninth degree member of the Ordo Templi Orientis (OTO), the masonic organization of which Crowley had seized control in 1922. The then-current head of OTO authorized Grant to begin a branch in London in 1951. That outpost of the OTO would serve as the home for Grant's spiritual explorations until 1962.

Grant established the new Isis Lodge in 1955, which he conceived as an OTO appendage. But the theology of the lodge developed to include ideas that were not orthodox within the OTO. In particular, Grant claimed that the earth was now being influenced by "the transplutonic planet Isis" and that his new organization would channel the power from that planet. The planet Isis was associated with the goddess Nuit, who was also mentioned in Crowley's *The Book of the Law* (1904).

Grant's innovations disturbed the head of the OTO, Karl J. Germer (1885–1962), who formally expelled Grant in 1955. Grant, however, continued to operate the lodge and meet with its few dozen members until 1962. By then, Grant was on his way to formulating his own idiosyncratic development of Thelema and the OTO, aided by texts that were channeled by members of the lodge.

Also in the 1950s Grant became involved with Hinduism, especially the teachings of Bhagwan Sri Ramana Maharshi (1897–1950). He was especially drawn to the Advaita Vedanta concept of nonduality. Grant also learned a version of Indian Tantra from the British esotericist David Curwen (1893–1984). Grant was especially impressed with the similarities between westernized Tantra and the sex magic of the higher levels of initiation into the OTO. Grant's emphasis on parallels between the esoteric traditions of East and West resembled the Perennialist philosophy's concept that all religions were originally unified in their fundamental insights.

During the 1960s and 1970s, Grant worked on editing some of Crowley's manuscripts for publication. In 1972, he published the first volume in his own set of three trilogies, of which the last volume would be published thirty years later. Through those volumes readers can trace Grant's development of what he called the Typhonian Tradition.

Claiming the prestige of antiquity, Grant presents the Typhonian OTO, which was renamed the Typhonian Order in 2011, as an ancient tradition. The female figure of Typhon, who also appears in Greek mythology as an antagonist of Zeus, is portrayed as the object of the original Egyptian cult that is the oldest known religion. Correspondingly, the Egyptian God Set is depicted as the earliest male God to have been worshipped who later evolved into Satan.

Over the course of the trilogies, Grant described various practices by which initiates could get into contact with the "Outer Ones." He argued that individuals must master the world of shadows or the hidden aspects of their psyches. He described the "nightside" as the reverse of the kabbalistic Tree of Life. He also asserted that individuals could gain access to entities beyond human consciousness by entering a zone between dreaming and wakefulness that he called the Mauve Zone. Grant aimed to provide humans with such strange concepts so that individuals would be able to develop their own intuitive insights and develop spiritually.

See also: Channeling; Crowley, Aleister (1875–1947); Kabbalah; Occultism and Esotericism; Ordo Templi Orientis.

Further Reading

Bogdan, Henrik. 2015. "Kenneth Grant and the Typhonian Tradition." In Christopher Partridge, ed., *The Occult World*, pp. 323–330. New York: Routledge.

Djurdjevic, Gordan. 2014. *India and the Occult: The Influence of South Asian Spirituality on Modern Western Occultism.* New York: Palgrave Macmillan.

Guénon, René (1886–1951)

Along with Frithjof Schuon (1907–1998) and Ananda Coomaraswamy (1877–1947), the French writer, intellectual, and convert to Sufi Islam, René Guénon is one of the founders of the traditionalist or perennialist philosophy. The traditionalists were highly critical of the modern world, particularly its reliance on science as a source of knowledge. They sought wisdom instead in primordial revelations, which they believed were transmitted by the world's oldest religions. They saw sacred wisdom as unified and universal, striving to move beyond the superficial diversity of the world's religions to identify and revivify the essential message that they all shared. Influences of perennialist or traditionalist philosophy can thus be seen in many new or alternative religions, such as various forms of New Age thought and practice, that emphasize the compatibility of apparently diverse and even conflicting religious practices and ideas.

Though he was born a Catholic, Guénon became acquainted with Hinduism and Taoism early in his life. His first published book was *Introduction to the Study of the Hindu Doctrines* (1921), which originally had been intended as a doctoral thesis but was rejected by his adviser. After a brief stint in teaching, Guénon quickly tired of academe and devoted himself to independent study and travel. During his student years in Paris, Guénon had become acquainted with various forms of Western esotericism. He joined the Gnostic Church of France (founded in 1890) for a time and even founded and wrote for his own journal, *La Gnose* ("Gnosis"). He also became a member of the Thebah Lodge of the French Masons. But he became dissatisfied with the diverse and uncoordinated ideas circulating in esoteric and Masonic circles and strove to find a surer foundation for his religious interests.

Guénon's study of Hinduism reinforced his impression that there was a valuable, ancient, and universal tradition that had derived directly from divine revelation. That gave him the firm foundation for religious exploration that he was seeking. It also led him to be very critical of both contemporary orientalist scholarship that he believed misconstrued the ancient sources and especially of contemporary religious groups that claimed to draw on those sources. Guénon was particularly critical of Theosophy, about which he wrote *Theosophy: History of a Pseudo Religion* (1921). His critiques also encompassed Allan Kardec's (1804–1869) Spiritism and neo-Masonic groups and other forms of contemporary esotericism.

Guénon is also notable for his impact on some influential figures in the contemporary study of religion, including the Romanian historian of religions Mircea Eliade (1907–1986), who discounted Guénon's influence, and Huston Smith (1919–2016), who embraced a perennialist approach to the study of religion. Through such influence, Guénon's perspective continues to shape scholarly and popular understandings of religion.

See also: Freemasonry; Gnostic Groups; Kardecism (Spiritism); New Age, The; Occultism and Esotericism; Theosophy.

Further Reading

Herlihy, John, ed., 2009. *The Essential René Guénon: Metaphysics, Tradition, and the Crisis of Modernity.* Bloomington, IN: World Wisdom.

Sedgwick, Mark. 2004. *Against the Modern World: Traditionalism and the Secret Intellectual History of the Twentieth Century.* New York: Oxford University Press.

Gurdjieff, G. I. (c. 1866–1949)

Of the Russian mystics emerging at the turn of the twentieth century, George Ivanovich Gurdjieff was one of the most prolific and multitalented. His precise year of birth is unknown, with some dating it as early as 1866 and others as late as 1877. What is known is that he was born in Armenia (then part of the Russian empire) in a town (Kars) known for its religious diversity. Like many occultists, he claimed to have seen unexplained phenomena at a young age, though he did not yet have the knowledge to explain what had occurred.

Gurdjieff traveled widely during the first decade of the twentieth century, which brought him into contact with a number of learned figures and mystics from whom he would claim to derive his esoteric religious knowledge. This has led to criticism as to the provenance or authenticity of his claims to mystical knowledge; a fact exacerbated by Gurdjieff's reticence to reveal where his knowledge came from. He simply stated that the knowledge had been hard fought and that he would not reveal its sources so easily. After returning to Russia in 1912 and jumpstarting his career as a composer, he began taking on his first students, including P. D. Ouspensky (1878–1947), who would become a prominent proponent and interpreter of his work (even though the two would part ways eventually). Unrest in Russia followed by two World Wars, led to a nomadic life during the heyday of Gurdjieff's occult work, even bringing him to the United States where he sought to win funding and pupils for his methods. Because of his unsettled life, he was unable to create a formal institution that would house his religious views during his lifetime. Thus, most of his works are preserved in his writing, many of which were published posthumously or in the form of interpretations by his students (such as Ouspensky's, *The Fourth Way* (1957)).

Chief among Gurdjieff's mystical discoveries was the belief that people currently existed at the nadir in terms of their grasp of deep, universal knowledge. Religious traditions, as they existed, bore no real connection to ancient truths, thus most people were spiritually lost. In lieu of current religious systems, Gurdjieff proposed his own system known simply as "The Work" (later Ouspensky would teach these ideas under the title *The Fourth Way*). At the center of Gurdjieff's work was the idea that, through self-development, people could achieve harmony and become whole. In contrast to other religions, which Gurdjieff believed only attended to one or two aspects of human life, Gurdjieff proposed a system that would attend to all three aspects of the person: the physical body, the emotions, and the mind. Each dimension corresponded to a particular path: the Way of the Fakir, which attuned the body; the Way of the Monk, which aimed to control the emotions; and the Way of the Yogi, which harnessed the power of the mind. A "Fourth Way," one that attended to all three components and combined all three paths, Gurdjieff argued, was possible. Once each aspect of human life was brought into harmony, then people could achieve even higher levels of consciousness and ability, becoming truly "awake" to the nature of the universe and to their own capacity as spiritual beings. Gurdjieff employed diverse methods to help his pupils achieve such focus, knowledge, and self-mastery, often calling upon his other talents, such as music and dance. This eclectic method also made his particular brand of self-development difficult to replicate, thus contributing to the lack of formal institution for his teachings.

During his later years, Gurdjieff was involved in two car accidents, one as late as 1948, which affected his health, but from which he made a seemingly miraculous recovery. He attributed these physical triumphs to his methods of self-development, proving that he had achieved dominion over his body. Nonetheless, his body finally gave out: he died in 1949 while living in France. He was survived by his six living children, but more significantly, by the Fourth Way, his students, and the belief that total self-mastery was possible.

See also: Fourth Way, The; Occultism and Esotericism; Ouspensky, P. D. (1878–1947).

Further Reading

Gurdjieff, G. I. 1999 [1950]. *Beelzebub's Tales to His Grandson: An Objectively Impartial Criticism of the Life of Man*. New York: Penguin Compass.

Ouspensky, P. D. 1957. *The Fourth Way: A Record of Talks and Answers Based on the Teachings of G. I. Gurdjieff*. New York: Knopf Press.

Shirley, John. 2004. *Gurdjieff: An Introduction to His Life and Ideas*. New York: Penguin Press.

Hassan, Steven (1954–)

In January 1974 while he was in college and suffering after breaking up with his girlfriend, Steven Hassan encountered members of the Unification Church. A self-professed avid reader who wanted to make a positive contribution to the world, Hassan was initially intrigued by the idealistic young people whom he met. Soon he was listening to Unificationist lectures and, though hesitant, he agreed to attend a weekend workshop. Hassan ended up leaving school and joining the church, spending two years in it.

While he was recuperating at home from a serious car accident, Hassan's parents arranged for him to be deprogrammed. Now seeing himself as having been deceived and exploited, he resolved to leave the church and to return to what he saw as normal life. Combating groups like the Unification Church, identified as "cults," became the focal point of Hassan's career. In 1979, after the deaths at Jonestown, he founded Ex-Moon, Inc. and then began to investigate the literature on thought reform and brainwashing. Psychiatrist Robert Jay Lifton (1926–), who developed eight criteria for mind control in *Thought Reform and the Psychology of Totalism*, was an important influence on Hassan's thinking.

Although Hassan initially spoke approvingly of involuntary deprogramming, clearly viewing his own deprogramming positively, and even practiced deprogramming early in his career, he came to see it as inadequate to the task of combating the "mind control" that he believed was practiced by cults. He eventually earned a Master's degree in counseling and turned to the therapeutic approach of exit counseling. Hassan now calls his method the Strategic Interactive Approach. It focuses on distinguishing what he calls a cult identity from an individual's authentic identity and involves family members in structured interactions with the person being targeted. Hassan professes a deep concern for religious freedom but also asserts that cultic groups constitute a serious social problem.

In 1999, Hassan founded the Freedom of Mind Resource Center (https://freedomofmind.com/), which has served as his base since then. Hassan's team offers a range of services, including resources, workshops, webinars, litigation and expert witness consultants, training materials, and even estate planning. Hassan remains one of the most prominent exponents of the anticult position.

Hassan's career mirrors those of others in the anticult movement who have also turned their negative experiences of cult membership into the basis for a new profession. His expertise and persuasiveness are grounded in his experience as a member of a group he identifies as a cult. Although he does attempt a rudimentary typology, he minimizes the differences among groups and assimilates them all to a general pattern of exerting illegal and illegitimate mind control. But, most of all, he knows about cults because he was in one.

See also: Anticult Movement, The; Brainwashing; Cult; Deprogramming; Exit Counseling; Jonestown; Patrick, Ted (1930–); Unification Church, The.

Further Reading

Hassan, Steven. 1990. *Combatting Cult Mind Control*. Rochester, VT: Park Street Press.

Shupe, Anson, & Susan E. Darnell. 2006. *Agents of Discord: Deprogramming, Pseudo-Science, and the American Anticult Movement*. New Brunswick, NJ: Transaction Publishers.

Healing, Health, and New Religious Movements

A famous scene in the documentary *Holy Ghost People* (1967)—a staple of college anthropology classes—depicts a Pentecostal preacher being bitten by one of the snakes he has been handling. The film ends with a shot of his swollen hand and his repeated refusals to seek medical treatment. Though not included in the film, it was learned, later, that the preacher died of his wound. This film has been employed to provide an intimate portrait of an obscure, often misunderstood, religious group and one of their most controversial practices, that of snake handling. This practice is based on the belief that if people are faithful, the Holy Ghost will protect them—a fact they prove by willingly holding venomous snakes. Were they to be bitten by these snakes, their survival is a mark of their faithfulness, hence their belief that any medical intervention should be eschewed in such an event. However, the fact of the pastor's death is often perceived as a condemnation of these views and employed to show the dangers of blind faith.

Though not all new religious movements that deny all or certain medical treatment invite the potential cause of their maladies in such a way, there are many that like the Holy Ghost Pentecostals, believe that God, spirit, or even the human mind will provide where modern medicine cannot.

MIND OVER MATTER

The notion that there is a direct connection between the body, the mind, and the soul is not new. The body houses the soul, thus sustaining the body is often seen as a necessary step to advancing the mind and soul. It is only through the mechanisms of the body—eyes to read texts, ears to hear truth, the brain to store knowledge and memory—that human beings are capable of acting upon higher, spiritual needs. However, religions have often cast the connection between body, mind, and soul as the root of humanity's plight or sinfulness: by giving in to bodily needs, the soul suffers. Major religious traditions have also eschewed the body for the sake of the soul. Asceticism spans traditions from Buddhism to Christianity, where devotees will deny bodily needs such as food and rest to focus the spirit or to show spiritual mastery over the body. In this sense, the body is an impediment to spiritual advancement and enabling the body to disconnect from the spirit and/

or mind ensures the ascension of the latter. Both the idea that mind, body, and spirit are intricately connected and the idea that they must be disconnected for purposes of spiritual evolution or salvation persist in new religious movements.

The nineteenth century witnessed the evolution of a number of religions that could be gathered under the category of New Thought. The origin of New Thought is traced to the discoveries of German physician, Franz Mesmer (1734–1815), who posited that a substance, called "animal magnetism," connected all living things. This substance could be manipulated by the use of magnets, which when properly placed on the human body, could release blockages and heal a variety of physical ailments. "Mesmerism," the system, became hugely influential for those seeking alternative methods for healing.

In the United States, Phineas Quimby (1802–1866) began experimenting with Mesmerism only to make a discovery of his own: that those patients who *believed* they were being healed were more likely to be healed than those who did not. Thus, it was not the healing method itself, but the power of the mind that cured; this led to Quimby's own contribution to the world of alternative medicine, the theory of "mind cure." Quimby began employing mind cure techniques on his patients to marked success, earning him a reputation that would attract those who had been let down by modern medicine, such as Mary Baker Eddy (1821–1910). Plagued by illness for much of her life, Eddy would ultimately combine Quimby's concepts of mind cure with Christianity in her own religion, Christian Science, which is perhaps the new religious movement best known for its views on medicine and healing.

Christian Science is based on the belief that God is mind and therefore all matter is spirit and hence illusory. Disease, then, is also illusory—the result of "sin" or wrong thinking, not an actual physical malady. Eddy discovered Christian Science following a near-death experience in 1866: she fell on the ice and, while on her deathbed, read a particular passage from the Bible (Matt. 9:2) that described Jesus's feat of healing a man from palsy. After meditating on that passage, she was healed. Eddy would go on to write her own sacred text, *Science and Health with Key to the Scriptures*, which promised to unlock the spiritual message of the Bible and enable all willing practitioners to be cured through prayer and the power of their own minds and souls.

In recent decades, Christian Scientists have experienced pushback for their practices from both the medical and legal community. Numerous court cases have arisen over the decisions of Christian Scientist parents to withhold medical treatment from a child. The issue is whether these children actually assented to the beliefs of their parents and whether they would have asked for medical treatment had they been able to advocate for themselves.

FAITH HEALING AND MODERN MEDICINE

Christian Scientists are not the only religious people to deny medical treatment, of course. The Watchtower Bible and Tract Society, more commonly known as the Jehovah's Witnesses, deny the administration of blood transfusions due to their particular interpretation of certain biblical passages (namely, Gen. 9:4 and Lev. 17:14). In certain cases, like those of the Jehovah's Witnesses, such medical exemptions have spawned medical innovations like bloodless transplants. Yet, many new religious movements have created and, depending upon the context, relied upon their own healing methods outside of and in some cases in direct opposition to the modern medical community.

For those forcibly removed from Africa and brought to the New World to labor, traditional religious practices were merged with Christianity and indigenous practices as a mode of resistance and autonomy from Western mechanisms of power. Often the spiritual and the medical merged, as many of the slaves who hailed from African traditional religions believed that there were usually spiritual causes for physical ailments. On the African continent, religious specialists were often sought to treat disease; on the slave plantation, though these practices were often regulated and heavily suspected, both slaves and white masters often sought the services of those believed to have special healing power (many of whom were women). In Haiti, Vodou priests and priestesses would perform healing rituals while "ridden" by particular deities known as lwa (spirits). Vodou is often conflated with Hoodoo, also known as "conjure," though the latter transcends denominational lines. Born in South Carolina and Georgia among the Gullah people, Hoodoo practitioners employ a pharmacopeia of herbs and substances to evoke and control divine power, which can be employed to heal a client as well as to "work" against someone. Finally, Santería emerged in Cuba, as a combination of Catholicism and African traditional religions, including Yoruba. Its practitioners, called "santero/as," can harness the power of the orishas (deities) for religious rituals, many of which involve healing.

Syncretic religious systems that focused on religious healing were not limited to the context or era of slavery. Kardecism (or Spiritism/Espiritismo) though emerging in Europe, found root in Latin America and the Caribbean in the late nineteenth and early twentieth centuries, where its central belief—that human beings could commune with and draw sacred knowledge from the spirit realm—merged with ritual healing. Mediums, or those who possess the ability to contact or channel the spirit realm, were sometimes capable of performing healings, often while in a trance-like state.

In the United States, the movement most associated with religious healing is Pentecostalism. Though various in its practices and denominations, this now-global religion was born in 1906 in Los Angeles, following a revival where spiritual gifts rained down on those present. The movement spread, as did these gifts, which included the ability to speak or translate foreign tongues and the ability to heal. Though miraculous healings were not an unknown occurrence in Christianity (the nineteenth-century "holiness movement" witnessed such healings and is often viewed as a precursor to Pentecostalism), suddenly instances of faith healing seemed to rise exponentially and with them the number of faith-healing preachers.

A number of new religious movements have focused on the importance of diet for both physical and spiritual health. The Church of Jesus Christ of Latter-day Saints had the "Word of Wisdom," a revelation that dictated the avoidance of certain substances (alcohol, "hot drinks") and advocated a predominantly vegetarian diet. The Seventh-day Adventists, for example, advocated for the importance of a plain, healthy diet. Though these practices reportedly derived from Jewish kosher laws, they extended to the advocacy of vegetarianism and avoidance of alcohol and tobacco. This "biblical" diet was believed to purify the body for the impending Second Coming of Christ. Far more extreme are the Breatharians, who believe that only air ("spirit") is necessary for survival, a belief that has been resoundingly panned by the medical community as dangerous.

NEW RELIGIONS AND MENTAL HEALTH

New religious movements are not only engaged in the practice of bodily but mental health as well. Since the mid-twentieth century, a number of religions have tied mental to spiritual wellness. Movements such as Transcendental Meditation and the Movement for Inner Spiritual Awareness have built on various Asian religious traditions and the practice of meditation and yoga as a means of aligning body, mind, and soul. Increasingly, these practices are employed outside of religious settings as complementary practices to traditional medicine and psychology; studies have shown that meditation, for example, is connected to lower blood pressure, sharpened focus, and decreased stress.

Perhaps no new religious movement has tackled the world of mental health more readily than Scientology. Its founder, L. Ron Hubbard (1911–1986), published the book, *Dianetics* (1950), which he intended to be a therapeutic system that worked "through" (dia) the "mind" (nous) and as an alternative to modern psychology, a discipline of which he was immensely critical. Hubbard posited that the mind comprised both analytic, or conscious, and reactive components; the latter stored "engrams," which were echoes of past trauma that, once discovered and released, would drastically improve a person's mental and physical health. The religious system of Scientology arose in part from the discoveries of those practicing Dianetics, when they began recounting memories of past lives. Hubbard revealed that each person was actually a Thetan—an immortal being whose lives went past centuries, but whose divine capabilities had been lost over many lives. The aim of Scientology practice is to rid oneself of all problematic engrams (to become "clear") and to reactivate the Thetan's innate capacities.

Scientology has been roundly criticized by the psychological community, particularly for its stance on the use of drugs to treat mental illness. Dubbed a "pseudoscience," Scientology is not alone in receiving the medical community's ire; many new religious movements have earned the same epithets. Nonetheless, these religious systems continue to present themselves as supplements to, if not replacements for, modern medicine.

See also: Breatharianism; Children and New Religious Movements; Christian Science; Church of Jesus Christ of Latter-day Saints, The; Courts and New Religious Movements; Dianetics; Eddy, Mary Baker (1821–1910); Food and New Religious Movements; Hoodoo; Hubbard, L. Ron (1911–1986); Kardecism (Spiritism); Mediums; Mesmerism; Movement for Inner Spiritual Awareness, The; New Thought; Pentecostalism; Quimby, Phineas

(1802–1866); Santería; *Science and Health with Key to the Scriptures*; Scientology; Seventh-day Adventism; Shamanism; Transcendental Meditation; Vodou; Watchtower Bible and Tract Society, The (Jehovah's Witnesses); Yoga.

Further Reading

Barnes, Linda L., & Susan S. Sered, eds. 2004. *Religion and Healing in America*. New York: Oxford University Press.

Brown, Candy Gunther. 2013. *The Healing Gods: Complementary and Alternative Medicine in Christian America*. New York: Oxford University Press.

Folk, Holly. 2014. "Healing." In George D. Chryssides & Benjamin E. Zeller, eds., *The Bloomsbury Companion to New Religious Movements*. London: Bloomsbury Publishing.

Murphy, Joseph M. 1994. *Working the Spirit: Ceremonies of the African Diaspora*. Boston: Beacon Press.

Saliba, John A. 2016. "Psychology and New Religious Movements." In James R. Lewis, ed., *The Oxford Handbook of New Religious Movements*. New York: Oxford University Press.

Heaven's Gate

FOUNDERS

The group that became known as Heaven's Gate only near the end of its lifespan spent most of its career in obscurity. But when thirty-nine members, including one of its founders Marshall Herff Applewhite (1932–1997), committed suicide in March of 1997 at a rented house in the San Diego suburb of Rancho Santa Fe, it became internationally notorious. Heaven's Gate grew out of the spiritual seeking of Applewhite and the group's other founder, Bonnie Lu Nettles (1927–1985). Applewhite had been raised a Presbyterian and briefly attended seminary but he later developed an interest in astrology, occult wisdom, and UFOs. By the time he met Nettles in 1972, she had developed much broader interests, including participation in the Houston branch of the Theosophical Society of America. The group that they would found bore the imprints of their combined religious searching.

Applewhite and Nettles quickly became inseparable. They devoted much of their time to spiritual pursuits, including opening a short-lived Christian Arts Center in 1972 and an equally short-lived retreat center, Know Place, in 1973. Applewhite and Nettles soon developed a sense that they had a special, joint, role to play in the world. They called themselves "the Two." Although their initial efforts at gathering followers did not bear fruit, that did not deter them. By July 1973, they became convinced that they were the two witnesses mentioned in Revelation 11. It would be their task to prophesy, perform miracles, be killed, and then after three and a half days to rise up to heaven in a cloud. Applewhite and Nettles never abandoned their sense of mission, even as they tried on different identities, often with playful names such as Guinea and Pig, Bo and Peep, and the ones on which they finally settled on, Ti and Do, for notes on a musical scale.

Initially, Applewhite and Nettles paid more attention to their own spiritual quests than to gaining converts. They had difficulty both in attracting and keeping followers. Only in April 1975, when they spoke to a group in Los Angeles did they attract a substantial group of some two dozen converts. In October, they gained another twenty followers from a meeting in Waldport, Oregon. The core of their message was that the earth was soon to be recycled or spaded over like a garden. To avoid destruction and qualify for transit into the Kingdom of God in the literal heavens, individuals would have to reduce their attachments to this world.

FROM AUDIENCE TO COMMUNITY

Initially, Ti and Do did little to form the loose audience of students that they had acquired into a cohesive group. They spent time in seclusion away from their followers and did not attempt to exercise consistent authority over them. That changed in April 1976 when Nettles declared that the "harvest" had closed and that there would be no more informational meetings. After that point, Heaven's Gate largely dropped out of public view and developed into a small, mobile, monastic community. In 1995, they attempted to establish a communal settlement called the "Launch Pad" in Manzano, New Mexico. But they sold the property after only ten months.

According to the Two, members constituted a "class"; they were supposed to learn who they truly were and to prepare themselves for a "final exam" and ultimate "graduation" into the kingdom in the heavens that was their true home. Those ideas meshed well with Applewhite's realization, achieved in early 1975, that he and Ti were, in fact, not really human but rather extraterrestrial beings who had incarnated in human bodies. They saw themselves as representatives of the "next level" or The Evolutionary Level Above Human. Their task on earth was to come to the full realization of their true identities, lead as many others as possible to the same realization, and prepare themselves and their followers to enter bodily the physical Kingdom of God. That gnostic religious system also led them to style themselves the "crew" of the "Away Team," since they were currently displaced from their true home.

Applewhite and Nettles instructed their followers to distance themselves from their human bodies, which were seen as mere vehicles. The souls they housed were their connection to the next level. Accordingly, the aim of life on earth was to undertake a process of self-transformation. Individuals were taught that they should slough off characteristics that tied them to this world. Ti and Do believed that next level beings did not have sex, eat, or die. Consequently, their followers were encouraged to practice celibacy and follow a carefully controlled diet, often vegetarian. Members were often assigned partners, who would monitor their behavior and encourage honest self-examination.

Applewhite and Nettles consistently used the metaphor of a caterpillar changing into a butterfly for the process they envisaged. The goal of life on earth was expressed in the early name of the group, Human Individual Metamorphosis, and the subsequent Total Overcomers Anonymous. A prayer composed by Nettles shows how the desire for self-transformation became expressed in ritual. The speaker of the prayer begins by claiming "I would like to know more than I now know" and ends with the assertion that "I am rapidly changing." In particular, the speaker urges her "vehicle" to change its chemistry (Zeller, 2014:166f.).

Members signaled their desire to change by adopting new names. The new names emphasized their distance both from their former lives and from their physical bodies. Each member adopted a name ending with the suffix "-ody." Two explanations of the names were offered. One claimed that "ody" combined reference to being a child "of God" with the diminutive "y." The other held that the suffix was a contraction of Do and Ti. Either way, the new name marked a rupture with a member's former identity.

REEMERGENCE AND THE END OF HEAVEN'S GATE

Throughout much of its existence Heaven's Gate avoided public notice. Nettles had declared the "harvest" of recruiting new members closed in 1976 and that curtailed further efforts at proselytization. When Nettles died in 1985, Applewhite was left alone as the leader of the movement and he needed to account for that unanticipated event, which could easily have destroyed the movement. Nettles's death did not conform to the scenario of the two witnesses from Revelation 11; she was not visibly resurrected after three and a half days. Applewhite eventually asserted that Ti was indeed alive, only on the next level. That in turn raised the question of whether Do and the rest of the class would need to enter the next level in their physical bodies.

Do explained some of his reasoning in a pamphlet called *'88 Update*, which explained the media's rejection of their message as a metaphorical killing of the two witnesses. In 1991–1992, the group made a series of satellite broadcasts that returned to the metaphor of the harvest, asserting that the time was at hand when the garden of earth would be spaded up in preparation for a new planting. The end of the age was at hand, and a fortunate few would be able to graduate to the next level. Intermittent communications from the group appeared in subsequent years. In 1994, they broached the possibility that the transit to the next level might require shedding the human body. In 1996, Do reaffirmed the group's stance against suicide, but reevaluation was still happening in years after Ti's death.

Several factors influenced the final decision to use suicide to reach the next level. First, despite a renewed engagement with the public, recruitment efforts were not very successful. Only seven new members joined in the period from 1991 to 1994. Last-ditch efforts to promulgate the group's message on the internet in 1995 and 1996, including the publication of an anthology of the group's writings and a videotaped lecture entitled *Last Chance to Evacuate Earth Before It's Recycled*, also failed to attract positive responses. Second, although the group anticipated violent persecution from the outside world, none occurred. Third, Ti's death indicated that the transit to the next level need not be accomplished in a physical body. Fourth, around 1994–1995 several members had taken the additional step of medical castration to further distance themselves from their physical vehicles. Finally, the members of Heaven's Gate took the appearance of the

Hale-Bopp Comet in 1996 as a sign that the end was nigh and that the class was about to graduate. The members bought material for the uniforms they would wear (including matching pairs of Nike shoes and purple shrouds) on March 1, 1997. On March 22 and 23, they made their exit, which they believed would convey them to the next level.

See also: Applewhite, Marshall (1932–1997), and Bonnie Lu Nettles (1927–1985); Millennialism; New Age, The.

Further Reading

Chryssides, George D., ed. 2011. *Heaven's Gate: Postmodernity and Pop Culture in a Suicide Group.* Burlington, VT: Ashgate.

Zeller, Benjamin. 2014. *Heaven's Gate: America's UFO Religion.* New York: New York University Press.

Hermetic Order of the Golden Dawn, The

In England at the turn of the twentieth century, there was a flurry of interest in the occult. As a result, a variety of secret religious societies arose, each purporting to have access to ancient strains of esoteric knowledge and sacred, often magic, rituals that could unlock humanity's potential. In this milieu, the Hermetic Order of the Golden Dawn emerged.

The Order was founded in 1888 by William Robert Woodman (1828–1891), William Winn Westcot (1848–1925), and Samuel Liddell Mathers (1854–1918). All were Freemasons (Freemasonry is an international secret society) with ties to Rosicrucianism (an esoteric religious movement that claims access to sacred knowledge of Christianity and a mystical branch of Judaism, Kabbalah). Similar to other esoteric movements, the Hermetic Order of the Golden Dawn promoted itself as an exclusive, secret society whose primary function was to study ritual magic as a means of spiritual advancement.

Like many other occult secret societies, its founders claimed that ritual knowledge of the Order was ancient. In reality, the Order was a mixture of multiple systems—some old, some new. Its practices mixed seventeenth-century Hermeticism—another Western esoteric tradition—Kabbalah, and mystical Christianity with astrology, tarot reading, and astral projection. The magic or "great work" was believed to be directed by "secret Chiefs," whose often unseen guidance helped Order members control their environment and develop inner magical ability. Some of their focus on ritual magic echoed the burgeoning Neopagan movement, specifically, Wicca.

Similar to the Freemasons, there were degrees of initiation; but, where the Freemasons had three, the Order had eleven. The first three levels were collectively referred to as "The Golden Dawn," perhaps referring to the dawning of secret knowledge in new initiates. Many of the levels mapped onto Kabbalah's degrees of knowledge, known as *sephiroth*. Also like Freemasons, the Order was organized into "lodges," which were often geographically based and served the needs of local members. Temples also exist, most notably the Isis-Urania Temple in London, where the most sacred rituals are performed.

The Order became the home for many famous British occultists, most famously, Aleister Crowley (1875–1947) and Dion Fortune (1890–1946). Additionally, the poet W. B. Yeats (1865–1939) was a member who often found literary inspiration from his involvement in the Order. Schisms did occur during the course of the movement. One of the original founders, Samuel Liddell Mathers split to form the Alpha et Omega Temple in 1903. Despite spawning competitors, however, the Hermetic Order of the Golden Dawn still exists today.

See also: Crowley, Aleister (1875–1947); Fortune, Dion (1890–1946); Freemasonry; Hermeticism; Kabbalah; Magic and New Religious Movements; Occultism and Esotericism; Rosicrucianism; Wicca.

Further Reading

Bogdan, Henrik. 2007. *Western Esotericism and Rituals of Initiation.* Albany: SUNY Press.

Bogdan, Henrik. 2008. "Women and the Hermetic Order of the Golden Dawn: Nineteenth-Century Occultistic Initiation from a Gendered Perspective." *Aries Book Series* 8: 245–264.

Graf, Susan Johnston. 2015. *Talking to the Gods: Occultism in the Work of W.B. Yeats, Arthur Machen, Algernon Blackwood, and Dion Fortune.* Albany: SUNY Press.

Hermeticism

Hermeticism, or Hermetism, derives its name from the collection of Greek sacred texts known as *Corpus Hermeticum* (the Hermetic corpus), which were likely written sometime between the second and fourth centuries and are attributed to a mysterious author named Hermes Trismegistus ("thrice-greatest Hermes"). As an ancient philosophical and religious tradition, Hermeticism emerged from and combined a variety of sources, including Egyptian paganism, Hellenistic philosophy, early Christian Gnosticism, and ancient Judaism. Though Hermeticism fell out of vogue with the rise of Christianity in Europe, it experienced a series of revivals, including during the late nineteenth through twentieth centuries, when it heavily influenced the Western esoteric tradition and a number of new religious movements associated with that lineage.

The notion of an ancient tradition that had been suppressed by dominant religious institutions, but somehow maintained its presence in secret proliferated among such movements, some of which claimed to be the descendants of a Hermetic order. As a cohesive religious system, Hermeticism has been interpreted variously; however, at its base Hermetic thought maintains that all religions are united, reflecting the idea that there is a single, universal reality. Hence the oft-repeated Hermetic phrase "as above, so below" implies that the earth is an echo of the divine realms. Hermeticists also maintain that the divine is both immanent and transcendent (thus, nature is a manifestation of the divine); all deities or supernatural beings are manifestations of one divine entity; and that human beings can interact with the realm of the divine through magico-religious practices.

The three primary magical practices—alchemy, theurgy, and astrology—correspond to a different source of power or wisdom in the universe, respectively, the sun, the gods, and the stars. Alchemy, though best known as the transformation of substances into gold, encompasses a multitude of techniques that manipulate matter through scientific and spiritual exercises. The phrase "hermetically sealed," which refers to the creation of airtight seal, evidently derives from Hermes Trimegistus's alchemical and magical experiments. Theurgy involves the practice of magic through invocation of gods or divine beings, with the ultimate goal being the unity of human and divine. And astrology employs study of stars and planets to divine the future and understand the present. It is the latter two, theurgy and astrology, that can be found most readily in modern Hermetic traditions.

One of the first traditions to incorporate Hermeticism into its belief system was Rosicrucianism, a seventeenth-century religious movement in Europe founded on the notion that there existed a secret order tasked with protecting esoteric knowledge (including that of the world's major religious systems, such as Christianity), which held the key to humanity's spiritual and physical advancement. Accessing this hidden trove would lead to a global reformation of the world's institutions and knowledge itself. Numerous Rosicrucian societies arose over the centuries, very often bearing the word "Hermetic" in the title, which signals the ancient nature of these groups, their secrecy, and their cultivation of magical practices This includes the Hermetic Order of the Golden Dawn, a secret religious society that arose in England in the early twentieth century and combined a number of occult, magical practices to hone the ability of practitioners to control their environment and unlock latent potential or power.

The occult milieu of England at the turn of the twentieth century, generally, drew much of its beliefs and practices from Hermeticism. Aleister Crowley (1875–1947), often viewed as the father of modern occultism, began his foray into the world of Western esotericism via the Hermetic Order of the Golden Dawn, before establishing his own tradition, Thelema. Crowley's writings as well as those of various other British occultists and ceremonial magicians influenced the burgeoning Neopagan tradition, which would emerge throughout the twentieth century. Certain strains of Neopaganism maintain that they are the continuation of an ancient lineage of witchcraft (Wicca is one) and many are devoted to the idea that nature is both the site and source of all magical power; both assertions reflect the ongoing influence of Hermeticism.

See also: Crowley, Aleister (1875–1947); Hermetic Order of the Golden Dawn, The; Magic and New Religious Movements; Neopaganism; Occultism and Esotericism; Rosicrucianism; Thelema; Wicca.

Further Reading

Berberi, Viktor. 2010. "Vision, Metaphor and the Metaphysical Horizons of Twentieth Century Hermeticism." *Forum Italicum* 44, no. 1: 97–118.

van den Broek, Roelof, & Wouter J. Hanegraaff. 1998. *Gnosis and Hermeticism: From Antiquity to Modern Times.* Albany: SUNY Press.

Versluis, Arthur. 2007. "Late Antiquity: Hermetism, Gnosticism, Jewish Mysticism, and Christian Gnosis." In *Magic and Mysticism: An Introduction to Western Esotericism*. Lanham, MD: Rowman & Littlefield Publishers.

Hindu New Religious Movements

Hinduism is one of the world's oldest religions—it is also one of the most varied in practice and belief. There are millions of Hindus, each of whose worship may vary from the next. However, there are also groups with ties to Hinduism whose practices would qualify them as new religious movements, either because they have adapted Hindu beliefs and practices to different contexts or because these same practices have been absorbed and transformed in new ways. Certain critics have disagreed with the categorization of such groups (particularly of the latter variety) as Hindu. Undeniable, however, is the fact that Hindu new religious movements have proliferated over the last few centuries.

WEST GOES EAST, EAST GOES WEST

The centuries-long colonial enterprise of Europe precipitated countless atrocities, both physical and cultural, against countries compelled to bend to imperial powers. At the same time as Europeans sought to enforce their own, supposedly superior, way of life, an extraordinary amount of cultural exchange, as well as appropriation, occurred. Perhaps nowhere was this clearer than in South Asia,

Many Hindu teachers who worked internationally also established ashrams for their followers in India. This is an image of the ashram of Maharishi Mahesh Yogi in Rishikesh. (Danmir12/Dreamstime.com)

particularly India. Increasingly over the nineteenth century, Europeans and later Americans came to India for its spiritual and religious resources, namely, Hinduism, returning home with texts and ideas that long predated Western religious systems. The Transcendentalists of New England, for example, began absorbing Hindu and Buddhist principles in their writings by the 1830s. As interest in Hinduism increased, so did the demand for such materials—a demand that eventually extended to the people itself. By the century's end, Hindu swamis and gurus began to travel to Europe and the United States, speaking to awestruck Western audiences. As interest grew, so did the proliferation of Hindu religious societies; some were satellites of similar institutions in India, while others represented new paths.

One of the first Hindu religious societies to emerge in the United States during the nineteenth century was the Vedanta Society. Vedanta Societies—so named for its members' focus on the Hindu texts known as the Vedas—were born from the Ramakrishna Mission, a Hindu monastic order. The first Western Vedanta Society was established by Swami Vivekananda (1863–1902), whose invitation to speak at the 1893 World's Parliament of Religion in Chicago made him a religious celebrity. In translating Hinduism to a Western audience through the Vedanta Society, Vivekananda emphasized the unity of all existence and of religious truth as well as the specific contributions of Hinduism, which held the key to ancient, esoteric truth: that each person's true nature was divine, a manifestation of "Atman." The realization of this truth occurred through the practice of yoga, primarily raja-yoga (or meditation). Vedanta societies still exist, though most have relinquished ties to any kind of monastic tradition.

COUNTERCULTURAL EXPLOSION

Hindu new religious groups witnessed a second wave of growth during the 1960s and 1970s, the product of a robust counterculture, relaxed immigration laws, and, once again, the symbiotic desire of Hindu gurus to spread their message and Western audiences to hear them. Perhaps the most iconic Hindu new religion of this period was the International Society for Krishna Consciousness (ISKCON), whose orange robes and efforts at proselytization both enticed and aggravated. Founded by Indian swami A. C. Bhaktivedanta Praphupada (1896–1977) in New York in 1966, ISKCON was a devotional and monotheistic sect of Hinduism, focused on worship and love of the Lord Krishna. The group became better known as the "Hare Krishnas," which derived from their constant repetition of the *maha-mantra*, which petitions God for awakening and begins "Hare Krishna, Hare Krishna, Krishna Krishna, Hare, Hare . . ." ISKCON members generally devote themselves to a particular lifestyle characterized by vegetarianism, abstention from alcohol and, occasionally, sex and gambling. Attractive to both men and women alike during the 1960s onward, the movement has maintained a belief in the spiritual equality of women, even while emphasizing that marriage and motherhood are the highest forms of worship that women can provide Krishna, a fact that has led to accusations of being retrogressive.

Similar to the attention paid to Swami Vivekananda in the late nineteenth century, very often people were drawn to a particular Hindu guru as much as a particular message. Such was certainly the case for Maharishi Mahesh Yogi (1918–2008), the founder of Transcendental Meditation, the practice of which is based on teacher-student relationships. The Maharishi claimed numerous celebrity acolytes, including the Beatles, some of whom claimed the Maharishi as their particular teacher or the one who discerns the proper, secret mantra for each student. The Osho Movement and its founder Shree Bhagwan Rajneesh (1931–1990)—another charismatic and magnetic figure—also drew the public's attention, not always in a positive sense. In the 1980s, Rajneesh and many of his followers established a city, Rajneeshpuram, in Oregon. The aim of this intentional community was to advance spiritually through certain meditative practices that, once mastered, would lead one to transcend the physical body, becoming divinized (like Osho himself).

HINDU-BORN OR HINDU-INSPIRED?

Not all Hindu new religious movements came West or were ultimately spurred by Western interest. Brahma Kumaris, the "Daughters" of Brahma, founded in Hyderabad, in northwest India (now Pakistan), combined Hinduism, millennialism, and trance mediumship in a movement that comprised and comprises primarily women. Through repeated chanting of "Om," those present for worship might fall into a trance, even becoming mediums for deities or spiritual entities. Though the movement does have a more robust international presence as of 2019, its spiritual and geographical home remain in India. However, the fact that Brahma Kumaris is distinctly syncretic in nature has invited critique as to its inherently Hindu core. Other Hindu-born religions have sought to distance themselves from that label, claiming to be nondenominational, such as the Sathya Sai Baba Movement. Members of all faith backgrounds are welcome with no expectation of conversion nor of adoption of specifically Hindu practices.

A number of new religious movements founded by white Westerners emerged during the twentieth century, which would fall under the scholarly umbrella of "Hindu-inspired Meditation Movements," or those religions that have adopted certain Hindu practices, such as meditation or yoga, without tying them to Hinduism specifically. The Movement for Spiritual Inner Awareness, for example, was created by John-Roger Hinkins (1934–2014) who combined Hindu beliefs and practices with New Age religiosity and his own revelations from what he called, the Mystic Traveler Consciousness. The religious aim of "soul transcendence" is equivalent to Hindu practices that focus on realizing oneness with God.

Other groups, such as the Self-Realization Fellowship, which was founded by Yogananda (1893–1952), form a middle ground between those religious movements considered Hindu-born versus Hindu-inspired. Similar to Swami Vivekananda, Yogananda was a Hindu transplant to the West who translated the Hindu beliefs that Atman is the only reality and merging with the "God-consciousness" is the aim of all religious practice with Western religious language, even theology. Following his death, however, all subsequent presidents of the movement have been white Westerners, reflecting its primacy outside of South Asia. Integral Yoga had a similar trajectory; following the death of its founder Sri Aurobindo (1872–1950), it came under the leadership of a Parisian woman, Mira Richard (1878–1972), known as "The Mother." Critics of these movements point to the divorcing of Hindu practices and principles from their historical, cultural, and geographical contexts, which is highlighted by the abundance of Westerners, often in direct contrast to the number of South Asians, who practice the religion. For those who do practice these religions, however, they maintain that the message is universal and timeless, which negates any need to pay homage to a specific religious or geographical lineage.

There are still other groups, such as Elan Vital (originally the Divine Light Mission), that have adapted Hindu principles to what its leaders and practitioners claim are entirely secular means. The goal of the movement is self-knowledge that inner peace is inherent in every person, which is achieved through techniques known collectively as "Knowledge." Though members practice these methods at "ashrams," a Sanskrit term for spiritual hermitage, the belief is that these practices are accessible to those even without religious intent.

See also: Aurobindo, Sri (1872–1950); Brahma Kumaris; Elan Vital (Divine Light Mission); Integral Yoga; International Society for Krishna Consciousness (ISKCON); Movement of Spiritual Inner Awareness; New Age, The; Occultism and Esotericism; Prabhupada, A. C. Bhaktivedanta (1896–1977); Rajneesh, Shree Bhagwan/Osho (1931–1990); Rajneesh/Osho Movement, The; Ramakrishna Mission; Sathya Sai Baba Movement, The; Self-Realization Fellowship (Yogananda); Transcendental Meditation; Transcendentalism; Vedanta Society, The; Vivekananda, Swami (1863–1902); Yoga; Yogi, Maharishi Mahesh (1918–2008).

Further Reading

Chyrssides, George. 1999. "New Religions in the Hindu Tradition." In *Exploring New Religions*. London: Cassell.

Thursby, Gene R. 1995. "Hindu Movements Since Mid-Century: Yogis in the States." In Timothy Miller, ed., *America's Alternative Religions*. Albany: SUNY Press.

Thursby, Gene R. 2011. "The Study of Hindu New Religious Movements." *Nova Religio* 15, no. 2: 6–19.

Urban, Hugh. 2015. "ISKCON (Hare Krishna): Eastern Religions in America and the 'Brainwashing' Debate." In *New Age, Neopagan, and New Religious Movements: Alternative Spirituality in Contemporary America*. Berkeley: University of California Press.

Williamson, Lola. 2010. *Transcendent in America: Hindu-Inspired Meditation Movements as New Religion*. New York: NYU Press.

Holy Order of MANS, The

New religions can often change rapidly, due to new insights received or developed by their leaders, responses to internal and external pressures, or other factors. The history of the Holy Order of MANS provides a dramatic example.

The Order was formally established in 1968 in San Francisco by Earl Wilbur Blighton (1904–1974). After encountering Free Methodism and Roman Catholicism early in life, Blighton had developed interests in Spiritualism, Freemasonry, New Thought, Rosicrucianism, the Subramuniya Yoga Order, Theosophy, UFOs, and alternative healing. In 1961, Blighton formed a group known as the Science of Man (see www.scienceofman.org) aimed at uniting science and the teachings of Jesus. By 1966, some members of the 1960s counterculture who learned from him about esoteric Christianity became the nucleus of the Holy Order of MANS and the predecessor group faded into the background. The meaning of MANS was originally for members only, but it stands for the Greek words *mysterion* (mystery), *agape* (love), *nous* (mind), and *sophia* (wisdom).

Blighton's Christian message was clearly inflected by New Age concepts. He saw himself as representing the ancient Christian Wisdom Tradition. Blighton taught that the earth was entering a new age of spiritual enlightenment and that his group of advanced students would prepare the world for the upcoming transformation. Blighton viewed Jesus as the Cosmic Christ and believed that the "Christ Light" was increasing in the world.

Bringing back ancient Christian wisdom entailed reforming the authentic priesthood. Blighton believed that he, as the reincarnation of the Apostle Paul, had the ability to ordain priests who could conduct the ancient Christian initiations that were the precursors of the seven sacraments. The Order practiced not only the rituals of Baptism and Communion but also the more esoteric rites of "illumination" and "self-realization." The rituals were designed to meld modern science with ancient wisdom so that individuals could realize the "divine self" within them, which represented a spark of the ultimate Divine light.

Blighton's followers were organized as a monastic order that devoted itself both to outreach and good works. By the early 1970s, the Order had centers throughout the United States and a few in Europe. It reached a high of some three thousand members. After Blighton's death in 1974, the Order went through a period of organizational instability that ended with many of the members converting to Eastern Orthodoxy as the Christ the Savior Brotherhood, in part as a response to being numbered among the dangerous cults that preoccupied public attention after Jonestown. A website maintained by former members (www.holyodrderofmans.org) preserves Blighton's original teachings.

See also: Freemasonry; Gnostic Groups; Millennialism; New Age, The; New Thought; Peoples Temple; Rosicrucianism; Spiritualism; Theosophy.

Further Reading

Lucas, Phillip Charles. 1995. "From Holy Order of MANS to Christ the Savior Brotherhood: The Radical Transformation of an Esoteric Christian Order." In Timothy Miller, ed., *America's Alternative Religions*, pp. 141–148. Albany: SUNY Press.

Lucas, Phillip Charles. 1995. *The Odyssey of a New Religion: The Holy Order of MANS from New Age to Orthodoxy.* Bloomington: University of Indiana Press.

Holy Piby, The

Published in 1924 by the prophet Robert Athyli Rogers, *The Holy Piby* was designed to be the foundational text for a new religion that would reconnect people of African descent in the diaspora with their true heritage and their own God. Although Rogers's Afro-Athlican Constructive Church initially gained adherents in the United States, the Caribbean, and South Africa, his new Bible had its most enduring impact in another religion developed in the African diaspora.

Although the origins of the Rastafarian movement are difficult to reconstruct with precision, it is clear that *The Holy Piby* played a role as the beliefs of the early Rastafari began to coalesce in Jamaica in the early 1930s. One of the pioneer Rastafarian preachers, Leonard Howell (1898–1981), distilled his teaching in a slim volume published around 1935, *The Promised Key*. Howell's work borrowed heavily from *The Holy Piby* and other texts that were then circulating in Jamaica.

Those texts shared a commitment to Ethiopianism, which identified all of Africa with Ethiopia and emphasized that Africa had long been home to great civilizations and noble peoples. A key image was the promise of Psalm 68:31 that "Princes shall come out of Egypt; Ethiopia shall soon stretch out her hands unto God." Ethiopianists also employed biblical themes such as exile, exodus, and the millennialist reversal of the status quo to interpret African diasporic experience. They aimed to construct new religious options that were in continuity with the biblical tradition yet distinct from the churches that supported slavery, colonialism, and the denigration of people of color.

The Holy Piby constitutes a selective retelling of the Bible, directly addressed to the "Children of Ethiopia." It includes a revised creation story, a new collection of twelve commandments, an elaborate account of the call and commissioning of a new prophet, Rogers himself, and even a section on the "facts of the apostles," of which the Black Nationalist Marcus Garvey was the foremost. One contemporary Rastafarian intellectual, Ras Miguel Lorne, has asserted that Rogers definitely intended for his own work to supplant the Bible among people of African descent.

The Holy Piby expresses the dramatic hope for the total renovation of the world. It counsels its readers to live hardworking and sober lives and to maintain their individual dignity. They should strive for independence and self-determination and aim to implement God's will on earth as it is in heaven. The promises that *The Holy Piby* extends to people of African descent still suffering from the effects of slavery and colonialism have continued to exert an attraction even after the demise of Rogers's short-lived church.

See also: New Scriptures and New Religious Movements; Rastafari.

Further Reading
Hill, Robert. 2001. *Dread History: Leonard P. Howell and Millenarian Visions in the Early Rastafarian Religion.* Kingston, Jamaica: Research Associates School Times Publications/Frontline Distribution Int'l Inc.

Rogers, Shepherd Robert Athyli. 2000. *The Holy Piby*, reprint of 1924 edition, with foreword by Ras Sekou Sankara and introduction by Ras Michael (Miguel) Lorne. Kingston, Jamaica: Research Associates School Times Publications/Frontline Distribution Int'l Inc.

PRIMARY SOURCE DOCUMENT

Excerpts from *The Holy Piby*, Proto-Rastafarian Text (c. 1928)

Selections from The Holy Piby, *written by Afrocentric religious leader Robert Athlyi Rogers in the 1920s, follows below.*

The Call of a Prophet

There is a great convention in heaven, saith the angels of the Lord, unto you this day we are sent by the Lord to felicitate. For thou art appointed the shepherd to lead Ethiopia's generations from the oppressive feet of the nations, and there are appointed also prophets to prepare the way before thee.

And it came to pass when Athlyi heard these sayings he feared with great astonishment and turned his face from the angels of the Lord. And there appeared unto him his divine highness Jesus Christ, Prince of the Kingdom of God, and said quickly behold the messengers of my Father.

At this saying Athlyi turned again to the angels of the Lord and said, thy will be done, O God of Ethiopia, but how can I be the shepherd, to lead millions of millions even from the end of the earth when as I am but a twig before the eyes of men?

The Heavens Open

And the angels of the Lord answered him saying, a twig that is made by the Holy Spirit, an instrument to lead men, is great in the sight of God, over which the armies of the earth or the hosts of hell shall not prevail.

And it came to pass that the angel who had the less to say lifted her eyes to heaven and stretched forth her arms over the earth and cried, blessed be thou Ethiopia, glory be the Father, thou Elijah, Hosanna, Hosanna to Jehovah, praise ye Douglas the convention have triumph.

There appeared a beautiful light on earth and when the light flashed Athlyi looked toward the heaven, and behold the heaven was open and there was a great host of saints robed in blue, millions of millions as far as his eyes could see there was a mighty host.

When Athlyi sought the angels of the Lord they were not and he heard a voice say "Athlyi" and another "Athlyi" and he looked up and saw two angels ascending towards the celestial host.

Ethiopia Anointed

And when the two messengers of the Lord were midways they cried out unto the earth saying, blessed be thou Ethiopia for this day thou art anointed, thou are blest with a blessing, be ye forever united and stand up, let the world know your God.

And when the two angels of the Lord neared the multitude the whole host roared with a thunder of joy that shook the earth like a mighty earthquake.

And it came to pass that an angel robed in four colours came forward to receive them and the whole celestial multitude stood and quietly formed an aisle.

And when the two messengers appeared before the heavenly host they bowed to the multitude and turned themselves around and bowed also to the earth.

Then came forward the mighty Angel robed in four colors and placed a gold ring upon their heads, and came forward also two mothers of Ethiopia, each with a star in their right hand, and pinned them on the left breast of the two messengers of the Lord.

And it came to pass that heaven and earth shook three times and the two angels marched up the aisle and joined with the multitude.

Rejoicing in Heaven

There was great rejoicing in Heaven and singing hosanna to Elijah; praise ye Douglas; blessed be thou Ethiopia forever and forever; the people at the end of the known world, and world unknown, shall look for the coming of thy children with food and with rainment.

And when the two angels had joined the multitude and the mighty angel had finished his performance the said angel who was robed in colors turned to the heavenly host and said: "Mothers of Ethiopia, the convention has triumphed, your sorrows have brought joy to Ethiopia, your tears have anointed her soil with a blessing, your cries have awakened her children throughout the earth, yea in the corners of the unknown world are they aroused, and is prophesying, saying prepare ye the way for a redeemer."

Shepherd Anointed

For unto Ethiopia this day a Shepherd is anointed, yea, as a shepherd gathers his sheep so shall he gather unto God, the generation of Ethiopia even from the end of the earth and lead them high, a nation among nations.

Then shall the inhabitants of the earth know that the Lord our God has not forsaken Ethiopia, and that the mighty is weak against his command, and unto no nation has he given power forever.

Verily I say unto you, woe be unto the persecutors of the shepherd for he is anointed by the Lord our God, therefore one drop of his blood or the least of his apostles whom he has anointed to administer the law to the generations of Ethiopia, or the blood of a prophet within the law, shall break to pieces the oppressors of Ethiopia.

The Mighty Angel

When the mighty angel had finished speaking to the heavenly host he then turned to the earth and said: "Children of Ethiopia, stand," and there flashed upon the earth a great multitude of Negroes knowing not from whence they came; then shouted instantly the whole heavenly host, "Behold, behold Ethiopia has triumphed."

And it came to pass that the mighty angel spoke to the multitude of Negroes, saying, "Woe be unto those who say to the shepherd, thou fool, or to the least of an apostle anointed to administer the law, for it is not the desire of the shepherd but the will of the Lord who is God."

Source: Rogers, Robert Athlyi. *The Holy Piby.* Newark, NJ, 1928. Available at: https://www.sacred-texts.com/afr/piby/index.htm.

Hoodoo

Hoodoo, also known as "conjure" or "root work" is a religious practice derived from West African religious roots and born in the crucible of slavery. Unlike the religion Vodou (more pejoratively called "voodoo"), with which it is often conflated, Hoodoo is a system of magic, divination or prophecy, and alternative healing that can transcend religious lines. Its creation is attributed to the Gullah people, whose African roots are various (most came from Angola), but who grew into a cohesive culture after being forcibly removed to plantations in South Carolina and Georgia during the eighteenth and nineteenth centuries.

At the center of Hoodoo practice is a pharmacopeia of herbs, minerals, and bodily substances employed to harness divine power. Most often hoodoo is employed for protection, healing, or, in the many moments of crisis peppering African American history, redemption. When harm befell an individual, it was often attributed to hoodoo being "worked" against that person. As a form of witchcraft—which meant something different to those of African descent than it did to Euro-Americans—Hoodoo practitioners, particularly under the fearful gaze of slave masters, were often accused of performing black magic. For this reason, hoodoo was usually banned on plantations; however, hoodoo practitioners maintained a steady trade in secret and were even visited by some of those same slave masters.

Much of Hoodoo aligns with Christian belief, a feature of the plantation environment in which the practice arose. For example, the Bible is often employed in Hoodoo ritual. Many believe that Hoodoo practice aligns with God's providence and that God is pleased with the results of Hoodoo. The aim of Hoodoo is peace with the realm of spirits, whose power is both appeased and invoked through ritual.

Individual clients seek out Hoodoo men or women (though there are no designated priests, per se) to restore balance in their lives or to cause something to happen. It is understood that the Hoodoo will not be effective unless the seeker has faith in the practice. The Hoodoo practitioner would provide a specific remedy or spell for the client's needs, which might involve creating a parcel of herbs and other elements that the client would wear for protection or power. Black women continue to make up a significant number of Hoodoo practitioners, as they did on slave plantations. Many West African traditions maintained equality in the genders in terms of religious practice, with a bent toward women priests, who they believed were better channels of the spirit world. Despite misunderstanding and, on occasion, outright persecution, Hoodoo maintains a vital presence in the American religious landscape today.

See also: African New Religious Movements; Healing, Health, and New Religious Movements; Magic and New Religious Movements; Vodou.

Further Reading

Anderson, Jeffery E. 2005. *Conjure in African American Society.* Baton Rouge: Louisiana State University.

Chireau, Yvonne P. 2003. *Black Magic: Religion and the African American Conjuring Tradition.* Berkeley: University of California Press.

Hazzard-Donald, Katrina. 2013. *Mojo Workin': The Old African American Hoodoo System.* Urbana: University of Illinois Press.

Hubbard, L. Ron (1911–1986)

Practitioners of Scientology revere Lafayette Ron Hubbard, affectionately known simply as Ron or LRH, as the "Source" of Scientology's distinctive technology or "tech." Over the course of his long career, Hubbard devised and revised the worldview and practices, as well as the organizational form, of what became a worldwide new religious movement: The Church of Scientology, International (CSI).

LIFE HISTORY

Although external critics have questioned many of the details, official publications of CSI attribute to Hubbard a colorful biography (see www.lronhubbard.org/). Though he was born in Nebraska, his family moved frequently. While living in Montana, he became friendly with local Blackfoot Indians and was made a blood brother at age six. During his teenage years, he traveled twice to Asia, making stops in Japan, China, and the Philippines, among other places. In 1930, he entered George Washington University. His talent for writing led to pieces being accepted in campus publications. He also wrote about his experiences as a pilot. Nonetheless, Hubbard left the university after two undistinguished years and married his first wife, Margaret Grubb.

Hubbard made a living by writing for popular "pulp" magazines in both western and science fiction genres. He also produced novels and wrote screenplays for Columbia Pictures, some based on his own works. Hubbard also continued his

L. Ron Hubbard was the author of *Dianetics,* which posited that human beings were stymied by existing trauma or "engrams" embedded in their minds and souls. Later he would determine through the practice of "auditing" that these engrams carried memories of previous lives, indicating that each human being was a spiritual being called a "Thetan." These ideas formed the basis of the Church of Scientology, which Hubbard founded in the early 1950s. (Special Collections, Davidson Library, University of California, Santa Barbara)

adventures and became a member of the Explorers Club in 1940. Among other trips, he led an expedition to Alaska, where he encountered native cultures of the Tlingit and the Aleutian Islanders. During World War II, Hubbard served in the Navy as a lieutenant. He apparently suffered injuries in the war and spent a period of convalescence in Oak Knoll Naval Hospital in Oakland, California.

Evidence produced by researchers outside of Scientology, some of which has come to light in lawsuits in which the Church was involved, has cast doubt on most of Hubbard's official biography. But his life story still plays a significant role within the Church. His adventures as a larger than life figure undergird the Church's claims about Hubbard's deep insight into human nature and the problems faced by individuals and societies. In Scientology's presentation, his diverse talents, which were evident from an early age, reinforce his image as a person of extraordinary accomplishment. The character of Hubbard's life is made to testify to the accuracy of his understanding of human nature and the wisdom of his remedies for personal, familial, social, political, and global difficulties.

The Church's presentation of Hubbard's biography, then, can be read as an effort to construct, maintain, reinforce, and defend the charismatic persona of its founder. From that perspective, the Church's account of Hubbard's life appears more as a hagiographical attempt to emphasize Hubbard's incomparable religious insight. The ongoing reverence for Hubbard is indicated in both large and small ways in the statements and practices of Scientology. For example, an exact replica of Hubbard's office is maintained in all Scientology Churches. In addition, the sermons, group practices, and other elements of Scientology's ritual life, contained in the large volume called *The Background, Ministry, Ceremonies and Sermons of the Scientology Religion*, are to be followed exactly as they were written by Hubbard, "without deviation." Following Hubbard's teaching to the letter is what makes Scientology's technology work. Hubbard's original words are sufficient in themselves; they need neither to be interpreted or supplemented, only followed.

Every word that Hubbard has uttered or written about Scientology or its predecessor Dianetics constitutes scripture for the Church. In 1982, Scientology formed a nonprofit corporation, the Religious Technology Center (RTC), that is charged with preserving the integrity of the trademarks, symbols, and texts of Scientology. In effect, the RTC is dedicated to maintaining the uniformity and orthodoxy of Scientology, wherever it is taught or practiced, by controlling the use of Hubbard's teachings. It issued new editions of Hubbard's many works in 2005, claiming to have recovered Hubbard's original teachings and corrected errors that had crept into them. Scientology has even taken steps to preserve Hubbard's teachings by placing his originals in blast-proof underground vaults and having his words etched onto steel plates and recordings of his talks transferred to compact disks designed to last for a thousand years.

FROM DIANETICS TO SCIENTOLOGY

Hubbard's time spent convalescing after the war plays an extraordinarily important role in the history of Scientology. His lengthy recuperation gave him the opportunity to reflect on both his personal life experience and human nature in general. Although Hubbard resumed his writing career when he was released from the hospital and left active duty, he continued to develop what he thought was his innovative approach to understanding the human mind.

Hubbard first distributed the conclusions he had reached in 1948 in a privately circulated book, *Dianetics: The Original Thesis*. The reception of that text led to the publication of an essay in the journal of the Explorers Club and then to the publication of "Dianetics: The Evolution of a Science" in *Astounding Science Fiction* in May 1950. *Dianetics: The Modern Science of Mental Health* appeared at the same time and soon hit the best-sellers list of the *New York Times*.

As the title of his book suggests, Hubbard saw his work as a breakthrough in psychology. At the heart of his system was the proposition that the sources of psychological and social problems can be located in the human mind. But through an innovative therapy, individuals can break free of the negative effects that plague them and reach a state Hubbard called "Clear." Specifically, Hubbard argued that what he called the "reactive mind," which he described as operating "below the level of consciousness," retains complex images or "engrams" of traumatic events. Those events can subsequently be reactivated and cause psychological, emotional, and other problems.

Hubbard claimed that he could bring such engrams to the surface and dissipate their negative effects through a process called auditing. By being led through a series of questions by a qualified auditor, an individual could encounter the stored engrams, diminish their negative effects, and proceed toward becoming "clear" of their ongoing impact.

Hubbard had high hopes that his new "science" would revolutionize mental health treatment. He was deeply disappointed when the medical establishment, particularly the American Medical Association and the American Psychiatric Association, failed to take his claims seriously.

Despite that rejection, *Dianetics* was gaining enthusiastic responses throughout the world. Some who had tried Hubbard's methods, however, reported unanticipated developments. In the process of auditing, some individuals claimed to unearth not only events that shaped their own lives but also past lives in which they had experienced traumas. Both the frustrations with medical gatekeepers and reports about past lives contributed to Hubbard's turn from Dianetics as a new science to Scientology as a religion.

ORGANIZATION AND SUCCESSION

Hubbard's organizational involvement with Scientology varied over his lifetime. He was initially deeply involved in developing the organization and related groups, in which his ideas could be put into practice. In 1967, however, he founded an elite group of dedicated Scientologists called the Sea Organization, or "Sea Org," partly in response to opposition he had encountered in the United Kingdom, Australia, and the United States. Until 1975, when it moved ashore in Clearwater, Florida, Scientology's "religious order" was housed on a fleet of ships.

By 1966, Hubbard had withdrawn from daily administrative responsibilities to focus on writing. After 1975, he stayed for a while in Clearwater and then moved to rural California, near San Luis Obispo, where he continued to apply his ideas to social problems, such as drug addiction, and continued his science fiction writing.

Hubbard's gradual withdrawal from administrative responsibilities allowed David Miscavige (1960–), who had become a Scientologist as a teenager when he served Hubbard as one of his "Commodore's messengers," to assume progressively greater responsibilities and consolidate his position after Hubbard's death in 1986. By 1987, Miscavige had become the Chairman of the Board of the RTC and as such the ecclesiastical leader of Scientology.

Miscavige has since consolidated his power within the Church. As a public face of Scientology, he enthusiastically extolls its virtues and details its expansion throughout the world. But he has also been harshly criticized, particularly by former members and individuals who had been part of the Church hierarchy, for secrecy, abusive behavior, coercion, and harassment of perceived church enemies.

See also: Charisma and Leadership in New Religions; Crowley, Aleister (1875–1947); Dianetics; Freezone Scientology; New Scriptures and New Religious Movements; Scientology.

Further Reading

Christensen, Dorthe Refund. 2005. "Inventing L. Ron Hubbard: On the Construction and Maintenance of the Hagiographic Mythology of Scientology's Founder." In James R. Lewis & Jesper Aagard Petersen, eds. *Controversial New Religions*, pp. 227–258. New York: Oxford University Press.

Corydon, Bent. 1992. *L. Ron Hubbard: Messiah or Madman?* rev. ed. Fort Lee, NJ: Barricade Books.

Friends of Ron. 1995. *L. Ron Hubbard: A Profile.* Los Angeles: Bridge Publications.

Lewis, James R., ed. 2009. *Scientology.* New York: Oxford University Press.

Lewis, James R., & Kjersti Hellesøy, eds. 2017. *Handbook of Scientology.* Leiden: E. J. Brill.

Melton, J. Gordon 2000. *The Church of Scientology.* Salt Lake City, UT: Signature Books.

I

I AM Activity, The

Tracing its origins to the revelatory encounters of Guy Ballard (1878–1939) with Saint Germain, an Ascended Master of the Great White Brotherhood, the I AM Activity emerged in 1930 and by the middle of the decade had attracted a substantial audience throughout the United States. Scholars see the movement as having developed out of a cultic milieu that included influences from Theosophy, New Thought, and other currents of esoteric thought. Both Ballard and his wife Edna (1886–1971) were well acquainted with that milieu.

BELIEFS AND PRACTICES

The fundamental insight of Ballard's movement is that every individual has an essential divine nature. The God Self is part of the Mighty I AM Presence who created and rules the universe. Unfortunately, humans have generally lost their consciousness of God and their own nature. But the Ascended Masters, particularly Saint Germain and Jesus, have resolved to encourage humans to recover the knowledge of who they really are through the agency of the Ballards, their chosen messengers.

From August through October of 1930, Guy Ballard interacted with Saint Germain at Mount Shasta in northern California. When he returned to his Chicago home and told Edna about his experiences, she eagerly joined with him to promulgate the message he had received. By 1932, they had founded the Saint Germain Foundation (www.saintgermainfoundation.org). In 1934 Guy published an extensive account of his meetings with Saint Germain, *Unveiled Mysteries*. In the same year, the Ballards began to hold classes, first in Chicago and then throughout the United States, to disseminate their teachings. Local groups devoted to studying the revelations from Saint Germain also developed. In addition to their classes, the Ballards made public appearances and conducted an extensive publishing program through the foundation.

The Ballards promoted a progressive millennialism that anticipated the dawning of a golden age that would recapture the past when God's children actually did live in perfection. The United States would play a central role in the coming new age, since the Ascended Masters had singled it out for particular attention. The Ballards also preached a conservative morality. Those who committed themselves fully to the teachings were expected to avoid meat, onion, garlic, tobacco, alcohol, narcotics, card playing, and all sexual activity. They were to focus only on the cultivation of their consciousness of their inner God Self.

Ritual life centered on the individual practice of making decrees and affirmations, which the Ballards frequently demonstrated in their public appearances and which were likely influenced by similar practices in the New Thought movement. These statements were designed to support and enhance individuals' convictions that within them is the beneficent Light and Presence of God, the I AM. One published example reads, "O 'Mighty I AM Presence'! I love Thee, I bless Thee for the joy of Thy Glorious Light that lifts me beyond my outer self."

The most noteworthy communal ritual of the I AM Activity is the annual "I Am Come" pageant, commemorating the life of the "beloved Jesus." It was designed by Edna Ballard herself and has been held at Mount Shasta since 1950, recently in the Guy W. Ballard Amphitheatre.

CONTROVERSY

As with any alternative religious movement, the success of the I AM Activity also provoked opposition. In 1940, Gerald Bryan published a comprehensive attack on the movement, *Psychic Dictatorship in America*. It featured particularly timely comparisons between the Ballards and Hitler and Mussolini. Anticipating the critiques of the contemporary anticult movement, Bryan accused Edna Ballard of using a "hypnotic spell" to capture followers. Bryan also orchestrated negative media coverage of the movement and encouraged some former students of the Ballards to file lawsuits.

The lawsuits, which accused the Ballards of mail fraud because their books contained some eighteen "false representations," dragged on from 1940 to 1946 and their aftereffects were still felt as late as 1957. Informed by the efforts of the movement's opponents, the United States Attorney in Los Angeles in 1940 persuaded a grand jury to indict Edna and her son Donald (Guy had died in December 1939) for mail fraud and conspiracy to commit mail fraud. The indictment initiated a complex chain of events that resulted in Edna and Donald being convicted in 1942. Despite the judge's statements to the contrary, that remains the only time in American history when the beliefs of a religious groups have been declared false in a court of law. The Supreme Court eventually overturned that verdict in 1946, but by that time the I AM Activity was irreparably weakened.

INFLUENCE

The I AM Activity continues to this day, though it has never recovered the large audience that it reached in the late 1930s. The group's website continues to present the teachings that Saint Germain delivered to the Ballards and to chronicle the group's activities. Active opposition to the I AM Activity also persists, notably on a website maintained by former students (www.tyob.info), which also includes a full copy of Bryan's 1940 book.

Beyond that, the I AM Activity has seen a number of splinter groups develop when individuals claimed that they, too, had received communications from the Ascended Masters. Perhaps the most consequential of those groups coalesced around Mark L. Prophet (1918–1973) in 1958 as the Summit Lighthouse. In 1974, that group would become the Church Universal and Triumphant, led by Mark's wife, Elizabeth Clare Prophet (1939–2009).

See also: Anticult Movement, The; Ballard, Guy W. (1878–1939); Church Universal and Triumphant, The; Courts and New Religious Movements; Cultic Milieu; Millennialism; New Age, The; New Thought; Theosophy.

Further Reading

Bryan, Gerald B. 1940. *Psychic Dictatorship in America.* Los Angeles: Truth Research Publications.

Chanera (Edna Ballard). 1937. *"I AM" Adorations and Affirmations,* Vol. 5, part 1. Schaumburg, IL: Saint Germain Press.

King, Godfré Ray (Guy Ballard). 1934. *Unveiled Mysteries.* Schaumburg, IL: Saint Germain Press.

Noonan, John T., Jr. 1988. *The Lustre of Our Country: The American Experience of Religious Freedom.* Berkeley: University of California Press.

Rudbøg, Tim, 2013. "The I AM Activity." In Olav Hammer & Mikael Rothstein, eds., *Handbook of the Theosophical Current,* pp. 151–172. Leiden: Brill.

Indigo Children

Although public references to the New Age movement declined toward the end of the twentieth century, concepts associated with the New Age and more broadly with various currents of Western esotericism have continued to exercise cultural influence. One that has gained a broad audience is the concept of Indigo Children, which draws most immediately on the idea that individuals have auras that have distinctive colors. In this case, an indigo aura supposedly surrounds special or unusual individuals who may even possess supernatural abilities.

The connection between colors and auras has been articulated most influentially by Nancy Ann Tappe in *Understanding Your Life Thru Color* (1986). But the idea that individuals had auras or energy fields around them draws on ideas from Spiritualism and Theosophy, particularly from Theosophist Charles Webster Leadbetter (1854–1934). Besides Tappe, other influential authors on the subject include Lee Carroll and Jan Tober (*The Indigo Children* [1999]) and Doreen Virtue (*The Care and Feeding of Indigo Children* [2001]). For a time, the American comic actress Jenny McCarthy also promoted the concept of Indigo Children.

The identification of some individuals as Indigo Children has taken shape in a context in which certain behaviors, such as inattentiveness or perceived excessive activity, have been increasingly medicalized (as attention-deficit disorder and attention-deficit hyperactivity disorder, respectively) and treated with drugs. The alternative identification of such individuals as Indigo Children constitutes both a different, spiritual, explanation of their distinctiveness and a critique of "Big Pharma." Some observers even traced acts of violence by young people, such as the Columbine high school shooting, to the frustration experienced by Indigos in a world that does not understand their gifts.

There is no agreed-upon list of traits for an Indigo Child; other kinds of special children, such as Crystal Children and Star Kids, have also been recognized. They are all generally portrayed to be in possession of a special wisdom and as harbingers of a new, better world. In a reversal of the typical parent-child relationship, their parents are counseled to learn from them and to take their extraordinary abilities seriously.

As is common with much of the New Age, a substantial commercial enterprise has grown up around Indigo Children, including books, films, seminars and workshops, companies dedicated to helping Indigo Children recognize their true nature and capabilities, and even specialized schools. The phenomenon has also attracted its share of critics. One line of critique, aligned with criticisms of the New Age in general, focuses on those who are profiting from Indigo Children in one way or another. Another critique attributes the vaunted abilities of the Indigo Children to wish fulfillment on the part of their New Age parents.

See also: Children and New Religious Movements; Millennialism; New Age, The; Theosophy.

Further Reading

Kline, Daniel. 2014. "The New Kids: Indigo Children and New Age Discourse." In Asprem, Egil & Kennet Granholm, eds., *Contemporary Esotericism*, pp. 351–371. New York: Routledge.

Whedon, Sarah W. 2009. "The Wisdom of Indigo Children." *Nova Religio* 12, no. 3: 60–76.

Info-Cult/Info-Secte

Like many other contemporary groups that formed to combat what was perceived as the growing negative influence of groups identified as dangerous cults, or in French "sectes," Info-Cult/Info-Secte grew out of a personal encounter with a new religious movement. In 1977, Mike Kropveld (1949–) had an encounter with the Unification Church. A friend of his had joined the Church and Kropveld spent a brief time living with Church members in California.

Kropveld soon left, however, and when he returned to Canada he helped his friend's parents arrange a successful deprogramming of their son from the Unification Church, which is chronicled in journalist Josh Freed's *Moonwebs*. From that experience, Kropveld developed a volunteer organization known as the Cult Information Center. In 1980, the group received funding from the Montréal Jewish community and from the federal and provincial governments and became known as The Cult Project. Kropveld estimates that the group handled between 250 and 1,000 calls each year from individuals who were concerned that they or their loved ones had become involved in a dangerous cult. Unlike some other groups in the loosely affiliated anticult movement, The Cult Project never advocated coercive deprogramming, either directly or indirectly.

In 1990, The Cult Project became a nondenominational, nonprofit, bilingual organization known as Info-Cult/Info-Secte. It has since been supported by small grants from the provincial Ministry of Health and Social Services, foundations, and individuals. Info-Cult/Info-Secte maintains a threefold mission. First, it aims to promote the study of what it calls the "cult phenomenon." The organization maintains an extensive collection of books, articles, and other materials related to the study of cults. As Executive Director, Kropveld has been very active as a public speaker and some of his presentations have been published. Info-Cult/Info-Secte's website (www.infosecte.org) provides a sampling of Kropveld's writings on cults, including digital copies of his book in both English and French.

Second, Info-Cult/Info-Secte sees itself as having a mission of public education. It intends its research to be useful to anyone who has a question about a particular group or about the processes by which individuals become members of new or alternative groups. However, the explicit focus of the organization is on the harm that can befall individuals in cultic groups. Over time, the group's understanding of the potential for harm has become more nuanced. Rather than painting all new and alternative religious with a broad brush, as some early cult opponents definitely did, it now contends that some people, in some groups, can sometimes suffer harm. But its focus remains on helping those who have suffered because of their or their loved ones' participation in new religions.

Consequently, the third goal of the organization is to assist people who experience problems with cult phenomena. That assistance includes efforts to raise public awareness through various media, including documentary videos, the maintenance and expansion of the group's website, and what it calls an "active listening" service that focuses on ex-members and the family and friends of current members of cults.

In its fourth decade of operation, Info-Cult/Info-Secte has nuanced its understanding of the "cult phenomena." It has tried to diminish the use of highly polarized dichotomies, in which all cults are alike and equally dangerous in favor of a more modulated understanding of what constitutes "cultic thinking" and how that can be dangerous to some individuals in some situations.

Since the late 1990s, Info-Cult/Info-Secte, like some other cult awareness groups, has also become more open to engaging in conversation both with members of new and alternative religious groups and with scholars who have in the past been critical of the excesses of anticult groups and individuals, such as the practice of illegal coercive deprogramming. Since Kropveld sits on the board of the International Cultic Studies Association, he has also participated in exchanges with scholars, identified by some as "cult apologists" or "procultists," who have attended the annual meetings of that group. Info-Cult/Info-Secte continues to focus on helping those who have suffered harm but acknowledges the need for more research and broader alliances in understanding the cult phenomenon.

See also: Anticult Movement, The; Cult; Cult Awareness Network, The; Deprogramming; Exit Counseling; International Cultic Studies Association, The (The American Family Foundation); Unification Church, The.

Further Reading
Freed, Josh. 1980. *Moonwebs: Journey into the Mind of a Cult.* Toronto: Dorset Publishing.

Kropveld, Mike, with Eileen Barker. 2015. "Understanding the Religious Landscape: The Info-Secte/Info-Cult Perspective." Interview available at: https://wrldrels.org/wp-content/uploads/2017/03/Interview-with-Michael-Kropveld.pdf.

Kropveld, Mike, & Marie-Andrée Pelland. 2006. *The Cult Phenomenon: How Groups Function*, Natasha DeCruz & Gwendolyn Schulman, trans. Montréal: Info-Secte.

INFORM (The Information Network on Religious Movements)

During the 1970s and 1980s, efforts to create alarm about new and alternative religions, called "cults" by their detractors, created a public discourse that relied on spectacular and overgeneralized narratives and that drew highly polarized distinctions between destructive cults and their frequently unsuspecting prey. Those stories were based on the experiences of individuals who came to regret their engagement with new religions. On the other hand, converts to new religions frequently extolled their virtues in extravagant terms and implored others to join. But popular media sources devoted much more attention to dramatic stories of loss and rescue than they did to routine tales of conversion and departure. In North America and Europe, there was a general clamor to "do something" about the apparent explosion of cults.

The public furor about cults created the need for reliable, accurate, comprehensive, and current information about groups called cults and the processes by which they attracted and retained members. Various groups vied to shape the public perception of new religions, their members, and family members who often felt that they had "lost" loved ones to strange groups. But many of those groups espoused very specific points of view, even when they professed only to be interested in the public good. The Information Network on Religious Movements (INFORM) was founded in 1988 at the London School of Economics (and in 2018 moved to King's College, London) to counter misinformation and provide trustworthy and up-to-date information about new, alternative, and minority religions to any who inquired.

Established by sociologist of religion Eileen Barker and supported by the British Home Office and by mainstream churches in Britain, INFORM was designed to provide a full array of information to any interested parties while refraining from making specific recommendations about what individuals should or should not do. The professional staff of INFORM undertakes field visits to new and minority religions, engages directly with former members, collects documents from and about various groups, and consults available research on every group it considers. It also maintains connections with an international group of experts to which it can make referrals. The goal is to include virtually every perspective on each group without endorsing any one of them, respect the decisions of individuals both within cultic groups and outside of them, and to reduce suffering wherever possible. But it acknowledges that there are multiple perspectives on what counts as respect or suffering.

INFORM, then, is a research-oriented group that neither endorses particular religious groups nor counsels attempting to extricate members from them. That stance distinguishes INFORM from four other types of "cult-watching groups" that Barker has identified but also situates INFORM in conversation with them. Both cult-awareness and countercult groups focus on the dangers posed by cultic groups. The cult-awareness groups have been secularly oriented and focus on the processes of brainwashing, coercive persuasion, or thought reform. Countercult groups, both Christian and Jewish, focus on theological deviations and less on the processes of conversion. Human rights groups, like research-oriented groups, take a neutral stance toward cults but seek to identify and remedy any violations of human rights that can occur either against minority religious groups or within them. Finally, cult-defense groups have been formed by new or minority religions themselves. They seek to portray such religious groups in a positive light and to defend them against both misunderstandings and direct attacks.

In addition to responding confidentially to inquiries about religious groups and carefully safeguarding the personal information of both inquirers and informants, the staff of INFORM strives to shape the broader understanding of new and minority religions in several ways. Members of the Management Committee, research fellows, and the professional staff all maintain active research and publishing agendas. Many of those individuals help to organize and also present at the twice yearly seminars on specific topics and occasional larger conferences that INFORM sponsors; they also give public presentations in a variety of venues. A running list of seminar topics is maintained on the INFORM website. INFORM also produces reports, short briefings, and data summaries that can be used in court and by individuals and government agencies.

The periodic INFORM conferences provide a clear example of how the organization attempts to develop a multidimensional understanding of any group. It is not uncommon to have the same session feature a speaker who is a current member of a group, followed by a scholar who researches the same group, followed by a former member, and then a member of a cult-watching organization. Staff members of INFORM, particularly Eileen Barker, have also participated in conferences sponsored by both academic organizations throughout the world and by cult-awareness groups such as the International Cultic Studies Association.

INFORM rejects the term "cult" as necessarily pejorative and prefers to use what it sees as more neutral terms, such as "movement" and "minority religion," but accepts that any religious group, in certain situations, can be harmful. Consequently, it suggests that potential members learn as much as possible about a group before committing to membership. It similarly cautions friends and relatives of potential or actual members to be equally thorough in accumulating information and also to be wary of making hasty judgments.

From INFORM's perspective information and context are key. In acknowledging that some new or minority religions can harm some people sometimes, INFORM rejects the overblown generalizations that have characterized some activists in the contemporary anticult movement and promotes more nuanced understanding of religious movements that are unfamiliar to many.

See also: Anticult Movement, The; Cult; Media and New Religious Movements; Sect.

Further Reading

Barker, Eileen.. 2002. "Watching for Violence: A Comparative analysis of Five Types of Cult-Watching Groups." In David G. Bromley & J. Gordon Melton, eds., *Cults, Religion, and Violence*. Cambridge: Cambridge University Press.

Barker, Eileen, with Catherine Wessinger & David G. Bromley. 2015. "How to Be Informed about Minority Religions: Celebrating INFORM on Its 25th Anniversary." Interview available at: https://wrldrels.org/wp-content/uploads/2017/03/Interview-with-Eileen-Barker.pdf.

Gallagher, Eugene V., ed. 2017. *"Cult Wars" in Historical Perspective*. London: Routledge.

PRIMARY SOURCE DOCUMENT

Excerpts of Interview with Eileen Barker, Founder of INFORM (2017)

INFORM (Information Network Focus on Religious Movements), a London-based charity focused on providing the public with unbiased information about up-and-coming religious movements, was founded by sociologist Eileen Barker in 1988. In 2017, the World Religions & Spirituality Project at Virginia Commonwealth University interviewed Dr. Barker about her organization. An excerpt from that interview follows below.

Eileen Barker Interview (2017)

WRSP: What was it that first led you to consider founding the organisation that became INFORM?

Dr. Barker: I had been studying new religious movements since the early 1970s, and was becoming increasingly concerned about the social reactions to them insofar as these were based upon ignorance or misinformation—the misinformation coming from the movements themselves, their opponents, and the mass media. By the mid-1980s deprogramming was rife. Parents were paying tens of thousands of dollars to a deprogrammer who would kidnap their (adult) children and hold them against their will until they managed to escape or say that they had renounced their faith. The main justification for such illegal practices was that the movements had acquired "brainwashing" techniques of a well-nigh irresistible and irreversible nature, which, it was claimed, meant they would never leave the movement of their own free will. At the same time, some of the movements were undoubtedly involved in illegal or antisocial behavior that was obscured by the gross and obfuscating generalizations that were being made.

The crunch came when I was attending an "anticult" meeting in London to which some former members had been invited to talk about their experiences. I thought they gave plausible accounts of their joining and their time in their respective movements, but the majority of the audience were highly dissatisfied and pressing them to say that they had been brainwashed and/or deceived and treated badly. Trying to pour oil on troubled waters, the organiser asked the former members whether they would like to say something that they thought would be helpful for the relatives in the audience. At this point, a woman stood up and started shouting, "We don't want to hear this! We don't want to hear this!"

I realized at that moment that the majority of members of anticult groups like the one I was attending really did not want to hear anything that threatened their own version of the movements. I also decided that something needed to be done to make an alternative version of what the movements were like available to the media and relatives—and, indeed, to policymakers, law-enforcement officers and others who were making decisions concerning the movements. It seemed that the most obvious thing was to create an organisation that would offer enquirers information that was as objective and reliable and up-to-date as possible, drawing on the methodology of the social sciences and the not inconsiderable network of scholars who had been conducting research in the area. . . .

WRSP: What has been the reaction to INFORM by the religious groups on which you collect information and the cult watching groups that also collect information?

Dr. Barker: At the beginning, there was suspicion all round. However, at that time the media and anticult groups were depicting the movements in such negative, and frequently inaccurate terms that the movements were quite relieved that someone was prepared to listen to them, even if we didn't always accept everything that they said. Many of them learned to trust us and began to cooperate with us when we presented them with problems. We were, for example, able to facilitate meetings between members and relatives who had not communicated for years. This was by no means always the case, however, and there have been occasions when one or other of the movements has threatened to sue. So far, I'm glad to say, this has not actually happened.

As time went on and some of the movements came to be more accepted in society, they became slightly chary of being associated with INFORM and thus, they feared, with "cults." Even more recently, as these movements became even more "established" they have felt secure enough to cooperate with us once again.

On the other hand, the existing cult watching groups seemed to consider that we were even more dangerous than the movements. They informed the media and anyone who would listen that we were "cult lovers," "cult apologists" or even that we were really cultists in disguise. A petition to this effect was presented to 10 Downing Street, demanding that the start-up funding INFORM had been granted by the Home Office should be withdrawn immediately. An enquiry was set up, which evidently reported back to the Prime Minister (it was Mrs Thatcher at that time) that INFORM was doing useful work and that its funding should be increased!

WRSP: Many social scientists who study new religions have dismissed what you have called "cult watching groups" as important to the study of new religions. INFORM seems to have made a point of including cult watching groups, families of converts, and former members in the conversation about new religions. Has this been a productive approach for INFORM and why do you think this is important?

Dr. Barker: Yes, I think it has been an extremely productive approach and I also think it is very important.

There are always many constructions of social reality, each person selecting what s/he considers relevant, often ignoring what is considered irrelevant. There is no single "Truth" out there when we are talking about social phenomena. There are, however, certain things that we can know are factually incorrect. The methods of social science are, I believe, in many respects more reliable than the methods used by others, but if we are to understand "the cult scene" we need to understand the different perspectives of the different actors in that scene. To my mind it would be ridiculous to ignore *any* understanding of the movements. Quite apart from anything else, there is always a very real possibility that other cult watching groups have access to information that would be otherwise unobtainable. Of course, all the information has to be assessed, and we need to be able to acknowledge when we don't know which is the "most correct"—assuming such a thing exists. Sometimes people (particularly media people) seem to think that the truth lies somewhere in the middle between two extreme positions. But this is as silly as saying "X thinks that 2+2 makes 4, while Y thinks that 2+2 makes 5, so the correct answer must be 4.5."

Furthermore, if we want to communicate our version(s) of reality to someone else who is coming from a different perspective, then we have to learn how to translate so that other people can "hear" what we are saying. To do this effectively, one has to understand where it is that they are coming from.

Source: Wessinger, Dr. Catherine, & Dr. David G. Bromley, interviewers. Interview with Eileen Barker, founder of INFORM. Conducted by the World Religions and Spirituality Project at Virginia Commonwealth University: https://wrldrels.org/wp-content/uploads/2017/03/Interview-with-Eileen-Barker.pdf.

Insider/Outsider Problem, The

The roots of what has come to be called the insider/outsider problem go back at least to the nineteenth century, but the set of issues that can be gathered under that umbrella term continues to spark vigorous scholarly discussions. Students of religion have long debated which sources to privilege in the interpretation and explanation of religious phenomena. Some, like the Romanian historian of religions Mircea Eliade (1907–1986), stressed that religion is a distinctive, *sui generis* phenomenon that has to be interpreted on its own, that is, religious, terms. Others, taking their cue from observers of religion like Sigmund Freud (1856–1939), argue instead that since religion is a human phenomenon, it not only could, but should, be interpreted from the perspectives of the human sciences. In that view, offering religious interpretations of religion constitutes making further theological assertions rather than analytical investigations.

Although it has been phrased as a simple dichotomy for the sake of convenience, the distinction between insiders and outsiders needs to be described with more nuance. There are multiple kinds of insiders, just as there are multiple kinds of outsiders. Although the insider/outsider problem was initially phrased with reference to scholarly interpretations and explanations of religion, it can also play out in public discussions of religions in which the voices of scholarly experts are either muted or absent. Thus, both scholarly and nonscholarly insiders and scholarly and nonscholarly outsiders may be engaged in making interpretive or explanatory statements about a particular religious group.

In the study of new religious movements, the insider/outsider problem takes on particular inflections. In public discourse, for example, new religions are almost always characterized by outsiders. Such outsiders exhibit a variety of relationships to the group under scrutiny, but they are most frequently hostile. From the 1970s on, for example, parents of young adults who joined new religions have often mobilized against those groups, contending that their offspring could not possibly have joined such groups willingly and therefore must have been manipulated into membership. Those parents have found allies in some psychologists and others from related professions and even, sometimes, from law enforcement and government.

Former members of new religions have long played outsized roles in the public controversies about them. Some who leave groups become convinced that they have dramatic cautionary tales that the public needs to hear. Their voices become amplified by the loose coalition of anticult activists and thereby contribute to the dominant perception of new religions as dangerous "cults." Cults, in the public stereotype, are led by deceitful and manipulative leaders, populated by vulnerable individuals who never would have joined had they been thinking clearly, and will inevitably lead to harm for their members and damage to society as a whole.

In public discourse, it is rare to see satisfied or even questioning members of new religions, two different kinds of insiders, receive anywhere near the attention that disgruntled former members receive. The inadvertent omission or outright suppression of their voices contributes to the one-sided view of new religions that appears in the news and entertainment media. Insiders, given access to a public platform, would of course tell different stories about the religious groups to which they belong.

Scholars who focus on the study of new religions have overwhelmingly rejected the simplistic public image of dangerous "cults." They have argued strongly against the brainwashing hypothesis advanced by a handful of professional psychologists and their supporters. They have also contributed to the brainwashing concept being rejected by professional organizations like the American Psychological Association and, after a brief period, by courts at every level.

Despite scholarly efforts, however, the negative stereotype persists in public treatments of new religions. In 2018, for example, *People* magazine began a series of articles and accompanying television shows investigating "cults." The perspective adopted and reinforced the negative image of cults as deceitful, manipulative, and dangerous to both their members and society as a whole. Those shows reinforced the message of Leah Remini's multiseason show, *Leah Remini: Scientology and the Aftermath* (2016–), which continued the excoriation of the Church of Scientology as a dangerous cult that had begun with her autobiography *Troublemaker: Surviving Hollywood and Scientology* (2015).

In addition, a small number of scholars have attempted to refine and rehabilitate the theory of brainwashing and related concepts to use them to render negative judgments on at least some new religions. Although their arguments have infrequently appeared in the most widely recognized scholarly journals, they have often found an outlet for their work in *The International Journal of Cultic Studies*, published by the International Cultic Studies Association (ICSA). In fact, both the organization and its journal and other publications represent a substantial professionalization of the formally loosely organized anticult network. The work of the ICSA attempts to connect the more popular treatments of cults with more substantial, but still negative, scholarly work.

Awareness of the insider/outsider problem in its various forms can help observers make sense of the welter of opinions that have been articulated about new religions. Anyone who wants to learn about a new religious group needs to assess carefully the kinds of information on which any statements are based. It is misguided simply to cast one's lot either with disgruntled former members or satisfied continuing members; neutrality and comprehensiveness are difficult to achieve.

See also: Anticult Movement, The; Brainwashing; Conversion; Cult; Disaffiliation and Ex-Membership in New Religious Movements.

Further Reading

Chryssides, George D. 2013. "The Insider/Outsider Problem." In George D. Chryssides & Benjamin E. Zeller, eds., *The Bloomsbury Companion to New Religious Movements*, pp. 29–32. London: Bloomsbury.

Lalich, Janja 2004. *Bounded Choice: True Believers and Charismatic Cults*. Berkeley: University of California Press.

McCutcheon, Russell T. 1997. *Manufacturing Religion: The Discourse on Sui Generis Religion and the Politics of Nostalgia*. New York: Oxford University Press.

McCutcheon, Russell T., ed. 1999. *The Insider/Outsider Problem in the Study of Religion: A Reader*. London: Cassell.

Zablocki, Benjamin, & Thomas Robbins, eds. 2001. *Misunderstanding Cults: Searching for Objectivity in a Controversial Field*. Toronto: University of Toronto Press.

Integral Yoga

Some would argue that there are no truly "new" religious movements, just variations of similar ideas and themes. This notion is taken to a different level in the case of Integral Yoga, since there are two different new religious movements that bear that name. Some would argue that one is a continuation of the other, linked by their founders, but the two act as distinct institutions and have different historical trajectories.

Integral yoga, as a practice, first emerged from the writings of political activist-turned-guru, "Sri" Aurobindo Ghose (1872–1950). Through sustained spiritual practice, Aurobindo came to the conclusion that all life progressed through an evolution of consciousness from simple matter to "supermind." The notion that matter and spirit are ultimately integrated, and that the advancement of the one means the advancement of the other, spawned the name "Integral" yoga. Those further advanced down the path could achieve consciousness of the supermind through the practice of yoga, specifically that which turned an individual inward. Some have described the practice as predominantly psychological, focused internal analysis and reflection.

Aurobindo eventually retreated from public life to focus on the transformation of his own human nature to the divine supermind. Settling at Pondicherry, in a place eventually called "Auroville," he met Mira Richard (née Alfassa; 1878–1972), a Frenchwoman who ultimately remained in India and took the helm of Sri Aurobindo Ashram during Aurobindo's seclusion and after his death. She came to be known as "the Mother." The Sri Aurobindo ashram at Auroville still exists today as a destination for religious seekers and as the repository for Aurobindo's writings; though, despite its presence, there was no formal Aurobindo "movement" that emerged from his practice of Integral Yoga.

The same cannot be said for the Integral Yoga of Swami Satchidananda Saraswati (1914–2002). Originally a member of the Ramakrishna Mission, a monastic Hindu order, Satchidananda began to develop his own religious philosophy. He did meet Aurobindo prior to his death, though it is unclear whether or to what extent the latter's own version of Integral Yoga influenced Satchidananda's. The name Integral Yoga, for example, comes from the notion that Satchidananda synthesized all six classical yogic paths: raja (concentration), hatha (physical exercise), bhakti (worship), karma (work or charity), jnana (wisdom), and japa (meditation or mantra).

Beginning in the 1960s, Satchidananda embarked on a world tour, ultimately prompting the establishment of the Integral Yoga Institute in the United States in 1966. During the height of the counterculture, youthful, Western audiences were seeking for new spiritual directions and Satchidananda quickly amassed a following (which exploded after he spoke at the Woodstock Festival in 1969). His message was particularly appealing to the burgeoning countercultural milieu, as he emphasized physical health, the mastery of the emotions and the will, and the expression of love toward oneself and others as equally important and necessary spiritual goals. Satchidananda became the first Hindu guru to gain permanent entry to the United States and ultimately become

An aerial view of the Satchidananda Ashram in Yogaville, Virginia, the international headquarters for the branch of Integral Yoga founded by Swami Satchidananda Saraswati in 1979. Satchidananda diverged from the Ramakrishna Mission, a Hindu monastic organization of which he was a member, to create a global religious movement that merged Hindu practice with Western counterculture. (Joe Sohm/Dreamstime.com)

a United States citizen. In 1979, he founded the Satchidananda Ashram, better known as "Yogaville," which remains the international headquarters of the movement. Though this may be an allusion to Aurobindo's Auroville. Satchidananda's global, specifically Western focus, and concern with spreading his particular brand of yoga differed markedly from Aurobindo's quieter, Indian-based spiritual retreat. Satchidananda also made ecumenical overtures to other world religious leaders, including several Popes and the Dalai Lama.

Unlike Aurobindo and Auroville, Satchidananda and Yogaville experienced a great deal more negative scrutiny. Much of the media spotlight focused on the general cultural concern about the profusion of new religious movements in the United States that seemed to be "entrapping" the impressionable youth of America. However, Satchidananda was also accused of sexual misconduct against female acolytes in the movement—allegedly leveraging spiritual guidance for sex. When Satchidananda returned to Woodstock in 1991, he was met with protests by those who wanted him brought to justice.

See also: Aurobindo, Sri (1872–1950); Hindu New Religious Movements; Ramakrishna Mission; Yoga.

Further Reading

Ghose, (Sri) Aurobindo. 1959. *The Integral Yoga of Sri Aurobindo*. Pondicherry, India: Sri Aurobindo Ashram Press Distributors for the U.S.A.

Killingly, Dermot. 2014. "Remembering Sri Aurobindo and the Mother: The Forgotten Lineage of Integral Yoga." In *Gurus of Modern Yoga*. New York: Oxford University Press.

Panya, Samta. 2018. "Auroville as an Intentional Spiritual Community and the Practice of Integral Yoga." *Cogent Arts and Humanities* 5, no. 1: http://dx.doi.org.libdb.fairfield.edu/10.1080/23311983.2018.1537079.

Satchidananda, Sri Swami. 1970. *Integral Yoga Hatha*. New York: Holt, Rinehart, and Winston.

International Cultic Studies Association, The (The American Family Foundation)

Beginning as an affiliate of the Citizens Freedom Foundation, which later became the Cult Awareness Network (CAN), The American Family Foundation (AFF) was founded in 1979 in Lexington, Massachusetts, by Kay Barney. In 2004, its name was changed to the International Cultic Studies Association (ICSA), to reflect the growing ties between North American cult-awareness groups and similar organizations in Europe and elsewhere.

Like many other parents, Barney first encountered new religions when his daughter joined one, in her case the Unification Church. He quickly became alarmed by the degree of control that he thought the group exercised upon his daughter and set out to learn more and then to counter the negative effects of the Unification Church and similar groups. Direct personal experience with new and alternative religious groups lent the statements of Barney and others in AFF a persuasive power that found an eager audience in the news media, which then amplified the public suspicion of groups branded cults.

Along with CAN, AFF became one of the two most prominent nation-wide anticult organizations in the United States. Unlike CAN, however, AFF generally avoided associating with freelance deprogrammers who often acted illegally in their efforts to remove individuals from groups they identified as dangerous cults. Instead, AFF focused on organizing professionals who took seriously the apparently growing "cult problem." Psychiatrists, psychologists, and social workers, some of them with academic appointments and many with advanced degrees, figured prominently among the professionals for whom AFF provided materials and from whom AFF drew information.

For its first few years, AFF focused on trying to enlist local, state, and national governments in the project of opposing dangerous cults. Although it succeeded in getting a few public hearings held, all attempts at writing legislation against cults failed. By 1984, AFF gave up trying to influence the government and focused instead on trying to educate professionals and the public.

AFF consistently has seen itself as having four constituencies: former members of cultic groups who may need counseling services to ease their transition out of the group; the families of members and former members of cultic groups who themselves could need both information and counseling; a variety of "helping" professionals who aim to provide both reparative services and preventive information; and researchers who want to develop further their understanding of how cultic groups operate.

To keep those constituencies informed, AFF quickly developed a wide-ranging and vigorous publishing program. The earliest publication, *The Advisor*, lasted from 1979 to 1984. Each issue was a short (eight and then sixteen pages) newsletter that included news clippings and reports from AFF events, among other things. In 1984, the *Cultic Studies Journal* debuted, taking the place of the earlier *Cultic Studies Newsletter* and assuming the format of a standard academic journal, with articles, comments, book reviews, and notes from the field. In 2002, the *Cultic Studies Journal* and other publications were merged into the *Cultic Studies Review*, whose first issue featured an explanation of the new publication by Michael D. Langone, a psychologist and the Executive Director of the AFF. In 2010, the primary scholarly outlet for the ICSA became the *Journal of the International Cultic Studies Association*. More popular and practically oriented materials appear in *ICSA Today*, also begun in 2010 and published three times a year. ICSA also sends out other materials through e-mail.

Unlike many other groups, AFF/ICSA has kept itself on relatively sound financial footing by charging at least nominal sums for the information it sends out as well as soliciting donations from individuals and foundations.

Beyond its publications, ICSA hosts an annual international meeting as well as other conferences, some devoted to gathering former members and their families. Since the late 1990s, ICSA has opened lines of communication both with members of new religious groups, such as the International Society for Krishna Consciousness, and with scholars who have been critical of at least some of the practices of the anticult movement and cult-awareness groups.

See also: See: Anticult Movement, The; CESNUR (The Center for the Study of New Religions); Cult; Cult Awareness Network, The; Deprogramming; Info-Cult/Info-Secte; INFORM (The Information Network on Religious Movements); Unification Church, The.

Further Reading

Langone, Michael D. 2002. "The History of the American Family Foundation." *Cultic Studies Journal* 1: 3–50.

Langone, Michael D., with Eileen D. Barker. 2014. "The Cult Awareness Movement in North America: Past, Present, and Future." Interview available at https://wrldrels.org/wp-content/uploads/2017/03/Interview-with-Michael-Langone.pdf.

Shupe, Anson, & Susan E. Darnell. 2006. *Agents of Discord: Deprogramming, Pseudo-Science, and the American Anticult Movement*. New Brunswick, NJ: Transaction Publishers.

PRIMARY SOURCE DOCUMENT

Excerpts from Interview with Michael Langone, Executive Director of the International Cultic Studies Association (2017)

Dr. Michael Langone is the executive director of the International Cultic Studies Association, an organization dedicated to the study of psychological abuse and mental manipulation within North American cults. In 2017, Dr. Langone was interviewed by the World Religions & Spirituality Project about his research and the Association's work.

Interview with Dr. Michael Langone (2017)

WRSP: The North American Cult Awareness Movement historically consisted of a number of small groups but has gradually coalesced into a few major groups. Would you briefly outline this movement history for us?

Dr. Langone: Your question suggests that the coalescing continued into the present. In fact, the coalescing to which you refer occurred in the late 1970s, when the Citizens Freedom Foundation (CFF) was formed (later renamed Cult Awareness Network—CAN). Prior to the formation of CFF, many small groups had been formed in various parts of the USA and Canada. Most of those groups joined together to form CFF, but a number of prominent groups retained their independence, including American Family Foundation (founded in 1979, renamed International Cultic Studies Association—ICSA—in 2004), Council on Mind Abuse (COMA) in Toronto, The Cult Project (later renamed Info-Cult/Info-Secte) in Montreal, and a number of programs of Jewish organizations in New York, Los Angeles, Baltimore, and Miami. Today, only Info-Cult and ICSA exist. When CAN went into bankruptcy because of lawsuits, it was taken over by people associated with the Church of Scientology, I believe. I do not know whether or not CAN still functions as an organization. However, if it does, the perspective it advances is probably very different from that expounded before the bankruptcy.

There were also dozens of (mostly very small) Evangelical cult watch organizations in the USA. I remember a handbook that used to be published annually in the 1980s that listed dozens, if not hundreds, of such Evangelical organizations; I do not know if such a handbook is still published. Most of these small organizations focused on evangelizing to one group, in particular either the Jehovah's Witnesses or Mormons.

During the past 35 years many other organizations critical of cultic groups have formed, e.g., FactNet, the Ross Institute, and Freedom of Mind. With the advent of the Internet, dozens of websites were created that focused on one particular group or leader. So far as I know, there is today no single directory of organizations and websites concerned about cultic groups.

Hence, to return to your question, the coalescing was a one-time phenomenon that occurred about 35 years ago and has not occurred since. Nor has here been any recent movement toward a second "coalescing."

WRSP: Do the separate organizations that make up the North American Cult Awareness Movement share interests and a mission in common, or are there important differences among them?

Dr. Langone: The common interest, in my opinion, is a concern for the casualties of cultic groups. However, there are sometimes marked differences in how these organizations conceptualize the issues and the actions they take to deal with the problems they perceive.

In my view, the so-called "cult wars" ("pro-cultists" vs. "anti-cultists") resulted from the fact that sociologists of religion and religious studies scholars did not study casualties, whereas mental health professionals and volunteers associated with cult awareness organizations worked almost exclusively with people and families who believed they or a loved one had been hurt as a result of a group involvement. Some so-called "pro-cultists" were aware that people were sometimes harmed by groups, and some so-called "anti-cultists" were aware that not everybody was harmed. However, nuance was not the norm, at least not until the past 10–15 years.

Within the North American cult awareness movement, ICSA and Info-Cult have championed, especially during the past 15 years, a more nuanced view of the phenomenon. All human beings have a tendency to overgeneralize. I believe that ICSA and Info-Cult differ from other organizations in this field in that we try, however imperfectly, to be aware of and resist the impulse to overgeneralize from one's limited experience. I believe that many individuals within the so-called "camps," would agree with a statement that I am fond of making: Some groups harm some people sometimes. We can disagree about the nature and magnitude of harm, the mechanisms by which it comes about, and the degree to which new religious movements are at risk of harming members. However, we ought to be able to agree that some people are harmed. My colleagues and I are concerned with this subgroup. We lose balance, however, when we act as though all "cults" harm all members. Such an overgeneralization usually results from heavy exposure to victims' sometimes harrowing stories of abuse and, for this reason, is an understandable lapse in balance. Most helping professionals I know, however, can return to a more balanced, objective perspective if they are reminded that individual variation is the norm, not the exception, and that their clients are selected from a subgroup of casualties.

I would add that during the days of deprogramming some "pro-cultists" made the same kind of overgeneralization error, but from the other direction. They sometimes described all "anti-cultists" as overzealous anti-religious bigots willing to do anything to rip people out of cults. Though this caricature may have fitted a few people, it was by no means an accurate description of the majority of workers in this field.

Source: Barker, Dr. Eileen, interviewer. Interview with Michael Langone, Executive Director of the International Cultic Studies Association, conducted by the World Religions and Spirituality Project: https://wrldrels.org/wp-content/uploads/2017/03/Interview-with-Michael-Langone.pdf.

International Peace Mission Movement
ORIGINS AND FOUNDER

The story of the International Peace Mission Movement (PMM) begins with George Baker (c. 1876–1965). Baker was born when segregation and fears of lynching were a normative piece of African American life. These experiences would fundamentally shape Baker's later religious ideology. While working as a gardener and as an itinerant preacher in the early twentieth century, Baker discovered New Thought, a religious movement that emphasized the ability of the mind to achieve both physical and spiritual salvation and to effect change in the world. Around this time, Baker also met and for a brief time partnered with a fellow itinerant preacher, Samuel Morris, who claimed to be God. Baker eventually rejected Morris's claim to Godship and instead asserted that *he* was God.

Soon after moving to New York, first to Brooklyn then to Sayville on Long Island and finally to Harlem, Baker took the name Rev. Major Jealous Divine or, more commonly among his disciples, Father Divine. While in New York the movement flourished and reflected the interracial ethos promoted by Father Divine. PMM was both a religious movement that merged Christian theology with New Thought and a social justice initiative that promoted the uplift of poor black communities. The movement also suffered from setbacks due to the entrenched racism of U.S. society and suspicion over the agenda and growing fame of Father Divine and PMM. Father Divine's very public arrest, trial, and imprisonment, ironically, served to catapult him and his movement to fame and renown. At its zenith in the 1930s, which was also the height of the Great Depression, the movement boasted around two million members.

Due to pressure on PMM from both within and without, Father Divine relocated the headquarters to Philadelphia, Pennsylvania, where it remained until his death in 1965. Following his death, his wife, Mother Divine (née Edna Rose Ritchings; 1925–2017) took over leadership of the movement, a position she held until her death. She continued to preside over the major PMM rituals and to distribute her late husband's teachings. However, the movement saw a sharp decline in new membership. And, as older members died, it became harder to sustain the initiatives of the movement financially.

BELIEFS AND PRACTICES

Central to the theological system of PMM is the belief that Father Divine is both God and Christ come again. As the divine personified, Father Divine hoped to direct the attention of his followers and the world to the fact that they can achieve heaven now, through the work of their own minds. This ideology was directed particularly at poor blacks in the country. At the same time that he promoted the idea that heaven was a state of consciousness anyone could achieve, he also used the money donated or earned through PMM to help black movement members find jobs or housing. Given the interracial makeup of PMM, Divine emphasized the need of white or affluent members of the group to help the less fortunate, both in and outside of the movement.

Then and now, PMM members abstain from alcohol, drugs, and tobacco. Many also practice celibacy, the rationale being that all are married to God. Father Divine had advocated for communal living (with strict gender segregation) and property ownership, which is practiced by the remaining PMM members at the Woodmont Estate today. This practice also had a practical purpose; through the pooling of their money, members were able to invest in businesses, which, in turn, would enable them to help themselves move up in society.

Most central to the movement, particularly during the Father Divine years, were the Holy Communion Feasts or Banquets where members of the movement were served large communal meals, often feeding thousands of attendees. During the feasts, Father and Mother Divine would sit at the head of the table and Father Divine would often speak extemporaneously. Besides being a conscious reenactment of the sacrament of communion (and the Last Supper), the meals represented the fact that during the 1930s food was scarce for many. PMM also holds weekly church services, which are now comprised primarily of listening to recorded sermons of Divine or other prominent figures in the movement, reading from the Bible, and encouraging members to give testimony of their own spiritual advancement or struggles. Additionally, Father and Mother Divine's wedding day (April 29) is celebrated as a religious holiday and is called "the Marriage of Christ to his Church," reflecting the fact that through Mother Divine, a church member, he is married to all his disciples.

CULTURAL LEGACY

Though the movement has never achieved the popularity of the 1930s nor truly recovered from the death of Father Divine, PMM still maintains various properties and maintains a website called "Father Divine's Peace Mission Movement" (www.peacemission.org). The Woodmont Estate outside of Philadelphia that Father and Mother Divine inhabited until their respective deaths is still the primary residence of PMM members and the site of the Palace Mission Church, the holiest site of worship.

The PMM as a religious movement and program of racial uplift operates at a much more modest level than it did in the early twentieth century. Now its primary function is to preserve the legacy of Father Divine and the teachings of PMM for posterity. On PMM's website, interested people are invited to "Visit Woodmont," where they may take a tour of Father Divine's home and see his living chambers, which are kept untouched in the event that his eternal spirit should return.

See also: Father Divine (1876–1965); Law Enforcement and New Religious Movements; New Thought; Race and New Religious Movements.

Further Reading

Divine, Mother. 1982. *The Peace Mission Movement.* New York: Anno Domini Father Divine Publications.

Mabee, Carleton. 2008. *Promised Land: Father Divine's Interracial Communities in Ulster County, New York.* Fleischmanns, NY: Purple Mountain Press.

Roof, Wade Clark, & Mark Juergensmeyer. 2011. "Father Divine and the Peace Mission Movement." In *Encyclopedia of Global Religion.* Thousand Oaks, CA: Sage.

Watts, Jill. 1992. *God, Harlem U.S.A.: The Father Divine Story.* Los Angeles: The University of California Press.

International Society for Krishna Consciousness (ISKCON)

During the 1970s, those visiting baggage claims in airports throughout the United States could easily encounter individuals dressed in orange, distributing smiles, pamphlets, and flowers. These figures, often called Hare Krishnas for their repetition of a particular chant, were possibly the most visible symbol of the rise of Asian, particularly Hindu, new religious movements in the Western Hemisphere during the decades following World War II. To the many religious seekers of this era, the International Society for Krishna Consciousness (ISKCON) and its orange-clad missionaries were a source of fascination and religious innovation. To those individuals whose relatives joined up, to the burgeoning anticult movement, and to the traveler who was simply trying to be on her way, they were a nuisance or, more seriously, a dangerous "cult."

ORIGINS AND HISTORY

Abhay Charan De (1896–1977) was born in Calcutta to Bengali parents who were devotees of the Hindu deity, Vishnu. Growing up, he attended schools run by Europeans, from which he graduated with multiple degrees—degrees that he would reject after becoming influenced by Mahatma Gandhi's (1869–1948) independence movement. By the time of his graduation, he was fluent in both English and Sanskrit.

In 1922, Abhay met his spiritual mentor, Bhaktisiddhanta Sarasvati Thakura (1874–1937), though he would not become his formal disciple until 1933. Very early in their relationship, Bhaktisiddhanta asked Abhay to disseminate his teachings to the Western, English-speaking world. Shortly after his guru's death, he began publishing prolifically, in both English and Sanskrit. In 1944, he founded *Back to the Godhead*, which is still the primary magazine of the Hare Krishna movement; it was published primarily in English until 2010. On the recommendation of Bhaktisiddhanta, much of his work involved the translation of Sanskrit texts into English and the publication of texts relating to Vaishnava religious life. In 1947, Abhay dispensed with his surname, adding the honorific "Bhaktivedanta" given to him by the Gaudiya Vaishnava Society as a commendation for his devotion (*bhakti*) to the Lord Krishna. He also added the name "Prabhupada," which meant "one who sits at the master's feet." Thus, the name by which he would be known in the West was A. C. Bhaktivedanta (Swami) Prabhupada.

In 1965, Prabhupada set sail for the United States. His trip was unsponsored and his visit unsolicited; he arrived in New York with seven dollars in his pocket, after having suffered two heart attacks while aboard. His mission to the West began humbly; he gave classes on the Bhagavad Gita and led devotional chants (*kirtan*) in public spaces or by invitation. Despite the lack of fanfare, his message soon caught on among young people, particularly those steeped in the counterculture. Soon, he was able to rent a small storefront in New York, which he used as a temple. In 1966, he formally established ISKCON.

During the last decade of Prabhupada's life, he witnessed the growth of ISKCON into a movement of international renown as well as an object of derision and censure. He traveled the world on multiple lecture tours, establishing temples, intentional agricultural communities, schools, and a publishing house along the way. His texts formed the spiritual basis for the movement, particularly his English translations of texts such as the Bhagavad Gita. Today, ISKCON has established over four hundred temples worldwide, along with numerous other facilities related to their mission, and counts around one million as members.

Hare Krishnas, the practitioners of the International Society for Krisha Consciousness, walk down a European street proclaiming the mantra for which they derive their name: "Hare Krishna, Hare Krishna, Hare Hare, Krishna Krishna." Notable for their shaved heads and often orange dress, Hare Krishnas became a symbol of countercultural religious innovation during the late twentieth century. (Anky10/Dreamstime.com)

BELIEFS AND PRACTICES

ISKCON is the largest Vaishnavic tradition, or a monotheistic strain of Hinduism. Vaishnavas believe that their ultimate goal is for every living being to become awakened to their love of Lord Krishna, or God, who is dubbed "the all-attractive one." Though Lord Krishna can have different avatars, these avatars as well as everything else in the world, emanate from Krishna who is the only reality. Thus, bhakti yoga, or worship, is due only to Krishna. To awaken this "Krishna consciousness," Hare Krishnas repeatedly speak their version of the maha-mantra, which asks for awakening from God: "Hare Krishna, Hare Krishna, Krishna Krishna, Hare Hare, Hare Rama, Hare Rama, Rama Rama, Hare Hare."

Unlike other branches of Hinduism, the consciousness achieved through Hare Krishna devotion will not result in absorption into God. Rather, each individual is an eternal, genderless, and discrete entity. Thus, this leads to the belief that the aim of Hare Krishna practice is not to become a part of Krishna, but to be filled with love for Krishna. This love will ultimately benefit the entire world, since love for Krishna produces love for all humanity. This idea is reflected in their seven-part mission statement, developed by Prabhupada in 1966, which encourages the spread of Krishna consciousness to bring people toward Krishna, toward each other, and toward a simpler, less materialistic way of life.

Bhakti yoga, the practice of Krishna consciousness, can be practiced at home and with others at a temple. There are also festivals, seminars, and classes where Hare Krishnas or potential converts can learn about Krishna consciousness. Aside from advancing their own spiritual journeys, Hare Krishnas are tasked with publicly preaching the message of Krishna consciousness. Hare Krishnas will often chant the maha-mantra in public and distribute preliminary pamphlets on the religion, though the aim is to sell the teachings of Prabhupada. There is an ISKCON Ministry of Education that is tasked with training Hare Krishnas in spreading the message as well as regulating the message itself.

Along with the practice of bhakti yoga and proselytization of its message, members of ISKCON are also encouraged to live in a particular way. In line with the "four legs of Dharma," *daya* (mercy), *tapas* (self-control), *satyam* (truthfulness), and *saucam* (cleanliness of body and mind), Hare Krishnas are prohibited, respectively, from meat eating, having illicit sex, gambling, and consuming intoxicating substances. Many of the initiatives of ISKCON relate to eating a vegetarian diet, such as the project Food for Life, which serves free vegetarian meals in sixty countries throughout the world.

Since the soul is genderless, this has led to the belief in total gender equality; men and women are equally venerated among Hare Krishnas and are enabled to perform religious duties. However, the almost exclusively male Governing Body Commission, the governing arm of ISKCON, maintains the view that women's primary means of advancing toward Krishna consciousness comes through motherhood. Marriage and motherhood are seen as spiritual acts of love for Krishna, thus both same-sex marriage and women seeking work outside the home are issues often debated by the institution itself. Nonetheless, this has not precluded members of the LGBTQI+ community from joining ISKCON nor has it prevented Hare Krishna women from joining the workforce. Given the diffuse nature of ISKCON's community and practices, such things would be hard to regulate in reality.

CULTURE AND CONTROVERSY

Though their presence in public places such as airports had already gained them a degree of cultural relevance, the Hare Krishnas were catapulted to fame when the Beatles popularized their beliefs in several songs (e.g., "Give Peace a Chance" and "My Sweet Lord"). George Harrison also became a devotee of Krishna Consciousness and contributed financially to ISKCON.

Unfortunately, the history of ISKCON has also met with institutional and cultural woes. Some were internal issues, usually regarding deviant interpretations of Prabhupada's teachings or the particular governance practices of certain members of the Governing Body Commission. However, ISKCON was also a frequent target of the diffuse anticult movement during its heyday of the 1970s through 1980s. Very often, the anticult movement used the Hare Krishnas as examples of the effects of "brainwashing," arguing that the movement gained members through involuntary coercion. In 1976, *People v. Murphy*, a case involving parents' accusations that the Hare Krishnas had brainwashed their children, reached the Supreme Court. The Supreme Court ruled that ISKCON was a viable religion and that no such brainwashing had occurred.

More damning, however, were accusations of child abuse and child sexual abuse filed against Hare Krishna devotees and monks from the 1970s through the 1990s. Though originating in the Texas branch of the movement, such abuses were evidently widespread, leading to rising legal costs and ISKCON filing for Chapter 11 bankruptcy protection; the movement rebounded thereafter. This ultimately resulted in the decision by the Governing Body Commission to strengthen its Child Protection Policy and Procedure in 2012.

Despite such scrutiny and setbacks, the movement persisted, recently celebrating its fiftieth anniversary.

See also: Anticult Movement, The; Brainwashing; Hindu New Religious Movements; Prabhupada, A. C. Bhaktivedanta (1896–1977); Seekers; Self-Realization Fellowship (Yogananda); Yoga.

Further Reading

Dwyer, Graham, & Richard J. Cole. 2007. *The Hare Krishna Movement: Forty Years of Chant and Change*. New York: I.B. Tauris & Co.

Goswami, Mukunda. 2001. *Inside the Hare Krishna Movement: An Ancient Eastern Religious Tradition Comes of Age in the Western World*. Imperial Beach, CA: Torchlight Publishing, Inc.

Prabhupada, A. C. Bhaktivedanta Swami. 1970. *The Nectar of Devotion: The Complete Science of Bhakti-Yoga*. Los Angeles: International Society for Krishna Consciousness.

Rochford, Burke. 2007. *Hare Krishna Transformed*. New York: New York University Press.

PRIMARY SOURCE DOCUMENT

Swami Prabhupada, Preface from *Bhagavad-gītā As It Is* by Swami Prabhupada (1971)

Bhagavad-Gītā As It Is, *a translation and commentary of the Bhagavad Gita, was written by ISKCON founder A. C. Bhaktivedanta Swami Prabhupada in 1968. This translation quickly became the touchstone of the Hare Krishna movement. The Preface to the 1971 edition follows below.*

Originally I wrote *Bhagavad-gītā As It Is* in the form in which it is presented now. When this book was first published, the original manuscript was, unfortunately, cut short to less than 400 pages, without illustrations and without explanations for most of the original verses of the *Śrīmad Bhagavad-gītā*. In all of my other books—*Śrīmad-Bhāgavatam, Śrī Īśopaniṣad,* etc.— the system is that I give the original verse, its English transliteration, word-for-word Sanskrit-English equivalents, translations and purports. This makes the book very authentic and scholarly and makes the meaning self-evident. I was not very happy, therefore, when I had to minimize my original manuscript. But later on, when the demand for *Bhagavad-gītā As It Is* considerably increased, I was requested by many scholars and devotees to present the book in its original form. Thus the present attempt is to offer the original manuscript of this great book of knowledge with full *paramparā* explanation in order to establish the Kṛṣṇa consciousness movement more soundly and progressively.

Our Kṛṣṇa consciousness movement is genuine, historically authorized, natural and transcendental due to its being based on *Bhagavad-gītā As It Is*. It is gradually becoming the most popular movement in the entire world, especially amongst the younger generation. It is becoming more and more interesting to the older generation also. Older gentlemen are becoming interested, so much so that the fathers and grandfathers of my disciples are encouraging us by becoming life members of our great society, the International Society for Krishna Consciousness. In Los Angeles many fathers and mothers used to come to see me to express their feelings of gratitude for my leading the Kṛṣṇa consciousness movement throughout the entire world. Some of them said that it is greatly fortunate for the Americans that I have started the Kṛṣṇa consciousness movement in America. But actually the original father of this movement is Lord Kṛṣṇa Himself, since it was started a very long time ago but is coming down to human society by disciplic succession. If I have any credit in this connection, it does not belong to me personally, but it is due to my eternal spiritual master, His Divine Grace Oṁ Viṣṇupāda Paramahaṁsa Parivrājakācārya 108 Śrī Śrīmad Bhaktisiddhānta Sarasvatī Gosvāmī Mahārāja Prabhupāda.

If personally I have any credit in this matter, it is only that I have tried to present *Bhagavad-gītā* as it is, without any adulteration. Before my presentation of *Bhagavad-gītā As It Is*, almost all the English editions of *Bhagavad-gītā* were introduced to fulfill someone's personal ambition. But our attempt, in presenting *Bhagavad-gītā As It Is*, is to present the mission of the Supreme Personality of Godhead, Kṛṣṇa. Our business is to present the will of Kṛṣṇa, not that of any mundane speculator like the politician, philosopher or scientist, for they have very little knowledge of Kṛṣṇa, despite all their other knowledge. When Kṛṣṇa says, *man-manā bhava mad-bhakto mad-yājī māṁ namaskuru,* etc., we, unlike the so-called scholars, do not say that Kṛṣṇa and His inner spirit are different. Kṛṣṇa is absolute, and there is no difference between Kṛṣṇa's name, Kṛṣṇa's form, Kṛṣṇa's qualities, Kṛṣṇa's pastimes, etc. This absolute position of Kṛṣṇa is difficult to understand for any person who is not a devotee of Kṛṣṇa in the system of *paramparā* (disciplic succession). Generally the so-called scholars, politicians, philosophers and *svāmīs*, without perfect knowledge of Kṛṣṇa, try to banish or kill Kṛṣṇa when writing commentary on *Bhagavad-gītā*. Such unauthorized commentary upon *Bhagavad-gītā* is known as *māyāvāda-bhāṣya*, and Lord Caitanya has warned us about these unauthorized men. Lord Caitanya clearly says that anyone who tries to understand *Bhagavad-gītā* from the Māyāvādī point of view will commit a great blunder. The result of such a blunder will be that the misguided student of *Bhagavad-gītā* will certainly be bewildered on the path of spiritual guidance and will not be able to go back to home, back to Godhead.

Our only purpose is to present this *Bhagavad-gītā As It Is* in order to guide the conditioned student to the same purpose for which Kṛṣṇa descends to this planet once in a day of Brahmā, or every 8,600,000,000 years. This purpose is stated in *Bhagavad-gītā*, and we have to accept it as it is; otherwise there is no point in trying to understand the *Bhagavad-gītā* and its speaker, Lord Kṛṣṇa. Lord Kṛṣṇa first spoke *Bhagavad-gītā* to the sun-god some hundreds of millions of years ago. We have to accept this fact and thus understand the historical significance of *Bhagavad-gītā*, without misinterpretation, on the authority of Kṛṣṇa. To interpret *Bhagavad-gītā* without any reference to the will of Kṛṣṇa is the greatest offense. In order to save oneself from this offense, one has to understand the Lord as the Supreme Personality of Godhead, as He was directly understood by Arjuna, Lord Kṛṣṇa's first disciple. Such understanding of *Bhagavad-gītā* is really profitable and authorized for the welfare of human society in fulfilling the mission of life.

The Kṛṣṇa consciousness movement is essential in human society, for it offers the highest perfection of life. How this is so is explained fully in the *Bhagavad-gītā*. Unfortunately, mundane wranglers have taken advantage of *Bhagavad-gītā* to push forward their demonic propensities and mislead people regarding right understanding of the simple principles of life. Everyone should know how God, or Kṛṣṇa, is great, and everyone should know the factual position of the living entities. Everyone should know that a living entity is eternally a servant and that unless one serves Kṛṣṇa one has to serve illusion in different varieties of the three modes of material nature and thus wander perpetually within the cycle of birth and death; even the so-called liberated Māyāvādī speculator has to undergo this process. This knowledge constitutes a great science, and each and every living being has to hear it for his own interest.

People in general, especially in this Age of Kali, are enamored by the external energy of Kṛṣṇa, and they wrongly think that by advancement of material comforts every man will be happy. They have no knowledge that the material or external nature is very strong, for everyone is strongly bound by the stringent laws of material nature. A living entity is happily the part and parcel of the Lord, and thus his natural function is to render immediate service to the Lord. By the spell of illusion one tries to be happy by serving his personal sense gratification in different forms which will never make him happy. Instead of satisfying his own personal material senses, he has to satisfy the senses of the Lord. That is the highest perfection of life. The Lord wants this, and He demands it. One has to understand this central point of *Bhagavad-gītā*. Our Kṛṣṇa consciousness movement is teaching the whole world this central point, and because we are not polluting the theme of *Bhagavad-gītā As It Is*, anyone seriously interested in deriving benefit by studying the *Bhagavad-gītā* must take help from the Kṛṣṇa consciousness movement for practical understanding of *Bhagavad-gītā* under the direct guidance of the Lord. We hope, therefore, that people will derive the greatest benefit by studying *Bhagavad-gītā As It Is* as we have presented it here, and if even one man becomes a pure devotee of the Lord, we shall consider our attempt a success.

A. C. Bhaktivedanta Swami
12 May 1971
Sydney, Australia

Source: Preface. *Bhagavad-gītā As It Is*. by Swami Prabhupada: https://vedabase.io/en/library/bg/preface/. © 2005–2012 The Bhaktivedanta Book Trust International. All rights reserved.

ISIS

ORIGINS AND BACKGROUND

ISIS or ISIL, which stand, respectively, for the Islamic State in Iraq and Syria or the Islamic State of Iraq and Levant, often known simply as "the Islamic State," is a Salafist group that blends nationalistic and apocalyptic aims with its practice of lesser, or defensive, jihad. Similar to other Salafist groups, such as al-Qaeda, ISIS believes that Western imperialism has ushered the world, and most Muslims, into a state of apostasy. Only by reclaiming both political and geographical territory can the world return to its godly, Sunni Muslim state. However, ISIS differentiates itself from many groups who see the expansion of Muslim society as an end in itself; for members of ISIS, the creation of a true Islamic State will precipitate the long-awaited apocalypse as predicted in the Qur'an.

In 1999, Abu Musab al-Zarqawi, a Salafist from Jordan, founded Jama'at al-Tawhid wa-al-Jihad (translated as The Organization of Monotheism and Jihad), in response to the U.S. presence in the Middle East. Following the advent of the Iraq War in 2003, Jam'at al-Tawhid began carrying out suicide bombings as a means of destabilizing the territory and beginning the process of reestablishing an Islamic caliphate. Through these efforts and by joining forces with various Iraqi insurgent groups, the group formally declared itself the Islamic State of Iraq (later adding "in Syria" and/or "in Levant"). Mistakenly, reports have often concluded that ISIS arose from al-Qaeda, given that Jam'at al-Tawhid was the precursor to an al-Qaeda affiliate known as al-Qaeda in Iraq. Al-Zarqawi also pledged a loath of loyalty to Osama bin Laden in 2004. Despite these early ties, ISIS and al-Qaeda distanced themselves from each other due to differences in their goals and al-Qaeda's assessment that ISIS was inflexible and too violent in its methods. It was the leader of the group, Abu Bakr al-Baghdadi (1971–2019), who precipitated the split between the two organizations in 2014.

IDEOLOGY AND AIMS

ISIS members adhere to a fundamentalist variety of Sunni Islam, which separates the Muslim world into a small group of devoted believers (themselves) and the apostate masses. Central to their Salafist worldview is the belief that they must restore the caliphate, which is a theocratic form of government led by a caliph, who is both the religious and political head of a given region. The last caliphate ended in 1918 with the fall of the Ottoman Empire, an event that precipitated the rise of Salafism and Islamic fundamentalism in response to this sudden loss of religious and political primacy. Those in ISIS believe that this caliphate must cover a very specific geographic area, most notably in Iraq and Syria, which corresponds to the original caliphate under Muhammad and his earliest successors. Though the caliphate will exist physically within certain borders, members of ISIS believe that its authority will extend across the globe, ruling not only Muslims but all citizens under a worldwide government premised on its interpretation of the Qur'an and sharia (religious law).

ISIS is a millennialist group, meaning that they believe in an imminent apocalypse. In fact, members of ISIS believe that the restoration of the caliphate will precipitate events prophesied in the Qur'an regarding the end of the world. Not only must the caliphate be geographically complete, but all Muslims living under the caliphate must be living lives of perfect devotion. This desire to create perfect, Sunni order has led ISIS, in particular, to persecute Shi'a Muslims (most notably in Syria) and to employ violence as a general means of "purifying" the world. Hearkening back to earlier Islamic caliphates, ISIS maintains that Christians who agree to pay a tax called "jizya," will be tolerated and allowed to practice their religion. This desire to restore the world to an earlier, pristine time is common among millennialist groups.

ISIS TODAY AND TOMORROW

Unlike other groups whose recruitment processes are shrouded in mystery, ISIS has been quite open in its use of social media and the internet as a means of attracting new members. When websites are swiftly shut down and seized, new sites appear in their place. Thus, despite a desire to recreate the caliphate of the past, ISIS is thoroughly modern in many of its methods and its willingness to adapt to modern techniques of communication and dissemination. Though constant skirmishes and a fluid membership base make it difficult to calculate the number of ISIS members, in 2015 it was estimated that there were between twenty thousand and thirty-two thousand active ISIS members around the globe.

Beyond providing a new face in the war on terror, the impact of ISIS is most directly seen in two ways: in its advances and losses in Syria and Iraq and in its perpetration of terrorist attacks, primarily in Europe and North America. As of 2018, ISIS has lost much of the territory it gained in Iraq, with the Iraqi government declaring victory after regaining Kabul. Yet, ISIS has not declared defeat, nor does it rest on efforts in the Middle East to sustain its goals. In recent years, ISIS has taken credit for many assaults on Western countries. Some, such as the 2015 Paris attacks, represented a coordinated attack by multiple ISIS operatives, whereas others, such as van attacks in Canada and the United States, are undertaken by individuals and appear more random in nature. The possibility of smaller, "lone wolf" attacks differs from groups like al-Qaeda, which favors larger, sustained efforts against the West and within majority-Muslim countries. In this way, ISIS persists in its efforts, working toward the world to come.

See also: Al-Qaeda; Apocalypticism in New Religious Movements; Millennialism; New Religions on/and the Internet; Salafism; Violence and New Religious Movements.

Further Reading

Byman, Daniel. 2015. *Al Qaeda, the Islamic State, and the Global Jihadist Movement: What Everyone Needs to Know.* New York; Oxford: Oxford University Press.

Gerges, Fawaz. 2016. *ISIS: A History.* Princeton, NJ: Princeton University Press.

Lister, Charles R. 2015. *The Syrian Jihad: Al-Qaeda, the Islamic State and the Evolution of an Insurgency.* New York; Oxford: Oxford University Press.

Japanese New Religious Movements

Since the early nineteenth century, Japan has seen the rise of so many new religious movements that one observer used the evocative phrase "the rush hour of the gods" to describe the proliferation of new groups. The religious landscape of Japan has long been dominated by Shintō and Buddhism, with individuals drawing from both traditions in their religious practice. New religions have drawn on both traditions and other sources of inspiration and, with few exceptions, do not make exclusive claims on individuals' affiliations.

Some observers have drawn distinctions between new religions, which originated in the period from the early nineteenth century through 1970, and "new, new" religions, which have developed since 1970. Others have distinguished four phases in the manifestation of new religions: nineteenth century, post–World War I, post–World War II (WWII), and post–1970, with a noticeable diminishment of activity after 1995. Both forms of rough categorization remain in use.

New religions in Japan, as elsewhere, are very rarely wholly new. They combine traditional elements with innovative ones, frequently based on the claims of their founders to extraordinary experiences. In fact, charismatic leadership is a prominent element in many new Japanese religions, along with a focus on the transformation of the self and the world, often through healing. Like other new religions, those in Japan have also codified their founders' teachings into texts that serve as scriptures for their movements. New religions in Japan typically endorse conservative, traditional values and focus on improving the situations of their followers in this world through addressing personal problems.

In addition to spawning its own new religious movements, Japan, particularly in the post–World War II period, has welcomed new religions from abroad. They include the Theosophical Society, the Baha'is, the Jehovah's Witnesses, and the Rajneesh (Osho) movement, among others. The Unification Church, which originated in Korea, has had a particularly strong presence in Japan virtually since its beginning. Japanese new religions have sought new members in diasporic communities in Brazil, the United States, and Peru, for example. Few of them, however, have succeeded in attracting a substantial non-Japanese clientele. Japan is thus fully involved in the global flow of people, goods, and ideas that has been accelerated by contemporary technologies. A few examples will give a brief introduction to the richness of Japanese new religions.

TENRIKYŌ

Founded in the nineteenth century after a farmer's wife, Nakayama Miki (1798–1887), began to receive revelations in 1838, Tenrikyō today claims over one million members worldwide (see www.tenrikyo.or.jp/eng/). The revelations were attributed to Tenri-Ō-no-Mikoto, "God the Parent." They identified Nakayama Miki, who had been a practitioner of Jodo Shin, or Pure Land, Buddhism, as the "Shrine of God" and declared that she would serve as a divine model for humanity and teach individuals how to provide healing.

Tenrikyō teaches that humans were created to lead joyous lives and that blessings come to humans according to how they use their minds. The Tenrikyō website declares that God wants to save all humans and that because the universe is the body of God, the world is filled with God the Parent's work. It is essential for individuals, therefore, to rid themselves of the "dusts of the mind," such as hatred, anger, and greed, because they can affect both one's present life and the conditions of one's rebirth. Thus, purifying one's thought aligns an individual with God the Parent's intentions and leads to living a joyous life.

Nakayama Miki also received divine instructions for the construction of a place for religious services and for the distinctive songs, dances, and hand gestures that in Tenrikyō rituals symbolize elements of divine reality. In 1875, she identified a place known as Jiba as the location where God created humans. It is located at the center of the main sanctuary of the Tenrikyō headquarters in Nara, Japan. The core ritual of Tenrikyō is performed around Jiba and members make pilgrimages to visit it.

During the nineteenth century, Tenrikyō struggled to achieve official recognition as a religious group. In 1908 Tenrikyō was formally recognized as a part of Shintō and the group experienced a growth in membership over the next decade. In the period leading up to WWII, however, the group again experienced official oppression, but it reconstituted itself in the postwar period. Accomplishments of the postwar period include the establishment of Tenri University in 1949, the ongoing publication of Tenrikyō's doctrinal and scriptural texts, substantial building projects, and engagement in interfaith dialogues with the Pontifical Gregorian University in Rome.

SOKA GAKKAI

Like Tenrikyō, Soka Gakkai is a lay Buddhist organization. It traces its lineage, however, to the Japanese Buddhist priest Nichiren Daishonin (1222–1282). Soka Gakkai grew out of an educational reform organization founded in 1930, the Soka Kyoiku Gakkai, or the Educational Society for the Creation of Value, by Tsunesaburō Makiguchi (1871–1944) and Josei Toda (1900–1958). Both were imprisoned during WWII for their opposition to observing the state religion, and Makiguchi died there. After the war, Toda, who had experienced a religious awakening while reading the Lotus Sutra in prison, turned the group into a religious organization, Soka Gakkai, of which he became president in 1951.

Acting on the conviction that Nichiren Buddhism is the only true religion, Toda urged his followers to undertake an extraordinary missionary effort. It succeeded and by the end of the 1950s Soka Gakkai claimed more than a million members.

The central practice of Soka Gakkai is chanting praise to the Lotus Sutra while focusing on a scroll called a *gohonzon*, which replicates one made by Nichiren himself. Through chanting individuals are supposed to recognize their own Buddha nature and cultivate the qualities of compassion and wisdom. Since Soka Gakkai teaches that the world is in the declining stage of the Buddha's dharma, spreading the message remains an important task for members. Due to its relatively simple ritual practice and the portability of its central ritual object, Soka Gakkai has proved more adaptable to different contexts throughout the world than some other Japanese new religions and has attracted practitioners beyond Japanese ex-patriots in Europe and North America, for example.

AGONSHŪ

The importance of healing in Japanese new religions is evident in the origins of Agonshū, which was established in 1978. The founder of Agonshū, Tsutsumi Masao (1921–2016) suffered physical maladies as a young man and was unable to serve in the Japanese army during WWII. He aimlessly turned to petty crime and was imprisoned in 1953 for the illegal manufacture of alcohol. After a suicide attempt in 1954, he claimed to have been saved by the bodhisattva of compassion, Kannon. He soon founded Kannon Jikeikai, changed his name to Kiriyama Seiyū in 1955, and began to practice asceticism. In 1970, Kiriyama received another communication from Kannon, in which he was told that he had "cut his karma," or escaped its negative effects.

Also in 1970, Kiriyama was instructed to hold the first "Star Festival" near Mount Fuji, a central activity of which was the fire ritual. That ritual involved individuals writing prayers on sticks, which were then put into the fire to be consumed. The prayer offerings were designed to pacify and potentially liberate the unhappy spirits of the dead. As Agonshū developed, the focus narrowed to those who had died in WWII and then, as the movement took a nationalist turn in Kiriyama's later years, to the spirits of Japanese who had died in the war. Kiriyama performed fire rituals throughout the world, including important WWII sites like Palau, New York, Paris, the site of the Auschwitz concentration camp, and Jerusalem.

By 1978, Kiriyama had dissolved Kannon Jikeikai and started Agonshū. The new organization focused on the teachings of the Āgama sutras and what Kiriyama had learned about esoteric Buddhism. Kiriyama argued that his teachings represented "original" or "complete" Buddhism, and thus constituted the clearest and fullest presentation of the Buddha's dharma yet developed. Rituals undertaken both at home and at festivals focus on the objectives of "cutting" one's karma or freeing oneself from spiritual impediments, pacifying and liberating the spirits of the dead, and achieving happiness in this life and afterwards. Agonshū also provides spiritual counseling for its members to help them achieve those goals and to further the broad objective of promoting world peace.

Kiriyama's position within Agonshū continued to be exalted throughout his lifetime. In 1980 he claimed to have received a message directly from the Buddha Shakyamuni, while at the site of the first Buddhist monastery in India, Sahet Mahet. In 1986, he received a Buddhist relic from the president of Sri Lanka, which his followers interpreted as recognition of Kiriyama's status within worldwide Buddhism. In 1988, he built a new temple at Yamashima, near Kyoto, and designated it the new Sahet Mahet. Eventually, Kiriyama was perceived by his followers to occupy the position of a second Buddha, and places of Agonshū worship included images of him along with images of the Buddha, Kannon, and Shintō deities.

Kiriyama's exaltation has continued after death. Soon after his passing, members of Agonshū claimed to have started to receive spirit messages from the founder. In that way, Kiriyama continues to lead the religion that he founded and to serve as an object of veneration within it.

FROM AGONSHŪ TO AUM SHINRIKYŌ AND BEYOND

Like other new religions everywhere, Agonshū has not avoided controversy. Perhaps most notably it became entangled in the fallout from Aum Shinrikyō's terrorist attack on the Tokyo subway in 1995. Shoko Asahara (1955–2018) had been a member of Agonshū before founding Aum Shinrikyō but left because he felt that Agonshū did not sufficiently emphasize ascetic practices. Aum, of course, notoriously subjected its most committed members to extraordinary bouts of self-denial. When Aum turned to violence in the 1990s, the negative social reaction cast an unflattering light on all Japanese new religious movements by association.

Although Aum's idiosyncratic blend of Buddhist and Christian millennialism held few similarities to the doctrine and beliefs of Agonshū, the exaltation of Asahara within the movement did parallel the treatment of Kiriyama within Agonshū at the same time that it reinforced public stereotypes about the roles of charismatic leaders within new religions.

After the arrests and convictions of Asahara and other Aum leaders for their roles in the subway attack and other crimes, Aum was essentially destroyed. A reformed version of Aum, called Aleph, was established in February 2000. One of Asahara's former lieutenants, Jōyū Fumihiro (1962–), rejoined the group when he was released from prison in 1999. By 2004, Fumihiro and a few others formed a small group within Aleph. In 2007, prompted by a series of visions, they left to form a new religious organization, Hikari no Wa, officially the Circle of Rainbow Light. It rejects Aum's excesses and promises a new spiritual wisdom for the twenty-first century. It aims at the cultivation of one's sacred consciousness in accordance with the models of God, the Buddha, Jesus, and Muhammad.

See also: Aum Shinrikyō; Baháʼí; Charisma and Leadership in New Religious Movements; Globalization and New Religious Movements; Millennialism; New Scriptures and New Religious Movements; Rajneesh/Osho Movement, The; Soka Gakkai; Theosophical

Society, The; Unification Church, The; Watchtower Bible and Tract Society, The (Jehovah's Witnesses).

Further Reading

Hardacre, Helen. 1986. *Kurozumikyō and the New Religions of Japan.* Princeton, NJ: Princeton University Press.

Kasai, Kenta. 2012. "Theosophy and Related Movements in Japan." In Inken Prohl & John K. Nelson, eds., *Handbook of Contemporary Japanese Religions*, pp. 433–458. Leiden: E. J. Brill.

McFarland, H. Neil. 1967. *The Rush Hour of the Gods: A Study of New Religious Movements in Japan.* New York: Macmillan.

Prohl, Inken. 2012. "New Religions in Japan: Adaptations and Transformations in Contemporary Society." In Inken Prohl & John K. Nelson, eds., *Handbook of Contemporary Japanese Religions*, pp. 241–268. Leiden: E. J. Brill.

Reader, Ian. 2015. "Japanese New Religions: An Overview." Available at: www.worldrels.org.

Susumu, Shimazono, & Tim Graf. 2012. "The Rise of the New Spirituality." In Inken Prohl & John K. Nelson, eds., *Handbook of Contemporary Japanese Religions*, pp. 459–486. Leiden: E. J. Brill.

Jediism

Religions are not always born in the most serious circumstances; sometimes a pronounced element of play is involved. The contemporary, online religion of Jediism, named for the Jedi Order in the widely viewed *Star Wars* films, grew out of e-mail campaigns to have individuals fill in "Jedi" as their religion in the 2001 and 2011 British Commonwealth Censuses. In 2001, nearly 400,000 people in the United Kingdom identified as Jedi as well as some 71,000 Australians and another 53,000 New Zealanders. In 2011, more than 175,000 people in the United Kingdom designated themselves as Jedi.

In general, observers saw those events as successful, large-scale pranks, but there do appear to be some respondents whose identification of themselves as Jedi expressed a real religious yearning. The movement from a group of fans to actual followers of Jediism took place over time, abetted by the development of the internet as a global way of storing and sharing information. By the end of the 1990s, clusters of individuals had moved beyond participating in role-playing games online to becoming virtual communities with a common focus on Jediism as a religious or spiritual philosophy and mode of practice.

Like other religions that exist solely or primarily online, Jediism has no central authority and no overarching organizational structure. Accordingly, there are multiple manifestations of Jediism and, as with many phenomena online, they can frequently pass into and out of existence. But while individual websites may be ephemeral, the phenomenon of Jediism persists and has begun to have effects in real life.

Jedi groups all draw on the imagined universe of the *Star Wars* films and their various spinoffs, but some Jedi groups also emphasize the similarities between their religious worldviews and those of Daoism and other Eastern religions. At the heart of Jediism is the concept of "the Force," which the Temple of the Jedi Order (see www.templeofthejediorder.org/doctrine-of-the-order), for example, describes as a ubiquitous and metaphysical power that is the underlying fundamental nature of the universe.

The Temple of the Jedi Order, which achieved official recognition of its status as a religion in Texas at the end of 2005, has developed an elaborate presentation of its doctrine. The Temple's doctrine includes a statement of Jedi beliefs (which begins with "Jedi believe: In the Force, and the inherent worth of all life within it"); the three main tenets of focus, knowledge, and wisdom; a code that expresses the Jedi view of the world; a creed modeled on a prayer of St. Francis Assisi; and lists of sixteen teachings and twenty-one maxims. The overall impression created by such expressions of doctrine is of a benevolent group dedicated, as the final statement in the list of teachings has it, to self-improvement and helping others.

Several online Jedi sites offer guided initiations into the Jedi order. The Temple of the Jedi Force (www.templeofthejediforce.org), for example, advises those interested first to make an introductory post to its website, requesting tutelage. A Jedi Master then reviews the request and directs the potential initiate to begin study of the Jedi doctrine and to record the results in a personal journal. The website also refers interested parties to an elaborate training manual that guides their progress through ascending ranks of initiation. As their progress continues, initiates gain greater access to the various forums on the website.

Jediism is not without foundation in the *Star Wars* universe. Although George Lucas, the director who did so much to create the cosmology in which the films unfold, has denied trying to form a new religion, he has admitted that he intended to tell a mythic story of a hero's journey that had significant religious and spiritual resonances. Thus, individuals who take religious meanings from the films have some basis for their efforts. The doctrinal and ritual structures that proponents of Jediism have developed indicate a serious intent, despite the frivolous beginnings of their religion.

See also: Anamadim; Dudeism; New Religions on/and the Internet.

Further Reading
Davidsen, Marcus Altena. 2017. "The Jedi Community: History and Folklore of a Fiction-Based Religion." *New Directions in Folklore* 15: 7–49.
Kosnáč, Pavel. 2017. "Pop Culture—A New Source of Spirituality?" In Eugene V. Gallagher, ed., *Visioning New and Minority Religions: Projecting the Future*, pp. 145–155. New York: Routledge.
Malaquais, Laurent, dir. 2017. *American Jedi: A Fan's Journey to Knighthood*. Freestyle Digital Media.
McCormick, Debbie 2012. "The Sanctification of Star Wars: From Fans to Followers." In Adam Possamai, ed. *Handbook of Hyper-Real Religion*, pp. 165–184. Leiden: E. J. Brill.

Jews for Jesus

Historically and traditionally, the primary difference between Christians and Jews is a simple one: Christians believe that Jesus of Nazareth was the messiah predicted in the Hebrew Bible and Jews do not. Thus, on the surface, being a "Jew for

Jesus" seems paradoxical, if not impossible. And yet there are those who claim to be exactly that.

ORIGINS AND HISTORY

The name, however, is somewhat deceiving. The movement is a form of Messianic Judaism or a Christian missionary movement aimed at converting Jews to a particular, some would say fundamentalist, version of Christianity. Its founder, Martin "Moishe" Rosen (1932–2010) was born to Jewish parents, but he and his wife Ceil converted to Christianity in the 1950s. Shortly after graduating from college, he was ordained a Baptist minister and joined the American Board of Mission to the Jews (now Chosen People Ministries). In this capacity, he presided over several "Hebrew Christian" or Messianic Jewish congregations—those that combine traditionally Christian beliefs with aspects of Jewish liturgical practice.

In 1970, Rosen founded Hineni (a Hebrew word translated as "Here I Am") Ministries, which would become Jews for Jesus in 1973. The movement is headquartered in San Francisco, though it has branches in thirteen countries around the world. Rosen served as director of the group until he stepped down in 1996; David Brickner succeeded him and continues to serve as director today. There are around fifty thousand people who identify as members of Jews for Jesus, mainly in the United States.

BELIEFS AND PRACTICES

Their website (www.jewsforjesus.org) states that Jews for Jesus "reject the stereotype that Jewish people cannot be followers of Jesus" and that they are "100 percent Jewish and 100 percent Christian," reflecting the self-proclaimed hybridity of the movement. Overall, most of the beliefs derive from Christianity, while many of the practices are Jewish, albeit with some modifications.

Most crucial to the belief system of Jews for Jesus is that Jesus is the Messiah; he is also considered divine and part of the triune God (the Trinity). Deviating further from traditional Jewish theology, Jews for Jesus believe that salvation comes through belief in Jesus alone and that a literal hell awaits those who are not saved in Christ. Jews for Jesus are Biblicist, meaning they hold the Bible to be the central religious authority. They are also traditionally fundamentalist in their view of the Bible, seeing both the Old (Hebrew Bible) and New Testament as verbally inspired and without error. Traditionally, Jews are as reliant on the Talmud or traditional rabbinic literature as they are on the Bible; for Jews for Jesus, the Bible takes precedent and only those extra-biblical Jewish texts that find support in the Bible are accepted.

The conversion of Jews during the "Last Days" is a biblically significant event. In certain passages of the Bible, such as Revelation 7:4, there will be certain number of Jews who will convert to Christianity and prophesy on behalf of Christ; this event will then precipitate others, which will usher in Christ's millennial reign. Thus, Messianic Jewish groups such as Jews for Jesus are almost always millennialist and focused on Christ's Second Coming in their message. Nonetheless, Jews for Jesus maintain that a Jew need not "convert" to be a follower of Christ; if a person is Jewish by birth and chooses to believe in Christ, then she or he is effectively a Jew for Jesus without undergoing a formal conversion process.

Alongside these Christian positions, Jews for Jesus practice a wide array of Jewish customs and rituals. They follow the Jewish liturgical calendar, but with some notable additions. Traditional holidays such as Passover, Yom Kippur, and Purim are celebrated, as well as Christmas, Chrismukkah (a hybrid of Hannukah and Christmas Eve), and Easter. Jews for Jesus practice Shabbat, which takes place from sundown on Friday through sundown on Saturday. Both weekly and annual services take place in "Messianic synagogues," which feature both Christian and Jewish elements, such as the cross and the ark, respectively. Hebrew is spoken at services, as is English, particularly when reading from the New Testament. Jews for Jesus also participate in traditional Jewish lifecycle practices, such as the Naming ceremony, Bris, and Bar/Bat Mitzvah; each service reflects the theological language of Messianic Judaism and traditional Judaism.

One primary practice that deviates from traditional Judaism is proselytization. Rosen founded the movement as a ministry to Jews, thus much of the work performed by its members is missionary in nature, primarily through the distribution of movement literature. Jews are traditionally nonevangelizing, thus this is again reflective of the Christian side of the movement.

CONTROVERSY AND CULTURE

Unsurprisingly, Jews, Christians, and Muslims have criticized Jews for Jesus. Jews from all major denominations have called Jews for Jesus a movement of "spiritual deception" that employs the word Jew as a means to lure Jews into a belief system that is fundamentally Christian in nature. In particular, mainstream Jews take umbrage at the fact that Jewish rituals are used as conversion tools and are mixed with Christian beliefs. They deny outright the fact that this is a Jewish group, despite the statements of its founder and the protests of its members.

Christians and Muslims have critiqued the movement for its evangelistic focus on Jews, believing that Jews have the right to practice their faith unmolested. Several Christian denominations and interfaith initiatives have issued statements against proselytization efforts toward Jews. Jews for Jesus has been the target of countermissionary groups, such as "Jews for Judaism" (www.jewsforjudaism.org), which focus their energies at debunking Hebrew Christianity. As a result, members of Jews for Jesus have expressed concern that their beliefs are being invalidated and their free expression violated.

See also: Messianic Judaism; Messianism and New Religious Movements; Millennialism.

Further Reading
Ariel, Yaakov. 2000. *Evangelizing the Chosen People: Missions to Jews in America, 1800–2000*. Chapel Hill: University of North Carolina Press.

Chyrssides, George D. 2011. "Jews for Jesus." In *Historical Dictionary of New Religious Movements*. Lanham, MD: Scarecrow Press.

Rosen, Ruth. 1987. *Jesus for Jews*. San Francisco, CA: Purple Pomegranate Productions.

Jones, Rev. Jim (1931–1978)

Jim Jones is notorious for leading more than nine hundred people in a murder-suicide at the Peoples Temple Agricultural Mission in Jonestown, Guyana on November 18–19, 1978. Jones has been vilified as the deranged head of a destructive cult. He has also been compared to Hitler and other mass murderers and put forward as a paramount example of a cult leader. Jones has been so prominent in the contemporary popular discussion of "dangerous cults" that a clear sense of who he was, what he taught, and how he and his followers came to their fateful decisions in Guyana has become difficult to achieve.

EARLY LIFE

James Warren Jones was born in Crete, Indiana, on a small farm on May 13, 1931. His family moved to nearby Lynn when Jones began school. Some of Jones's most prominent personality traits as the leader of Peoples Temple, the group that grew out of his work as a pastor in Indianapolis in the early 1950s, were all in evidence during his early years and were incubated in his family, particularly in his relationship with his mother. They included his love of dramatic ritual performances, tendencies toward paranoia and fantasy, claims to have special powers, fascination with sex, and preaching of racial equality.

During his time in grade school, Jones attended a local congregation of the Church of the Nazarene with a neighbor, Myrtle Kennedy. By the time he was in high school, Jones was occasionally traveling to nearby Richmond, Indiana, to preach, especially to African Americans in that city's poorer districts. As his preaching in Richmond shows, Jones took an early interest not only in religion but also in racial equality, which set him at odds with many citizens of Indiana in the 1950s. A concern for those on the margins of U.S. society characterized Jones throughout his life.

INDIANA YEARS

Jones married Marceline Baldwin on June 12, 1949. By 1951, the new couple moved to Indianapolis, where Jones worked a variety of odd jobs and Marceline worked as a nurse. They eventually started their own "rainbow family," including adopted African American and Korean children.

Jones became a student pastor at Somerset Methodist Church. Also in the early 1950s, Jones attended many religious revivals. Those meetings nurtured his preaching style and developed his interest in performing dramatic "healings" that might attract believers to his ministry.

By 1954, Jones started his own church, Community Unity, ministering primarily to the disenfranchised African American population of Indianapolis. Community Unity was briefly known as Wings of Deliverance, but, with the purchase of its own building, became known as Peoples Temple (with no apostrophe), emphasizing its openness to all. In 1960, Peoples Temple formally became part of the Disciples of Christ denomination and Jones was ordained a Disciples minister in 1964, a status he never relinquished.

By the time that Jones started Peoples Temple, his personal theology had already begun to push the boundaries of mainstream Christianity. He was sympathetic to the egalitarian goals of communism and socialism and identified them with the portrait of the early Christian community in Acts 2:44 where the believers were said to hold "all things in common" (see Acts 4:32). In Peoples Temple, Jones strove to address not only the spiritual but also the practical needs of his congregation, including things as mundane as dealing with the electric company. Jones's vision of "apostolic socialism" had its roots in his reading of both the contemporary situation and the New Testament.

Jones's concern with the social welfare of a population that was regularly discriminated against also led him to question the good faith of Christians who ignored the plight of the poor. In a more radical move, he also began to question the God who would allow such conditions to persist. Throughout the rest of his life Jones would develop and extend that critique of the biblical creator whom he came to identify as a mere "Sky God."

Beginning in 1956, Jones had several meetings with the founder of the International Peace Mission, known as Father Divine. Jones was intrigued by all that Father Divine had done for African Americans and probably more so by the extraordinary status that Father Divine had among his followers, who recognized him as God in the flesh. Jones was clearly angling to merge Father Divine's followers with his own and perhaps to present himself as the reincarnation of Father Divine after his death. Jones's efforts, however, only produced a few converts for Peoples Temple. But Jones did borrow from Father Divine the custom of having his followers address him as "Father" or even "Dad."

In the 1960s, Jones became preoccupied with the possibility of a nuclear holocaust, even at one point predicting that it would happen on July 15, 1967. During the 1960s, he briefly moved to Belo Horizonte, Brazil, perhaps as a safe haven from the impending destruction. But he returned to Indiana, only to initiate a move with around one hundred followers to Ukiah, California, in the summer of 1965.

IN CALIFORNIA

Both Jones's message and the demographics of his followers changed when Peoples Temple moved to California and extended its reach into the Bay Area and Los Angeles. The members who joined in California were whiter, better educated, and more well off. Jones adjusted his message to focus his critique on the unjust actions of the government; the focus on immediate practical help for his congregants diminished. In addition, Jones's critique of the Sky God of the Bible also came to include the idea that Jones himself was now animated by the same spirit that once inspired Jesus. Jones's healings also faded from prominence in California as Peoples Temple moved further away from its Christian roots. Jones kept up a hectic pace in promoting Peoples Temple and in the early 1970s began relying on drugs both to keep up his energy and to help him sleep.

With the added income from some of its new members, Peoples Temple was able to extend the services that it provided for the less fortunate. As he had in Indiana, where he was appointed director of the Indianapolis Human Rights Commission in 1961, Jones gained considerable recognition for Peoples Temple's philanthropy. His support was courted by George Moscone in the San Francisco mayoral election of 1975, which Moscone won in a runoff. Jones was eventually rewarded with a seat on the San Francisco Housing Authority. But the losing candidate, John Barbagelata, claimed that members of Peoples Temple had voted illegally.

His increased prominence earned Jones lavish praise from some, like political operative and State Assemblyman Willie Brown. But others developed a more critical perspective. In 1972, Lester Kinsolving published an exposé in the *San Francisco Examiner*. Among other things, he detailed Jones's shocking contempt for the creator God of the Christian Bible. Jones had members counter the negative press, but his image began to fray.

The next press salvo against Jones came in 1977. A reporter from the *San Francisco Chronicle*, Marshall Kilduff, and a writer for *New West* magazine, Phil Tracy, published a devastating article that called for the investigation of Jones for financial fraud, physical abuse of Peoples Temple members, and harassment of former members. Weeks before the appearance of the August edition of the magazine, Jones left San Francisco for Guyana.

JONESTOWN

In 1974, Jones had leased three thousand acres in the dense jungle of northeast Guyana to establish the Peoples Temple Agricultural Mission. In mid-1974, volunteers had begun to hack a space for the utopian settlement out of the unforgiving vegetation. When Jones left California, around one thousand members of Peoples Temple soon followed him to Jonestown. Jones's preaching became even less focused on Christianity as he touted the precarious settlement as a socialist utopia.

Fueled by his increasing drug use, negative press, and also a bitter custody dispute over a child he had fathered with one of the members, Jones's anxiety about the future of Jonestown increased. He repeatedly portrayed Jonestown as being under siege and encouraged residents to be willing to lay down their lives for the cause. When a group known as the Concerned Relatives prompted an onsite visit by Representative Leo Ryan (D-CA), during which a handful of members expressed their desire to leave Jonestown, Jones saw his community crumbling from external pressures and internal betrayals. Jones ordered a lethal attack on

Ryan and then led the members of Jonestown in what he identified as an act of "revolutionary suicide." Jones saw the dramatic dissolution of his community as a final testament to the values it espoused, but in the wake of the mass deaths few others saw it that way.

See also: International Peace Mission Movement; Millennialism; Peoples Temple.

Further Reading

Chidester, David. 2003. *Salvation and Suicide: Jim Jones, the Peoples Temple, and Jonestown*, rev. ed. Bloomington: Indiana University Press.

Guinn, Jeff. 2017. *The Road to Jonestown: Jim Jones and Peoples Temple*. New York: Simon & Schuster.

Moore, Rebecca. 2009. *Understanding Jonestown and Peoples Temple*. Westport, CT: Praeger.

Judge, William Quan (1851–1896)

Often overshadowed by his larger than life cofounders, Helena Petrovna Blavatsky (1831–1891) and Henry Steel Olcott (1832–1907), William Quan Judge brought necessary organizational skill to the Theosophical Society. Judge was born in Dublin but immigrated to the United States in 1864. In his early twenties, he passed the New York bar exam, thereafter specializing in trade law.

Though raised a Methodist, Judge showed early interest in occult religious ideas, particularly those of Asian origin. The beginning of his law career coincided with his attendance at various occult, often Spiritualist, religious circles. It was in this context that he met Blavatsky and Olcott. In 1875, the three of them founded the Theosophical Society based on the teachings of Theosophy. Theosophy was a religious system that argued that human beings could communicate with the Great Masters or Mahatmas, higher beings who occasionally returned to earth in various avatars to help humanity evolve spiritually.

While Blavatsky and Olcott were seen as the spiritual leaders of the Theosophical Society, it was Judge who shouldered the majority of administrative duties. When Blavatsky and Olcott left New York for India in 1878, the management of the American branch of the Society was left to Judge. This was a difficult task, first because Judge also found reason to travel abroad until 1885 and, second, because he did not claim to be a medium in the way of Blavatsky, he could not rely on divine communication or revelation to retain old members or to attract new converts. What he lacked in charismatic authority, however, he made up for in organizational and literary ability.

His most important contribution to the Theosophical Society was the founding of *The Path*, Theosophy's first magazine, which became the primary means of disseminating information about the Society and in keeping the various Theosophical "lodges" connected with one another. He also wrote *The Ocean of Theosophy*, which still acts as a foundational text to American Theosophists. Whereas Blavatsky's writings were often filled with complicated theological language and mystical flights, Judge wrote plainly and simply about the beliefs of Theosophy.

By 1895, Judge could count six thousand active members of the Society and over one hundred lodges.

Following Blavatsky's death, Judge sparred with Olcott and new leader, Annie Besant (1847–1933) about certain interpretations of the Mahatmas' teachings. This prompted a split between the Indian (Adyar) and American branches of Theosophy. The American branch, known simply as the Theosophical Society, is the largest sect of Theosophy, due in great part to the work of Judge, who died suddenly in 1896.

See also: Blavatsky, Helena Petrovna (1831–1891); Occultism and Esotericism; Olcott, Henry Steel (1832–1907); Spiritualism; Theosophical Society, The; Theosophy.

Further Reading

Judge, William Q., & Dara Eklund. 1893. *The Ocean of Theosophy.* London: Theosophical Publishing Society.

Judge, William Q., & Dara Eklund. 2009–2011. *Echoes of the Orient: The Writings of William Quan Judge.* 4 Volumes. Pasadena, CA: Theosophical University Press.

Lavoie, Jeffrey D. 2012. *The Theosophical Society: The History of a Spiritualist Movement.* Boca Raton, FL: BrownWalker Press.

Kabbalah

Depending upon who you ask, Kabbalah is either very old or very new, open to an elite few or open to all who are interested, a mystical branch of Judaism or a mystical movement for the modern religious seeker. Both the ancient branch of Judaism known as Kabbalah and the twentieth-century American institution the Kabbalah Centre claim access to special, spiritual knowledge that, when mastered, will provide its recipients with a new perspective on the world and their places in it. Yet, the path and method for arriving at such knowledge as well as the various interpretations of that knowledge diverge significantly, causing "traditional" Kabbalists, or *Mekubals*, to rail against the New Age adaptation of Kabbalah by the Kabbalah Centre and its acolytes.

ORIGINS AND HISTORY

Kabbalah means "corresponding or received tradition," which reflects the traditional Jewish understanding of Kabbalah as a discipline for extracting mystical meaning from Hebrew texts, namely, the Tanakh and the Talmud. It also designates the mystical knowledge itself. Though Kabbalah is often said to comprise part of the Oral Torah given to Moses by God on Mount Sinai, most scholars date the beginning of Kabbalah to the appearance of the Zohar in the thirteenth century in Spain. Published by Rabbi Moses de Leon (1240–1305), the Zohar was attributed to a second-century rabbi named Rabbi Shimon bar Yochai (?–160); that the text was written in Aramaic seemed to confirm its authenticity as a text written during the early Rabbinic period. The Zohar is made up of several books, each providing commentary on the Torah (the Five Books of Moses). The commentary contained four different levels of biblical interpretation: *Peshat* (the literal meaning), *Remez* (the allegorical meaning), *Derash* (the rabbinic meaning), and *Sod* (the esoteric or hidden meaning). Of the four exegetical methods, the Zohar emphasized Sod as the most important, since it revealed mystical knowledge of God, the universe, the human soul, among other things.

Following the appearance of the Zohar, mystical Jewish practice began to coalesce around the text. Soon thereafter, the term "Kabbalah" became associated most regularly with those teachings derived from the Zohar. However, it was Rabbi Isaac Luria (1534–1572) who streamlined the knowledge and practice of Kabbalah, which is now known as Lurianic Kabbalah. With the posthumous publication of Luria's Kabbalist teachings, most notably *Etz Chayim* ("The Tree of Life"), by

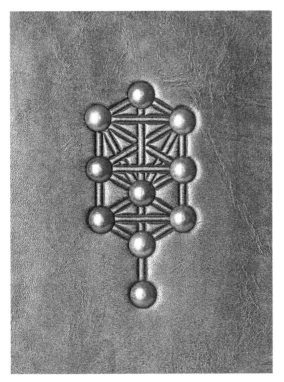

Kabbalah is a branch of Judaism that derives its knowledge from a mystical reading of the major Hebrew texts. The tree of life, pictured here, symbolizes the creation of the universe and the past, present, and future spiritual progression of humanity. The symbol is claimed by both the "traditional" Kabbalists, Mekubal, and those who belong to the modern Kabbalah Center. (Alexlibris/Dreamstime.com)

several of his former students, Luria cemented his status as father of modern Kabbalah and one of the greatest Jewish mystics in history. Not only that, but the study of Kabbalah achieved a celebrated status, open to only the most experienced and well-intentioned Rabbis and Talmudic scholars. Since the information found in the Zohar was so complex, even dangerous, it was crucial that only an elite group could access it; otherwise, Kabbalah could be misinterpreted, misused, or corrupted. Soon there were yeshivas (Orthodox Jewish rabbinical schools) devoted solely to the study of the Zohar and Kabbalah.

Over time, with the proliferation of Kabbalist schools and the increasing availability of the Zohar and Kabbalist teachings, it became harder to regulate who was teaching Kabbalah—and who was learning it. The diffusion of Kabbalist ideas created a context where different versions of Kabbalah could coexist or conflict.

BELIEFS AND PRACTICES

There are multiple branches of Jewish Kabbalah as well as several branches of non-Jewish Kabbalah that emerged alongside but independent of the Jewish tradition. The most famous and popular is Lurianic Kabbalah, which sought deeper knowledge of God and his mystical divine realm. Contemporaneous to Lurianic Kabbalah was Ecstatic Kabbalah, often associated with the rise of Hasidism, whose practitioners courted union with God, not simply knowledge of the divine. This branch produced a rich ritual as well as intellectual tradition focused on creating opportunities to merge with the divine. Taking this a step further were those who partook of magical Kabbalah (often called "Practical Kabbalah"), whereby practitioners sought to manipulate and alter both earthly and divine realms through prayer and magical ritual. Though both ecstatic and magical versions of

Kabbalah were looked down upon by Lurianic Kabbalists, they formally shunned the latter. There are also Christian Kabbalah groups and Hermetic Kabbalah groups that also emerged out of a general cultural interest in the Zohar and the notion of a mystical, secret message embedded in the text.

Though the specific beliefs and practices of each branch of Kabbalah vary, at least among the Jewish Kabbalists, there are certain commonalities. Kabbalists envision a rich cosmological universe in which God exists in two forms—as a transcendent, incomprehensible being and as a manifested persona that interacts with humanity. This persona is manifested in ten emanations known as Sefirot; there are also evil spiritual entities, called Kelipot, which inhabit an evil realm, the Sitra Achra, and oppose the Sefirot. This posits an alternate theory regarding the origin of evil, wherein Sitra Achra is a necessary contrast to God and the heavenly realm and was created apart from God. Thus, Kabbalists believe in multiple spiritual realms, proceeding from the highest, where the transcendent God resides, and descending down to earth and to the lowest realm of evil. Human beings exist as echoes of God, spiritual beings in their own right, who through the performance of mitzvoth (commandments) help to create the world anew. Most Kabbalists also believe that the soul has multiple components—a lower, animal soul; a spirit that acts as conscience and moral center; and the higher soul that has knowledge of God.

THE KABBALAH CENTRE AND NEW AGE KABBALAH

The late twentieth and early twenty-first centuries saw the emergence of Kabbalah as a pop cultural phenomenon. When Madonna, followed by a slew of other celebrities, was seen emerging from a "Kabbalah Centre" wearing a red string around her wrist, Kabbalah was catapulted to the status of tabloid fodder. Though the initial craze has died down, one can still purchase Kabbalah "red strings" (which reputedly ward off the evil eye) on Amazon and follow the Kabbalah Centre on twitter. Philip Berg (1927–2013) and Yehuda Tzvi Brandwein (1904–1969) founded the Kabbalah Centre in New York in 1965; the Los Angeles Centre (now headquarters) was founded in 1984 when the movement was formally incorporated as a nonprofit organization and renamed the Kabbalah Centre International. Philip Berg was succeeded by his wife Karen (1942–) and son Michael (1973–) as directors of the Kabbalah Centre; Michael has written extensively on Kabbalah and is now the primary proponent of the New Age Kabbalah promoted by the Kabbalah Centre. He is also renowned as a screenwriter, most notably for the popular *Ice Age* animated films.

Unlike its more selective namesake, the Kabbalah Centre welcomes all and does not require formal membership. However, the Kabbalah Centre purports to disseminate the same information as Lurianic Kabbalah, namely, the teachings of the Zohar. But it maintains that such mystical knowledge is universal and should be made accessible to everyone. Students at the Kabbalah Centre are not required to study the Torah, Talmud, or rabbinical teachings prior to learning Kabbalah and are not expected to know Hebrew. As for the concepts taught, some converge with

Lurianic Kabbalah, such as the existence of Sefirot and Kelipot, whereas others diverge, such as the belief that it is not knowledge of God that is taught, but of God's essence or the "Light."

The Kabbalah Centre, while clearly laying claim to its Jewish roots via the Zohar, also promotes itself as teaching "spirituality for the modern world" (www.kabbalah.com). Many, including celebrities, have been drawn to its promise of ancient wisdom packaged in a New Age form. However, most Jews, particularly Orthodox Jews and Lurianic Kabbalists, have criticized the Kabbalah Centre for peddling a fraudulent form of Kabbalah. The Bergs have been roundly lambasted as money-hungry hucksters who have gotten rich on the backs of credulous religious seekers looking for the next spiritual fad. The Centre has been investigated by the Federal Bureau of Investigation and Internal Revenue Service for financial crimes and has been hit with multiple lawsuits by former practitioners. This is not the first, nor will it be the last time a new religious movement will claim to be an old religion reborn in a shinier guise; nor will it be the last that an old religion has sought to push back against claims to such a lineage. However, whether Kabbalah or the Kabbalah Centre, the desire to unlock secret knowledge, to come closer to the divine, and to achieve personal transformation will continue to appeal to many, Orthodox Jew and Hollywood starlet alike.

See also: Essene Groups; Mysticism; New Age, The; Occultism and Esotericism.

Further Reading

Ariel, David S. 2006. *Kabbalah: The Mystic Quest of Ancient Judaism.* Lanham, MD: Rowman & Littlefield Publishers, Inc.

Berg, Michael. 2002. *The Way: Using the Wisdom of Kabbalah for Spiritual Transformation and Fulfillment.* Hoboken, NJ: John Wiley & Sons.

Myers, Jody. 2007. *Kabbalah and the Spiritual Quest: The Kabbalah Centre in America (Religion, Health, and Healing).* Westport, CT: Praeger.

Scholem, Gershom. 1995. *Zohar: The Book of Splendor: Basic Readings from the Kabbalah.* New York: Schocken Books.

Kardecism (Spiritism)

Kardecism, or Spiritism, differentiates itself from its popular cousin, Spiritualism, as the "scientific" religious alternative to Spiritualism's smoke-and-mirror show. In the mid-nineteenth century, Spiritualism, or the belief that contact was possible between spirits and the living, spread rapidly in Europe and the United States, propelled by the experiences like those of the Fox sisters, Kate (1837–1892) and Margaret (1833–1893). Kate and Margaret were reportedly contacted by spirits, an event that revealed themselves to be mediums. Soon, Spiritualist circles began forming around various mediums, who would lead members or a bereaved client in a ceremony to contact the dead.

French educator Hippolyte Léon Denizard Rivail (1804–1869) was interested in the truth of communication with spirits and began attending Spiritualist séances in the 1850s. At the same time, he also began investigating the effects of Mesmerism, or animal magnetism. With a background in science, Rivail was intrigued by, but also skeptical, of the claims made by Spiritualism and Mesmerism. He began investigating these phenomena, determined to prove (or disprove) them through precise scientific methods. He came to the conclusion that while most Spiritualist and Mesmerist phenomena were the result of human means, spirits did communicate with the living and true mediums did exist.

From these authentic mediums, Rivail gathered knowledge about the truth of the universe, of the realm of spirits and human existence. Writing under the nom de plume, Allen Kardec—a name given to him by a spirit he only called "Truth"—he published his findings in a series of books. Most famous among them was *The Spirits Book* (1857) in which he laid out the principles of Spiritism, which he followed with books devoted to instructing mediums and unpacking the occult truth hidden in the Bible and Christian theology. Though most practitioners of Kardec's doctrines call themselves Spiritists not Kardecists, his works are foundational to the movement and have been translated in as many languages as countries in which Spiritism has emerged.

BELIEFS AND PRACTICES

Kardecism purports to combine science, religion, and philosophy. Its scientific basis comes from the methodical examination and training of mediums. Spiritists believe that spirits are constantly in contact with human beings, but only a select few have the wherewithal to notice; these are mediums. Even for those who have such abilities, their spiritual sensors must be trained and contact with spirits must occur in carefully constructed spaces and along specific guidelines. The effects wrought by the Spirits may vary, from possession to automatic writing to visions of the spirit realm or, in the case of Latin American Spiritism, to physical healing.

From a religious and philosophical standpoint, Spiritism engages the idea that the lower nature, one's human instincts and passions, must be subordinated to the higher nature, that which is instinctively connected to the spirit realm and God. Spiritists maintain that God (or Universal Intelligence) exists and is an eternal, omnipotent, and omniscient being, albeit a distant one. The God of Spiritists is not the historical God of the Bible who has interacted with humanity. Rather, those interactions recorded in books like the Bible were spirits (or lower deities, as understood in some Latin American interpretations) who are still interacting with humanity to help them along the path to spiritual advancement. Spiritists believe in reincarnation or the belief that spirits are born and reborn on earth and in various spiritual realms on a path to achieve perfection. Human beings are simply incarnate spirits. Unlike Hindu belief systems, where a spirit can be reincarnated as a lower life form or with greater spiritual baggage (karma), Spiritists believe that the spirit only progresses forward through each lifecycle. However, there are "intranquil spirits" that are lower on the spectrum of spiritual evolution and can cause turmoil in the lives of human beings.

Spiritist practice varies from society to society, often depending upon the degree to which a particular group has absorbed the religious tendencies of other traditions. Kardec maintained that Spiritists should follow Jesus as an example of a perfect moral life. In fact, beyond the teachings of Kardec and later Spiritist mediums, Christian teachings such as the Bible and particularly the Gospels are employed often by Spiritists as sacred texts. Beyond these general moral guidelines, there is very little formal practice required of Spiritists. Prayer or meditation is recommended as means of focusing the mind and body on messages from the spirit realm; this is the most regular practice for Spiritists. Meetings with mediums, however, are the most intensive of rituals and involve either a collection of experienced mediums communicating with the spirits or an impromptu gathering based on the need of a particular individual.

LEGACY

Institutionally, Kardecism comprises a loose affiliation of Spiritist societies that are concentrated in Europe and North America, but particularly in Latin America. Kardecism has also greatly influenced Cao Dao, a Vietnamese religious movement, founded when three Vietnamese mediums separately claimed to have been visited by Allen Kardec in the early twentieth century.

Kardecism found a permanent, if somewhat reimagined home, in Espiritismo, a creole religion born in Cuba, which spread to Brazil, Puerto Rico, and the United States. Espirtisimo mixed Spiritist, indigenous, and Afro-Caribbean religious influences to create a movement that focuses on contact with or possession by spirits as a means of altering one's external circumstances, particularly through healing. Brazil has one of the largest modern Spiritist movements—counting forty million practitioners—which arose due to the efforts of the Brazilian medium Chico Xavier (1910–2002), who wrote hundreds of books and claimed contact with the deceased relatives of thousands of Brazilians.

See also: Cao Dai; Fox, Kate (1837–1892), and Margaret (1833–1893); Ghosts, the Paranormal, and New Religious Movements; Mesmerism; Occultism and Esotericism; Science, Technology, and New Religious Movements; Spiritualism.

Further Reading

Hess, David J. 2007. *Spirits and Scientists: Ideology, Spiritism, and Brazilian Culture.* University Park: The Pennsylvania State University Press.

Kardec, Allen. 2006 [1857]. *The Spirits Book: The Principles of Spiritism.* New York: Cosimo, Inc.

Kardec, Allen. 2011 [1864]. *The Gospel According to Spiritism.* Miami, FL: Edicei of America.

Kimbangu, Simon (1887–1951)

Born on September 12, 1887, in Nkamba in the Belgian Congo (now the Democratic Republic of Congo), Simon Kimbangu became the founder of one of the largest African-Initiated Churches. Many of the details of Kimbangu's life are embedded in hagiographical accounts that reflect the continuing reverence of his followers. But the general outlines of his career can be identified.

Although his father was a traditional healer, Kimbangu was baptized into the Christian Church in 1915. He later served as a catechist for the Baptist Missionary Society in the area around Nkamba. In 1918, Kimbangu experienced a vision in which Christ informed him that it would be his task to bring wayward Christians back to the true faith. Like many other prophets, Kimbangu initially tried to resist his call, claiming that he was insufficiently educated and that others were much better qualified. He even briefly fled Nkamba to the capital city of Leopoldville (now Kinshasha), but soon returned as his experiences of being called to prophesy continued.

Ultimately, Kimbangu began a public ministry that lasted only five months. On April 6, 1921, he obeyed a command that he had received in a vision and healed a woman in the name of Jesus. Other miracles quickly followed. Kimbangu developed a reputation that drew many people to Nkamba, which became known as the New Jerusalem, to seek help from the African prophet. Kimbangu insisted that the only power he had was Christ working through him. He preached against the traditional cults of the area and preached a conservative morality, exhorting his followers to abandon polygamy, traditional religious dances, and all forms of immorality.

Kimbangu's followers came to see him as the Comforter promised in John 14:12–18 and the "envoy" of Jesus Christ. They believed that he had a special mission for oppressed Africans that had been ordained from the beginning by God (citing John 1:1–5). They do not profess that Kimbangu is God, but rather believe that in every age God chooses someone from each race to spread His message. Although Kimbanguists often make the story of Kimbangu's life conform to that of Jesus, they insist upon the orthodoxy of their Christianity, depicting their religion as Christianity resulting from the actions and teachings of Simon Kimbangu.

Kimbangu's preaching raised concerns both among the mission churches and the government. The mission churches were concerned with competition and theological innovation. Also, the Belgian government was troubled, since some of his followers saw in Kimbangu a new Moses who would liberate them from an oppressive colonial regime. The colonial administration became wary that Kimbangu could spark a mass political uprising. Those fears were amplified when some of the minor prophets, *ngunzists*, associated with Kimbangu appeared to be predicting a divinely sanctioned religious war in which a fire from heaven would consume the white colonialists.

The authorities quickly resolved to arrest Kimbangu. He initially evaded captured. But, prompted again by a divine vision, he eventually surrendered himself and counseled his followers not to react violently to his arrest. After a trial during which he was denied legal representation, Kimbangu was condemned to death, but his sentence was later reduced to life in prison by the Belgian king. Kimbangu died in prison thirty years after his arrest on October 12, 1951.

To the surprise of the Belgian authorities, Kimbangu's movement continued after his incarceration and even after his death. The government continued to hound the movement, deporting thousands of believers between 1925 and 1957. But, contrary to the colonialists' intentions, that only helped make Kimbangu's church an intertribal and international phenomenon. The church has prospered in central Africa and through immigration beyond Africa.

Only in 1959 did the Church of Jesus Christ on Earth through the Prophet Simon Kimbangu achieve formal recognition by the Belgian government. The church's movement toward Christian orthodoxy culminated with its admission to the World Council of Churches in 1969. The church now estimates it has more than five million members in central and southern Africa, Europe, Canada, Brazil, and the United States.

On Kimbangu's death, leadership of the church passed to his third son, Joseph Diangienda. When he died in 1992, Kimbangu's grandson and son of Solomon Dialungana, Simon Kimbangu Kigani, assumed leadership of the church. Other groups revere Kimbangu as a prophet but are not formally a part of the church.

Further Reading
Kimbanguisme.net (French).
Martin, Marie-Louise. 1976. *Kimbangu: An African Prophet and his Church*, D. M. Moore, trans. Grand Rapids, MI: Eerdmans.

PRIMARY SOURCE DOCUMENT

Excerpts from the "The Kimbanguist Catechism" and the "Psalms of Kimbangu"

Simon Kimbangu was a Congolese religious leader who started The Church of Jesus Christ on Earth Through the Prophet Simon Kimbangu in 1921. Kimbangu saw himself as a "Special Envoy of Jesus Christ and the Holy Spirit," and was praised by his disciples as the Holy Spirit sent by Jesus Christ described in the Gospel of John in the Bible. What follows are excerpts from Kimbangu's Catechism and Psalms.

The Kimbanguist Catechism

1. Who is Tata Simon Kimbangu?
2. Tata Simon Kimbangu is the envoy of our Lord Jesus Christ.
3. How do we know that Tata Simon Kimbangu is the envoy of our Lord Jesus Christ?
4. Jesus Christ himself promised us to ask his Father to send us another Comforter who should do still greater things than he (John 14:12–18).
5. What did Tata Simon Kimbangu do?
6. He raised the dead, gave sight to the blind, caused the dumb to speak and the lame to walk and fulfilled all the Lord's promises (Matthew 8:1–10).

7. When did Tata Simon Kimbangu begin?
8. He was in the beginning with God (John 1: 1–2).
9. Who was the mother of Tata Simon Kimbangu?
10. His mother was Mama Lwezi, who was married to Tata Kuyela.
11. In what village was Tata Simon Kimbangu born?
12. In Nkamba, now the new Jerusalem, in the lower Congo.
13. What does Kimbangu mean?
14. It means the sure Witness (*mbangi*) of the gospel of the Lord God, the True Interpreter (*mbangudi*) of the hidden and obscure.
15. But were Tata Kuyela and Mama Lwezi believers?
16. No, they did not believe; but there was love in their house. Therefore the Pathfinder (*muntu a nsongi*) came thence (I Corinthians 13:1–5)....
17. From whom did he receive his work as a prophet?
    From our Lord Jesus Christ....
19. Was Tata Simon Kimbangu a believer?
    Yes, he was a believer, baptized at the BMS mission of Ngombe Luteta, as everyone is (Matthew 3:15).
20. What did he say when he was given his work as a prophet by our Lord Jesus?
    He said Lord I am not worthy; choose one who desires this gift [*ndwenga*; "intelligence, capacity"].
21. What did Jesus say?
    Don't be afraid, I shall be with you.
22. In what year was this?
    In 1918 ...
24. When Tata Simon Kimbangu was afraid of the word he was given, where did he go?
    He went to Kinshasha, to look for other work.
26. Why did he leave Kinshasha and where did he go?
    He left because he got word that his foster-mother Mama Kinzembo had fallen ill in the village.
27. What was the first wonder that occurred when he was in the village?
    He was told by the Lord Jesus to go to Ngombe Kisuka to heal someone seriously ill there....
30. How did he heal (*saasukila*) her?
    He laid his hands on her and healed her in the name of Jesus the Savior.
31. When the news spread, whom did he meet on the road?
    He met the teacher Samuel, who said to him Greetings healer of men.
32. Why was he involved in this story?
    Because he was the catechist who had baptized [Kimbangu].
33. What reply did Tata Simon Kimbangu make?

He said, Do you not want people to be healed in the name of Jesus Christ?

34. What was the second wonder he performed, and where did he do it?
In Lukengo he raised a dead child, whose name was Nzuzi.

35. Before raising this child where did he spend the day?
He stayed at the place of Nsumbu Simon in Lukengo. They discussed the Bible, beginning at Genesis 37, from the story of Joseph to the escape of the children of Israel. . . .

45. Who was the first helper given him?
The first helper given to him was Ntwalani Thomas of Mbanza Ngoyo.

46. Who else were with him as helpers or apostles?
1) Ndanga Pierre 2) Manika Paul 3) Mikala Mandombe 4) Mukoko Jean 5) Mbanga Thérèse 6) Mbaki André.

47. What help did these apostles give him?
They healed the sick in the name of the Lord Jesus and at the command (*lutumu*) of Tata Simon Kimbangu. . . .

53. Why was he arrested?
To fulfill the testimony of Our Lord Jesus Christ (John 17:14).

54. Will he come again? What will be the end of all this?
Surely he will come again, for all that he began must be accomplished (John 16:19–33).

55. Where is Tata Simon Kimbangu now, who was sent to Upper Congo by the government?
After being sent to Upper Congo by the government, Tata Simon Kimbangu died and rose again and is with us in the Spirit. . . .

59. Why is the name of Tata Simon Kimbangu put foremost? Is it because he is God?
No, Tata Simon Kimbangu is not God, but in every age God chooses one man from each race to enlighten his people (Exodus 3:7–17).

Source: The Kimbangu Catechism. Reprinted in John M. Janzen & Wyatt MacGaffey, *An Anthology of Kongo Religion.* Lawrence: University of Kansas, 1974, pp. 125–127.

Psalms of Kimbangu

Psalm 07: Tona muna lubantiku, Nzambi wazola nge ndombe
From the beginning,
God's love for the black race is manifest.
As proof, Adam and Eve are blacks.
This revelation we have from daddy "Mfumu'anlongo." He is the true Paraclete.
But, the blacks made fun of it,
Hardening their hearts.

Pity for you black race!
For not recognizing Kimbangu.
Oh my God!
Pity for you black race!
Because you have to die for
Win in wisdom.

My brothers, you who continue to sleep,
Wake up!
Let's go begging the Lord.
Who knows, he can answer us.
Come! Let's carry bags
for him to have mercy on us.
He revealed to us that he wants to do
Come back to the Garden of Eden.

Go away! Go away!
Fools!
Do you really read the scriptures
to be trusted!
Go yourself!
Blind of Diangienda!
Go away! Go away!
Fools!

My little children!
I complain because of your brothers,
Blacks like you!
Have the truth like a tight belt
Around your waist
and follow me blindly so that
you have access to the entrance.
Our "Nvualas" came down from Heaven.
They are the hope of the whole world.

Psalm 11 (1) Mansueki ma Yave mu nkanda ndombe wau

The mysteries of Yahweh in the black race
Reveals the kingdom of heaven.
The promises of Yahweh are the ones we expect,
Christ will be glorified
The Kingdom of Saints has revealed itself on earth
According to the promise of Jesus, the savior.
This promise has come true in Africa,

In N'kamba-Jerusalem.
This is the reason that leads me to go with you
the whole world so that nobody will fix fake shifty.

Source: "Psalms of Kimbangu." Kimbanguisme.net.

Knight, JZ (Ramtha) (1946–)

Since her public debut in the late 1970s, JZ Knight (née Judith Hampton; 1946–) has become one of the most popular channels in the world. Channeling is the term used in New Age circles to refer to contact with disembodied entities who either have lived before or exist only as personalities or consciousnesses in other realms. In Knight's case, she was contacted by an ancient warrior named Ramtha who lived thirty-five thousand years ago in Lemuria on the northern part of the continent of Atlantis. In Knight's telling, Ramtha has a complex biography, which centers on his conquering his self and ultimately transforming into God. He thus serves as a model for what his audience can accomplish themselves.

As Knight recalls, she led a generally unremarkable life as a suburban housewife and mother prior to her being contacted by Ramtha. But she did have a few experiences that in retrospect prepared her for meeting Ramtha, including the promise from a fortune-teller that she would meet "The One" sometime in the future, a statement from a psychic that she had an awesome power within her, and an experience of religious healing. It was a dramatic event in 1977 at her home in Tacoma, Washington, however, that enabled her to make sense of all of those events. When the large and impressive figure of Ramtha appeared in her kitchen, he was suffused in light and exuded peace. Ramtha identified himself to Knight as "The Enlightened One" and promised that he was there to help her overcome fear and limitation. Ramtha also informed Knight that she would become a light to the world. Her inaugural vision thus paralleled the calls of many others who went on to initiate religious innovations.

As Knight progressively came to grips with her encounters with Ramtha, she began to immerse herself in the metaphysical subculture, and her abilities as a channel soon attracted a growing clientele. Ramtha's message had many similarities to ideas then circulating through the New Age subculture. He informed individuals that they had the ability to create their own reality and urged them to fulfill their highest potential, which is to realize that they themselves are actually gods. In a video on Knight's website (www.ramtha.com), for example, Ramtha greets the audience as "you Christs."

Ramtha's teachings closely parallel the religious systems of ancient Gnosticism, which in a well-known formulation promised that individuals could learn who they (really) are, where they come from, what birth is, and what rebirth is. Ramtha argues that over time, however, individuals have forgotten the fundamental truth that they contain a spark of the divine, and the difficulties that they experience in life all derive from their ignorance. Ramtha's mission, then, is to help people remember who they really are and put that realization into action.

As Knight continued her work as a channel, she developed an extensive corpus of revelations from Ramtha, which are available through her website in various formats. Like the materials produced by other channels, they are authoritative for their audience, but do not necessarily preclude the search for wisdom from other sources, even other channels.

In 1988, Knight opened Ramtha's School of Enlightenment at her headquarters in Yelm, Washington. The school gives Ramtha's teachings a distinctive institutional home and serves as the setting for courses, workshops, and the ritual practices that Ramtha has devised to raise students' consciousness and energy. Knight also lectures and holds workshops in other locales and online.

Like other religious innovators, Knight has acquired her own share of detractors. Vocal and disillusioned former students of Ramtha have questioned Knight's motives and even Ramtha's existence. They briefly formed a group, Life after Ramtha's School of Enlightenment, and some appealed to the familiar anticult arguments about brainwashing to buttress their case against Knight. Knight's former husband joined the fray and accused her of seeking profit rather than enlightenment. In response, Knight has characterized her opponents as a disgruntled few among the more than one hundred thousand who have benefited from Ramtha's teaching. As with other conflicts over religious innovations, no certain resolution seems likely.

See also: Channeling; Mediums; New Age, The; Pursel, Jach (Lazaris) (1947–); Ramtha's School of Enlightenment.

Further Reading

Brown, Michael F. 1999. *The Channeling Zone: American Spirituality in an Anxious Age.* Cambridge, MA: Harvard University Press.

Knight, JZ. 2004. *A State of Mind: My Story / Ramtha: The Adventure Begins.* Yelm, WA: JZK Publishing.

Melton, J. Gordon. 1998. *Finding Enlightenment: Ramtha's School of Ancient Wisdom.* Hillsboro, OR: Beyond Words Publishing.

Kopimism

Many, if not most, religions employ the internet. Sparkling websites welcome members or potential converts, explain beliefs and practices, and provide access to a religious community. Some religions exist mostly virtually, such as Vampirism, whereas others employ online networking tools to recruit new members, such as ISIS. Rarely is a religious community, old or new, untouched by the internet. It is perhaps not surprising, then, that the internet and the sharing of digital information has spawned its own religious movement: Kopimism.

The movement was founded in Uppsala, Sweden, by university students Isak Gerson and Gustave Nipe in 2010 under the name the Missionary Church of Kopimism. Both Gerson and Nipe had roots in Piratbyran, a Swedish political group and online collective that advocated for the sharing of art and information online and arose in response to the growing antipiracy movement in Sweden. The Church was successfully recognized as a religious group by the Swedish government in 2012, following two failed application attempts. "Kopimism" derives from the phrase "copy me," which is reflected in the primary creed (or constitution) of the religion. As described on its website, Kopimists are those who believe that the search for knowledge is inherently sacred, knowledge is universal, and "the copying and sharing of information" is a sacred right (http://kopimistsamfundet.se/english/). "Copymixing," or the reworking of copied information with new data, is also considered sacred and ethically sound, since it helps to expand the field of knowledge. Kopimists object to copyrights and view one of their major aims as doing away with copyrighting entirely. Monopolies on information and failure to disclose information are sacrilege.

Despite this focus on the need for openness when it comes to information, the privacy and secrecy of Kopimists is held as a holy and necessary right. Kopimist priests, known as operators or "ops," are tasked with protecting the identities of their members as well as combating copyrights and other laws that infringe upon the free sharing of information. More recently, ops have presided at Kopimist weddings, wearing masks to conceal their identities and reading tenets of Kopimism that align with themes of the holiness of sharing. The Church has a primarily virtual presence, nonetheless. When they do gather together, temporary "interaction points" are created, designated by the Kopimi pyramid and declared a sacred site by an op. Beyond this, members are connected through a mutual devotion to information sharing (called "kopyacting"), exemplified by their espousal of sacred symbols "CTRL+C" and "CTRL+V," the keyboard strokes for copy and paste, respectively. Kopimists maintain that only through copying is there an afterlife: since all life exists as information, if it is not copied, then it ceases to exist. Replication ensures eternal life. Along these lines, the soul only exists online and through sharing.

The Church is not without its critics. There are some who feel that, like the parody religion Pastafarianism, Kopimism does not qualify as a religion. It lacks a belief in a higher power, a centralized institution, a clear infrastructure, and most elements that generally smack of a religion. For this reason, there are those who swiftly protested the Swedish government's recognition of the Church as a religion. Others critique the legality of Kopimism's practices, which seem to accept, if not advocate, virtual piracy (or illegal file sharing) of information. The phrase "Kopimi" first appeared on Piratbyran before it was claimed as a religious name and symbol by Gerson and the Church. Ironically, both Gerson and Nipe participated in antipiracy rallies, thus differentiating themselves from and igniting tension with other illegal file-sharing groups. The Church argues for information sharing as a sacred act: since information is universal and the nature of the universe is an infinite array of replicated cells, the copying of knowledge simply mirrors these broader processes.

In Sweden, there are between three thousand and four thousand Kopimists, and the religion has spread to nearly twenty nations around the globe, including United

States (where it is incorporated as the United Church of Kopimism), Canada, and Israel.

See also: ISIS; New Age, The; New Religions on/and the Internet; Pastafarianism (Church of the Flying Spaghetti Monster); Science, Technology, and New Religious Movements; Vampirism.

Further Reading

Baraniuk, Chris. 2012. "The Pirate and the Priest: How Digital Turned into Divine." *The Machine Starts.* Available at: http://www.themachinestarts.com/read/2012-01-the-pirate-and-the-priest-how-digital-turned-into-divine.

Nilsson, Per-Erik. 2016. "Techniques of Religion-Making in Sweden: The Case of the Missionary Church of Kopimism." *Critical Research on Religion* 4, no. 2: 141–155.

Sinnreich, Aram. 2016. "Sharing in Spirit: Kopimism and the Digital Eucharist." *Information, Communication, & Society* 19, no. 4: 504–517.

Korean New Religious Movements

The proximity of the Korean peninsula, divided since 1945 into the Democratic People's Republic of Korea in the North and the Republic of Korea in the South, to both China and Japan has facilitated the flow of people and ideas across the borders. In the fourth century CE both Buddhism and Confucianism came from China into Korea. They were joined by Daoism, although it has played only a minor role in Korean religious history. Buddhist and Confucian ideas and practices interacted with Korean folk beliefs, such as the local deities of rural villages and reliance on shamans. Koreans drew upon whatever traditions were available to them to shape their religious lives. Only in the late eighteenth century did Christianity come to Korea in the form of Roman Catholicism. Protestant missionaries arrived in the late nineteenth century.

Christianity introduced ideas, such as monotheism, the concept of religious freedom, and emphasis on clear boundaries between one religious community and another, that challenged the fluid forms of religious practice that had long characterized Korean life. The importation from Japan in the late nineteenth century of the concept of a religion as an identifiable community distinct from others added to that challenge. In response, a variety of new religious movements developed, starting in the mid-nineteenth century.

TONGHAK AND CH'ONDOGYO

The first new religious movement of Korean origin was established in 1860, likely in response to the earlier arrival of Roman Catholicism. Ch'oe Cheu (1824–1864) claimed that God, or the Heavenly Emperor, had appeared to him in 1860 and given him the mission of saving humankind. His religion, which he called Tonghak or "Eastern Learning," as opposed to the Western Learning borne by Christian missionaries was monotheistic, endorsed traditional Confucian morality, and included elements of traditional Korean shamanism. In anticipation of the dawning of a new era, the group focused on bringing righteousness and peace to this world by meditation, prayer, and ritual actions, including Sunday worship of God. Both its monotheism and its status as a separate group constituted challenges to the religious status quo and the ruling Confucian elite. Continuing conflicts with civil authorities led to Ch'oe Cheu's execution in 1884. In 1905, the group changed its name to Ch'ondogyo ("Teaching of the Heavenly Way"). Ch'ondogyo still has a presence in South Korea, though its membership is declining.

TAEJONGGYO

Founded in 1909, Taejonggyo is a nativist new religious movement that describes itself as the original religion of the Korean people. That religion, it claims, had been forgotten for centuries and Koreans' collective amnesia, along with their reliance on foreign religions like Buddhism and Confucianism, has contributed to the contemporary weakness of Korea. But the original religion has been brought back to light by Na Ch'ŏl (1863–1916), who had been active in political efforts against Japanese imperialism and for Korean independence.

Na Ch'ŏl argued that Koreans had to return to the worship of their original God, Hanŏllim, in whom there are three persons. Hwanim is the Lord of Heaven and the creator; Hwanung is His son and the educator of human beings. Hwanung had been dispatched to earth where he mated with a bear who had turned into a beautiful woman. She then gave birth to Tan'gun, who is recognized as the first ruler of the Korean people, some four thousand and three hundred years ago. Tan'gun's goal was to establish a paradise on earth, and Taejonggyo argues that Korea should return to his philosophy of government. Such sentiments contributed to the Korean independence movement in the early twentieth century. Taejonggyo has produced a group of sacred texts that give advice about how to achieve spiritual and physical health through self-cultivation.

Founded by Ilchi Lee (1950–) the Dahn World School, Danhak, is an offshoot of Taejonggyo that focuses on internal alchemy and the practice of yoga. It has a substantial following in the United States, where it is now known as Body and Brain (see www.bodynbrain.com).

CHUNGSAN RELIGIONS

A cluster of religious groups focused on the worship of Kang Chŭngsan (1871–1909) as the supreme God, called Sangjenim ("Supreme Ruling God"), constitutes one of the largest new religious movements in Korea today. These groups believe that God descended to earth in the nineteenth century in Kang Chŭngsan's human form to teach humans the rites of cosmic renewal that will bring about the great transformation of the current imperfect world into one of peace and harmony. Religions focused on Chŭngsan differ from established and new Korean religions.

One of the contemporary Chŭngsan religions, Jeung San Do, which has a robust missionary presence beyond Korea, identifies Chŭngsan as God the Ruler and as the same being that is worshipped by Christians, Buddhists, and Daoists (see www.jeungsando.org). Established in 1974, it espouses the mission of spreading the millennialist teachings of Chŭngsan throughout Korea and the rest of the world.

Daesun Jinri-hoe, another Chŭngsan group, claims as many as six million members in Korea today. It focuses on efforts to improve the world, advocating the Confucian virtues of sincerity, reverence, and trust in both other humans and God. Its website recommends the practices of the resolution of grievances and the grateful reciprocation of favors as ways of achieving harmony between humans that will eventually lead to the establishment of an earthly paradise (see http://eng.idaesoon.or.kr/.)

WON BUDDHISM

Won ("Perfect" or "Completed") Buddhism, which has a large contemporary following, was also founded at the beginning of the twentieth century. Pak Chung-Bin (1891–1943) experienced an "awakening to truth" in 1916. His experience happened without the guidance of a teacher, and only later did he conclude that what he learned aligned best with the teachings of the Buddha. Consequently, he believed that his group, which was first known as the Buddhist Dharma Research Association and only became Won Buddhism in 1947, constituted a new religion rather than an offshoot of any existing Buddhist group.

Like other Korean new religions, Won aims at a revitalization of Korean culture. It presents itself as a reformed and modernized form of Buddhism, focusing on clear and accessible presentation of Buddhist teachings (see www.wonduddhism.org). Its veneration of the founder and his successors, however, is a distinctive feature. Won teaching is laid out in a set of scriptural texts that are available in multiple languages at www.wonscripture.org. The central practice is meditation on the Il-Wŏn-Song symbol, a circle (won literally means "circle") that replaces images of the Buddha in Won temples. Won claims that the circular symbol conveys the origin of all things in the universe, the truth to which all sages have aspired, and the original nature of all beings.

THE UNIFICATION CHURCH

Internationally, the best-known Korean new religious movement is the Unification Church. It is Korean in origin and some of its beliefs and practices remain culturally Korean, but it has become a globalized religious body. The Church traces its origins to a vision of Jesus experienced by Sun Myung Moon (1920–2012) on Easter morning, 1936. After a substantial delay, Moon began his public ministry in 1946. He ultimately established the Holy Spirit Association for the Unification of World Christianity on May 1, 1954. In 1952, Moon had already completed the first written account of his teachings, *Divine Principle*, a reinterpretation of the biblical narrative from Genesis to Revelation. The central point of Unificationism is that humanity stands in need of a third Adam or the Lord of the Second Advent. Adam and Eve, and then Jesus, failed to establish the perfect, loving family that God has envisaged for them. Consequently, humanity remained in need of salvation. In the 1990s and 2000s, Moon finally confirmed what many of his followers had expected and hoped for; he and his wife, Hak Ja Han Moon (1943–), were the True Parents of humankind and jointly served as the Messiah.

From the start, the Unificationist movement was strongly involved in proselytization. It quickly established a presence in Japan and by the late 1950s came to the West coast of the United States. After a slow start, the movement began to attract members in the 1960s and soon became one of the most prominent "dangerous cults." Despite concerted opposition from the anticult movement, Unificationism now has outposts throughout the world, including in states of the former Soviet Union. By numerical counts alone, its missionary efforts have been a success.

Since the nineteenth century, Korea has had a dynamic religious economy that has both produced new religions and welcomed others from abroad.

See also: Anticult Movement, The; Charisma and Leadership in New Religious Movements; Globalization and New Religious Movements; Millennialism; Shamanism; Unification Church, The.

Further Reading

Baker, Don. 2008. *Korean Spirituality*. Honolulu: University of Hawai'i Press.

Buswell, Robert E., ed. 2007. *Religions of Korea in Practice*. Princeton, NJ: Princeton University Press.

Chryssides, George D. 1991. *The Advent of Sun Myung Moon: The Origins, Beliefs and Practices of the Unification Church*. London: Macmillan.

Pokorny, Lucas, & Franz Winter, eds. 2018. *Handbook of East Asian New Religious Movements*. Leiden: E. J. Brill.

Pye, Michael. 2001. "Won Buddhism as a Korean New Religion." *Numen* 49: 113–141.

Koresh, David (1959–1993)

Born Vernon Howell on August 17, 1959, David Koresh gained public attention as the leader of a small Christian Adventist sect known as the Branch Davidians. After the U.S. Bureau of Alcohol, Tobacco, and Firearms (BATF) executed a disastrous military-style raid on the Mount Carmel Center in search of illegal weapons on February 28, 1993, Koresh quickly became portrayed in popular media as the unstable and manipulative leader of a dangerous cult.

Little in his past would seem to have prepared Howell for religious leadership. He was a high school dropout and had a learning disability. But he knew the Bible very well and could recite many passages from memory. After Howell was excommunicated from his Seventh-day Adventist congregation, he eventually joined a group living outside of Waco, Texas, at the Mount Carmel Center, under the leadership of Lois Roden (1916–1986). The group had been in the Waco area since the 1930s.

Howell quickly learned the distinctive theology of the group, but a crucial transformation came on a visit to Israel in 1985. Although he was never very forthcoming about what happened, it appears that Howell experienced an ascent into the heavens. He returned from Israel convinced that he was the Lamb of God mentioned in Revelation 5 as the only one capable of unsealing the scroll sealed with seven seals. Howell thus received full knowledge of the events that would set in motion the end of the world as each seal was opened. Ultimately, the new heaven and new earth prophesied in Revelation 21:1 would be established.

Soon after his return from Israel, Howell assumed the leadership of the Branch Davidians, a small but international and multiracial group of Bible students, most of whom had been members of the Seventh-day Adventist Church. The transition was not easy, since Lois Roden's son George thought that he should have assumed the role of leader after her death. But by 1988, Howell was securely situated as the leader of the group. In August 1990, Howell officially changed his name to David Koresh. His new first name signaled his connection to the biblical King David and his hope to reestablish a Davidic monarchy. His new last name linked him to the Persian king Cyrus, who was hailed as a "messiah" in Isaiah 45:1 for allowing the Jews to return from captivity in Babylon.

BIBLE STUDIES

The central activity at Mount Carmel was the daily Bible study session, which could sometimes last for hours. Howell was convinced that for the first time in history it was possible to achieve a full understanding of the Bible under his guidance. His Bible studies focused on the interpretation of the Book of Revelation. As Koresh put it in his unfinished manuscript that survived the April 19, 1993 fire, "every book of the Bible meets and ends in the book of Revelation" (Tabor & Gallagher 1995: 197).

Because he understood the Bible as preaching a single message, Koresh's Bible studies assembled mosaics of passages that he believed interpreted and confirmed each other. He actually provided little commentary of his own, preferring instead to arrange the texts so that they cumulatively reinforced his message that the events described in the seven seals were unfolding even as he spoke. Even though the Federal Bureau of Investigation (FBI) agents who conducted negotiations with the Branch Davidians during the fifty-one-day siege quickly decided that Koresh's teaching was merely "Bible babble," those who accepted Koresh as their teacher saw him as revealing unprecedented insight into God's plan for the end-times. They eagerly attended the Bible studies and often asked Koresh to extend them, no matter how long they went on.

NEW LIGHT

The Adventist tradition in which Koresh and the Branch Davidians located themselves had long been accustomed to prophetic figures offering "present truth" or "new light." When Koresh revealed his own new light in 1989, it almost destroyed the community. Although he was already married with children, Koresh revealed that all women in the group would now become his wives and that all men other than him would have to practice celibacy. Koresh believed he was to father children who would assume the roles of the twenty-four elders (see Rev. 4:4; 11:16; 19:4) who would rule over the coming Kingdom of God.

Koresh's new light proved hard to take for many. It provoked some departures, most notably by Marc Breault and his wife Elizabeth Baranyai. Breault would then become a dedicated opponent of Koresh. But among those who stayed their acceptance of the challenging new light only increased their dedication to and dependence upon Koresh.

THE BATF RAID AND FBI NEGOTIATIONS

Koresh was in the Mount Carmel Center when the BATF raid began. They had apparently made no plans for a peaceful serving of the search warrant nor had they planned on taking Koresh into custody during one of his many trips into town. On February 28, six Branch Davidians and four BATF agents died. After the FBI took control the next day and began negotiating with the barricaded Branch Davidians, Koresh spent hours on the phone, trying to explain his theology to uncomprehending negotiators. Almost immediately, FBI negotiators tuned out his biblical exegesis. They also doubted that he was actually writing his exposition of the seven seals and that he would ever come out. Despite the efforts of both sides, negotiations quickly devolved into a stalemate. The FBI Special Agent in Charge at the scene decided on April 19 to initiate the insertion of CS gas into the Mount Carmel Center using armored vehicles. When a fire, whose origins remain disputed, broke out around noon, Koresh and all but nine of those inside perished.

See also: Branch Davidians; Millennialism; Seventh-day Adventism.

Further Reading

Haldeman, Bonnie. 2007. *Memories of the Branch Davidians: The Autobiography of David Koresh's Mother* Catherine Wessinger, ed. Waco, TX: Baylor University Press.

Newport, Kenneth G. C. 2006. *The Branch Davidians of Waco: The History and Beliefs of an Apocalyptic Sect.* Oxford: Oxford University Press.

Tabor, James D., & Eugene V. Gallagher. 1995. *Why Waco? Cults and the Battle for Religious Freedom in America.* Berkeley: University of California Press.

PRIMARY SOURCE DOCUMENT

David Koresh's Last Letter to His Attorney (April 14, 1993)

Hello Dick,

As far as our progress is concerned, here is where we stand: I have related two messages, from God, to the F.B.I.; one of which concerns present danger to people here in Waco.

I was shown a fault line running throughout the Lake Waco area. An angel is standing in charge of this event. Many people, here in Waco, know that we are a good people, and yet, they have shown the same resentful spirit of indifference to our "warnings of love."

I am presently being permitted to document, in structured form, the decoded messages of the Seven Seals. Upon the completion of this task, I will be freed of my "waiting period." I hope to finish this as soon as possible and to stand before man to answer any and all questions regarding my actions.

This written Revelation of the Seven Seals will not be sold, but is to be available to all who wish to know the Truth. The four Angels of Revelation 7 are here, now ready to punish foolish mankind; but, the writing of these Seals will cause the winds of God's wrath to be held back a little longer.

I have been praying so long for this opportunity; to put the Seals in written form. Speaking the Truth seems to have very little effect on man.

I was shown that as soon as I am given over into the hands of man, I will be made a spectacle of, and people will not be concerned about the truth of God, but just the bizarrity of me—the flesh (person).

I want the people of this generation to be saved. I am working night and day to complete my final work of the writing out of "these Seals."

I thank my Father, He has finally granted me the chance to do this. It will bring New Light and hope for many and they will not have to deal with me the person.

The earthquake in Waco is something not to be taken lightly. It will probably be "the thing" needed to shake some sense into the people. Remember, Dick, the warning came first and I fear that the F.B.I. is going to suppress this information. It may be left up to you.

I will demand the first manuscript of the Seals be given to you. Many scholars and religious leaders will wish to have copies for examination. I will keep a copy with me. As soon as I can see that people, like Jim Tabor and Phil Arnold have a copy I will come out and then you can do your thing with this Beast.

I hope to keep in touch with you by letter, so please give your address.

We are standing on the threshold of Great events! The Seven Seals, in written form are the most sacred information ever!

David Koresh

Source: David Koresh's Last Letter to His Attorney, 1993. Activities of Federal Law Enforcement Agencies toward the Branch Davidians (Part 2). Committee on the Judiciary, One Hundred Fourth Congress, First Session. Washington, D.C.: Government Printing Office, 1996, p. 211.

L

Landmark Forum, The (est)

In various ways, religions consistently strive to address the total well-being of their participants. Consequently, they address psychological, moral, social, and economic issues as well as spiritual ones. In so doing, they inevitably enter areas of life where other social or professional institutions, such as the practice of psychology or economics, claim expertise. As a result, the borders between specifically religious expertise and other kinds of expertise can become blurred. For example, just as some forms of religion may express psychological messages or insights, so also some forms of psychology may express or draw upon originally religious insights. Such border-crossing was particularly evident in the 1970s and 1980s when humanistic psychology and the broad New Age movement developed in parallel and sometimes intersected.

est, the acronym for Erhard Seminars Training but also Latin for "it is," developed out of the intellectual ferment of the 1960s. It was founded in 1971 by Werner Erhard (né John Paul Rosenberg, 1935–). In 1960, Rosenberg had left his first wife and children behind in the Philadelphia area to begin a new life, for which he took a new name. During the 1960s, the self-taught Erhard engaged with a wide variety of ideas, including Dale Carnegie's (1888–1955) positive thinking, which was shaped by the New Thought movement; the humanist psychology of Abraham Maslow (1908–1970) and Carl Rogers (1902–1987); and the seminar programs of Mind Dynamics, Subud, Scientology, and Zen Buddhism (through its British interpreter Alan Watts [1915–1973] whom he met in San Francisco).

According to Erhard, the generative moment for the formation of est occurred in 1971 while he was driving in Marin County, California. In the terminology of est, Erhard "got it" and he resolved to help others achieve the same realization. By October 1971, Erhard had held his first training session. The training sessions soon reached their standard form of sixty hours spread over two weekends and were soon being offered throughout the country. By 1979, Erhard had expanded to Europe and then to Israel. Erhard stopped offering est seminars in 1984.

The goal of the seminars was "personal transformation." The activities in the seminars are designed to help participants experience past patterns of living that constrained their ability to be satisfied with their lives and therefore experience themselves in a new, more gratifying way in the present time (see www.wernererhard.net). The seminars thus bore some resemblance to Scientology's therapeutic attempts to rid participants of the continuing harmful effects of past experiences on their way to becoming clear.

At least half a million people went through the training during est's lifetime and most of them reported extraordinarily positive effects. A website maintained for est graduates collects a sample of testimonials (see www.erhardseminarstraining.com).

The strong control that trainers exercised over participants during the seminars, including prohibitions against keeping their watches on during the seminar, leaving the seminar room for any reason except during the scheduled breaks, talking to other participants during the training, and talking without being called upon, led some disgruntled participants, their sympathizers, and receptive journalists to describe est as an authoritarian "cult." That brought Erhard's seminars, which he consistently denied were religious, to the attention of the anticult movement. Erhard had charges of financial malfeasance and personal misconduct leveled against him, but the latter were eventually rescinded and the former were resolved in his favor by the Internal Revenue Service.

When Erhard stopped offering seminars in late 1984, a new, modified course called "The Forum" began to be offered at the beginning of 1985. est became an educational corporation and then Werner Erhard and Associates. In 1991, the intellectual property rights of Erhard's group were purchased by former students who continued to offer similar courses as Landmark Education and later Landmark Worldwide. They reduced the length of Erhard's original course to three days and renamed it The Landmark Forum. Landmark has developed many other training courses, which focus on improving the productivity and satisfaction of workers by enhancing their productivity, communication skills, and decision-making.

As the later transformation of est indicates, Erhard's methods of training have had a substantial impact in the world of business. In fact, the later stages of Erhard's career have been marked by his integration into the corporate world and business education, as is evidenced by his work with the Harvard Business School and several Fortune 500 companies. Erhard has also founded several charitable organizations, including The Hunger Project, a nongovernmental organization that aims to generate awareness of global hunger and develop ways to end it (see www.wernererhardfoundation.org).

The acceptance of Erhard's ideas into the mainstream has generally occurred without the acknowledgment of the religious ideas and practices that inspired them. Although Erhard claimed that his experience with Zen made a deep impression on him and the practices of his seminars bear strong resemblances to the type of rationalized "protestant Zen" purveyed by teachers like D. T. Suzuki (1870–1966), those influences are muted or entirely excluded when his ideas are communicated in trainings for businesses. A similar observation applies to related programs like Lifespring, which claimed to have provided training to over four hundred thousand people during its career, and many other leadership and business training organizations. Erhard's wide-ranging influence in contemporary life shows again how ideas and practices formed in the counterculture of the 1960s and 1970s have continued to exert an impact even as their origins, and ties to alternative religions, have been obscured.

See also: Anticult Movement, The; New Age, The; New Thought; Scientology; Subud.

Further Reading

Bartley, William W. 1978. *Werner Erhard: The Transformation of a Man.* New York: Clarkson N. Potter.

Fenwick, Sheridan. 1977. *Getting It: The Psychology of est,* 2nd ed. New York: Penguin Books.

Laycock, Joseph 2014. "Zen Meets New Thought: The Erhard Seminars Training and Changing Ideas about Zen." *Contemporary Buddhism* 15: 332–355.

Rupert, Glenn A. 1992. "Employing the New Age: Training Seminars." In James R. Lewis & J. Gordon Melton, eds. *Perspectives on the New Age,* pp. 127–135. Albany: State University of New York Press.

LaVey, Anton Szandor (1930–1997)

Anton LaVey remains the most influential figure in contemporary Satanism. On April 30, 1966, he founded the first organized Satanic group, the Church of Satan. Although the Church was loosely structured and never made sustained efforts at recruitment, through his writings, media appearances, and publically staged rituals, LaVey attracted a considerable audience for his ideas.

For LaVey, Satan was a metaphor rather than an anthropomorphic being. His most influential book, *The Satanic Bible,* laid out a religious philosophy that viewed human beings as carnal and appetitive, no different than other animals. LaVey railed against the repression of natural instincts by many religions, particularly Christianity. In a creedal statement that he formulated for *The Satanic Bible,* "The Nine Satanic Statements," LaVey asserted, among other things, that Satan represented indulgence, vital existence, undefiled wisdom, kindness to those who deserved it, vengeance, responsibility to those who act responsibly, and all of the so-called sins that lead to physical, mental, and emotional gratification.

LaVey's ideas were far from original. He borrowed freely from thinkers like Aleister Crowley, Friedrich Nietzsche, Ayn Rand, and the English occult philosopher John Dee (1527–1608). One section of *The Satanic Bible* depends heavily on the social Darwinist tract *Might is Right* written by New Zealander Arthur Desmond under the pseudonym Ragnar Redbeard. But LaVey did not borrow indiscriminately despite accusations that his major work is wholly plagiarized. He carefully edited and arranged his sources to construct his message.

Although the Church of Satan intermittently experimented with sponsoring groups outside its home base in San Francisco, LaVey's primary influence on other Satanists came through his writings and public statements. *The Satanic Bible* remains the most prominent gateway through which individuals have entered Satanism. Similarly attractive to many was the persona that LaVey fashioned for himself.

THE "BLACK" POPE

The facts of LaVey's biography are difficult to pin down. In his own comments and in biographies written by Church of Satan insiders, he revealed a colorful life.

He claimed to have left high school early to work in circus and carnivals, including working as a "cage boy" for big cats. Later, he worked as an organist in bars, nightclubs, and burlesque houses, and even purported to have had an affair with Marilyn Monroe when she was working as a dancer early in her career. In addition, Jayne Mansfield was said to have been a paramour of LaVey and an active participant in the Church of Satan. LaVey claimed to have worked as a crime scene photographer for the San Francisco police department and also as an investigator into the paranormal. He also said that he had played oboe in the San Francisco Ballet Orchestra.

The dramatic persona that LaVey developed for himself helped him to attract a diverse group into his social circle. With a group that attended the "magic circle" discussions held frequently at his home, he founded the Order of the Trapezoid to structure his investigations into psychic phenomena and unconventional ideas. That group quickly evolved into the Church of Satan.

LaVey complemented his embellished biography with his physical appearance. When he founded the Church of Satan he also shaved his head, while leaving on his distinctive goatee. He frequently dressed in all black or in elaborate ritual robes, with a Satanic symbol hanging from his neck on a chain. For a time, he also kept a lion, Togare, as a pet.

The Church of Satan was headquartered on 6114 California Street in San Francisco, which LaVey painted black and decorated with artifacts reflecting his eclectic and esoteric interests. It served as the site for Satanic rituals, such as the baptism of LaVey's daughter Zeena and a Satanic wedding at which LaVey officiated, and lectures and discussions on subjects related to Satanism.

LaVey's status as the founder of the Church of Satan and his flamboyant self-advertisement earned him the nickname the "Black Pope" from journalists, which only added to his notoriety. But LaVey was ambivalent about capitalizing on the substantial charisma that his followers attributed to him. He was, in many ways, a reluctant leader. For one thing, his emphasis on individuals' capacity to determine the truth for themselves made it difficult to impose much order on the Church of Satan, since it empowered others to achieve the same insights that he had. LaVey was also as much a provocateur and jokester as he was a religious leader. He took great delight in mocking social conventions and pretensions of all sorts. It has accordingly sometimes been difficult to determine whether some of his more outrageous actions and statements were to be taken seriously.

Unlike many other founders of new religions, LaVey did not depend on prophetic inspiration for his authority. Instead, he relied on his own intellectual insight, which he forthrightly asserted could be equaled by anyone else who rejected inherited dogma and made the effort to see things as they really were. LaVey urged others to employ the scalpel of doubt as rigorously as he had. But he had no illusions about how many would be able to follow his lead. Satanists, for him, constituted an intellectual elite; they were the few who were willing to examine established verities critically and to embrace the consequences when accepted truths were shown to be false.

In his carefully constructed persona and in his writings and public statements, LaVey thus became more of a symbol of Satanism than its organizational leader.

His influence has continued after his death, with many being drawn into the Satanic milieu through their encounters with *The Satanic Bible.*

See also: Church of Satan, The; Satanism.

Further Reading

Barton, Blanche. 1992. *The Secret Life of a Satanist: The Authorized Biography of Anton Szandor LaVey.* Los Angeles: Feral House.

Dyrendal, Asbjørn, James R. Lewis, & Jesper Aa. Petersen. 2016. *The Invention of Satanism.* Oxford: Oxford University Press.

LaVey, Anton Szandor. 1969. *The Satanic Bible.* New York: Avon Books.

Wright, Lawrence. 1991. "Sympathy for the Devil." *Rolling Stone*, September 5.

Law Enforcement and New Religious Movements

Ideally, law enforcement agents protect citizens: from crises or chaos, from each other, and, occasionally, from themselves. To do so, police and federal agents are trained in tactics such as negotiation and deescalation as well as the use of weapons and self-defense. When agents are called, strict protocols are in place to ensure the safety of all involved; violation of these protocols should, in theory, lead to censure or termination on the part of officers. Yet, what if the interactions between police officers and civilians begin with a fundamental misassumption?

This has often been the case for law enforcement officers interacting with new religious movements, or "cults." In fact, it is the very use and application of the term "cult" by law enforcement when engaging with certain religious groups that can lead to miscommunication and misunderstanding and, sometimes, tragic results.

The term "cult," though disavowed by scholars of religion, has been used to describe supposedly dangerous religious groups whose leaders are cast as fiendish, sex- and power-driven megalomaniacs and whose members are brainwashed followers with no ability to distinguish right from wrong. When a group is labeled a "cult," either by the law enforcement themselves, by the media—building on the language of the anticult movement—, or by the public, the presumption is often that those involved in the group need stopping, if it's the leader, or saving, if it's the group's members. Conversely, those in the religious groups rarely see themselves as manipulators or manipulated, but as genuine believers.

When law enforcement officers, however well-meaning they may be in their desire "to protect and to serve," treat new religious movements as cults, they may actually *cause* groups to retaliate with violence or hostility, or to retrench, when those in the religious group were not likely to have done so if not provoked. In some cases, the actions of law enforcement officers actually confirm the beliefs of the group, who expect to be persecuted, even martyred, for their beliefs.

Thus, encounters between law enforcement and new religious movements are fragile. Even when the accusations against a group appear airtight and the interjection of law enforcement justified, such as in instances of alleged child abuse, the reality is often far more complex and requires everyone involved to proceed with caution.

ARRESTS, RAIDS, AND STANDOFFS

When and how law enforcement become involved with new religions is determined by a variety of factors, including the relative size of a particular group, whether the public or the media has determined them to be a menace, or whether the rhetoric or actions of the group are deemed dangerous or threatening to the public or established institutions. Of course, many of these factors, particularly the latter, are up for interpretation. A group that speaks of imminent destruction of the world might seem to justify intervention, even if the group is no more likely to cause this destruction than mainstream religions that speak of similar events.

Arguably Joseph Smith Jr. (1805–1844), the founder of the Church of Jesus Christ of Latter-day Saints, was arrested for the challenge that his "true Christian church" posed to one particular mainstream religion, Protestantism. Smith and his followers had been inciting critiques and government pressure prior to the Church's founding and rumors of immorality had been swirling since the early 1830s (regarding the Church's still secret practice of plural marriage). However, it was his indirect involvement in the destruction of a printing press, a federal crime, that led to his arrest and imprisonment in an Illinois jail cell, where he and his brother Hyrum (1800–1844) were murdered by an angry mob. Either the jail was left unguarded or, conspiracy theorists attest, the mob was allowed into the jail by the law enforcement officers tasked with guarding Smith. Others, like the Congolese preacher Simon Kimbangu (1887–1951), have been arrested for posing similar "threats" to the dominant religions and local culture, meaning that law enforcement becomes an arm of established institutions, acting as maintainers of the "status quo."

In other cases, law enforcement agencies may be acting on what they believe is a viable threat by a new religious movement, while lacking key information or expertise. Such was the case for the Bureau of Alcohol Tobacco and Firearms (BATF) when they went to serve a warrant to the Branch Davidians at the Mount Carmel Center in Waco, Texas, leading to a fifty-one-day standoff between the religious group, BATF, and Federal Bureau of Investigation (FBI) that would ultimately lead to the death of four BATF agents and over eighty Branch Davidians. The Branch Davidians were an offshoot of the Seventh-day Adventists, a millennialist sect of Christianity, who believed that Christ would soon return and the events predicted in the Book of Revelation would come to pass. This theological worldview fundamentally shaped how the Branch Davidians viewed the actions of law enforcement, who were agents of "Babylon," and thus sent there to persecute the righteous (a.k.a. them). During phone conversations with the leader of the Branch Davidians, David Koresh (1959–1993), negotiators became increasingly frustrated with Koresh's insistence on speaking in biblical terminology (what they deemed "Bible babble"), which they felt was a stalling technique. In fact, for Koresh, making clear the urgency of his biblical message was all that mattered. Sufficiently frustrated, the BATF and FBI initiated a raid on April 19, 1993, which resulted in a fatal fire.

Not all such sieges and standoffs result in tragedy, of course. In 1996, the Montana Freeman, members of the Christian Patriot Movement whose leader LeRoy

Schweitzer (1938–2011) was influenced by the white supremacist religion, Christian Identity, refused to vacate farmland from which they had been evicted. The FBI, having faced a public relations nightmare after Waco, proceeded with caution to avoid violence and another tragedy. After eighty-one days, the Freemen surrendered to the FBI, having avoided bloodshed, though members of the Christian Patriot Movement were highly critical of the intervention of law enforcement in the first place.

There are cases where intervention may be necessary. Rajneeshpuram, the incorporated city in Oregon founded and inhabited by the Osho Movement during the 1980s, was raided by law enforcement after its members were involved in the salmonella poisoning of 751 people in Wascoe County. At the compound, they found evidence of illegal wiretapping, leading to the dissolution of the group and the flight of its leaders to India and Germany.

Very often, in such instances where intervention may be required, concern for the safety of children is involved. Tony Alamo (1934–2017), founder of Alamo Christian Ministries, was the target of a 2008 police raid on suspicion of child pornography; he was eventually convicted of sex trafficking and sentenced to 175 years in prison. In a more publicized event, the Yearning for Zion Ranch, which was home to the Fundamentalist Latter-day Saints, was subject to a police raid in 2008, leading to the arrest and prosecution of numerous church leaders, including prophet Warren Jeffs (1955–), for statutory rape, sexual assault, and child abuse. Nonetheless, there was a public outcry when it came to light that children had been separated from their mothers during the raid, leading to critiques of sweeping police involvement.

However, the mere whiff of child abuse has led law enforcement to overstep in certain cases. During the Satanic Panic, numerous individuals were falsely accused of Satanic practices, often against infants and children, and arrested for their "crimes." Most of these supposed Satanists were later exonerated when the information law enforcement acted upon was found to be erroneous. Also in the 1980s, reports of child sexual abuse in the Children of God (COG) (now the Family International) emerged, leading the group to disavow and discontinue any problematic relationships between adults and minors; nonetheless, COG communes were subject to international raids during the 1990s, years after they had reportedly abandoned these practices.

POLICING NEW (BLACK) RELIGIONS

Not every interaction between law enforcement agencies and new religions is so overt. Various new religious movements, particularly those involving African Americans who are already frequently targeted by law enforcement, have been surveilled for decades at a time. Throughout the twentieth century, various black ethnic religions, particularly those with ties to Islam, were surveilled by the FBI under the guise of their "un-American" character. The Moorish Science Temple of America attracted many African Americans on its platform that they were not "Negroes" but "Moors," the descendants of the biblical Moabites whose true religion was Islam and who represented the true "chosen people" of the Bible. Their attempt to create a nation within a nation appeared suspicious to the government, which prompted the FBI to surveil its members.

During the latter half of the twentieth century, the Nation of Islam (NOI) was surveilled as a potential threat to the nation. The NOI was historically critical of the U.S. government, Christianity, and the civil rights movement, believing that all upheld white supremacy. Though no acts of violence were perpetrated, the militance of the NOI against "white devils" spooked the white public, leading to surveillance by the FBI. In fact, many believe that the assassination of Malcolm X (1925–1965) came not by the hands of NOI leadership but by the FBI who perceived X to be a threat to white racial hegemony.

For these new religions, it is clear that their members were targeted not just because they were members of fringe religions but because they were black. Such was certainly the case for Father Divine (1876–1965), whose practice of holding "love feasts"—huge, interracial banquets held at his home in Sayville, New York—led to his arrest for "disturbing the peace." His predominantly white neighbors had complained about the nuisance, though the diversity of the feast's participants was more likely the cause.

A BETTER UNDERSTANDING?

In light of past events, particularly incidents like the 1993 Mount Carmel fire, law enforcement officers and agencies have sought to improve tactics and increase understanding of new religious movements. In the United States, for example, the FBI has consulted with scholars of religion to better understand the language, mindset, and belief systems of new religious movements.

Nonetheless, law enforcement officers often find themselves in difficult, seemingly unwinnable situations. Fail to act, they fear, and members of the group may take violent action; act too soon or without proper preparation, and tragedy may ensue. Hopefully, with better information and proper training, there can be more peaceful outcomes in interactions between the law and new religious movements.

See also: Alamo, Tony (1934–2017); Anticult Movement, The; Brainwashing; Branch Davidians; Children of God (The Family International); Christian Identity; Church of Jesus Christ of Latter-day Saints, The; Conspiracy Theories; Courts and New Religious Movements; Cult; Father Divine (1876–1965); Fundamentalist Mormons; Kimbangu, Simon (1887–1951); Koresh, David (1959–1993); Malcolm X (1925–1965); Media and New Religious Movements; Millennialism; Moorish Science Temple of America, The; Nation of Islam, The; Race and New Religious Movements; Rajneesh/Osho Movement, The; Satanic Panic; Satanism; Seventh-day Adventists; Smith, Joseph (1805–1844); Violence and New Religious Movements .

Further Reading

Docherty, Jayne Seminare. 1999. "Bridging the Gap between Scholars of Religion and Law Enforcement Negotiators." *Nova Religio* 3, no. 1: 8–26.

Evanzz, Karl. 2017. "The FBI and the Nation of Islam." In Sylvester Johnson & Steven Weitzman, eds., *The FBI and Religion: Faith and National Security Before and After 9/11*, pp. 148–167. Berkeley: University of California Press.

Johnson, Sylvester. 2017. "The FBI and the Moorish Science Temple of America, 1926–1960." In Sylvester Johnson & Steven Weitzman, eds, *The FBI and Religion: Faith and National Security Before and After 9/11*, pp. 55–66. Berkeley: University of California Press.

O'Leary, Stephen. 1999. "Law Enforcement and New Religious Movements." *Nova Religio* 3, no. 1: 54–59.

Wessinger, Catherine. 2003. "New Religious Movements and Conflicts with Law Enforcement." In Derek H. Davis & Barry Hankins, eds., *New Religious Movements and Religious Liberty in America*, 2nd ed., pp. 89–106. Waco, TX: Baylor University Press.

Wessinger, Catherine. 2017. "The FBI's 'Cult War' against the Branch Davidians." In Sylvester Johnson & Steven Weitzman, eds., *The FBI and Religion: Faith and National Security Before and After 9/11*, pp. 203–243. Berkeley: University of California Press.

Lee, (Mother) Ann (1736–1784)

RELIGIOUS BEGINNINGS

Ann Lee better known as "Mother Ann" or "Ann the Word" by believers was a religious leader who defied both theological and gender convention. Claiming that she was Christ reborn, Mother Ann presented herself as the female Messiah—the living embodiment of the Second Coming predicted in the Book of Revelation. Her assertions invited censure but also praise from those desirous of living as though the millennium—the one-thousand-year reign of Christ—had finally arrived.

Mother Ann was born to Quaker parents in Manchester, England. The Quakers, or the Society of Friends, were then known for their effusive worship style (which often caused members to "quake") as well as their spirit-driven system of authority, which invited congregants to know God through the "inner light" within. Beyond this rather unconventional religious upbringing, her parents could afford little in the way of formal education and Mother Ann began working in her youth. By the late 1750s, she had joined Jane and James Wardley, whose religious group, the "Shaking Quakers" (later known simply as Shakers under Mother Ann—both names ascribed to them from the outside) would serve as a space for her to begin testing some of the ideas that would form the basis of her own religious group following her death, the United Society of Believers in Christ's Second Appearing. Mother Ann reportedly was repulsed by sex and sexuality, avoiding marriage until she was effectively forced into it, marrying Abraham Stanley. Further, having suffered through four painful labors, followed by the deaths of all of her children in infancy, she had come to fear not just sex, but procreation. While with the Wardleys and following a religious vision, she began to propose that one could achieve perfect holiness by practicing celibacy and through the dissolution of marital ties.

A PROPHET BORN

Throughout the 1760s, Mother Ann gained a reputation as a prophet. Becoming a fixture at religious revivals, she began prophesying about the imminent arrival of Christ, which meant, she argued, that all people must look to their own sinful behaviors and seek to eradicate sin in their hearts. Revivalism, in general, was a generative space for religious visionaries—both men and women; revivals generally promised intimate experience of the divine, even extending to new, divine knowledge. Thus, for Mother Ann to claim authoritative knowledge of God received in a moment of religious ecstasy was far less controversial than the content of her message, which railed against marriage and touted celibacy.

In 1770, Mother Ann had a vision that changed her life. At the time, she was in prison for having partaken in a raucous religious service, which "disturbed the peace." In this vision, she saw Adam and Eve in the midst of intercourse, which confirmed for her that it was their sexual act that precipitated humanity's fall from the Garden of Eden and, therefore, was the source of all sin. Soon after, she received a second vision wherein Jesus Christ confirmed the truth of the first—and helped to explain her own experiences as wife and as mother—and told her to spread her message around the world. This ultimately led Ann (spurred by another vision), along with the remnant Shaking Quakers, now Shakers—of which she was now definitively the leader—to leave England in 1774 for the soon-to-be United States.

INTRODUCING THE MESSIAH

Arriving in the colonies, Mother Ann and her followers settled first in New York City, where they remained for five years. During this time, she was abandoned by her husband. His absence did not particularly perturb her, given her own aversion to their union in the first place and her stance that marriage perpetuated sexual lust and therefore impeded the work of Christ. Finding city life less than ideal to their communitarian and celibate lifestyle (coupled with suspicion that these English immigrants were "Tories," and thus loyalist sympathizers to the crown), Mother Ann and the Shakers departed for Niskayuna (now Watervliet), New York, outside of Albany. It was here that Mother Ann was truly able to implement her vision for a utopian religious society, where the bonds of marriage were dissolved and all lived in anticipation of the coming Kingdom of God.

Soon after moving, however, it became clear that the time of God's Kingdom was already upon them. In 1780 (though the precise date is unknown), Mother Ann gave a sermon, during which she appeared to be suffering greatly; the source of her suffering, it would be revealed, was the revelation of a world-shifting truth: that she was Christ come again. "It is not I that speak," she was reported to have said: "it is Christ who dwells in me" (Gal. 2:20). Mother Ann had asserted previously that the world was suffused with male and female counterparts. So, just as Christ had been embodied in the masculine form of Jesus, she embodied Christ in the feminine. And since Christ had now returned and the millennium arrived, this meant that all should begin living as they would in heaven. This meant, first and foremost, that all marital and sexual relations were dissolved and celibacy was the only suitable state.

With such traditional institutional boundaries transformed, Mother Ann preached absolute equality of the sexes and communitarian living, where all lived for each other and none for the self. This led her to become a rather vocal and, for her time, early proponent of economic justice. Additionally, echoing her Quaker roots, she argued for religious tolerance on the ground that religious truth speaks to people in different ways at different times through their inner light. Much of her rhetoric echoed her context; as war raged and the nation turned to new methods of governance, questions of tolerance, equality, and democracy abounded. That these ideas came from a woman claiming to be the Messiah set her apart, even if her ideals were germane to the cultural and political zeitgeist.

TRIALS AND TRIUMPHS

For Mother Ann, the years following the settlement of the Shakers in upstate New York and the revelation of her true identity were a veritable roller-coaster of stressors and successes. In 1780, Mother Ann was imprisoned once again, this time for treason. The fact that she was a recent English immigrant meant that her colonist neighbors perceived her pacifist views and outright refusal to sign an oath of allegiance to the colonies not as the result of her millennialist Christianity (there are no nations and no wars in heaven, after all) but as the product of her loyalist sympathies.

Once released, Mother Ann and a few of her most devoted disciples, including her brother, William Lee, set about on a preaching mission to New England, which lasted from 1781 to 1783. During that time, she witnessed the growth of a number of new Shaker communities throughout New England, with Harvard, Massachusetts, serving as the New England base for the movement. Mother Ann had particular luck in converting religious people or sometimes entire communities who already existed on the margins of religious society, such as the Quakers. At the same time, her progress was marred by escalating mob violence toward the Shakers, generally, and her, personally. New Shaker converts were reportedly horsewhipped and, once, she was dragged out of her house and into an awaiting carriage where she was beaten and berated. The effects of the mission, though positive for the community, would precipitate a terminal decline in Mother Ann's health.

LEGACY

After having returned from the mission in September of 1783, both Mother Ann and her brother William languished. When William died in July of 1784, Mother Ann retreated from the world, spending her days speaking and singing in tongues alone in her rocking chair. Her death soon followed, with her passing away in September 1784 at the age of forty-eight. She was buried in a simple wooden coffin following a heartfelt celebration of her life and her contributions to the spread of the divine Kingdom.

Following her death, her followers formally organized themselves into a church called the United Society of Believers in Christ's Second Appearing. As indicated by its name, Mother Ann was certainly not forgotten in death, but formed the centerpiece of Shaker thought and practice. Christ *had* appeared in her and the millennium continued apace. Still, without their leader and without the promise of producing future generations through procreation, the Shakers' membership would plateau and ultimately dwindle to the point of near extinction in the early twenty-first century.

See also: Millennialism; Sex, Sexuality, and New Religious Movements; Shakers, The.

Further Reading
Blinn, (Elder) Henry C. 2017. *The Life and Gospel Experience of Mother Ann Lee*. London: Forgotten Books.
Foster, Lawrence. 1984. *Religion and Sexuality: The Shakers, the Mormons, and the Oneida Community*. Urbana: University of Illinois Press.
Francis, Richard. 2013. *Ann the Word: The Story of Ann Lee, Female Messiah, Mother of the Shakers, the Woman Clothed with the Sun*. New York: Arcade Publishing.

Lévi, Éliphas (1810–1875)

Éliphas Lévi Zahed, born Alphonse Louis Constant, was a prolific French occultist and socialist, whose work would influence prominent occultists such as Helena Petrovna Blavatsky (1831–1891) and Aleister Crowley (1875–1947). He is often cited as the individual most responsible for revitalizing interest in magic during the nineteenth century.

Lévi was born in Paris and at the age of twenty entered seminary to become a Roman Catholic priest, a pursuit he would ultimately abandon in 1836. He was increasingly influenced by socialist thought and began writing about Christianity and the Bible as sources of socialist protest; he would argue that socialism was "true Christianity." And though he had reportedly been influenced by occult and magical practice in his youth, his interests began to grow apace with his interests in socialism. Lévi was heavily influenced by a growing subset of French writers examining different magical theories and their connection to certain occult branches of knowledge. For his part, Lévi was particularly interested in Kabbalah, the Jewish mystical tradition (hence the adoption of the name Éliphas Lévi).

It was Lévi who reportedly differentiated between two types of pentagrams: one that represented evil (one point down, two points up) and one that represented good (two points down, one point up). Lévi also reportedly introduced the use of Tarot cards into his individual magical practice, which have now become regular components of occult religious practice overall. However, it was his many writings that ensured Lévi's lasting legacy. Besides his socialist writings, he published prolifically in the areas of magic and occult knowledge. His works on magic were seminal to a revitalized magical milieu, particularly since he proposed clear definitions of what magic entailed and who magicians were. His most famous, and first work, on magic was *Transcendental Magic, its Doctrine and Ritual* (1854–1856), which he followed with *The History of Magic* (1860). Though Lévi made a living from lecturing and publishing on magic, arguably, his works became more influential after his death. For example, his writings would be adapted by the

Hermetic Order of the Golden Dawn, whose own magical rituals and levels of occult knowledge would be mimicked by others.

Not everyone was enamored of Lévi or his work, however. Lévi reportedly sparred with Spiritualists whose belief in sentient, autonomous spirits went against his belief that, after death, all that remained of a person were memories or mental projections. Squabbles aside, Lévi's contributions to magic are indisputable and have lived on after his death in 1875, forever imprinted on the modern magical and occult religious world.

See also: Blavatsky, Helena Petrovna (1831–1891); Crowley, Aleister (1875–1947); Hermetic Order of the Golden Dawn, The; Kabbalah; Magic and New Religious Movements; Occultism and Esotericism; Spiritualism.

Further Reading

Hanegraaff, Wouter J. 2010. "The Beginnings of Occultist Kabbalah: Adolphe Franck and Éliphas Lévi." In Marco Pasi, Boaz Huss, & Kocku von Stuckrad, eds. *Kabbalah and Modernity*, pp. 107–128. Leiden: Brill.

Lévi, Éliphas. 2012 [1860]. *Magic: A History of its Rites, Rituals, and Mysteries*. Newburyport, MA: Dover Publications.

McIntosh, Christopher. 2011. *Éliphas Lévi and the French Occult Revival*. Albany: SUNY Press.

Love Israel Family, The

Utopian experiments in communal living have a long history. In the United States, such experiments have often been motivated by religious principles. The observation in the book of Acts 4:32 that in an early Christian community "no one claimed private ownership of any possessions, but everything they owned was held in common" has led many groups to try to reestablish the practices of Jesus's first followers. For example, the Oneida Community, founded by John Humphrey Noyes (1811–1886) in 1848 in Oneida, New York, practiced such communalism and the Peoples Temple Agricultural Mission in Jonestown, Guyana, begun in 1974, practiced "apostolic socialism." The Love Israel Family, initiated in Seattle, Washington, in late 1968, was another utopian community.

The Love Israel Family developed out of the experience of Paul Erdman (1940–2016). Despite an initial antipathy to the hippie counterculture, Erdman spent some time in San Francisco in 1967, and his apartment became a place for others to crash. Some of them later became members of the group. He returned to Seattle in 1968 and moved to the Queen Anne Hill neighborhood with his girlfriend; they were soon joined by four others. Those six became the nucleus of what would become the Love Israel Family.

During a trip seeking spiritual truth, Erdman experienced a vision that he had before but had been unable to interpret. He saw a pyramid formed of arguing people; God urged him to reach the top, and there he saw what appeared to be Jesus, but may actually have been Erdman as Jesus, and a stone on which "LOVE" was written. When Erdman returned to Seattle, he informed the others that he was

Love. He urged the others to take names that represented the virtues that they embodied, such as Patience or Strength. Eventually, members of the community would all take the last name of Israel to signal that they were all children of God (see Isa. 44:5).

By the end of 1969, others had joined the communal dwelling, and in the early 1970s, the group expanded into more homes in the same neighborhood. Members gave their possessions to the group upon joining, cut off most contact with people outside the group, and adopted a simple lifestyle. In addition to its homes, the Love Israel Family started several small businesses, including an Inn and a guesthouse where visitors could stay for free for three days. As the group grew, reaching a peak of around 350 members, so did its business interests. It also acquired land in rural areas outside of Seattle.

During its Seattle years, the Family was dogged by anticult activists, including the notorious deprogrammer Ted Patrick (1930–), who capitalized on the drug use of early members to raise alarms.

The beliefs of the Love Israel Family were summed up in three statements: "love is the answer; we are all one; now is the time." The group believed that God was in all persons and that the Family as a whole manifested the Second Coming. Appealing to John 2:25–26, early Family members believed that they were eternal. But deaths of several members led to a revised concept that they were all united in an eternal love. Baptism was used to confirm membership in the group after an initial period of mutual acquaintance. Dreams and visions, in which Love Israel often appeared, were an important part of communal life.

As the group grew, and members occupied a variety of locations, both in and outside of Seattle, it became harder to maintain the initial communal spirit. In 1983, seven members wrote to Love Israel, detailing the ways in which he had become spiritually, socially, and economically distant from the group. Love's response, reasserting his ultimate authority, led to the departure of many members. In the summer of 1984, the remaining members left Seattle for a farm in Arlington, Washington. They were later joined there by Love Israel and maintained a modestly self-supporting community on the farm until 2003 when it had to be sold. The membership then dispersed and dwindled to a small core.

See also: Farm, The; Oneida Community, The; Patrick, Ted (1930–); Peoples Temple; Utopianism in New Religious Movements.

Further Reading

Israel, Rachel. 2018. *Counterculture Crossover: Growing Up in the Love Family: A Memoir.* Maple Valley, WA: Life Story Press.

LeWarne, Charles P. 2009. *The Love Israel Family: Urban Commune, Rural Commune.* Seattle: University of Washington Press.

Miller, Timothy. 1999. *The 60s Communes: Hippies and Beyond.* Syracuse, NY: Syracuse University of Press.